B+T 1
$30.00

DISCARD

D0712363

Madhouse

Madhouse

A Tragic Tale of Megalomania and Modern Medicine

Andrew Scull

DISCARD

Yale University Press
New Haven and London

616.89
ScU

Pacific Grove Public Library

Copyright © 2005 by Andrew Scull

All rights reserved. This book may not be reproduced in whole or in part, in any form (beyond that copying permitted by Sections 107 and 108 of the U.S. Copyright Law and except by reviewers for the public press) without written permission from the publishers.

For information about this and other Yale University Press publications, please contact:
U.S. Office: sales.press@yale.edu yalebooks.com
Europe Office: sales @yaleup.co.uk www.yalebooks.co.uk

Set in Minion by Northern Phototypesetting Co. Ltd, Bolton
Printed in Great Britain by Cambridge University Press

Library of Congress Cataloging-in-Publication Data
Scull, Andrew T.
  Madhouse: a tragic tale of megalomania and modern medicine/Andrew Scull.
     p.   cm.
  Includes bibliographical references and index.
  ISBN 0–300–10729–3 (cl.: alk. paper)
  1. Cotton, Henry Aloysius—Career in psychiatry. 2. Psychiatry—United States—History.
  I. Title.
  RC443.S395 2004
  616.89′00973—dc22
                                                                              2004028567

A catalogue record for this book is available from the British Library.

10 9 8 7 6 5 4 3 2 1

Contents

List of Illustrations   vii

Acknowledgments   ix

Prologue   1

Part One

1. No Bughouse Doctor   13
2. The Perils of Pus Infection   28
3. The Mecca of Exodontia   41
4. Selling the Cure   61
5. Fighting Focal Infection   81
6. The End of the Affair?   97
7. An American Abroad   108

Part Two

8. Making a Medical Career   133
9. Cotton Under the Microscope   159
10. Averting a Scandal   180
11. Showdown   192
12. Playing for Time   203
13. The New Lister   225
14. Betrayals   235
15. Death in the Trenches   250

Epilogue: Psychiatry and Its Discontents   273

Notes   300

Index   350

Illustrations

1. Henry Cotton in middle age.   6
2. Trenton State Hospital.   16
3. Meyer, Cotton, and the staff at Worcester State Hospital.   22
4. Henry Cotton and the medical staff of the Trenton State Hospital,
    1915.   26
5. John Harvey Kellogg's Battle Creek Sanitarium.   35
6. Taking X-rays of a patient's teeth.   47
7. An exploratory laparotomy at Trenton State Hospital.   50
8. Stewart Paton as a young man.   70
9. An admission ward at Trenton State Hospital.   71
10. Injecting Salvarsan into the cranial cavity of a patient with tertiary
    syphilis.   72
11. A tonsillectomy.   73
12. The laboratory at Trenton State Hospital.   74
13. The laboratory for fecal analysis at Battle Creek Sanitarium.   85
14. Thomas Chivers Graves in fancy dress.   111
15. The auditorium at Lettsom House, London.   114
16. The sites of focal sepsis.   115
17. Treating psychosis: chart of a patient with paranoia.   116
18. Phyllis Greenacre as a young woman.   134
19. Meyer's staff at Johns Hopkins, 1916.   139
20. Adolf Meyer, 1916.   142
21. Curt Richter and Phyllis Greenacre testing the grasp reflex of an
    unidentified infant.   148
22. The Phipps Clinic.   151
23. The staff of the Phipps Clinic, mid-1920s.   156
24. Riven Rock, the McCormick mansion in Santa Barbara.   162
25. The entrance to the main building of Trenton State Hospital.   164

26. Adolf Meyer. 195
27. Henry Cotton at work at his desk. 211
28. Adolf Meyer, with an unidentified companion. 223
29. Thomas Chivers Graves. 226
30. Dr. Joseph Raycroft. 242
31. Dr. Robert Stone. 258
32. "End Results" of 645 Major Operative Cases and
    407 Non-Operative Cases. 265
33. The Cotton Award for Kindness. 298

Thanks are due to the following organizations and individuals for permission to reproduce the images contained in this book: New Jersey State Archives, Department of State, Trenton, New Jersey (1, 2, 4, 6, 7, 9, 10, 11, 12, 16, 17, 25, 27, 31, 33); The Alan Mason Chesney Medical Archives of the Johns Hopkins Medical Institutions (3, 19, 20, 21, 22, 23, 26, 28); Historical Collections, Willard Public Library, Battle Creek, Michigan (5, 13); University Archives, Department of Rare Books and Special Collections, Princeton University Library (8, 30); Mr. Frederick Chivers Graves (14, 29); Medical Society of London (15); Dr. Peter Richter (18); Santa Barbara Historical Society (24).

Acknowledgments

What follows is, as my title suggests, a horror story, the story of the depredations visited upon thousands of psychiatric patients by the New Jersey psychiatrist Henry Cotton and his followers over two decades and more. Unlike most gothic tales, though, it is not fictional or fictionalized. The events recounted here, and the actors on this particular stage, however far-fetched and extraordinary some of them may seem, are not the ghosts of some gothic nightmare, but are – may the postmodernists forgive me – real events and real people: all dead, but now given such semblance of new life as my prose can muster. I have not invented, nor gone beyond, what interviews with some of those who participated in what happened and twenty years of toil in the archives have revealed to me. Only the names of the patients, whose fate lies at the heart of this story, have been changed, in an effort to protect the innocent. Or rather – since it is much too late for that – to avoid inflicting yet more gratuitous violence (though here of only a symbolic sort) on those who by any measure have already suffered mightily at the hands of others who professed to be motivated by their welfare. I can only hope that this tale of twentieth-century psychiatric abuse will serve as a salutary warning to the psychiatric practice of the twenty-first century.

Inevitably, I have accumulated a huge number of debts in the course of the many years I have worked on this project, and I can thank only a small handful of those who have made my work possible and assisted me with my researches. I hope those I neglect to mention here will forgive me. I first conceived of this project during my tenure as a Guggenheim Fellow in the early 1980s. Grants from the Academic Senate of the University of California, from the American Council of Learned Societies, and from the American Philosophical Society helped to defray some of the costs of my visits to a variety of archives in the United States and in Britain, as did a University of California Presidential

Humanities Fellowship. I hope these various entities will think that their moneys were well spent.

I should particularly like to express my gratitude to the late Phyllis Greenacre and to her son Peter Richter for the invaluable information they provided over a period of years. Dr. Greenacre's memory of the Trenton affair was extraordinarily sharp, even after six decades had passed. Historians are rightly cautious about the pitfalls of oral history, but in this instance, wherever I had the opportunity to check a person's memory against contemporary written records, her recall was remarkably accurate. Peter Richter has been enormously helpful in a variety of ways and I am grateful to him for permission to draw on his memories, for supplying a rare picture of his mother (who hated to be photographed), and for giving me permission to quote freely from her published and unpublished writings. Dr. Greenacre's role as a would-be whistleblower, and the problems that she faced, as a junior, female clinician, have their obvious analogues today, when similarly placed subordinates may be tempted to go public about the ethical and scientific lapses of senior figures in positions of authority. All too frequently, the scientific and medical establishment promptly closes ranks, and those seeking to expose scientific and clinical misconduct find their own reputations under attack and their career prospects blighted or in ruins.

I should also like to thank another participant in the focal infection saga, Dr. Ferdearle Fischer, for sharing with me his memories of Henry Cotton and Trenton State Hospital. Originally appointed as the hospital dentist in 1918, Dr. Fischer served in that capacity until his retirement in 1960 and always remained convinced of the value of Dr. Cotton's work. In Britain, Thomas Chivers Graves's son Frederick, and the widow of his other son John, Dr. Valerie Graves, shared with me their memories of the leading advocate of focal sepsis among British psychiatrists, and some of Dr. Graves's former staff kindly showed me around his hospital and operating theater at the Rubery Hill Mental Hospital in Birmingham. I am very grateful to all of them.

One of my key informants, and someone who greatly facilitated my access to a variety of records in New Jersey, is a former high official in its mental health services who prefers to remain anonymous. I would nonetheless like to thank him publicly for his extraordinary assistance in bringing this story into the public domain. I also received much help and cooperation from several people in the administration of the Trenton Psychiatric Hospital, and am grateful for their assistance. Among archivists, I would particularly like to thank Nancy McCall and Andrew Harrison at the Alan Mason Chesney Medical Archives at Johns Hopkins University for assisting my work in the Adolf Meyer Papers.

Staff at the Rockefeller Archives in Tarrytown, New York; the George Washington University Medical Library; the New York Public Library; the Special Collections Department of the Rutgers University Library; the Santa Barbara Historical Society; the Willard Public Library at Battle Creek, Michigan; and the Yale University Library, were helpful in many ways, as was Joanne Nestor of the New Jersey State Archives.

My friend Stephen Cox has been an invaluable source of support and encouragement over the years it has taken to produce this book. An extraordinary editor, he has taken great pains to improve my prose, and I hope he knows how much I appreciate his efforts to discipline my sometimes wayward pen. Many of Britain's leading psychiatrists listened to an early version of this history as long ago as 1986, when I gave a Squibb lecture at the Institute of Psychiatry. They were a polite audience, as I presented a story that does not represent their specialty's finest hour, and I am happy to count at least some of them as my friends. Gerald Grob, with whom I have enjoyed a long and contentious scholarly relationship, was his usual generous self when it came to providing advice and even copies of archival material to assist me in my work. I am honored by the fact that our relations have remained friendly even in the face of our often acrimonious scholarly debates. Other historians of psychiatry have also been extremely helpful in a variety of ways over the years. It is invidious to mention only some of them, but I will anyway. Thanks especially to Bill Bynum, and to Joel Braslow, the late Roy Porter, Edward Shorter, Sander Gilman, Michael Neve, Charles Rosenberg, Nancy Tomes, Carla Yanni, Elaine Showalter, Ruth Leys, Alison Winter, Trevor Turner, and the late Michael Shepherd. Steven Shapin is a much-missed colleague and friend who had the audacity to leave the charms of La Jolla for Harvard, and he too deserves my thanks – along with Tim McDaniel, who *has* had the sense to remain in Southern California. And Sylvia Nasar has been extraordinarily generous with her help, providing both encouragement and access to materials on Irving Fisher and his daughter Margaret.

My long-time editor at Yale University Press, the estimable John Nicoll, waited with preternatural patience for this manuscript. It is my own fault (and my regret) that I finally delivered what I had promised only weeks before his retirement, for John is a prince among editors. I am fortunate, however, that his successor Robert Baldock has enthusiastically adopted the project as his own. Ewan Thompson has provided splendid assistance with the manuscript, and Tina Weiner at Yale's New Haven office has been a constant source of support. Warm thanks are also due to my long-suffering agent at Peters, Fraser and Dunlop, Caroline Dawnay.

I want to make one comment on what follows: the interventions of the New Jersey psychiatrist Henry Cotton at Trenton State Hospital, which occupy the center of this narrative, were motivated by his assumption that his patients' mental symptoms were purely epiphenomenal, merely symptomatic of what was actually wrong with them. In his view, their real illness was purely physical, and could and should be treated only with measures directed at the cure of their bodies. Though distinctive, his interventions formed part of a much broader set of somatic remedies in which his profession invested during the 1920s, '30s, and beyond.

It is perhaps worth reminding ourselves that, three-quarters of a century later, we once more live in an era where simplistic and biologically reductionist accounts of mental disorder enjoy widespread currency. Patients and their families have learned to attribute their travails to biochemical disturbances, to faulty neurotransmitters, and to genetic defects, and to look to their doctors for the magic potions that ensure "better living through chemistry." Pills have replaced talk as the dominant response to disturbances of emotion, cognition, and behavior. The revolution in treatment has been fomented and furthered by the vast expansion of a massively profitable psychopharmaceutical industry.

The psychiatric profession has done its part. Abandoning the flirtation with psychoanalysis that characterized the 1940s, '50s, and '60s, psychiatrists have embraced the neo-Kraeplinean approach embodied in the successive editions of the American Psychiatric Association's *Diagnostic and Statistical Manual of Mental Disorders*. The conceptual shift has eased the path of a profession eager to get its hands on the financial bonanza offered by the drug companies for those willing to do their bidding. Simultaneously, it has entailed the adoption of a concept of mental illnesses as specific, identifiably different diseases, each allegedly amenable to treatment with particular drugs or "magic bullets." Yet the whole conceptual edifice rests on the shakiest of foundations, and the treatments themselves are decidedly less efficacious than the public relations representatives for the industry would have us believe. Meanwhile, at the level of language, both psychiatry and popular culture have become saturated with biological talk: in David Healy's words, biobabble has replaced psychobabble. As someone no more enamored of Kraepelin than of Freud, I hardly regard this move as an improvement.

And talk, ironically, is mostly what the real foundation of the biological revolution in psychiatry amounts to. The etiology of most mental disorders remains as mysterious as ever. Despite all the recent advances in basic neuroscience, we have made remarkably little progress in understanding depression; and the sources of schizophrenia, or the schizophrenias, remain wrapped in the same obscurity. As for therapeutics, though there can be no question but that the new drugs – Thorazine, Prozac, and the rest – modify behavior, cognition, and emotion, sometimes in profound ways, we are a long way from understanding *how* they do so, or from having a balanced assessment of what it is they accomplish, desirable or undesirable.

I remain deeply skeptical that psychiatric science has at last succeeded in cutting nature at the joints. And I suggest that even in the aftermath of the so-called "decade of the brain," the tale of Dr. Cotton and his treatments has some salutary lessons to teach, not least to those who promote or credulously accept the latest siren songs about the biological bases of mental disorders.

Prologue

It is in the nature of an hypothesis, when once a man has conceived it, that it assimilates everything to itself, as proper nourishment; and, from the first moment of your begetting it, generally grows the stronger by every thing you see, hear, read, or understand.

Laurence Sterne, *The Life and Opinions of Tristram Shandy, Gentleman*

The rain that arrived before daybreak on Wednesday August 5, 1925, finally brought a measure of relief from the sweltering heat and humidity of an all-too-typical New Jersey summer. The storm's most violent downpour had abated by six that morning, to be replaced by a steady drizzle.[1] The grey light softened the profile of the bleak stone and brick buildings that sprawled behind the wrought-iron fence marking the boundary of the state hospital.

Anyone glancing through the hospital gates at that early hour would have observed a heavy-set, white-haired, middle-aged man walking rapidly between two houses set off to the side of the main buildings. Distinguished-looking and far too well dressed to be one of the inmates, the figure hurrying through the rain was nonetheless visibly nervous and disturbed. Reaching the second house, he banged on the front door and yelled to be admitted. A few minutes elapsed before the occupant, the hospital's warden and business manager Sam Atchley, appeared at the door and let his unexpected visitor in.

Wet and bedraggled, the white-haired man could not disguise how tense and upset he was. Ordinarily, Atchley would have been taken aback at being roused from his bed at such an early hour, and by the agitated appearance his boss presented. Not so on this occasion. For weeks, the hospital administration had been under siege. A runaway legislative committee, led by Senator William Bright, had focused its investigations of waste in state government on the hospital's affairs, and a surfeit of gothic horrors had tumbled into view. Ex-patients, their families, and disaffected former nurses and attendants had surfaced, and a litany of lurid tales had filled the pages of the state's newspapers. The scandal had even begun to draw the attention of the august *New York Times*. Stories of patients being beaten, kicked, and dragged screaming into the operating room, of trolleys filled with body parts and not a few corpses streaming in the opposite direction, had aroused the archetypical fears of the horrors of the madhouse that always linger just below the surface in our collective unconscious. Weekly, the situation seemed to worsen, and the stress had now driven Dr. Henry Cotton himself to the brink of a breakdown. Atchley had observed that "for several days previous to this time he seemed to be in a highly nervous condition ... caused largely by the Bright investigation and on account of his having the misfortune to lose a couple of patients who have people who are trying to make trouble for the institution."[2] To have one such patient mysteriously die in the midst of the inquiry was bad enough; to have two corpses on their hands was close to catastrophic.

Overnight, Atchley now saw, Dr. Cotton had become even more over-wrought. "He was very much excited and wanted to go away somewhere," and all Atchley's efforts to calm him down seemed to be of no avail. The concerned warden tried "to impress on him that there is nothing to worry about and that he must conserve his health and not allow himself to get in such a condition so as not to be able to do his work and not to be able to go before the investigating committee to prove to them that his work is right and should be carried on. I also tried to impress on him that the people who have made these charges are those who have had the misfortune to lose their friends and felt very sore about it; but that, of course, goes with all hospital work and sometimes cannot be avoided." But by way of response, Cotton kept insisting over and over again that "he would be arrested by some government detective and taken from the State. I told him this was impossible as he had the right to demand a hearing from the nearest Justice of the Peace, and in any case I would stand right with him and furnish bail if such a thing should become necessary." Growing steadily more concerned at how worked up his boss seemed to be, the warden "talked with him quite awhile and had him stay for breakfast." Still the doctor's excited state had not subsided, and he next announced his intention of going into town to see his lawyer, Mr. Kafes. Clearly, he was in no condition to drive himself, so Atchley promptly offered to go with him – an offer, he noticed, that Cotton accepted with pathetic eagerness.

The ten-minute trip to the lawyer's downtown office did nothing to allay the warden's apprehensions. Cotton's conversation verged on the incoherent, and he kept muttering to himself that they were not going to get him. Atchley grimly told himself that at this rate they undoubtedly would – hardly a reassuring prospect from his point of view. The two men had both secured their posts nearly two decades earlier, in the aftermath of an earlier asylum scandal. History seemed on the verge of repeating itself.

At Kafes's office they had to wait. Apparently Cotton was not due to testify until ten that morning. Sitting for what seemed like an eternity did nothing for either man's nerves, and it finally became too much for Henry. He abruptly announced he was going to walk over to the Capitol to join the other witnesses outside the hearing room, and would see Kafes and Atchley there.

News of the deaths of the two patients over the weekend had obviously leaked to the outside world, and a crowd of witnesses, journalists, and spectators were already packed into the legislative hearing room and the corridor outside by the time Cotton got there. It was as well that the rainstorm just before dawn had brought temperatures down by some twenty degrees, for certainly with this crowd the handful of fans creaking overhead would have made little impression on the previous day's suffocating temperatures. With Wednesday's thermometer struggling to reach seventy degrees at noon, at least those assembled either to record or to take part in the proceedings would mercifully be spared the physical discomfort that had plagued earlier sessions of the committee's work.

So far as Cotton was concerned, however, the welcome break in the weather apparently went unremarked. While the investigating committee headed by Senator Bright prepared behind the closed doors of the hearing room for yet another grueling day of testimony, he paced nervously up and down the hallway, sweating profusely and growing visibly more agitated as the start of the session drew nearer. He could be observed muttering to himself and glaring angrily towards several of the people gathered on the benches. Finally, he stopped in front of a man he apparently recognized and informed him that if he was there as a potential witness, his services would not be required until a later date.

The failure of this ploy to produce the desired effect only increased Cotton's uneasiness and agitation. Already bristling with hostility as he entered the hearing room, he sat at the back amidst the reporters and at once commenced heckling and interrupting the witnesses, challenging their veracity and impugning their motives for testifying. Initially ignored, his increasingly erratic outbursts soon drew fierce rebukes from the chair. But neither censure nor promises that he would soon be allowed to give his side of the story seemed to elicit any change in his behavior. At length, an exasperated Senator Bright called abruptly for a recess. As the committee prepared to move to an anteroom to consider how to proceed, it could be seen conferring with the rather nondescript man who had been approached in the hallway before the day's proceedings began. Observing the interchange, Cotton slipped quietly from the room, and on the committee's return to recommence its hearing, was nowhere to be found. The sergeant-at-arms promptly dispatched his minions to search the capital, and a few minutes later they returned, superintendent in tow.

Requested to take the witness's chair and sworn in, the truculent doctor found himself subjected to some distinctly unfriendly questioning. Asked directly whether he had attempted to intimidate and influence witnesses in the hallway prior to the opening of the day's hearing, he responded indignantly and belligerently that he had done no such thing. Immediately, he was asked to step down, and was replaced on the stand by the person he had approached before the day's session began. That anonymous-looking fellow, it now transpired, was affiliated with the county prosecutor's office. Indeed, Detective Leedom now testified, Dr. Cotton had used a ruse to try to prevent him testifying, and he had at the same time observed evident attempts at non-verbal intimidation of other potential witnesses. Once again, Cotton began to hector and interrupt, shouting out that Leedom was lying, and part of a sinister plot to "get" him. When these antics met with still another rebuke from the chair, he rose and, gesticulating wildly, stalked angrily from the room.[3]

The drama scarcely ended when Dr. Cotton removed himself from the scene. The morning's testimony about brutality by attendants and suspicious deaths at the nearby state hospital was now amplified by a string of witnesses, each of whom provided fodder for the next day's newspaper headlines. The son of Mrs. Emmeline White appeared, accompanied by the local chief of police and a nurse who had treated her at home, to testify to the harmless woman's sudden demise under highly questionable circumstances a mere two weeks after her admission to Trenton State Hospital "because of slight mental trouble." Ten days after her arrival Connover White had been summoned to see her because she had suffered "an accident . . . She did not recognize him, he said, but lay in bed groaning, with her eyes black and swollen." Attendants questioned about her injuries gave conflicting accounts of the source of her injuries, one claiming that she had fallen down stairs, another that she'd collided with a wall. Four days later, she was dead.

Next, a Mrs. Georgiana Phillips appeared, a former patient who had been committed to the asylum "on grounds of . . . immorality . . . indigency and moral insanity" – apparently a euphemism for engaging in prostitution. Claiming she had been sane when shut away, Phillips alleged that in direct violation of a court order she had been "compelled to undergo a delicate operation while a patient at the state hospital," despite the fact that she had "tried by every means within her power to avoid the knife." In response to questions, "she ridiculed the idea that there had been any misunderstanding as to her wish in the matter" and pointed out that the asylum superintendent Henry Cotton and his assistant Robert Stone had been cited for contempt of court for operating on her, only to have another judge subsequently set the matter aside on the grounds that "the whole affair was the result of a misunderstanding."[4]

Unquestionably the day's most dramatic testimony, however, concerned the case that had been the central focus of the Bright Committee's attention only a week before. Alive, if battered, at that time, Mrs. Bloom had been found dead four days later, her body a mass of bruises and contusions – wounds that the asylum authorities continued to insist were self-inflicted.

At that earlier committee session, family members had testified that Mrs. Bloom was convinced that she would not long survive, that the hospital's brutal attendants would beat her to death. Now that her fears had proved so prophetic, the Bloom case naturally moved to center stage once more. None of her relations was present on this latest occasion, for the funeral had been scheduled for the same time as the hearing. Their testimony was thus reserved for a later session. But in place of the bereaved, the committee heard from the county physician, Charles Mitchell.[5]

Mitchell was a brusque but unimpressive witness. He acknowledged that he had been called to the asylum by Dr. Cotton at midnight on Sunday to provide a second opinion about the cause of Mrs. Bloom's death. He at once made it plain that he was convinced that he had only been brought in "because of the furore caused by the Bright Committee's inquiry into the woman's treatment in the hospital," and that he bitterly resented the resulting imposition on his time. Pressed about how he had gone about determining the cause of death, he acknowledged that he had barely glanced at Bloom's bruised and battered corpse. The information recorded on the patient's hospital chart was, he insisted, entirely sufficient to show that "the woman died from natural causes and not from the effects of violence."

Subjected to a withering cross-examination, Mitchell was forced to admit that after he informed the family members of his conclusions, a bitter argument had ensued. Mrs. Bloom's children had demanded that he examine the condition of the victim's stomach. They had balked, however, when he indicated that further inquiries would necessitate a post-mortem examination. His vehement denial of the committee's most lurid allegation – that he had responded angrily with a threat to cut off Mrs. Bloom's head and rip her body open from head to toe if her daughters didn't desist arguing with him about the cause of death – evidently carried little conviction with many in the room,

1 Henry Cotton: the mad-doctor in middle age

particularly in light of his subsequent acknowledgment that the family had refused to sign a paper he had prepared for them that stated that they "voluntarily withdraw any accusations as to any internal injuries." Ominously, too, Bright announced that the relatives would attend a future session to rebut his testimony.

Meanwhile, another drama had unfolded outside the hearing room. Henry Cotton's abrupt departure after his confrontation with the committee on the witness stand had initially caught both his lawyer and the hospital warden by surprise. By the time they followed him outside, he was nowhere to be seen. Turning the corner on to State Street, however, they stumbled across their erstwhile companion.

Cotton was dripping wet. In departing so precipitously, he had evidently forgotten the rain, and had left his coat behind him. Even now, he seemed oblivious to his surroundings, disoriented about both time and place. At first he was mute, failing to respond at all when the warden asked him why in the world he was standing in the rain; and when Atchley finally did get him to talk, his mental confusion was pitiful. He kept pacing up and down, shouting that he could not find his car and that he had to get away. Apparently he had no recollection that he had come down in Atchley's automobile.

The spectacle had begun to attract an uncomfortable degree of attention from passers-by, and Atchley realized he had to take quick and decisive action. Trenton still had many of the characteristics of a small town, for all that it was the capital of the Garden State, and Cotton was a very prominent man. If they did not act immediately, word would soon be out that the superintendent of the local mental hospital had gone mad himself.

Mercifully the superintendent was not belligerent, and Atchley managed, without too much trouble, to coax him back into the car. Ironically, once the doctor could be conducted safely back on to the asylum grounds, he would temporarily be beyond the reach of prying eyes. Still, the crisis was far from over. He could hardly be just hidden from sight, and yet by the time they reached the hospital, his confusional state had deepened and he was acting like a stroke victim, or someone who was suffering from a severe form of hysteria.

Cotton's descent into madness obviously constituted a major problem for the hospital authorities. A quick telephone call alerted Professor Joseph Raycroft. The Princeton man, long one of Cotton's staunchest supporters on the asylum board, proved useful in an emergency. He agreed to contact Senator Bright and inform him that Cotton had been taken ill. Next, he and Atchley arranged to call in specialists from New York and Philadelphia, hoping thereby to keep the details of Cotton's condition from surfacing publicly. In the meantime, Bill Clark, one of the hospital doctors, was called upon to see if he had any clues about how to proceed or what was wrong.

Since the press had been on hand for the day's hearing and was clamoring for Cotton's reaction to the testimony, some sort of public announcement had to be made. Early that evening, therefore, the hospital released a prepared statement. Dr. Cotton, it indicated, had been in poor physical health for about a week and his health had temporarily broken down under the strain of the hearings. He was now confined to bed under doctor's orders and specialists from out of town had been sent for to treat him.

The next medical bulletin, released on Friday, was carefully phrased. The medical director had had a restful night and was much improved. Along with the nervous prostration induced by his run-down physical condition, months of overwork, and the stresses he had been under, his physicians announced that they had discovered that he was suffering from Bright's disease (the kidney disorder, not persecution by the investigating committee – though privately the medical men vented some gallows-humor about the coincidence). Dr. Cotton would in all probability be confined to bed for some weeks. He should by rights have given up all but the lightest work weeks ago, and he had paid for his dedication to his patients with his own health. To avoid a relapse, once he began to convalesce, they planned to order him to spend some time away from the hospital recuperating.[6]

Cotton's temporary removal from the stage seemed to make little difference to the politicians. Over the next three weeks, as he had promised to do, Bright produced a further succession of witnesses to testify about conditions at the asylum. Not one or two, but five of Leah Bloom's relatives surfaced and publicly contradicted Mitchell's account of the events surrounding her death.[7] One of her daughters, Iola Sleber, commented that throughout the ordeal the county physician gave the impression that he was dealing "with nothing more than animals." Edward Parent, her brother-in-law, provided more graphic details of the events in the asylum that night. Mitchell had been called to attend at about eleven o'clock, and on arrival had briefly scanned the body with the aid of a flashlight before announcing that Mrs. Bloom had died of Bright's disease. Her sons had remonstrated with him, pointing to her black eyes and the severe bruises covering her body. Surely she had been the victim of foul play. Mitchell had been furious: "I will cut off her head and show you, if necessary," he snapped. "Then I will rip her from head to feet and show you that." The very idea was so revolting that the family members returned home for a conference about how to proceed.

Attempts to find another physician willing to examine the body were unavailing (they were informed that "it would be a breach of professional etiquette for one physician thus to interfere with the affairs of another"), and by two o'clock in the morning the distraught family had reassembled at the hospital. Helpless to secure outside assistance and desperate to avoid mutilation of the corpse, they had agreed to sign a paper releasing the hospital from claims that abuse had been responsible for Mrs. Bloom's death, insisting only that the word "voluntarily" be deleted from the document they found prepared for their signatures. And, they reported angrily, after they had first testified about the incident before the Bright Committee some weeks before, adding insult to injury, they had been approached by Henry Cotton, who had previously avoided all contact with them. Berating them for raking up such a scandal, he had told them that "it is just such things as this that keeps us from getting money to carry on the hospital work."[8]

A series of other families subsequently appeared, testifying about loved ones they contended had been killed by neglect or active abuse. James Edmunds alleged that his sister had "practically starved to death" at the hospital. Her weight fell from 130lbs. on admission to less than 100lbs. by the time of her death, reducing her to "a mere skeleton." When he came to the hospital on receiving a telegram reporting that his sister was ill, he was shown on to the ward where she was confined: "I examined all the patients in her room, but did not recognize her. A nurse had to point her out. It was the most horrible sight I have ever seen." Two other witnesses spoke of the loss of a husband and mother respectively, their bodies when released to them being a mass of bruises, apparently the result of an attack by another patient. Both had been told that the injuries were the result of a fall. In turn, they were followed to the stand by the undertaker who was contracted to dispose of corpses from the hospital, who admitted under questioning that a regular part of his duties when dealing with asylum bodies was "covering up wounds and abrasions."[9]

But damaging as these allegations undoubtedly were, a whole range of other scandalous allegations were of still greater concern to the hospital authorities. After all, though hardly welcome, given the body-blow they inflicted on the asylum's reputation, instances of staff or patient violence could and would be used as evidence that the institution's problems were the result of inadequate funding by the state, and hence could be transformed into testimony of the need for more generous appropriations. It was far more difficult, however, to deal with suggestions that Dr. Cotton was illegitimately diverting his energies, while on the state payroll, to making money from the treatment of private patients.

Misses Gertrude Smith and Grace Fields, the joint proprietors of the Charles Private Hospital, reluctantly appeared in response to a Bright Committee subpoena. Cotton, they acknowledged, had supplied virtually all the hospital's patients since its opening a few months previous – a total of forty, eighteen of whom he had already operated on. Reproductive organs, stomachs, spleens, caeca, and colons had all been subjected to the surgeon's knife. The doctor visited his patients on the average of twice a day and was frequently consulted by telephone about their treatment.[10]

Next, an assistant attorney general, Theodore Backes, appeared to give more details in the case of Mrs. Georgiana Phillips, the patient who had been sterilized against her will. Mrs. Phillips, it transpired, had then been a ward of the Court of Chancery and, when he had learned of the plan to operate on her, Backes noted that he had explicitly instructed Cotton and Stone "to refrain from using the knife" unless and until they had secured permission from the court. That a complaisant judge had subsequently accepted their defense that the operation had just been "a misunderstanding" on their part should not obscure what had really gone on: surgery on a patient who had refused her consent. Nor, apparently, was this an isolated incident, as Bright and his colleagues soon heard from two ex-patients. Miss Annie Rogers of East Orange spoke of two operations that had been performed on her despite her vociferous objections, the second of which had left her with life-long pain and disability. And

Frank Hill, formerly confined in the criminally insane wing, testified that he had regularly seen patients being dragged, kicked, and punched as they resisted being taken into the X-ray room.[11]

By late August 1925, therefore, these and other witnesses had created the impression that Trenton State Hospital was a house of horrors. Worse still, the hospital board could not produce Henry Cotton in an effort to dispute and refute their allegations. For the unmentionable truth was that their superintendent, having literally taken leave of his senses, remained as disturbed and irrational as ever. Two more weeks passed and still Cotton's mental state had not improved sufficiently to risk his appearance in public. Writing to Adolf Meyer, who was professor of psychiatry at Johns Hopkins and Cotton's long-time mentor, Raycroft sought to keep him abreast of developments, speaking confidentially about the breakdown and Cotton's continuing mental infirmity:

> Dr. Cotton broke down about six weeks ago following a considerable period of nervous excitement and instability. He was greatly confused and apprehensive. He was found wandering about the streets in Trenton following a session before the Bright Committee of the State Legislature. Examination showed a serious kidney condition and a weak heart. He has been gradually improving but is still unable to work . . . I have just returned from an absence of six weeks during which these conditions came to a head. I've not seen Cotton who is down at Spring Lake but apparently in such a condition that he cannot defend himself or the hospital.[12]

The hospital managers were beside themselves. Still convinced that the surgical treatments for psychosis that Henry Cotton had pioneered at Trenton constituted an epoch-making breakthrough in the therapeutics of mental disorder, they had watched with dismay as the legislative committee "accepted and invited testimony from irresponsible persons regarding alleged abuses in the State Hospital due to brutal attendants and forced operations." Public airing of these charges in the media had left the hospital's image in tatters and now they could not even rely on Cotton himself to put the politicians straight. Like it or not, the managers recognized that they had "to meet some of the more serious of these charges at a special session of the Committee on September 23",[13] and that they must do so themselves. After all, nothing more would be required to destroy the last vestiges of public confidence in their establishment than to place on the stand a mad-doctor who was himself self-evidently mad.

Part One

1

No Bughouse Doctor

Who can envy the fate of the mad and the mopish, the distracted and the deranged, the delusional and the troubled in mind? By turns the objects of pity and punishment, of fear and fascination, they have over the centuries been seen as constituting a symbolic and practical threat to the very fabric of the social order. The distress and disturbance of the unhinged remind us all too clearly of the fragility of the rule of reason. Simultaneously, their looming presence constitutes a source of profound stress on the lives of those forced to cope with them. Whether ranting and raving, or melancholy and withdrawn, madmen and madwomen have experienced and provoked an explosive mixture of commotion and disarray, guilt and despair, stigma and shame. For hoi polloi and literary folk alike, the crazy may on occasion become figures of fun, but in the shadows lurks a darker perspective, from which they are viewed as an explosive mix of menace and misery.

The very intractability of the problems of the mad is compounded by the common view of them as creatures no longer responsible for their actions, as *non*-entities whose behavior can never attain the dignity and status of human action. To be considered insane is, in many respects, to have suffered a kind of social, mental, and metaphysical death. If their madness leaves them bereft of their status as moral agents, the lunatics' loss of civilized standards of conduct and of contact with our common(sense) reality likewise becomes the occasion for seeing them as less than fully human, and for treating them accordingly.

Even if they escape being seen and dealt with as brutes, the extremity of their condition is seen to justify the most desperate remedies. Small wonder that the nineteenth-century lunacy reformer Lord Shaftesbury concluded that "madness constitutes a right, as it were, to treat people as vermin."[1]

If madness itself conjures up the most profound sorts of existential anxiety, the madhouses to which we have traditionally consigned its victims have inspired their own set of gothic fantasies about what happens behind their walls, nightmare images that circulate and re-circulate, haunting our imaginations. In the words of the late eighteenth-century mad-doctor William Pargeter,

> The idea of a *mad-house* is apt to excite, in the breasts of most people, the strongest emotions of horror and alarm; upon a supposition, not altogether ill-founded, that when once a patient is doomed to take up his abode in these places, he will not only be exposed to very great cruelty, but it is a great chance, whether he recovers or not, if he ever more sees the outside of the walls.[2]

However loudly and insistently some may proclaim the therapeutic virtues of the lunatic asylum, to its inmates and to the public at large it is only a tomb for the living dead.

So it is, too, with the mad-doctors, those captains of confinement who make their living from speculating in this species of human misery and lay claim to special powers to identify, to manage, or even to resurrect those victimized by the corruption and death of the mind. Few other practitioners of the healing arts find their pretensions so steadily mocked and ridiculed, their motives so traduced, their own sanity so much the subject of sneers and speculation. "Shrinks," "mad quacks," "bughouse doctors," "smiling hyenas" – over the centuries, alienists have been subjected to more than a modicum of the stigmatizing labels routinely aimed at their patients. And on more than one occasion, they have earned the opprobrium.

For many readers, the gothic tale I am about to tell will confirm their worst imaginings about asylums, the mad, and those who claim to care for them. It links madness, mayhem, and manslaughter (and occasionally murder itself). Its protagonists are some of the leading figures in Anglo-American psychiatry and medicine, including the man who was perhaps the most eminent American psychiatrist of the first half of the twentieth century, Adolf Meyer. Though the events I recount might once have constituted a medical scandal of major proportions, they were quite deliberately and unceremoniously swept from sight along with the thousands of victims who were experimented upon, maimed, eviscerated. Hundreds of casualties paid with their lives for this particular episode of medical hubris. Perhaps even now they can serve as a warning, a reminder that the intrusions of the medical *savoir*/savior into the realm of mental disorder have not always been blessings. Be that as it may, the story of the disastrous large-scale experimentation at the New Jersey State Hospital at Trenton certainly deserves to be rescued from the oblivion into which it has hitherto been cast.

These days, anyone wandering on to the grounds of Trenton State Hospital will find buildings almost as derelict, dilapidated, and decayed as the handful of patients who still call it home. Like most of the Victorian museums of madness, those monuments of moral architecture that their founders hailed as "the most blessed manifestation of true civilization the world can present,"[3] New Jersey's first mental hospital has fallen on hard times. The once handsome trees that adorn its grounds are tangled, neglected, and overgrown. Their heavy foliage casts the buildings beneath them into gloomy shadows. Within their sepulchral shade, one breathes a dank and dismal atmosphere where mold and putrefaction seem to be everywhere. Iron bars on the windows deposit brown rust stains onto the stone and brick beneath. Behind them are the remains of rotting metal screens, encrusted with nameless dirt and filth, the deposits left behind over the preceding century and a half by the now departed denizens of the back wards of this desolate place.

Broken panes of glass allow the trespassing visitor to gaze on empty wards bereft of furnishings, human and inanimate. Where once two thousand and more inmates were consigned to this noisy and noisome cemetery for the still-breathing, now an eerie silence and emptiness reigns. No one strives any longer to sustain the previously inviolable boundary between the worlds of the mad and the sane. Cast loose from the fetters of their confinement, those who would once have inhabited this place have been consigned to the tender mercies of what our Orwellian masters call "community care." Lunatics at large are now dumped into the most deteriorated zones of our inner cities. Here they find themselves repressively tolerated alongside a variety of other kinds of human jetsam and flotsam. Some have become exemplars of that new urban phenomenon, the sidewalk psychotic. Others serve as easy prey for a new trade in lunacy, inhabitants of board and care homes, many of which were set up by entrepreneurs eager to profit from this species of human misery. Left behind, and at least as forlorn and forsaken as those who once crowded their wards, the old buildings barely endure. Amidst the detritus left behind by the despairing and the despaired of, they offer mute testimony to the abandonment of an earlier generation's enthusiasms for the supposedly curative properties of the madhouse.

Hidden further back, behind the stone-fronted original buildings that date from 1848, placed at a strategic remove from the public road past the old asylum, there remains one still fully functioning portion of this previously self-contained universe, the forensic unit that houses the criminally insane. Where the gatehouse to the main hospital now lies empty and unguarded, the boundaries of this secure unit are still starkly defined by high walls topped with razor wire. Searchlights are mounted on the walls, canine units patrol the no man's land that surrounds the forbidding grey buildings. No pretense or architectural contrivance seeks to disguise the purpose of their slab-like sides. And along the perimeter guard towers and the glint of high-powered rifles signal a determination to keep those who personify society's worst nightmares safely under lock and key.

A century ago, the main hospital at Trenton had just celebrated its fiftieth anniversary. Dubbed "her first-born child" by Dorothea Dix, the patron saint of the lunacy reform movement in nineteenth-century America, the grim buildings served as her own final refuge for the last half-dozen years of her long life. Like its counterparts elsewhere in the United States, Trenton found its early therapeutic ambitions swamped by legions of the poor, the aged, and the chronically disabled. Here, under the nominal guidance of the complacent and indolent John Wesley Ward, the "tainted creatures" whom he and his colleagues dismissed as degenerate and biologically inferior lingered out their days. Ward had been at Trenton since 1867 and had served as its superintendent for more than three decades. These had been largely somnolent years, marked by the slow accretion of chronic cases and the remorseless growth of the asylum population, which had reached almost 1,300 by 1907. Once installed in his post, the good doctor was content to tend his collection of prints and sea-shells,[4] and to spend as little time as possible with the patients, who were left instead to the tender mercies of the ruffianly attendants.

2 *Trenton State Hospital: a view of the main building, which dates from 1848. This idealized view of the asylum in its extensive grounds was frequently reprinted in the institution's annual reports.*

For the forty years Ward had been associated with the recently renamed Trenton State Hospital, he had kept a low public profile, warehousing the unwanted and seeking to avoid trouble or public notice. There had been the odd controversy that provoked a small ripple of attention. The press had briefly paid some attention in 1901, for example, when one of his assistant physicians alleged that an attendant had choked a patient to death.[5] But such incidents were few and far between. Like most of his colleagues running state hospitals, Ward had little difficulty keeping his institution out of the headlines and turning his own job into a sinecure.

Without warning, however, the isolation of life in his asylum was disturbed. Oddly enough, the precipitating cause of the dissolution of the seemingly impenetrable barrier between the asylum and the outside world was not the ordinary sort of moral panic that all such institutions gave birth to from time to time – the patient released prematurely who proceeds to murder his nearest and dearest; the allegedly sane person confined improperly in the company of the mad. Instead, it was a minute, seemingly insignificant organism, invisible to the naked eye, one of those mysterious "germs" that the public had recently learned to blame for all manner of diseases.

Dysentery and diarrhoea were an almost endemic feature of mental hospital life, one of the many unattractive but seemingly ineliminable aspects of life in an overcrowded and underfinanced receptacle for society's unwanted. When symptoms surfaced in a handful of patients in the spring of 1907, the hospital authorities saw no cause for alarm. Within days, however, events took a more serious turn. More and more patients became ill, and the gravity of their illness became ever more apparent. Along with nausea, vomiting, and uncontrollable diarrhoea, many of the victims developed prolonged high fevers and chills, symptoms that were accompanied by agonizing muscular pains and seizures. Several of the afflicted suffered from gross intestinal hemorrhaging, and in early April the first fatalities occurred. Belatedly, Ward and his assistants realized that they were confronting an epidemic of typhoid fever.

As with other awkward and inconvenient administrative matters, however, even once the diagnosis had been made, news of the outbreak was kept from outsiders. Nor did the hospital authorities exhibit any sense of urgency. Ward's carelessness and complacency, coupled with his evidently weak grasp of the nature of bacterial infections and his long-standing feud with the hospital's warden and business manager William Hayes meant that no effective steps were taken to discover and eliminate the source of the outbreak. Conditions in the hospital steadily worsened and by June typhoid had become epidemic, infecting staff as well as patients and threatening to produce hundreds of casualties.

Uncertain as to how to proceed, Ward summoned the State Department of Health for a consultation. But beyond ceasing to draw water from an open and possibly contaminated spring, he made little effort to act on their recommendations. A month later, as the number of cases continued to grow, panicky headlines began to appear in the local papers and Henry Mitchell, secretary of the State Board of Health, openly voiced fears that the outbreak would soon spread to Trenton itself. How strange that an insane asylum, of all places, should thus threaten public health! For if the asylum's mission had originally been proclaimed to be therapeutic, it had long since become primarily concerned with quarantining the crazy and segregating the biologically defective and degenerate lest they spread the taint of madness to future generations.

Delay and dissension in dealing with the outbreak soon proved fatal to the careers of both Ward and Warden Hayes. The state legislature launched an inquiry. A relentless train of revelations surfaced – tales of neglect and maladministration; corruption, both physical and financial; and worst of all, patient abuse at the hands of attendants, extending even to murder – crimes, Ward now acknowledged, that he had deliberately covered up.[6]

The medical director, it transpired, had deeply resented the curtailment of his authority some fifteen years earlier, when in an effort to drive down costs a lay warden had been hired to manage the hospital's business affairs. The doctor's simmering resentment of his diminished role had been translated into a deliberate policy of non-cooperation, indeed of barely speaking to his rival.[7] He and Warden Hayes now seized the occasion to blame the other for failure to contain the epidemic – the upshot being that both men's reputations were left in ruins.[8]

The legislators heard evidence of how lucrative contracts for food and clothing had been steered towards relatives of the asylum staff and board of managers. As for the outbreak of typhoid, it was difficult to determine which of the many sources of filth and physical corruption that were exposed to view might bear ultimate responsibility: a water supply shown to be contaminated by leaks from the asylum and city sewers; a dairy whose floor was encrusted with human and animal excrement, and whose milk containers swarmed with flies gorged on nearby piles of sewage; the filth and disorder found throughout the wards; or the manifest failure to disinfect the contaminated clothing of those already victimized by the disease.

Then there was the aging Dr. Ward's performance on the witness stand, where he appeared bemused and befuddled, claiming that the piles of human and animal waste in the dairy posed no threat to the milk supply (which he proudly asserted he made use of himself) and conceding in the face of hostile questioning that he had never so much as seen a typhoid "germ." His acknowledgment that the excreta from the first typhoid patients had been dumped, undisinfected, into the Delaware River, the source of the city's water supply and that this "might have been dangerous to Trenton" caused only slightly more of a sensation than his simultaneous revelation that more than six weeks had elapsed between the time he had been informed that one of the asylum's springs was contaminated and his order to discontinue using it. Capping the portrait of the mental hospital as a Bedlam over which he exercised little or no effective control were revelations of patients who had been beaten and abused by attendants. At the climactic moment, Ward was forced to acknowledge on the stand that he and the managers had conspired, a year and a half earlier, to conceal the murder of a patient by two particularly vicious attendants. Small wonder that by July 29, 1907, the asylum board of managers, pressed by Governor Stokes, had demanded the resignation of Ward (to be followed ten days later by Hayes) and had promised a complete overhaul of the institution's administration. In the meantime, a team of outside workers was ordered into the asylum to clean up the filth and ordure, and the attorney general announced that he was considering the indictment of Ward and his assistant physicians for covering up a murder.[9]

Within a matter of days, the board of managers had selected a new warden, the politically well-connected Samuel Atchley, formerly sheriff of Mercer County.[10] But the search for a new medical director took far longer, with the managers apparently torn between their desire to appoint someone from within the state and their acknowledgment of the need to hire an alienist, as mad-doctors had now come to be called, with unimpeachable credentials. Henry Cotton's appointment, first rumored in the press on October 5, and only confirmed publicly after the committee had visited the Danvers State Hospital in Massachusetts, signaled their reluctant acceptance of reality: they must give priority to countering the massive damage the scandals of the summer had inflicted on the hospital (though Cotton's chances certainly were not harmed when the committee learned that he had spent most of his summers as a child just a few miles from Trenton, at the Princeton home of his aunt, Mrs. Samuel Van Cleve).[11] Unlike his predecessor, he assured the board of managers, he was happy to cede oversight of the business affairs of the hospital to a lay manager, since he wished "to devote his whole time to the treatment and care of the patients."[12]

Trained at the University of Maryland and at Johns Hopkins, Cotton had apprenticed in psychiatry at the Sheppard and Enoch Pratt Hospital under Henry Hurd and the eminent Princetonian Stewart "Felix" Paton, before obtaining an even more prestigious post at the Worcester State Hospital, where he worked under the Swiss neuropsychiatrist Adolf Meyer. Meyer, together with Cotton's superior at Danvers State Hospital, Charles Page, served as the young psychiatrist's two professional references in support of his application and spoke glowingly of his accomplishments and his promise.[13] If John Wesley Ward had seemed as mystified and at sea with modern medical science as many of his lay audience, Henry Aloysius Cotton could boast of scientific credentials that would put most American physicians at the turn of the century – let alone his poorly educated fellow alienists – in the shade.

Meyer, Cotton's august mentor, had been educated at Zürich and then at Paris, Edinburgh, and London, and had recently moved to his post at Worcester after spending three years as a pathologist at Kankakee State Hospital in Illinois. With his extensive European training in neurology, he was determined to revolutionize "old fashioned asylum practice" by introducing serious and sustained clinical and pathological research that aimed at laying bare the biological roots of mental disorder.[14] Modeling his approach on the best German clinics and mental hospitals, Meyer had established positions for four new assistants a year, recruited from the best medical schools in the country on the basis of their academic record and performance in a competitive examination. To these jobs he succeeded in attracting those who in many instances went on to become the leaders of the next generation of American psychiatrists. Three of them, indeed, were subsequently to serve as presidents of the American Psychiatric Association.[15]

Cotton's selection for one of these posts and his exacting training under Meyer provided him with an important set of credentials as someone in the vanguard of the application of science to psychiatry. The circle was scarcely a large one. So far as most of the medical profession was concerned, the words "science" and "psychiatry" scarcely belonged in the same sentence. In the last quarter of the nineteenth century, anesthesia and antisepsis on the one hand and the discovery of the bacteriological basis of many diseases on the other had transformed the status and prospects of surgery and general medicine. But no comparable breakthrough had occurred in the understanding or treatment of mental disorder. Just months before Cotton had won his post at Trenton, Charles Hill, the physician-in-chief at the Mount Hope Retreat in Baltimore, had risen to deliver his presidential address to the nation's alienists, who were assembled at the annual meeting of the American Medico-Psychological Association (soon to rename itself the American Psychiatric Association). Ruefully, Hill felt driven to confess an unpalatable truth that the profession naturally sought to obscure and ignore, the dismal reality was that "with all our boasted advancement, our therapeutics is simply a pile of rubbish."[16]

For a quarter of a century and more, the psychiatric profession had sought to explain away its therapeutic failures by declaring that the mad were degenerates and defectives, tainted creatures whose blighted minds were but a reflection of their hopeless heredity. But for those claiming to possess expertise in the diagnosis and management of the mad to employ such tactics to excuse their failures was, in a wider perspective, the counsel of despair. With madness viewed as "the necessary organic consequence of certain organic antecedents," and the lunatic dismissed with the observation that "it is impossible he should escape the tyranny of his organization,"[17] those who superintended the institutions of confinement were condemned out of their own mouths to the status of boarding-house keepers or prison wardens. Hill's confession of alienists' helplessness in the face of the condition they purported to treat was news to no one save the most naive, but the dismal reality it reflected was a major source of the thinly veiled contempt with which the rest of the medical profession viewed their psychiatric colleagues.[18]

Trapped within the walls of the asylum as surely as most of the patients, alienists remained members of an isolated and stigmatized specialty coping with what they themselves insistently proclaimed was a congenital and essentially incurable condition. Asylum doctors were, as even a sympathetic observer remarked, "too much overburdened with the details of management, the reception of visitors, replying to correspondence, preparing returns and reports, or other mere clerical duties, to have time or inclination for scientific studies, or even the proper medical care of the patients."[19] Others had rendered an even harsher judgment: the New York neurologist Edward Spitzka spoke scathingly of work that "is not only without value, but absolutely misleading; . . . claims advanced are founded on that happy combination of effrontery and ignorance, which currently passes under the designation of . . . charlatanism." Asylum superintendents, he sneered, were "experts at everything but the diagnosis, pathology, and treatment of insanity."[20]

The bright and brash young men in Meyer's circle thought of themselves as harbingers of a very different future. They were the shock troops of the coming revolution in their profession, men who would bring the tools and techniques of the new scientific, laboratory-based medicine to bear upon the recalcitrant problem of madness, dispelling etiological ignorance and overcoming therapeutic impotence.[21] They applauded when Edward Cowles, superintendent of the private McLean Asylum in Boston, spoke of how essential it was that the treatment of mental diseases be "brought more closely than ever to common ground with general diseases." After all, under Meyer's tutelage, they were already pursuing the new pathways Cowles urged upon his fellow professionals:

3 *Meyer, Cotton, and the staff at Worcester State Hospital. This group portrait dates from the turn of the century. Meyer, with his arms folded, is the second figure from the left. On the other side, the second figure from the right in the back row is a jaunty-looking, dark-haired Henry Cotton. In the middle, in the doorway at the back of the picture, is the asylum superintendent Hosea Quinby, an administrative psychiatrist par excellence: unimaginative, remote from his charges, and content to immerse himself in bureaucratic routine, leaving the patients and their troubles to the tender mercies of his underlings.*

pioneering "new methods of investigating the anatomy and physiology of the nervous system," and searching for "the toxic causation of disease."[22]

Henry Cotton was among Meyer's most devoted disciples. Distressed when his mentor left Worcester to assume a post with greater national visibility as director of the Pathological Institute of the New York state hospital system,[23] young Henry kept in frequent touch by mail,[24] repeatedly thanking Meyer for the training he had provided and assuring him that "I shall always feel that to you I owe my inspiration in this work."[25] Eighteen months after Meyer's move to Manhattan, Cotton wrote to him in order to announce a transfer of his own – a promotion to second assistant physician at the Massachusetts State Hospital at Danvers "at a considerable advance in salary" – that was essential in the light of the other piece of news he had for Meyer – that he was engaged to be married to a certain Alice Delha Keyes of Baltimore. Marriage often forced ambitious young psychiatrists to seek more lucrative alternatives to work in a state hospital, but Cotton was determined that his scientific career would come first. "I could not bear the idea of going into [private] practice," he told Meyer, and assured him that he planned to continue his laboratory researches on the general paralysis of the insane.[26] Periodically, Cotton wrote to report on his progress, and on one occasion even arranged to spend several weeks of his vacation extending his researches under Meyer on Ward's Island, the isolated spit of land in the East River to which New York City had long consigned its mad folk.[27]

Soon, Cotton's zeal led him to seek still more advanced training, of a sort even fewer of his contemporaries and rivals in psychiatry could match. For at least a quarter of a century, virtually all the most talented and ambitious young doctors in America had flocked to German universities and clinics. They were the epicenter of the new scientific medicine.[28] Would-be psychiatrists, however, had not featured prominently in the ranks of these medical pilgrims. Cotton was determined to change that. In the fall of 1905, he wrote an excited letter to Meyer: the hospital authorities had granted his request for nine to twelve months of study leave, and he proposed to spend it at the most advanced center of research in biological psychiatry in the world.[29]

American psychiatry remained an essentially isolated, institution-based specialty, with scarcely more than a token connection to universities, and one that in any event largely lacked any systematic connection to organized programs of research. Its German counterpart, in sharp contrast, from the mid-century had cultivated the same sort of links to university-based polyclinics and research institutes as the rest of German medicine, embracing from the outset Wilhelm Griesinger's doctrine that mental diseases are brain diseases.[30] To be sure, German psychiatrists appeared to have neither time for nor interest in therapeutics and they manifested still less concern for their patients. Inmates were viewed as little more than interesting specimens. Nowhere outside these German institutes, however, was there a more intense commitment to organicism, a greater determination to trace the roots of mental disturbance to underlying neuropathology, or a more sustained commitment to making manifest the microscopic anatomy of the brain.

With Meyer's help and encouragement, and armed with letters of introduction from him, Cotton was able to depart in the New Year.[31] Arrangements had been duly made for him to spend 1906 in Munich, working on brain pathology and histology under the world-famous Kraepelin, Nissl, and Alzheimer, an experience that cemented his commitment to tracing the biological roots of mental disorder. Emil Kraepelin's textbook had already revolutionized psychiatric nosology, transforming the very categories within which psychiatrists thought, and establishing the notion that there were several distinct forms of psychosis, each with its own characteristic course and outcome.[32] Franz Nissl and Alois Alzheimer pioneered the study of the microscopic structure of the brain. Nissl had discovered stains that allowed the structures of nerve cells to be seen under the microscope, and in 1907 Alzheimer would identify the neurofibrillary tangles, neuritic plaques, and shrinking of the brain that are associated with the form of senile dementia that now bears his name. Working alongside these men and gaining their imprimatur gave Cotton a professional pedigree few could match. On his return to America, his promotion to the position of assistant superintendent at Danvers then constituted the penultimate step on his rapid rise to one of the richest prizes in his profession.

For once the local Trenton paper was engaging in something more than local boosterism when it announced that the local asylum's new superintendent "stands high in his profession." Few of the *Trenton Evening Times'* readers would have had any idea about the contents of Cotton's reported publications on such subjects as "The Relation of General Paralysis and *Tabes Dorsalis,*" "Central Neuritis," "The Cytological Study of the Cerebro-Spinal Fluid in Mental Diseases," or "Unilateral Mono-Radicular Regeneration of the Posterior Roots of the Cord in General Paralysis." But that was precisely the point. A listing of this sort was self-evident proof that the community had attracted into its midst someone intimately familiar with the microscopic miracles of modern medicine. It offered a promissory note that scientific intelligence would now be brought to bear upon the mysterious ravages of madness.[33] As soon as he had privately learned that the job was his, Cotton had written to his mentor to thank him, and to boast that he planned "a complete reform at Trenton."[34] October was a month filled with good news. Barely two weeks before Cotton formally assumed his new position, his first child, Henry junior, was born,[35] and then, almost before he had time to absorb his changed circumstances, Cotton's move to New Jersey was upon him and the hospital's 1,600 patients became his responsibility.

He was appalled by what he found. "Such a deplorable condition of affairs," he told Meyer, "one would not believe could exist in an insane hospital today." Ward's virtual inertia had allowed the attendants to rule unchecked over the patients, controlling them by means of a sub-culture of violence and brutality. "Patients [by the hundred] had been restrained for years and no one knew why."[36] The whole place had the atmosphere of a prison, a place, like so many other similar establishments, where, in the words of the eminent Philadelphia neurologist Weir Mitchell, "in the sadness . . . of the wards . . . the insane, who have lost even the memory of hope . . . sit in rows, too dull to know despair, watched by attendants: silent, grewsome machines which eat and sleep, sleep and eat."[37]

Cotton immediately made it clear that the old regime was at an end. Though most American psychiatrists had long disputed the claims of their English counterparts that even the most violent lunatics could be managed without recourse to mechanical restraints,[38] the ambitious young superintendent at once adopted this controversial approach as his own. Within two months of his arrival, more than seven hundred pieces of restraining apparatus had been confiscated from the wards and relegated to the hospital's museum. Efforts were already under way to retrain and discipline the attendants, a program soon expanded into a fully fledged training program for psychiatric nurses. Strong rooms were torn down, and fire alarms installed to protect against one of the great dangers of institutional life. Occupational therapy was introduced to try to eliminate the problems associated with patient idleness and, as far as his limited budget allowed, the new superintendent sought to add to the number of ward personnel.

But all of these changes, symbolic and practical, were in Cotton's eyes but the preliminary groundwork that had to be accomplished before he could undertake a more vital set of reforms. Convinced that insanity was fundamentally a biological disorder, he was determined to remake the old asylum into a modern hospital. If only one could fully mobilize the resources of modern scientific medicine, the scourge of madness would soon be lifted, just as surely as Koch, Pasteur, Lister, and their allies had triumphed over other forms of deadly and hitherto incurable disease. And perhaps he, too, would join that august pantheon of medical heroes.

If Trenton's assistant physicians had hitherto been sunk in a somnolent routine, now they would find their medical skills stretched to the limit. "What he taught his staff," a later medical recruit commented, "was simple, but very important. He believed that you should take a good hard look at the patient, not just write him off as crazy. He was no bughouse doctor, not one of those fellows that knew the routine and that's all. He was a *real* doctor. He wanted you to *study* the patient's condition."[39]

Real rather than bughouse doctors, though, needed access to the tools and techniques of modern medicine. That meant improved physical facilities: a new operating theater, improved laboratories, an infirmary and isolation ward for tuberculous patients, a professional library filled with the current medical literature, and regular staff conferences to discuss its contents. Previously parsimonious politicians were somehow persuaded to make the necessary funds available, assured that their investment would rapidly pay off in dollars and

4 *Henry Cotton and the medical staff of the Trenton State Hospital in an image dating from 1915. Henry Cotton is in the front and center of the group, with Clarence Farrar, one of his assistant physicians who had trained at Johns Hopkins, standing on the far right of the picture.*

cents. For if the biological roots of madness could be laid bare, effective therapies would surely follow, and the burden of the chronically insane would thus be lifted from the backs of long-suffering tax-payers.

Critics had long charged that many of psychiatry's deficiencies derived from its isolation behind the walls and bars of the asylum. On a variety of fronts, Cotton moved to address this problem as well. Local physicians were engaged as consultants. The hospital's medical staff were encouraged to attend professional meetings, to take professional leaves of absence to further their scientific education, and to undertake original research and publication. By 1913, Cotton was able to collect the resulting papers into two sizeable bound volumes.[40] That same year, he attracted Clarence Farrar, an associate professor at Johns Hopkins who was widely viewed as one of the most promising psychiatrists in the country, to join his staff as an assistant physician – a remarkable coup considering that Farrar was two years his senior, had at least as distinguished a scientific pedigree, and occupied an academic post at what was widely seen as the leading medical school in the country.[41] Here was confirmation that Cotton was enjoying at least partial success in moving Trenton from its status as a provincial backwater to a leading place in American psychiatry.

As insistently as he sought to link his institution to the medical mainstream, Cotton aggressively restructured his staff's approach to those they were called upon to treat. Meyerian principles were introduced into patient care: reworked and far more detailed case histories were started; stenographers were employed to record the ravings of psychotic patients for further study; and in 1911 two full-time social workers were hired. Initiatives like these would surely soon demonstrate the value of modern psychobiological psychiatry.

Except that they did not – at least not in any obvious, statistically measurable ways. To be sure, the elimination of physical restraints, the reinvigoration of the hospital's professionals, and the improved training of the attendants improved the patients' lot in a variety of not inconsiderable respects. And Cotton's periodic reports of his activities to his mentor, now installed as the first professor of psychiatry at America's premier medical school, Johns Hopkins,[42] brought him repeated marks of the great man's favor, including permission to name his second son Adolph Meyer Cotton.[43] But these modest rewards were, in his own eyes at least, only a poor substitute for the sort of therapeutic breakthrough he was convinced must proceed from his determined application of the principles of modern medicine. Somehow, the scourge of insanity had to be made to yield to his energy and ambition.

2

The Perils of Pus Infection

The frustration Henry Cotton felt at the failure of all his efforts to produce therapeutic gains for his patients can only have become the more intense when he contemplated the position and status of his chosen specialty, especially when psychiatry was compared with other branches of the medical enterprise. Though the medical profession had initially greeted the claims of Lister and Pasteur with skepticism and ridicule, by the turn of the century its entrenched conservatism had rapidly given way in the face of the powerful practical advances that flowed from their work: gains in both etiological understanding and therapeutic efficacy. In surgery, antisepsis (and the routine employment of anesthesia) prompted rapid advances in the technical capacities of surgeons, and equally striking therapeutic breakthroughs. Regions of the body that had hitherto been off limits now provided ever-expanding opportunities for surgical intervention, investing the most skilled modern operators with a capacity to ward off disability and even death in a way that would have been unimaginable only a few years earlier. Surgeons, for the first time, could invade the body cavity with relative impunity, and the standing of their specialty rose accordingly.[1]

For a variety of acute and life-threatening diseases treated by their physicians, similarly remarkable breakthroughs occurred within a short time. Within a five-year period, the typhoid bacillus, the plasmodia parasites that cause malaria, the tubercle bacillus, cholera vibrio, and diphtheria bacillus were all identified in the laboratory, and with the development of antiserums for diphtheria and tetanus, the medical outlook seemed completely transformed.[2] In the early years of the twentieth century, general medicine's prestige (and the prospects of its practitioners) soared, along with expectations that medical science would soon extend its dominion over yet-wider realms of disease and debility. Potentially, the practical payoffs of the bacteriological revolution seemed limitless.[3]

Alienists had long proclaimed that insanity in its various forms was rooted in disorders of the body. In their hands, though, somatic theories of mental illness had scarcely been linked to dramatic therapeutic advances. Rather, they had been used in precisely the opposite fashion, to account for the essential incurability of most serious forms of mental disorder and to explain away the profession's apparent therapeutic failures. During the last third of the nineteenth century, those specializing in the management of the mad had increasingly moved to adopt a grim determinism. Borrowing from evolutionary biology (albeit of a Lamarckian rather than a Darwinian sort), alienists had portrayed insanity as the product of a form of phylogenetic regression, a degenerative series of changes whose roots in defective heredity were essentially irreversible. Violation of "natural law" damaged body and brain, and whether in the sinner or in his or her offspring it led to inexorable physical and moral decay. Tainted and defective, these morbid varieties of humankind displayed problems that were rooted in "an inward and invisible peculiarity of cerebral organization."[4]

Complacently, Cotton's colleagues on both sides of the Atlantic consoled themselves and their public with the thought that, under the circumstances, it was perhaps as well that so small a proportion of their charges were cured and discharged back into the community. After all, "no human power can eradicate from insanity its terrible hereditary nature, and every so-called 'cure' in one generation will be liable to increase the tale of lunacy in the next . . . it is [thus lamentable but] inevitable that the higher the percentage of recoveries in the present, the greater will be the proportion of insanity in the future."[5] In an attempt to rationalize a regime of extended custodial care, G. Alder Blumer, the superintendent of the private Butler Asylum in Providence and president of the American Medico-Psychological Association, spoke darkly to his colleagues of the threat their charges posed to the very future of civilization. The mentally ill, he noted, were "notoriously addicted to matrimony and by no means satisfied with one brood of defectives."[6] The not-so-distant consequence, as others hastened to point out, was that "the transmission of insanity leads gradually to the abasement and ultimate extinction of the race."[7]

In a similar vein, an English psychiatrist warned that "every year thousands of children are born with pedigrees that would condemn puppies to the horsepond."[8] Ironically, misguided attempts to care for and cure the mad threatened to worsen the situation by "prevent[ing] . . . the operation of those laws which weed out and exterminate the diseased and otherwise unfit in every grade of natural life."[9] Hence Blumer's public lament about the demise of the ancient Scotch "rough and ready method" of burying babies and their disturbed mothers alive: putting aside sentimental concerns, "from the point of view of science the cruel and remorseless Scot was more advanced than his descendants of our day."[10]

In practice, however, while their language promoted visions of the Apocalypse, Anglo-American alienists shied away from actually implementing a program to exterminate their charges. For the most part they instead remained content with demands for eugenic tactics such as constraints on who could marry, efforts to secure the "violent extrusion" of "morbid varieties or degenerates of the human kind" into institutions that allowed for permanent confinement,[11] and (in the United States and elsewhere) a deliberate and partially successful attempt to impose involuntary sterilization on the mentally ill.[12] However vile and violent their words now seem, their actions were comparatively – and I stress "comparatively" – restrained.[13]

Cotton, though, refused to join this pessimistic consensus. He had not become a psychiatrist in order to preside over a custodial holding operation or to peddle eugenic advice to those nervous about the prospect of matrimonial alliances with possibly tainted bloodlines. As convinced as any of his colleagues that mental illness was rooted in biology, he nonetheless refused to countenance the notion that insanity was simply the result of hereditary defect and sought instead to uncover some alternative and more hopeful linkage between disorders of the body and those of the mind.

Much of Cotton's earlier laboratory work had focused on the microscopic analysis of the brains of patients who had died from paresis – the paralytic disorder that accounted for as many as 15 to 20 percent of male asylum admissions in the early twentieth century. Here was a group of patients whose dramatic physiological, neurological, and psychiatric symptoms had long been recognized as comprising a distinct syndrome: their grandiose delusions, manic elation and exaltation (or, more rarely, profound depression), restlessness, excitability, and sudden violence all progressed remorselessly and inevitably to dementia; even as subtle and often overlooked disorders of speech and gait proceeded towards epileptiform convulsions, physical deterioration, progressive paralysis, and death.

By the late nineteenth century, as increasing attention was focused on studying the pathology of this appalling disorder, suspicions were widespread that paresis represented the terminal stage of syphilis. Such suspicions now hardened into certainty through a series of developments that Cotton saw as a rebuke to those psychiatrists who had so blithely embraced hereditarian accounts of insanity. Here was a precursor of the gains that would result from the application of laboratory science to the problems of psychiatry. First, just before Cotton took up his new post at Trenton, August von Wasserman had created a reasonably reliable test for the presence of the syphilitic parasite, *Spirochaeta pallida*, in the bloodstream.[14] Then, in 1913, shortly after the introduction of Paul Ehrlich's "magic bullet" Salvarsan, the first modestly useful treatment for syphilis, Hideyo Noguchi and J. W. Moore published results that definitively confirmed that the corkscrew-shaped syphilitic spirochete led to brain lesions, which in turn caused paresis.

Cotton was scarcely alone in embracing the notion that the pathology of general paralysis provided a paradigmatic model of the origins of mental disorder, a harbinger of what harnessing the new science would bring to the understanding and treatment of mental illness. He was certainly, though, one of the more aggressive alienists in using the new Salvarsan treatment on his paretics, and when the normal lumbar injections of salvarsanized serum produced disappointing results, he experimented with introducing it directly into the cerebral cavity.[15] More importantly, the idea that this particular form of insanity was connected to infection by microbes exercised an ever-greater hold over his imagination. Perhaps, he mused, other forms of mental disorder had a similar etiology. Might this at last provide the key to effective therapy for the psychotics who thronged his wards and refused to recover their wits?

For all the gains the new science of bacteriology had brought in its train, in the first decades of the new century a number of chronic, debilitating disorders – and not just those that preoccupied psychiatrists – had remained frustratingly recalcitrant in the face of every attempt to unravel their secrets. For these diseases, the source of much distress, suffering, and premature death, even effective palliative therapies were in short supply, while their etiology remained speculative at best. Given the spectacular advances in the understanding and treatment of a variety of previously deadly diseases that had flowed from germ theory, it is not surprising that leading medical men on both sides of the Atlantic succumbed to the temptation to extend the bacteriological paradigm. Increasingly, a variety of influential voices suggested that such chronic diseases as arthritis, rheumatic fever, nephritis, and degenerative diseases of the arteries "might be caused by bacteria disseminated through the lymph or blood-streams from a hidden primary focus of infection."[16]

It was well established, for example, that the painful and often deadly muscular contractions of tetanus or lock-jaw were produced when bacteria in a wound stimulated the production of powerful toxins, which then spread through the body. Through the same mechanism, might not hidden reservoirs of infection, obscure sites of chronic focal sepsis, similarly prove responsible for a whole range of other baffling diseases? Such views found a particularly powerful advocate in Frank Billings, one of the most prominent figures in early twentieth-century American medicine.

Serving as dean of the School of Medicine from the amalgamation of Rush Medical College and the University of Chicago in 1901–24, Billings had been elected president of the American Medical Association in 1902 and of the elite Association of American Physicians four years later. From the first years of his tenure at Rush, with his enthusiastic leadership, much of the research and clinical care at the school and its affiliated hospitals and institutes was devoted to the pursuit of focal sepsis. Billings's ability to tap into the massive new wealth of the Chicago plutocracy to build his medical school and its affiliated institutions made his insistence on the importance of focal sepsis unusually consequential.[17] From 1904 onwards, he boasted, the "etiological relationship of Focal Infection to Systematic Diseases has been a subject of study in the clinical material of Rush Medical College, in affiliation with the University of Chicago and the Presbyterian Hospital," and the new research units he helped to create, the Memorial Institute for Infectious Diseases and the Sprague Memorial Institute at St. Luke's Free Hospital, joined the search.

And his enthusiasm for the doctrine did not diminish with time. Invited to deliver the Lane Lectures at Stanford Medical School in September 1915, he seized the occasion to advocate the vital importance of converting a new generation of physicians to the war on sepsis. In almost apocalyptic language, he urged his listeners "to make sure that all sources of focal infection have been obliterated."[18] Warming to his task, he warned darkly of the hidden dangers that lurked within: "The existence of focal infection of the jaws . . . without the manifestation of much discomfort is remarkable . . . often not discoverable by inspection and escapes the attention of the physician and dentist. Properly made Röntgen ray films of the jaws will enable one to recognize the real morbid and anatomical condition."[19] Once pathology was uncovered by that new and remarkable medical technology, intervention must then be ruthless and thorough-going: "Deplorable as the loss of teeth may be, that misfortune is justified if it is necessary to obliterate the infectious focus which is a continued menace to the general health."[20] "Too often," he continued, "the tonsillar tissue in children and also in some adults is a culture medium of pathogenic bacteria and as such is a constant source of danger as a portal of entry of infectious bacteria through the lymph and blood streams to the tissues of the body."[21] Again, since "infected tonsils cannot be successfully sterilized by any known method of treatment . . . entire removal is the only safe procedure."[22] Moving down the digestive tract, intestinal stasis "should have proper medical management or, if necessary, surgical treatment . . . [and] the focal acute and chronic infections of the pelvic organs of woman ... should be rationally managed and surgically treated when necessary to safeguard health and life."[23]

Such beliefs were not only the peculiar province of the medical elite of the Windy City. Similar views were held in the bastions of early twentieth-century scientific surgery and medicine: at the Mayo Clinic, for example, where Edward Rosenow had brought the doctrine with him from Chicago and converted Charles Mayo himself; and at Johns Hopkins, where the sainted William Osler's successor as professor of medicine, Llewellys Barker, along with his colleague William Thayer, became prominent and vocal proponents of focal infection theory. At their clinic in Rochester, Minnesota, Will and Charles Mayo had built a world-wide reputation for surgical skill in the years between 1889 and 1906, and by the latter year, they and their staff were undertaking more than 5,000 operations a year. More than half of these were intra-abdominal procedures, an extraordinary number for the period, a volume of surgery made possible by their unusually low mortality and morbidity statistics, and one that drew a string of professional observers to their establishment. Initially scornful of clinical medicine and skeptical of the value of laboratory data, the Mayos had eventually begun to modify their views, and Rosenow's recruitment reflected their conscious decision to augment the quality of medical diagnosis and care offered at the clinic, and to push forward into the new area of experimental bacteriology.[24]

Johns Hopkins, self-consciously modeled on German academic medicine and ambitious to raise the scientific status of American medical institutions and medical education, had swiftly established itself as the leading medical school of the age. Though many of its faculty remained skeptics,[25] in Lewellys Barker, who served as its chief physician, focal sepsis had gained still another prominent and strategically vital convert – just how vital is suggested by what Joel Howell's research has shown about the changing patterns of surgical practice at the New York and Pennsylvania Hospitals, prominent institutions that were increasingly serving an affluent clientele, but establishments that were nonetheless far from the academic vanguard of medicine. At the Pennsylvania Hospital, the clinical records show that the number of operations rose from 870 in 1900 to 4,180 in 1925, and the increase in surgery followed a similar pattern in New York. Revealingly, while only 0.52 percent of the surgery at the Pennsylvania Hospital in 1900 was for diseases of the tonsils, the proportion had risen to 19.02 percent in 1920; and whereas 2.09 percent of surgery at the New York Hospital was performed on tonsils in 1900, the figure was 25.51 percent in 1925.[26] Here, starkly revealed, is the penetration of the ideas associated with the doctrine of focal infection into the center of routine American medical practice.

Across the Atlantic, leading figures in British medicine and surgery hastened to add their voices to the chorus, invoking Lord Lister and calling repeatedly for the development of a "surgical bacteriology."[27] In later years, the prominent society surgeon Arbuthnot Lane would come to be seen as something of a crank on the subject of the connections between civilization and the malfunctioning of the bowels, but in the first two decades of the twentieth century, his dark warnings about the dangers of autointoxication and the "flooding of the circulation with filthy material" as a result of "chronic intestinal stasis" (constipation to the layman) were accorded the respect due to a newly minted baronet whose appendectomy had saved the life of England's monarch.[28] Men like Sir Berkeley Moynihan, less flamboyantly scornful of tradition and more solidly part of the Establishment, provided a perhaps more respectable endorsement of the health dangers of chronic sepsis and sluggish colons.[29] And outside the ranks of the knife-happy surgeons, one could look to figures like the immunologist Elie Metchnikoff (director of France's prestigious Pasteur Institute and winner of the 1908 Nobel Prize for Medicine) for passionate testimony on behalf of the value of Bulgarian yoghurt as the key to warding off autointoxication. Such yoghurt, he proclaimed, was a magical substance that produced a purified and healthy gastrointestinal tract, and slowed the aging process.

The popular appeal of all this proselytizing makes apparent a crucial part of the attraction the doctrine of focal infection possessed: its correspondence with deep-seated and ancient folk beliefs about the importance of "regularity" and thorough cleansing of the cloacal regions of the body, beliefs that had long been given the warrant of professional respectability in the teachings of humoral medicine and that survived intact into the bacteriological age (and indeed right down to the present day). Thus it was that when Lane set aside his lucrative practice "of ten thousand [pounds] a year to propagandize for his New Health Society, the masses flocked to hear him preach the virtues of fruits, nuts and fiber, and of defecating three times a day, the keys to health, long life, and the avoidance of cancer." At Oldham, in Lancashire, for instance, he boasted that his talk was "packed by three thousand or more people" – so large a crowd "that many had to be carried out fainting, while outside mounted policemen were kept busy holding back and controlling the crowd who wished to force their way into the hall."[30]

Popular belief in the intimate interconnections of health and alimentary hygiene was at least equally prevalent in the United States. Indeed, a whole succession of dietary reformers, from Sylvester Graham through Horace Fletcher and Ellen White to the Kelloggs (and more recently the proponents of organic food and farming), have attracted legions of followers by preaching the virtues

5 *John Harvey Kellogg's Battle Creek Sanitarium. Originally founded as the Health Reform Institute in 1866 by Ellen White, the prophet who created the Seventh Day Adventist Church, Battle Creek struggled to survive in its early years, but was transformed when it passed into the hands of one of her acolytes, the master publicist John Harvey Kellogg, in 1875. By 1888, the newly renamed Sanitarium (a term coined by Kellogg) contained between 600 and 700 patients, and was rapidly expanding. This aerial view dates from c.1900, just two years before a major fire necessitated a complete reconstruction of the facilities. At the Sanitarium through the first three decades of the twentieth century, a staff of between 800 and 1,000 ministered to the needs of United States presidents, celebrities, and rich neurasthenics from across the country. A further, ill-advised expansion in 1928, just before the stock market crash, placed the Sanitarium on a shaky financial footing, though it struggled on through the Great Depression, ministering to minds diseased (or at least discombobulated) by what its founder insisted were the poisons and toxins loosed upon the land by a modern, meat-filled diet.*

of dietary discipline and the horrors of intestinal putrefaction. At Battle Creek Sanitarium, John Harvey Kellogg spoke loudly of the evils of consuming animal flesh and the virtues of fruit and fiber. Civilized diet, civilized leisure, civilized defecatory positions and practices had clogged the gut, "flooded [it] with the most horrible and loathsome poisons" and produced that most damaging of outcomes, the "civilized colon," an unequalled source of premature debility and death.[31] Kellogg's establishment advertised itself as a "University of Health," "the largest, most thoroughly equipped and one of the most favorably located in the United States" and boasted of its "eight physicians . . . all that pertains to modern medical treatment . . . trained nurses, regular dietaries, [with] every desirable advantage." Under his leadership, and with his relentless flair for publicity and his culinary inventiveness, the business boomed. From the dozen patients at the failing Seventh Day Adventist institution he had inherited in 1876, then known as the Western Health Reform Institute, Kellogg fashioned an enterprise that "was soon attracting several thousand patients a year."[32] On a still-larger stage, his breakfast cereal business, and a whole array of other proprietary products – Prutose, the delightfully named Nuttose, Battle Creek "Steaks," Battle Creek Skallops, and peanut butter – brought some of the benefits of dietary reform and intestinal regularity within the reach of the masses, to the great benefit of his bank balance (though at some cost to his reputation among mainstream medical men).

The scientific physicians who made much of focal infection recoiled from being identified with the "health faddists" such as Graham and Kellogg. They insisted that their theories were rooted in the authority of the microscope and the laboratory, and spoke in a language that mystified the masses (and perhaps in the process lent their utterances more weight amongst the "respectable classes"). The appeal of their pronouncements to the profession at large may have rested in part on their conscious distancing of focal infection doctrine from its populist overtones (and almost certainly was further aided by their refusal to adopt Kellogg's hostility to the consumption of meat, for "muscular vegetarianism" was always destined to have a limited appeal to the carnivorous American mainstream). Besides, who could dissent from the notion of controlling and eliminating chronic infections as the royal road to increased vitality and improved general health?

It is not clear quite where and how Henry Cotton first became acquainted with the notion of focal sepsis in relation to disease. Perhaps it was Billings's early paper on the relationship of infected teeth to arthritis,[33] or the published version of his Lane Lectures, which appeared in 1916, that first alerted the ambitious psychiatrist to the subject. Alternatively, he may have been introduced to these notions, the cutting edge of medical science, by one of his former teachers, Stewart Paton, now installed as professor of abnormal psychology at Princeton, and in frequent contact with Cotton as a member of the Trenton State Hospital board of managers. Paton was Llewellys Barker's brother-in-law, so the link here would have been a direct and personal one. Barker, Billings, and the Mayo Clinic's Edward Rosenow were all among those Cotton would later credit for alerting him to the dangers of focal infection.[34]

Or perhaps Cotton was telling the truth, and not just flattering his hosts, when he subsequently claimed that his primary inspiration came from British sources.[35] Certainly, a number of eminent British medical men, unlike their American counterparts, had already begun to extend the range of diseases in which focal sepsis might be causally implicated to include psychiatric disorders. The venerable Henry Maudsley, doyen of British alienists in the closing decades of the nineteenth century, had first intimated a possible connection more than fifty years earlier, claiming that

> there is no want of evidence that organic morbid poisons bred in the organism or in the blood itself may act in the most baneful manner upon the supreme nervous centers. The earliest and mildest mental effect by which a perverted state of blood declares itself is not in the production of positive delusion or incoherence of thought, but in a modification of mental tone. The further effect is to engender a chronic delusion of some kind. A third effect of its more acute action is to produce more or less active delirium and general incoherence of thought.[36]

And more recently, the well-known British surgeon William Hunter had warned repeatedly of the perils of "intestinal stasis," particularly its likely effects on mental stability, and had urged his colleagues to respond by developing a "surgical bacteriology."[37]

Cotton was not the first psychiatrist to adopt these new ideas and make them part of his practice. The Scottish alienist Lewis Bruce had advocated careful attention to the problem of focal sepsis as early as 1906, and Henry Upson, the superintendent of the Cleveland State Hospital, had written articles in 1907 and 1909 on the relation of tooth decay to focal infection and thus to insanity.[38] But these men, it seemed to Cotton, had to some degree failed to have the courage of their own convictions. Bruce, for example, had insisted that, "in all forms of early acute mental illness, disorders of the alimentary canal are almost invariably present, and must be treated. Carious teeth are a source of continuous toxaemia, and must be removed as early as possible."[39] But while contending that these "toxines" were "exciting causes of insanity," the Scotsman had insisted still more emphatically that "the chief predisposing factor is hereditary predisposition," the source of "an unstable brain, which is easily thrown out of gear by the direct action of moral or physical causes upon the brain and nerve fibres."[40] Like Upson, Bruce implicated focal sepsis as an etiological factor in only a handful of cases of psychosis, when in Cotton's view it ought rather to have been seen as the master key to unravelling the mysteries of madness. Besides, both men, despite what he contended was their extraordinary prescience,[41] had not been taken seriously by their colleagues.

Cotton had apparently toyed with notions of autointoxication even as a young man at Worcester, and in 1916 he had embraced the theory of focal infection with an enthusiasm no one else could match. His annual report that year reported cryptically that "we have found that focal infection and the absorption of toxins may appear in the etiology of certain groups [of patients] primarily held to be purely psychogenic in origin." The first fifty patients he treated with tooth extractions were all chronic occupants of the back wards, and initial results were disappointing. Already, though, the X-ray apparatus being used to detect infected teeth "is also used in determining abnormal intestinal conditions which we believe play some part in the etiology of certain mental conditions."[42] A year later, however, having extended the treatment to include the removal of diseased tonsils as well, he began to report extraordinarily favorable outcomes: twenty-four of the twenty-five patients who had received the full treatment were discharged as recovered, and with results like these to boast of, "we started literally to 'clean up' our patients of all foci of chronic sepsis."[43] The operating theater and the laboratory facilities that he had previously installed at Trenton would now, he hoped, become the center of a thorough-going scientific assault on the root causes of psychosis.

Almost immediately, however, a crisis loomed on several fronts. Many hospital employees strongly objected to the extra work that the pre- and post-operative care of patients imposed on them. Rumors began to circulate about excessive patient mortality associated with Cotton's increasingly elaborate surgical interventions. Even the young dentist Cotton had hired to augment his staff, Ferdearle Fischer, was initially reluctant to embrace Cotton's planned campaign to substitute a policy of wholesale teeth extraction for crowns and cosmetic dentistry.[44] Sensing trouble ahead, Cotton confided in Adolf Meyer about some of his difficulties: "I know I hold some rather radical views and in order to bring my work to a successful conclusion I have had to overcome the opposition of my Staff. This has not been an easy task . . . for the last two years I have tried to get them interested to look for these sources of infection which I feel existed but were masked and not found by an early examination."[45]

But when, in the early summer of 1918, Cotton found his very tenure at the head of the hospital under threat, his problems did not come from disaffected staff. Fueled by their perception that, like other mental hospitals, Trenton had few effective therapies on offer and essentially constituted little more than a holding pen for the delusional and the demented, the institution's new governing board sought to reorganize daily operations and cut costs. Having decided to elect a new "chief executive officer" who would have overall charge of the care, treatment, and custody of patients, they announced that they had settled upon a lay warden to occupy the post. The effect, of course, was to render Cotton's position untenable, and in something of a panic he appealed to his mentor Adolf Meyer for assistance. Three days after his first letter, he reported that he and the entire medical staff were threatening to resign if the board's proposals were implemented, the implied insult to their professional pretensions being too much to bear.[46] Meyer hastened to offer his assistance, suggesting that his protégé consider joining his staff at Hopkins if the Trenton board failed to see reason.[47]

Within weeks, however, the immediate threat vanished. The Governor had just installed a new state commissioner of institutions and agencies, Burdette Lewis, an ambitious executive who had previously served as commissioner of corrections for New York City. Only thirty-six, Lewis was a typical Progressive-era reformer with graduate training from Wisconsin and Cornell in political science and economics, a serene sense of his moral and intellectual superiority to the "grafters and lazy incompetents" associated with machine politics, and an equally unshakeable conviction of his own disinterestedness. Though his own career had been wholly within the public sector, he pronounced himself keen to bring the efficiencies of modern business management to bear upon the management of public agencies and, most importantly, to import into public administration the "method of modern advertising adopted by business." Like a chief executive in the private sector, he had a product that needed "selling" – in his case "good government" – and to that end one of his first acts was to raise private funds to hire a full-time public relations director.[48]

Fortunately for Cotton, he and Lewis quickly hit it off, and the commissioner, persuaded of the immense promise of Cotton's revolutionary program of surgical treatment for psychosis, pressured the hospital board to reverse their position.[49] Still, the episode constituted a chilling reminder for Cotton of the low esteem in which his chosen specialty was held by outsiders, and how rapidly the near autocratic power of a superintendent could disappear. In the long run, only a heightened appreciation of the value of medicine in the treatment of insanity could ensure that he would not face further assaults on his position.

With renewed vigor, Cotton attacked the sources of sepsis. By October, he was writing to Meyer to report remarkable successes from the expanding program of defocalization, and to inform him that, with Lewis's support, he was seeking to add a bacteriologist to his staff.[50] Soon, his annual reports could boast an array of outside consultants unmatched by almost any other mental hospital in the country: four physicians, four surgeons, three gynecologists, a gastroenterologist, a neurologist (his long-time supporter, Stewart Paton of Princeton), a laryngologist, a rhinologist, two ophthamologists, a dentist, a genito-urinary surgeon, a pathologist, and the promised bacteriologist. With six other assistant physicians, a roentgenologist (what we would now call a radiologist), and an oral surgeon on staff,[51] here was a mental hospital that could claim triumphantly to mobilize the full array of modern medical specialists against the scourge of insanity. If Cotton's fellow alienists were willing, and in many cases apparently anxious, to isolate themselves within the walls of their asylums, his string of consultants testified to his ambition to tear down these barriers and bring psychiatry into the medical mainstream.

3

The Mecca of Exodontia

With the crucial support of Commissioner Lewis, Cotton now moved aggressively to implement his attack on focal sepsis. During the first twelve months following his near resignation, he managed to appoint four new assistant physicians and someone he referred to as a "woman physician" (obviously a separate species). The personnel changes were a vital step in minimizing internal sources of opposition to the therapeutic interventions from his own staff. "Their work," he noted happily in June 1919, "has been most satisfactory principally because they had no preconceived ideas regarding mental conditions and were willing to accept the theories of the Medical Director and work on the physical condition of the patient."[1] He had also secured the services of two bacteriologists, one of whom, William Striefler, had been on the faculty at Cornell Medical School for the past nine years, where he had worked on focal infection under T. W. Hastings, trying to link rheumatism and dental decay. And Drs. Draper and Lynch, consulting gastroenterologists from New York who served there as attending surgeons at St. Bartholomew's Hospital for Diseases of the Alimentary Canal, had begun visiting Trenton weekly. Together, they made up a formidable team, and one that rapidly expanded its field of operations.

Cotton framed his work in the context of "the alarming increase in insanity recently documented by the National Committee on Mental Hygiene."[2] One source of the swelling numbers was perhaps temporary, but substantial, and had profoundly raised public consciousness of mental disorder. The epidemic of mental breakdowns among the troops fed into the slaughtering machine that the politicians proclaimed was "the war to end all wars" had proved impossible to conceal. Trench warfare had produced millions of dead soldiers and hundreds of thousands of psychological casualties – men who had lost the ability to see, to sleep, to speak, to hear, to walk, to function; who screamed or wept uncontrollably; who hallucinated and became disoriented about time and place; who, most disturbingly from the standpoint of the authorities, had lost the will, and apparently the ability, to fight.[3] Dismissed initially as malingerers, cowards, and degenerates, they were treated harshly, and sometimes even shot, for their pains. Nonetheless, their numbers had grown frighteningly large, and once their condition had acquired a new name – "combat neurosis" or (the name the military tried desperately to suppress)[4] "shell shock" – public awareness of a new wave of psychiatric casualties rapidly rose.

But as the publicists of the new doctrine of mental hygiene proclaimed, even apart from the mental wreckage the war left in its wake, there was a relentless rise in the incidence of madness in the population at large. Institutionalized psychotics seemed to proliferate at an ever-increasing rate. In Illinois the increase over just the preceding eight years had been of the order of 113 percent, and, as Cotton noted, "there are over 417,000 insane confined in institutions in this country."[5] Worse still, "in a large majority of such hospitals, no attempt whatsoever is made to treat such patients."[6] The accumulating mass of chronic, deteriorating patients in the back wards was an ever-increasing burden on the taxpayer, and a standing reproach to the specialty.

From many points of view, Cotton felt that a "great opportunity for synthesizing psychiatry with scientific medicine" had been lost during the First World War.[7] Foolish infatuations with psychologically based explanations and therapies had led many down a blind alley, while at the opposite end of the spectrum the inclination of many other psychiatrists to dismiss those breaking down as physiologically degenerate had produced a therapeutic impasse. At Trenton, however, the growing understanding of the importance of focal infection had perforce required a thorough-going commitment to laboratory analyses, antitoxins, X-rays, and operative interference in an aseptic environment – all the most up-to-date trappings of modern medicine.

Cotton was thus convinced that a new opportunity was opening up to break down psychiatry's isolation from the rest of medicine. Furthermore, if his own results could be replicated, such a rapprochement could be expected to have a spectacular effect on cure rates – and hence also on hospital populations and state mental-health expenditures. Within twelve months of adopting aggressive techniques to counter infection, Cotton claimed that his recovery rate had grown by some 23 percent,[8] and with greater experience and more extensive intervention to excise other sites where sepsis lurked, he began to claim cure rates as high as 85 percent of those he treated.[9] And these were not, he asserted, temporary remissions. Beginning in the spring of 1921, a "special survey has been made of the patients discharged during 1918 by the two social service workers." Gratifyingly, he reported that the number of recoveries had actually increased over the three-year period, from the 360 originally reported to 370, and "we have found that those we consider recovered are earning their living, taking care of families, and are normal in every respect."[10]

Such spectacular results had another happy outcome: they produced major savings for the state budget. Cotton calculated that in just three years his efforts had reduced the burden on New Jersey's taxpayers by more than a quarter of a million dollars.[11] Even this underestimated the financial windfall that he had produced, for as word spread of the dramatic effects of his surgical bacteriology the hospital attracted more and more private, paying patients, many of them from out of state. Where private admissions had amounted to only 11 percent of total admissions in 1916, by 1920–21 they had increased to 349, or 45 percent of all new patients. The hospital census taken on July 1, 1921 revealed that as many as 317 of the 2033 patients present were private, paying patients, a change that, as Cotton hastened to point out, had a correspondingly large and favorable impact on the hospital's bottom line.[12]

In early April 1918, Meyer had remonstrated with his protégé about the tone of one of his recent presentations on focal sepsis, and had expressed the hope that Cotton would modify the paper before it appeared in print. The problem, it appeared, was the younger man's single-minded insistence on a monocausal account of mental disorder. On this early occasion, Cotton scrambled to repair the breach: "I certainly cannot be accused of being antagonistic to any of your teachings and it would be very unfortunate if the paper gave any such impression." He would, he promised, go over the text and "eliminate" the offending portions.[13]

The compromising spirit did not last many months. Though there was the occasional ritual genuflection in the direction of Meyer's emphasis on the multiple determinants of behavior – environment, hereditary make-up, and individual psychology, as well as organic factors – Cotton increasingly stressed a thoroughly reductionist biological account of mental disorders. He dismissed the very concept of "functional" mental disorders as incoherent and "untenable."[14] By 1919 he was confidently asserting that "we believe that [heredity] has very little influence either in the etiology or in the prognosis of mental diseases . . . [and] as in heredity, many cases occur in which we can find no psycho-genetic factors." At best, for Cotton, these two factors played a subordinate role, being neither necessary nor sufficient to produce psychosis. By contrast, the Trenton staff had become convinced that "infection is by far the most important influence and that, without this factor, the chances for the development of psychosis are very slight."[15] In many ways, it was fortunate that this was so. Heredity, after all, was all but impossible to alter, except indirectly and over several generations, through a program of eugenics – and even here the difficulties were formidable, if those prone to spawn mental defectives refused (as they were all too likely to do) to rein in their propensity to breed. "Infection, however, has been present in all our cases [and] . . . it can be removed by the knife or by vaccine."[16]

Psychoses, as the discovery of the syphilitic origins of general paresis had begun to make clear, were *symptoms*, not diseases. Earlier generations of alienists had misguidedly attempted to treat the dreadful symptoms of what they termed "general paralysis of the insane" with the same sorts of psycho-social therapies they employed for other forms of mental disorder. The results were, in Cotton's view, predictably dismal, for such methods did nothing about the malignant micro-organism that was the real source of the pathology. By contrast his work, he claimed, was now in the process of demonstrating that the same was true of manic depression, of dementia praecox, or schizophrenia, and all the other subtypes of mental illness the psychiatric profession spent so much effort distinguishing from one another.

Heavily influenced by Emil Kraepelin, the eminent German psychiatrist under whom Cotton had once worked, American psychiatrists devoted much of their efforts to the task of differential diagnosis. Cotton was increasingly certain that this was a mistake, the result of a misplaced focus on the diverse epiphenomenal manifestations of madness, to the neglect of the single etiology that gave rise to all of them. "Our studies," he noted, "have led us to conclude dementia praecox is not a distinct entity but is rather a chronic stage of the acute psychosis." This discovery was, he asserted, grounds for optimism about what most had concluded was an essentially incurable condition: "We are convinced that the early stages of dementia praecox offer us no greater difficulties in the treatment than the manic depressive group."[17] But delay could be fatal since the longer the condition persisted, the more likely that the poisoning of the brain would lead to irreversible structural changes, and hence to hopelessness. Were one to wait even two or three years to intervene, one was likely to find that "the brain tissue has probably become permanently affected," so that even the most extensive and aggressive intervention would be doomed to failure. And since "nothing can be done for the chronic patient," early and wide-ranging intervention was mandatory if there was to be any prospect of "arresting the ever-increasing number of human derelicts."[18]

One should not blame earlier generations for blundering down the wrong pathways, for it was only now, with the advent of laboratory-based scientific medicine, that it had proved possible to bring the true state of affairs to light. Trenton's success where others had failed depended upon the exploitation of "all the methods of modern diagnosis" that were the hallmark of modern medicine.[19] It was the X-ray and the microscope that made manifest the crucial fact that "the insane are physically sick . . . Our researches prove the presence of an unusual amount of pathology among the insane, due to bacteriological invasion."[20] And, in the light of the bacteriological revolution, these findings should not occasion surprise. After all, "the theory of bacterial specificity, now so generally accepted, lends much plausibility to the belief that certain strains of the colon bacillus and the streptococcus may produce toxins specific for the brain."[21]

Indirectly, Cotton insisted, it was the presence of these microscopic organisms that provided the key to understanding the mystery that was madness. Ordinarily, one might expect sufferers to complain of illness and debility. But not here. The lesions he saw as the source of insanity had hitherto gone undetected and unsuspected because they were not the sort of acute, fulminating disorders "in which the patient, by reason of pus, pain, temperature, and other symptoms, is only too well aware of the presence of infection."[22] Instead, the damage was done by chronic, latent, masked infections, which lurked unnoticed in the body, only occasionally directly invading the brain (as with tertiary syphilis), but more commonly and insidiously poisoning the system through "the toxin, generated by the bacteria and transmitted to the brain by the bloodstream."[23] Their tendency to "produce neither subjective nor objective symptoms" made such pathology exceedingly "difficult to establish by the ordinary methods of examination."[24] Fortunately, however (and so far as laymen were concerned, almost magically), the scientific physician had recently armed himself with novel tools and techniques that provided him with the power to penetrate to the most hidden recesses of the body. Utilizing these "modern methods of clinical diagnosis – such as the X-ray, bacteriological and serological examinations – in conjunction with a careful history and a thorough physical examination, will, in the majority of cases, bring to light these hidden infections of which the patient is usually blissfully ignorant,"[25] providing an invaluable guide to effective therapy. And, unlike the work of the generations of psychiatrists who had preceded him, "we believe that it can easily be seen that our work is not of the haphazard, hit-or-miss sort, but every method adopted is based on definite pathological concepts and results of clinical laboratory research."[26] Science, Cotton aggressively and repeatedly insisted, was on his side. At Trenton, unlike virtually all its counterparts elsewhere throughout the country and abroad, the modern marvels of bacteriology, immunology, chemotherapy, medical physics, and biochemistry were all mobilized in the assault on psychosis.

It was vital, of course, to proceed expeditiously: "By eradicating these foci at the outset of mental symptoms, a large portion of such cases may be arrested and cured." Better still, one could intervene prophylactically, removing troublesome tissue before it had had time to provoke mental imbalance.[27] But the task was not easy, even for the physician alert to the problem: "I can state," said Cotton, "that not only is the difficulty of locating foci of infection a tremendous one, but the problem of eliminating them when found is almost stupendous. It takes patience and ability to stick to the work of elimination"[28] – an ominous choice of words, as later evidence would show.

In principle, the doctrine of focal sepsis provided an almost unrestrained field for active therapeutic intervention. Infection might lurk in the most obscure nooks and crannies of the body, pumping forth its poisons and wreaking havoc on mental and physical health. From the outset, to be sure, Cotton's favorite target was the teeth, soon enough joined by the tonsils. Careful examination disclosed that "without exception, the functional psychotic patients all have infected teeth,"[29] and the only solution in such cases was extirpation. He boasted that even chronic patients recovered in some instances and could be released once their dental problems were attended to. One long-term patient, who had lingered for years on the back wards, had a single problem-tooth attended to, and promptly recovered her wits. "The only reason we can find for her recovery, after five years in the Hospital, is the extraction of an infected molar."[30] For another patient, whose stay had extended over as long as seventeen years, and about whose recovery all hope had long been abandoned, the removal of two infected molars had been followed by a pattern of steady work and eventual recovery.[31]

Bearing such marvelous results in mind, "if a tooth is at all suspicious, we are of the opinion that it should be extracted."[32] Conscious of the fact that not all his audience would find such a prospect palatable, Cotton hastened to reassure his readers that "this does not mean that every patient should have all his or her teeth extracted."[33] Yet without question, "all teeth with apical abscesses should be extracted. While this opinion may seem radical, it is the only rational viewpoint."[34] One needed to look still further: even "apparently toothless" patients needed careful scrutiny with X-rays, lest they have some remaining impacted or unerupted molar lurking unseen to make mischief and perpetuate their madness;[35] work in Cotton's laboratories had demonstrated that such impacted teeth "are all infected," even where the mouth remained asymptomatic.[36] More generally, "we extract all capped and pivot teeth, and remove all bridge work . . . I am willing to admit that 5 percent of such work is good; but unfortunately for us and for the patient we cannot afford to run the risk of leaving these crowns and bridges in place."[37]

Nor was the need for vigorous intervention confined to those who found themselves already in a mental hospital. Many adolescents suffered unknowingly from incomplete dentition, and their parents had been taught to see this situation as harmless. Cotton knew better: "Our viewpoint differs somewhat from that of the dentist as he claims that unerupted teeth in young people are normal and if left alone will finally come through."[38] On the contrary, Cotton argued that failing to intervene carried grave risks to their mental health and necessitated an effort to search out and treat all cases of this sort as quickly as possible. Such thoroughness, to his mind, might provoke misguided criticism, or even ridicule in some quarters: "Perhaps we shall be accused of being too radical in our opinion . . . but, after many serious mistakes in not extracting such teeth, and with the good results obtained in the patients by reconsidering our decision and later extracting all such teeth, our position is impregnable."[39] And the patients themselves did not object, at least after the fact: "during an experience extending over a period of three years, I have been berated by only one patient for extracting her teeth, irrespective of the number of teeth that had to be sacrificed."[40]

In an age when X-rays were only beginning to be employed on an extensive basis even in the best general hospitals,[41] Cotton kept the Trenton machine humming. In June 1920, he reported that his technicians had taken 4,201 X-ray films in the preceding twelve months, and the dentistry department had then

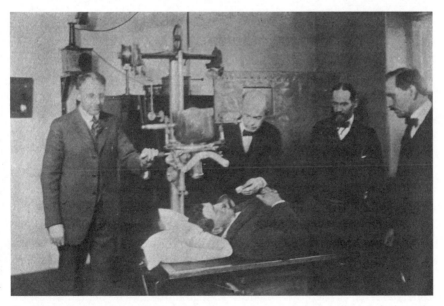

6 *Taking X-rays of a patient's teeth. X-rays were a relatively recent arrival on the scene in the 1910s, and their use at Trenton signaled the hospital's determination to use the most advanced diagnostic techniques of modern medicine in the hunt for hidden sepsis.*

performed 4,317 "ordinary" tooth extractions, and had operated to remove an additional 75 impacted molars. The following year, the dentists were busier yet and the total number of extractions soared to 6,472, an average of about 10 extractions per admission.[42] Cotton insisted, however, that "no teeth were removed without ample justification"[43] and that there was no "excessive" extraction of teeth at his establishment.[44]

Some of the sheer volume of work that needed doing reflected patients' neglect of their mouths. (Cotton noted that "it has been estimated that eighty percent of the population have infected teeth and this is, indeed, a conservative figure.")[45] But even those who religiously sought to care for their teeth might inadvertently be storing up trouble for themselves. Root canals and crowns preserved dentition, but at what cost? "We want to emphasize our view (shared by many progressive medical men) that modern dentistry is a serious menace to the whole country."[46] Pandering to their patients' vanity, dentists were covering up reservoirs of infection with "wonderful cosmetic work" that left germs behind to wreak havoc. Indirectly, these efforts produced "incalculable damage" by producing "serious systemic disease"[47] Often, the patient experienced no pain from what were in reality still decaying teeth, and yet the subterranean pathology continued to undermine their health, eventually leading to death, "or a condition worse than death – a life of mental darkness."[48] "It seems incredible," Cotton continued, "but it is nonetheless a fact, that the dental schools of today are teaching the installation of gold crowns, fixed bridge work, pivot teeth or Richmond crowns, all of which have been definitely proven to be a serious menace to the individual's health. To paraphrase an old proverb, 'Unhealthy is the tooth that wears a crown.'"[49]

Instead of being seduced by promises that played on the vanity of appearances, Cotton felt that the public should be taught that once decay had begun, removal of the offending molars was the only safe course of action. For this to occur, of course, the dental profession must first be convinced of the menace of focal sepsis. "We can then truly look forward to an era when all dentists will realize the importance of not doing what the patient wants in saving his teeth, but what is best for the patient – extracting all infected teeth."[50]

In these first pioneering years, Cotton acknowledged that his approach "seems entirely fanciful to the majority of professional men, both physicians and dentists" – a skepticism he planned to counter with "facts, substantiated by concrete cases."[51] There were signs of change though: "The dental profession has shown that it is progressive and wide awake to a degree that we should like to see in the medical profession." To their credit, "while members of the medical profession still doubt the results of our work and are skeptical as to the validity of the theories discussed, men [in the vanguard] of the dental profession have taken an almost unbelievable interest in the subject and are endeavoring, by every means possible, to correct an evil which has been evident to the leaders of the profession for years."[52] A sea change in public attitudes would surely follow once both professions were fully alerted to the dangers of putting cosmetic concerns ahead of the demands of conserving health. In light of the realities uncovered with the aid of modern medical knowledge, for instance, "instead of creating the impression of advancing age and as ushering in a period of decline, artificial dentures are in reality the greatest possible safeguards against premature old age."[53]

Teeth, then, were initially the primary site for therapeutic intervention, and Cotton's vigorous efforts to clean up his patients' mouths attracted widespread attention, much of which he himself helped to generate. "Unfortunately," though, as he reported with considerable asperity, "the impression has gotten abroad that we claim infected teeth to be the sole cause of insanity" – the upshot of which had been much snickering in some quarters: "We have been dubbed by one Philadelphia neurologist as a 'mecca of exodontia.'"[54]

It was, he protested, a thoroughly misleading mischaracterization. To be sure, the teeth, all too frequently decayed and in close proximity to the brain, were indeed very often the source of the trouble. But they were far from being the only culprits, as his critics ought to realize. As early as June 1919, he had reported that he had found it necessary to extract the tonsils of 337 of the 699 patients he had admitted to Trenton in the preceding twelve months,[55] and the following year, the number of tonsillectomies had risen to 542, "usually [performed] under a local anesthetic."[56]

This alone, Cotton felt, should be enough to give the lie to his antagonistic critics, but, of course, the infected tonsils were only one of many other foci of infection that required his attentions. Cotton acknowledged that when he and his staff began to grapple with the problem of focal sepsis and discovered that oral surgery alone often sufficed to produce "marvelous results," they had at first been somewhat taken aback to discover that on other occasions it produced "no results whatsoever."[57] It rapidly dawned on them, however, that there was an obvious explanation for their failure: the infection must have spread elsewhere, either through the lymph glands or (more rarely) through the bloodstream, or secondarily through swallowing bacteria in the saliva. Consequently, those committed to a "surgical bacteriology" must turn their attention to "stomach, duodenum, small intestine, gall bladder, appendix, and colon, as well as to the genito-urinary tract."[58] Failure to follow through aggressively in this fashion necessarily meant that "there are failures that tend to discredit the whole theory of focal infection, whereas the cause of our failures may be found in our lack of attention to these secondary foci."[59]

In 1918, when the importance of searching for these secondary sites of infection first became manifest, Cotton mobilized to track them down. Using the new Rehfuss method to extract the contents of the stomach for laboratory analysis, he determined that 451 of the 934 patients he examined showed evidence of infection, and attempted to treat 277 of these patients with autogenous vaccines, developed especially for him from cultures of the patients' own bacterial flora by the nearby Squibb Company.[60] The laboratory data had convinced Cotton that "the cases which tend to become chronic or have rapid recurrences are the ones in which [infection has spread from] the teeth and tonsils to the gastro-intestinal tract,"[61] and when the vaccines failed to add greatly to his tally of cures, he decided that more radical measures were called for.

Joining forces with the New York abdominal surgeon J. W. Draper (the former director of surgical research at Columbia and at the Mayo Clinic), Cotton commenced a more wide-ranging investigation of possible sites of focal sepsis. Playing upon the somatic prejudices of their colleagues, they raised the question of whether "there is any proved difference between the transient delusions arising from typhoid and alcoholic intoxications, and the fixed delusions of dementia praecox or manic depressive insanity? Have we not taken the

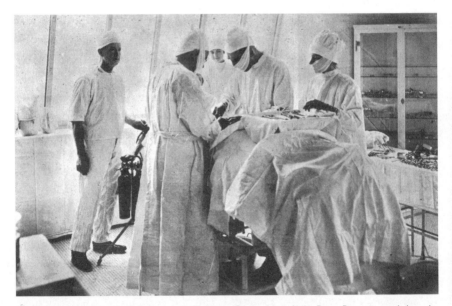

7 An exploratory laparotomy at Trenton State Hospital. Drs. Draper and Lynch, Cotton's outside consultants, are here pictured performing abdominal surgery at Trenton State Hospital. Cotton would later take on these operations himself.

freudian [*sic*] theories regarding the cause of insanity altogether too seriously?"[62] For them, of course, the answers were obvious. By June of 1919, they had accordingly undertaken 57 exploratory laparotomies (operations invading the abdominal cavity) and reported that 7 of these patients (or 12 percent) had died in the aftermath of surgery.

Cotton and Draper's published reports indicated that they had firstly operated on a dozen chronic, deteriorated cases, finding "a great variety of intestinal lesions" in all of them. Cotton's private correspondence and a subsequent review of his cases strongly suggest, however, that from the outset these claims were dubious. Their very first case was a Florence B. who had been admitted on February 26, 1916, having suffered what the patient herself called "a hysterical spell." Her symptoms were rather more serious than that, but scarcely ones that justified the labels "chronic" and "deteriorated." Married to someone her mother disapproved of, and rapidly thereafter pregnant, Florence B. had become depressed and anxious in the aftermath of her mother's death and, when upbraided by her sister, had tried to gas herself, the event that precipitated her hospitalization. Over the succeeding months, as Cotton later informed his former assistant Clarence Farrar (who had treated her in the first months after her admission), "she never got any better, in fact got very much worse and it was the first case on which we operated, resection of the colon. Unfortunately, her physical condition was so bad and her heart so weak that she did not survive, although she lived a week. It served to confirm my opinion, however, that her trouble was largely in the intestinal tract."[63]

While reporting this setback, Cotton assured his former assistant that in general, "our surgical work at the present time is developing very nicely. Drs. Draper and Lynch, who I consider know more about intestinal pathology than anyone in the country, come to the hospital from New York once a week and we have operated on about forty cases."[64] With what were alleged to be good results with these chronic patients, the surgeon and the psychiatrist were emboldened: "we were convinced it would be conservative surgery to explore the abdomens in the more recent cases," and again they found clear evidence of pathology in their first 12 cases.[65] Though compelled to acknowledge that "sufficient work has not been done as yet to make any definite conclusions," both men were sure they were on the right track,[66] and the range and quantity of the surgery undertaken now began to increase rapidly. Fortified by laboratory analyses[67] that demonstrated to their satisfaction that "the bacteria have entered the tissues," and recognizing that "they cannot as yet be successfully eradicated without radical surgical measures to remove the infected area,"[68] over the following twelve months they completed a total of 238 operations. By 1921, Cotton confidently pronounced that, as a result of their courageous work, "many psychopathic patients in the State Hospital are thus proven, in reality, to have been chronic intestinal invalids in whom the psychic phenomena were purely secondary to an unrecognized, but nevertheless extensive, disease in a congenitally misshapen and deformed bowel."[69]

Cotton and Draper's investigations had led them to conclude that "there is no shadow of a doubt that the segment of the bowel most prone to infection in the ratio of at least 10 to 1 is that developed from the hind gut and lying on the right side," a troublesome piece of tissue that "because of its decadent tendencies" well deserved the title of "the wisdom tooth of the gut."[70] The surgical solution in this case was to remove the terminal portion of the ileum, the caecum, and the first portion of the colon, an operation Cotton referred to as the "developmental reconstruction of the colon."[71] Such operations, fortunately, were only needed in about 20 percent of functional cases – the necessity being indicated by the presence of any or all of a wide variety of symptoms: a history of constipation or bilious attacks, any "pain or tenderness in the right or left lower quadrants", or where "X-ray studies . . . demonstrate conclusively the presence of marked delay in the test meal" – an indication of stasis and infection.[72]

That there were obvious hazards associated with these procedures, Cotton did not seek to disguise. Of the 79 resections of the colon he and Draper had performed between mid-1919 and mid-1920, they reported that 21 had recovered, and 23 "died as a result of the operation," generally from peritonitis – though he hastened to inform his colleagues that "the cases which have died have been those of long-standing mental disease."[73] In the professional literature, he reported the results of a first series of 50 cases of "developmental reconstruction of the colon," acknowledging that, while 10 of these had recovered sufficiently to leave the hospital, 14 more (or 28 percent of the total) had died. (Only 3 of these 50 cases were listed as "not benefited" by the operation. Apparently, the dead were to be counted among those who had "benefited" from surgical intervention.)[74] A year later he was sounding a more optimistic note, acknowledging that, until recently, the mortality rate from the hospital's abdominal surgery had been "about twenty-five percent," with "many" of the deaths being caused by "peritonitis," but now claiming that, with the recent decision to use anti-bacterial serum pre-operatively, mortality had fallen to less than 10 percent. The optimism did not last. A 1922 paper presented to the American Psychiatric Association reported on a series of 250 colon operations. Of these, he reported, 25 percent had recovered, 15 percent were improved, 30 percent were unimproved, and 30 percent had died.[75]

Such high mortality rates naturally demanded attention and explanation. Prior to acting as Cotton's consultant, in his large "general surgical practice," Draper had first undertaken these "developmental reconstructions" on a series of "chronic intestinal invalids," removing, as with his mentally disturbed patients, up to two feet and more of the gut, and he noted that "many of the patients are now enjoying good health five years after the time of operation."[76] Among the "invalids" he had treated in general practice, though, he acknowledged that his recorded mortality rate was only 7.7 percent, a marked contrast with the elevated death rate of his patients at Trenton. For some, the outcome statistics for the latter group might seem disturbing, but for Cotton and his staff, the increased mortality among the insane simply reflected "a much lower vitality" for those suffering from mental pathologies.[77] Would-be critics were admonished to remember that "psychotic patients in whom the infection has been long-standing and of great and specific virulence, are not good surgical risks and [naturally] yield a higher mortality rate."[78]

If the results of all this work were initially not startlingly positive,[79] Cotton regarded them as "at least encouraging" and as a sign that he was on the right track. To be sure, given the documented hazards associated with the abdominal procedures, "this research work should not be undertaken by novices or even by general surgeons but, until standardized, should be left in the hands of a highly specialized gastro-intestinal surgeon."[80] Cotton hastened to assure his colleagues that "in competent hands this procedure may properly be looked upon as a conservative preventive measure."[81] "Conservative" obviously had a somewhat idiosyncratic meaning for Cotton, for in a variety of publications, as we have seen, his own data showed an operative mortality rate of between 25 and 30 percent, with "many" of the deaths resulting from post-operative peritonitis. And as for the need for a specialized gastro-intestinal surgeon, Cotton soon regarded himself as fitting the bill: when Draper unexpectedly died, the psychiatrist took over many of his duties in the operating theater. Cotton insisted that, while one would obviously have preferred that the risks be lower (and recent improvements in operative technique promised dramatic advancements in this regard), "where there is no question as to the outcome of the psychoses being terminal dementia, we feel justified in performing a colectomy, with the possibility of a recovery."[82]

The emphasis here should clearly have been on the word *possibility*, for even though Cotton noted that the most likely candidates for bowel surgery were manic-depressive cases[83] (widely perceived by the psychiatric profession as having a relatively favorable prognosis), his claimed cure rates with this group were only on the order of 20 to 25 percent.[84] Two explanations for this unfortunate state of affairs suggested themselves to him. First, it might simply be that the surgical bacteriology remained incomplete. This, of course, implied a need for further surgery, a conclusion Cotton did not shrink from. In some instances, where only the right side of the colon had been resected, "examination, in the unsuccessful cases, proved that the left side was infected, so that it was wiser to remove it"[85] – a procedure that henceforth became a routine practice. In other cases, infection must surely still lurk elsewhere, and careful detective work was needed to ferret out the source of the trouble. Mental hospitals thus required "a diagnostic clinic similar to those established in progressive medical centers ... All the latest methods of internal medicine must be enlisted," requiring new equipment, new laboratories, and new staff.[86] And once this work had begun, there were, it became increasingly clear, simply too many different lesions present for a single surgical procedure to suffice.

Even organs that others mistakenly saw as untouchable might need the attention of the surgeon's knife, though Cotton stressed "the need for the exercise of the most mature and deliberate judgment in the choice of surgical procedures."[87] Fortunately, this still left wide latitude for the necessary intervention. Experiments at the hospital had demonstrated, for instance, that the stomach "is one of the least important organs in the body ... The principal function of the stomach is storage and motility, each easily dispensed with ... The stomach is for all the world like a cement mixer often used in the erection of large buildings and just about as necessary. The large bowel is, similarly, for storage and we can dispense with it just as freely as with the stomach."[88] The thyroid gland had begun to come under suspicion and in 1921 Cotton reported his first half-dozen thyroidectomies.[89] In female cases (and for some strange reason that Cotton was unable to explicate, but facts after all were facts, "in female patients the colon is involved twice as often as in the male cases"), the "gynecological complication ... is also very important. The cervix is infected in about 80 percent of the cases. The good results obtained from enucleating the cervix have convinced us of the importance of this lesion."[90] Usually, he reported, the surgeons had found it possible to spare the ovaries and fallopian tubes – an occasion for self-congratulation because, as he pointed out, these organs produced "secretions" important to the maintenance of women's health. Unlike an earlier orgy of sexual surgery to head off women's insanity,[91] during which "unfortunately a great many ovaries were removed,"[92] Trenton's operations respected the findings of modern medical science, and in Cotton's hands, "gynecological surgery becomes, as it should be, essentially and primarily protective."[93]

Not that the male reproductive organs were neglected. Here Cotton turned matters over to another of his array of outside consultants: "During the last year the genito-urinary field in the men has been investigated by Dr. Frederick W. Smith of New York, who has found that at least fifty percent of the chronic cases show infection of the seminal vesicles. In a certain number of cases these infected vesicles have been enucleated [i.e., the patients have been castrated] with gratifying results."[94] For both sexes, such regions as the gall bladder and the sinuses might also require attention. Consequently, "in many of the cases it has been necessary to do several operations, such as resection of the colon . . . enucleation of the cervix, cholecystecomy, hysterectomy, oophorectomy, and repair of the perineum."[95]

One particularly fortunate patient, Mrs. Lewellyn, was admitted to Trenton for a second time to be treated for depression and anxiety. Previously resident before the attack on focal sepsis had fully developed, she now experienced the benefits from the new emphasis on surgery. In the months following her admission, she underwent a gastroenterostomy for her stomach ulcer, followed by a right-side colectomy. When she remained depressed, she then received, successively, a thyroidectomy, a complete colectomy, a double oophorectomy and salpingectomy (removal of both ovaries and fallopian tubes), enucleation of her cervix, three series of vaccine treatments, and two series of serum treatments, following which she was discharged as "recovered."[96] By one subsequent count, Cotton and his staff undertook some 2,186 major operations between the first exploratory abdominal surgery in July 1918 and the beginning of July 1925.[97]

Such wide-ranging interventions, as Cotton blithely confessed, did not always meet with unanimous consent from patients and their families. Years later, stories surfaced in the local press of patients being dragged, resisting and screaming, into the operating theater. The hospital authorities would dismiss these as the malevolent imaginings of disaffected employees and paranoid ex-patients, but even Cotton's earliest publications on the need for surgery suggest otherwise. Protests from patients and their families, he insisted, must be ruthlessly pushed aside as short-sighted preferences reflecting the patient's mental disturbance and incompetence, or the imperfect knowledge of their families. "If we wish to eradicate focal infections, we must bear in mind that it is only by being persistent, often against the wishes of the patient . . . [that we can] expect our efforts to be successful. Failure in these cases at once casts discredit upon the theory, when the reason lies in the fact that we have not been radical enough."[98] More revealingly still, on another occasion Cotton boasted of one of many advantages his surgical approach offered over the quack remedies of his psychoanalytic rivals: psychoanalysts, he noted, often blamed their therapeutic failures on patients' resistances and refusals to cooperate with the talking cure.

"We offer no such excuse for our work because patients who are resistive and non-cooperative can be given an anesthetic and the work of deseptization thoroughly carried out."[99] Informed consent being a chimera, given the ignorance and incapacity of those who would have to be consulted, the benevolent physician must perforce rely upon his superior understanding and proceed with the work of elimination, protests notwithstanding.

There was, though, one variety of insanity that even Cotton's professional critics conceded had infectious origins: general paralysis of the insane or paresis had, as we have seen, been recently reinterpreted as a form of tertiary syphilis. While not dissenting from the newly established medical consensus, Cotton simultaneously sought to link the diagnosis more tightly to his claims about the etiological and therapeutic implications of focal sepsis. To be sure, "in connection with our specific treatment in paresis," like their counterparts elsewhere, the Trenton staff had employed lumbar puncture and intraventricular injections of Paul Ehrlich's magic bullet Salvarsan in a last-ditch effort to poison the offending corkscrew-shaped syphilitic spirochete. But Cotton's underlings had also gone further, seeking to improve upon the dismal results of these heroic efforts by undertaking a rigorous search for complicating factors: "we have also been removing all sources of focal infection . . . [since] we are of the opinion that while paresis is due to syphilis, at the same time many of the cases are complicated with serious chronic infections."[100]

Focal sepsis, Cotton suggested privately, might even be the villain of the piece in debilitating neurological conditions that the profession as a whole treated as mysterious, incurable, and deadly. In September 1921, he wrote to Adolf Meyer, not for the first time, about one such patient: "You will be glad to know that Elsie Schumann, the multiple sclerosis case, is entirely well and today does not show any symptoms whatsoever of her trouble. As we diagnosed the condition as colon infection we had the courage of our convictions and in August we resected the right side of her colon, which was very badly involved. She made a rapid convalescence with no complications and is today surprisingly well." Conscious that his mentor might find his claims in this instance a little far-fetched, he hastened to add: "Of course, we do not wish to claim too much for her, but the fact that she is better than she has been for the past two years certainly speaks well for the treatment."[101] He must have been gratified when, instead of expressing skepticism, Meyer responded that he was very interested in the case, and would like more details of the therapy and its outcome.

Even someone as "radical" as Cotton eventually had to concede that there were prudential limits to the kinds and quantity of surgery to which a given patient could be subjected. Where one physically could not remove further organs or parts thereof, recourse was had instead to inoculations with a special serum prepared by the local pharmaceutical firm Squibb's Laboratories by injecting horses with up to eight strains of streptococci and with colon bacilli.[102] Such "vaccines," while not the treatment of choice, could be expected to boost the immune system and assist the body in fighting off the infection that undoubtedly lay at the root of the mental troubles. Most especially, they were an essential adjunct in those cases in which the whole intestinal tract was involved, since obviously one could not remove all of it. Ten doses of 10cc of this magic potion usually sufficed.[103]

Unfortunately, even with such extensive surgical and medical treatment, some recalcitrant patients obstinately refused to recover. At first sight, such cases served as a reproach to the theory. In reality, however, their failure to improve was yet another demonstration of the centrality of sepsis in the producing of mental disturbance. Delayed treatment was the real villain: "the longer the duration [of the psychosis] the less effective detoxification is in restoring the patient's mental health. Such failures can be explained on the grounds that the brain has become permanently damaged, and no amount of detoxification has any effect in restoring the mental condition."[104] Since "nothing can be done for chronic patients" because "the brain tissue has probably become permanently affected," the work of "arresting the ever-increasing number of mental derelicts" must necessarily embrace efforts at prophylaxis rather than cure.[105]

"Cases of long-standing constipation," for example, "should be treated by preventive surgery long before the psychosis develops."[106] Children were an especially important target for early intervention, with at least 40 percent of juvenile delinquents showing "some very marked pathological lesions or physical disturbances which we think account for their delinquency. Many of them are entirely unfit for disciplinary institutions, being, in fact, hospital cases."[107] Advancing scientific knowledge had demonstrated the fallacy of moralistic accounts. On the contrary, "it is much better to explain the waywardness and incorrigibility on the basis of physical disturbances than on a suppositional inherent badness of the individual."[108] And once seen in its proper light, "the problem of this group becomes one for the psychiatrist, physician, and surgeon"[109] – a conclusion Cotton had already begun to put into practice. With Commissioner Lewis's unswerving support, Cotton and his staff were by now extracting teeth and tonsils at the Jamesburg State Home for Boys (where they had found that 75 percent of the juvenile delinquents had infected teeth and tonsils), as well as at the Trenton and Rahway Prisons, and had secured state funding for an X-ray laboratory and a bacteriological laboratory at Jamesburg so as to extend the valuable outreach work.[110] The difficulty of securing adequate equipment and staff at Rahway Prison had meant they were unable to "fully carry out the recommendations" made by Cotton, but in a single year, Dr. R. G. Stone, one of Cotton's most trusted assistants, had managed to complete 34 tonsillectomies and 195 dental extractions.[111]

Even these interventions, Cotton later decided, came too late in the process. Far better results could be anticipated if one were to intervene still earlier, before the systemic infection had produced any symptoms of mental disorder. "Why," Cotton mused, "should [the patient] run the risk of developing a psychosis when, by eliminating all foci of infection, this danger may be minimized or avoided?"[112] He therefore recommended the screening of all schoolchildren, who "may be harboring infection at that time which will later produce a psychosis."[113] The task was almost as enormous as the potential pay-off, since even apparently the best-adjusted child might turn out to be a candidate for future mental troubles. Perverse as it might seem to the lay person, for example, defective children were frequently abnormally bright since "the first effects of cerebral toxemia is [sic] to stimulate the mental activity in the same way as a small amount of alcohol."[114] One illustration of this principle was the infamous Leopold and Loeb case, where two precocious and well-to-do adolescents had randomly picked up and cold-bloodedly murdered a young child just for the thrill of committing the perfect crime: Cotton confessed that he had not personally examined the perpetrators of a crime that had shocked and enthralled the nation, but he "would unhesitatingly say they were suffering from chronic sepsis and toxemia."[115]

Cotton boasted that he himself had operated with great success on the colons of a six- and an eight-year-old.[116] Begging his audience's indulgence for being personal, he reported that when his son Henry reached the age of thirteen, he "showed a marked change of disposition." Clearly, it was imperative to discover the roots of the problem, and intervention was swift: "X-rays of the teeth showed impacted lower third molars. Finally these were removed and all his symptoms disappeared."[117] So convinced did he become of the importance of prophylactic steps to head off future trouble that he subsequently moved still more aggressively, taking the unusual step of having all his two boys' permanent teeth extracted and then undertaking abdominal surgery on his younger son, Adolph Meyer Cotton, when the boy displayed symptoms his father interpreted as indicating an abdominal infection.[118] Other parents, he proclaimed with typical expansiveness, should be counseled to be on the alert for any signs that their child needed similar surgical treatment. Abnormal childhood sexuality, for example, *pace* the bizarre speculations of the Freudians, was an equally strong clue to the presence of "chronic sepsis and toxemia ... [and] in a number of these cases the colon has been resected with improvement in the individual and cessation of abnormal sex practices, such as masturbation."[119]

Here at last was a set of medical and surgical interventions that might lend some substance to the empty vessel that was "mental hygiene," the new shibboleth of the most advanced and "progressive" alienists. With most of the profession wedded to an increasingly pessimistic hereditarian metaphysics and psychosis viewed as the all-but-hopeless end-state of a process of biological degeneration and decay, mainstream psychiatry at the turn of the century had virtually abandoned the prospect of active therapeutics – indeed, in its darker moments leading figures had suggested that "curing" patients simply multiplied the prospects for future generations of defectives. Such thoughts had led Henry Maudsley, the most eminent English-speaking psychiatrist of the previous generation, to lament openly his choice of a career:

A physician who has spent his life in ministering to diseased minds might be excused if, asking at the end of it whether he had spent his life well, he accused fortune of an evil hour which threw him on that track of work. He could not well help feeling something of bitterness in the certitude that one half of the diseased he had dealt with never could get well, and something of misgiving in the reflection whether he had done real service to his kind by restoring the other half to do reproductive work.[120]

Such claims had the distinct advantage of explaining away the profession's dismal therapeutic performance, but possessed the distinct *dis*advantage, on the other hand, of leaving but little scope for expert intervention, and running counter to the central "duty of every physician to exhaust all sources at his command to cure or relieve disease."[121] It was to meet this problem that the doctrines of mental hygiene had been promulgated: if insanity could not be cured, it must be prevented. Such schemes were an ideological chimera the profession could not be inhibited from pursuing just because it lacked much reliable knowledge of the etiology of insanity, or any obvious weapons by which to achieve the desirable objective of heading it off. One might opt, perhaps, for the near-hopeless task of urging the unfit to refrain from "attend[ing] upon the calls of their instincts and passions as does the unreasoning beast."[122] Or else, like many psychiatrists, embrace eugenics and urge that social policy be modified to permit "the operation of those laws which weed out and exterminate the diseased and otherwise unfit in every grade of natural life."[123]

Adolf Meyer himself had been in the forefront of efforts to lend a kinder, gentler face to this whole movement, working diligently for years to co-opt the patient activist Clifford Beers (whose *A Mind that Found Itself*, with its chilling tales of psychiatric abuses, had won for him a national audience), and persuading him over time to serve as little more than a figurehead of his own organization, the National Committee for Mental Hygiene. Meyer had originally sought to discourage Beers's plans for a national movement,[124] and then to bury Beers in a sinecure out of harm's way, fearing that the fledgling crusader would act in ways that harmed psychiatry's interests. In a letter of March 10, 1910 Meyer suggested that Beers should consider working as "inspector of the male wards at Trenton State Hospital," where a series of accidents needed investigation. "It would," he assured him, "be a remarkable experience" and his friend Stewart Paton had already been in touch with Cotton to make the necessary arrangements. But Beers was for once not so easily duped, angrily rejecting what the historian Norman Dain has called "this job as a glorified attendant."[125] Blaming this episode on the relatively innocent Paton, not the real culprit, Meyer, Beers then allowed the distinguished professor to transform the committee's goals, moving them away from his original interest in stopping the abuse of institutionalized patients towards the more amorphous goal of preventing mental illness.

But for all the financial support the National Committee eventually accumulated from the plutocrats and their foundations, and notwithstanding its quintessentially Progressive-era role in conducting fact-finding surveys, in setting up child and marriage guidance clinics, and in launching campaigns to "educate" the public on the principles of mental health, mental hygiene remained essentially empty of content, and Beers's organization itself an enterprise dressed in little more than the emperor's new clothes. With typical belligerence, Henry Cotton now sought to revolutionize the whole movement. As he delighted in pointing out, his theory and practice promised to supply an endless field for prophylactic efforts of a substantial and quite conventional sort, directed along pathways that were properly biomedical and practical – a program of scientifically guided action that stood in marked contrast to the rhetorical hot air that had hitherto passed for a serious assault on the problems of epidemic insanity.

4

Selling the Cure

Henry Cotton had never been one to hide his light under a bushel, having been convinced from his earliest days as a young psychiatrist that he was destined for greatness. He had found a kindred spirit in Commissioner Lewis, for whom Cotton's work was the epitome of what scientifically guided reform and good government could do to alleviate society's problems. Cotton's own propensities towards self-promotion found a ready echo in his superior's up-to-date insistence on the value of public relations, and the two of them worked together to make as broad an audience as possible aware of the great breakthroughs the work at Trenton was producing. Much as the modern advertising industry was transforming economic prospects and underpinning the emerging consumer society, a campaign to educate the public about the perils of pus infection promised dramatic pay-offs in improved public health, while simultaneously saving both the state and society the economic costs and existential misery that madness inevitably brought in its train. Publicity was vital, for "in no other field of medicine can such results be obtained by educating the laity to the dangers of chronic infection."[1]

At least as important, of course, was spreading the gospel to Cotton's fellow professionals, and in the first years following the adoption of a fully fledged assault on focal sepsis, Cotton worked indefatigably to enlighten psychiatrists and the medical profession at large. Beginning with papers in two successive issues of the *New York Medical Journal* and another in the *Journal of Dental Research*, both in 1919, Cotton published a string of papers on the subject in state and national medical and dental journals. Seizing opportunities to address local and national meetings, he spoke before the Northwestern, New York State, and New Jersey Medical Societies between February and April 1920,[2] and addressed the Neurological Association on "The Dementia Praecox Problem" in New York in June. In the spring he also traveled to Iowa to address the American Academy of Applied Dental Science, and then on to New Orleans for the annual meeting of the American Medical Association. For this occasion he had prepared a particularly elaborate presentation, and besides a formal paper on "What is Being Done for the Insane: A Statistical Study of 150 Laparotomies," he set up a "scientific exhibit" devoted to the laboratory and surgical work being undertaken at Trenton that "was visited by a great many physicians." Twice daily, he employed the latest technology to reinforce his message, with "moving pictures of the work of the hospital and another demonstration of lantern slides showing pathological conditions found in the teeth, tonsils, and gastro-intestinal tract."[3] Such tactics, he reported with pleasure, "attracted considerable attention" to his work, and at the 1921 annual meeting of the American Psychiatric Association in Boston, "it was gratifying to learn that many of those engaged in this work who were extremely skeptical three years ago volunteered the information that they were attempting to carry on similar work in the institutions under their care."[4]

These formal presentations at professional meetings and his publications in peer-reviewed journals were, however, but the tip of the iceberg. Cotton also took it upon himself to travel to a substantial number of mental hospitals up and down the East Coast – Brooklyn, New York City, the Norristown State Hospital in Pennsylvania, and the vast Milledgeville State Hospital in Georgia, with its ten or twelve thousand patients – "to discuss with members of the staff the work and the practical details of examining patients in order to demonstrate the presence of focal infection."[5] In early 1920, "Thos. B. Aiken, visiting dentist for the Hospital for the Insane, Sydney, Australia . . . made a trip to this country, the principal object of which was to investigate our methods in order to introduce the same in [his own hospital],"[6] and by July 1921, a very sizeable number of psychiatrists, surgeons, and administrators from around the United States had followed in his footsteps.[7] The Governor of New York sent a three-man commission to examine Cotton's work, and in 1920 added a special state appropriation to fund a resident dentist at all the New York state mental hospitals.[8]

Cotton's passion for publicity and his propensity for insistent self-promotion were not calculated to sit well with many of his professional colleagues, particularly since he laced his presentations on his achievements with acid asides about the failings of much of mainstream psychiatry. To be sure, his attacks on the new psychoanalytic psychiatry could be expected to fall on receptive ears among many of his professional brethren, who preferred to refer to Freud as Fraud, and looked askance at the very notion of talk as therapy. When Cotton asked rhetorically, "does not psychoanalysis, in its extreme form, bear a somewhat similar relation to the science of psychiatry as christian science [*sic*] bears to scientific medicine?" a majority of his colleagues would have nodded in assent. But assaults on their own preferences and prejudices were another matter entirely.

Cotton took delight in acknowledging that by insisting on the purely somatic roots of mental disorder, "we have to some extent antagonized those who believe that psychogenic factors are the only ones to be considered in the causation of the psychoses."[9] He graciously granted that the study of abnormal human psychology was all very well in its way, and it "should not be curtailed as long as it is confined to a study of symptoms and is not permitted to wander in the field of causation and treatment."[10] But when it meddled beyond its proper sphere, it amounted to quackery, a therapeutic fraud that predictably fell flat on its face. Small wonder then that he insisted, given madness's roots in the disordered body, that "the Freudian school . . . has led nowhere in the successful treatment of patients."[11] Psychoanalysis had committed the unpardonable sin "of disregarding or discarding all anatomical or physiological factors, either somatic or cerebral."[12] The magnitude of the error this represented was apparently demonstrated for all to see by the success of Trenton's surgical bacteriology. "More in truth than in jest," he concluded, "may it be said that psychoanalysis will in time be superseded by gastric analysis."[13]

But if Cotton shared the disposition of many alienists to dismiss patients' psychological disturbances as purely epiphenomenal, he was equally scathing about the degenerationist doctrines that most of his somatically-inclined colleagues had embraced. "We maintain," he announced, "that the doctrine of 'hereditary transmission of psychiatric diseases' is very unstable from a scientific viewpoint."[14] It was a "malevolent" approach that "is not in harmony with modern biological knowledge and is, therefore, obsolescent." The profession had embraced these "detrimental and destructive" ideas to hide its own impotence and explain away its therapeutic failings, and hereditarian accounts of insanity had served it all too well in these respects: "this fatalism assumes the role of a cloak to hide our ignorance and stifle initiative in the investigation of causation looking to prevention and relief." The price paid by both doctor and patient was a heavy one, "for if we believe firmly in these doctrines of heredity and the 'inherited constitution' . . . then evidently it would be futile to try to arrest the disease or search for methods of relief except along eugenic lines . . . [whereas] we are in no such dilemma as regards the effect on [the insane] of pathogenic bacteria and their toxins."[15]

Here was a full-blown assault on the received wisdom of the field, reflective of Cotton's characteristically robust confidence in the impregnability of his own findings, and expressed with the belligerence and pugnacity that were so central a feature of his personality. Not for him the subtleties or subterfuges of the diplomat. But on other fronts as well, Cotton's behavior was calculated to raise the hackles of many of his fellow alienists. In particular, his efforts to capture lay attention led him in directions that threatened to produce professional censure.

As early as April 1918, Cotton had addressed the New York Psychiatric Society on the importance of "extracting infected teeth, removing infected tonsils, and clearing up the gastro-intestinal infection," and in July he submitted a revised version of this paper to August Hoch, who had succeeded Meyer as head of the New York Psychiatric Institute, for publication in the *Psychiatric Bulletin*. Owing to "the amalgamation of this journal with the *Archives of Neurology and Psychiatry*, [his] paper was held up" and was to appear in the first number of the new *Archives*.[16] Impatient of the delay, Cotton now committed a serious violation of professional ethics by allowing Commissioner Lewis to abstract his "annual report to the [New Jersey] State Board of Charities and Corrections and [give] it to the Press." Cotton acknowledged in a letter to Hoch's successor, George Kirby, that "I knew that he intended doing this," yet pleaded that he had done his best to persuade his superior to ensure "that this report be withheld until my paper appeared in the Medical Journal."[17]

Kirby was not mollified by this rather disingenuous claim. As he noted in a letter to Meyer, it was not just that "extensive notice of his [Cotton's] work appeared in the lay press," but also that Cotton had gone so far as to place "an article in the *Literary Digest* with his photograph."[18] Anything that verged on advertising had long been anathema to organized medicine. Such activities smacked of the quack or of the tradesman and threatened to inflict grave wounds on medicine's claims to gentlemanly status and disinterested professionalism. The taboo against discussing "purely professional" matters in front of a lay audience had ancient roots and had long been sustained by a habit of communicating to one's fellow medical men in Latin or Greek. In the new world where medicine bound its fortunes ever more tightly to its credentials as a science, an additional norm had come to be rigorously enforced: the need for new knowledge to run the gauntlet of criticism by one's peers (or at least publication in a professional journal – not always quite the same thing), before being broached before a lay audience.

It was not, therefore, the extraordinary published mortality rates associated with Cotton's abdominal surgery or the ethics of operating on unwilling bodies that first attracted the ire of his fellow professionals, but rather his temerity in seeking lay approval and in rousing lay opinion to demand that the treatment of focal infection become a priority for psychiatry. Aware that publication of his paper was now threatened, Cotton appealed to his influential mentor to intervene on his behalf, and despite his misgivings (for the straight-laced Swiss had to acknowledge that journal editors had an obligation "to see to it that the rules of publication are not overlooked"), Meyer made every effort to do so. On January 15, 1919, he wrote to Kirby confessing that "I do not know whether the paper by Dr. Cotton will appear in the *Archives* after what has happened. I have done all I could in its favor and so has Dr. Hoch, but the other members of the Board are very set and I do not know what their action has been."[19] Three days later, a note from Cotton dispelled his uncertainty – the paper had been unceremoniously rejected and he had had to find a new home for it – in Smith Ely Jelliffe's *Journal of Nervous and Mental Disease.*[20]

Neither discomforted nor discouraged, Cotton pressed forward. He was by now giving a regular class on psychopathology to Princeton undergraduates,[21] and the close ties he already enjoyed with Stewart Paton (dating back to his days as a medical student and now further reinforced by Paton's appointment as the consulting neurologist at Trenton State Hospital) extended to other influential faculty members at the university, most especially the prominent biologist who chaired the Princeton department for a quarter of a century, Edwin Conklin. Less than two years after his unfortunate experience with the editorial board of the *Archives*, the powerful sponsorship of these two men secured him a glittering prize: Cotton was invited to deliver the Louis Clark Vanuxem Foundation Lectures at Princeton University. Vanuxem's bequest to the university, made in 1912, had specified that the lectures he endowed were to be given annually, at least half of the time "on subjects of current scientific interest," and that they were "to be published and distributed among schools and libraries generally."[22] Over the years, many distinguished scientists and scholars lent luster to these lectures: in the years before Cotton gave his series of lectures, such scholars as the French philosopher of science Emile Boutroux, the eminent Italian mathematical physicist and biologist Vito Volterra, and Thomas Hunt Morgan, the biologist who would go on to win the Nobel Prize for Medicine in 1933; in the inter-war years, figures like the philosopher A. N. Whitehead, the astronomer Edwin Hubble, and the novelist Thomas Mann; and, in the second half of the twentieth century, the father of the atom bomb Robert Oppenheimer, the polymath John von Neumann, and such Nobel laureates as Linus Pauling, Harold Urey, and Francis Crick. For Cotton, then, here was a remarkable forum in which to publicize his ideas, an enormously prestigious platform from which he could present his findings to a broad lay audience, and for once without fear of criticism from his professional colleagues for doing so.

Cotton seized the opportunity with both hands. On January 11, he gave the first of four lectures, the others following on the 13th, 14th, and 15th, expounding upon the potentially revolutionary significance of his work, not just for the cure of serious mental illness, but for the prevention of much crime and delinquency – forms of deviance he attributed to psychiatric disturbances that were themselves in turn rooted in disorders of the body. Tying his findings firmly to the rise of "scientific medicine" and "the epoch-making work of Pasteur ... who ... laid the foundations of the germ theory of disease and revolutionized the practice of medicine," he pointed out that "these great truths have had to fight their way to recognition through a maze of opposition and apathy due to the conservative disinclination of mankind to be uprooted from fixed and crystallized hereditary ideas." His own innovations, though resting firmly on the foundations of a newly scientized psychiatry produced by the work of Stewart Paton, Kraepelin, Alzheimer, and above all "the pioneer work of Adolf Meyer," were equally likely to encounter some initial resistance. "But there is a distinct difference between fancy and fact, and if a new conception of the etiology or nature of a given disease is advanced, no matter how much that conception may deviate from traditional teachings, if based upon scientific evidence and proof, it is not to be condemned simply because it upsets all previous conceptions and traditions."[23]

Indirectly addressing the controversy his earlier attempt to court a lay audience had caused, he reminded his listeners that "formerly ... the mysteries of medicine were sacred to the physician ... To further shroud his hypnotic power he wrote in Latin ... [and] the public was kept in ignorance of the nature and cause of disease." But with the advance of scientific medicine "public enlightenment [had become] necessary to prevent disease" and "the progressive physician" had now abandoned these outmoded guild practices.[24] Consistent with these views, he was to devote a substantial portion of one of his subsequent lectures to the need to alert the community to the vital importance of proactively fighting the menace of chronic sepsis.

Placing his work in a broad historical context and proceeding to a frontal assault on alternative accounts of psychosis, Cotton next turned to an outline of the theory of focal sepsis, followed by an extraordinarily detailed recital of the possible sites of infection: teeth in all manner of manifestations (unerupted and impacted teeth, teeth with infected roots and apical abscesses, decayed or carious teeth, apparently healthy teeth with peridontitis, poorly filled teeth, pyorrhea, exostosis and sclerosis of teeth, children's teeth); infected tonsils and sinuses; infections of the stomach and the duodenum, and of the lower intestinal tract and the genito-urinary tract. For such protean problems, he and his dedicated staff had fortunately developed an array of therapies, whose results, he claimed, were little less than miraculous. The impact of his surgical bacteriology was dramatically demonstrated with a series of twenty-five illustrated case histories that were remarkable for their uniform termination in dramatic recoveries from often long-standing and devastating mental illnesses. Briefly reviewing the possible extension of the work to address the problems of the feeble-minded and mentally retarded, the juvenile delinquent, and even the adult criminal, Cotton concluded with a call for a mental hygiene with teeth (or rather without teeth): an aggressive pursuit of sepsis through all the nooks and crannies of the body, searching out the earliest manifestations of infection and snuffing them out before they had the chance to poison the system and bring about mental disorder and collapse.

Within months, an expanded version of the lectures appeared in print, graced by the imprint of the Princeton University Press in North America, and Oxford University Press elsewhere. For the published version, Cotton had successfully solicited a foreword from his mentor, the person praised so fulsomely on its opening page as the man to whom primary credit was due for the "effort to apply scientific principles to the study of mental disorders."[25] Meyer returned the favor. He had followed "the energetic and aggressive work," he announced, "with interest and admiration." It represented "an outstanding contribution of twentieth-century medicine" and "fortunately [proceeded] . . . without elimination of vital functions, such as we experienced in the days of wholesale ovariotomies and the like." "Dr. Cotton," he claimed, "has been among the foremost in pushing to its logical end the freeing of the organism of the insidious infections. He appears to have brought out palpable results not attained by any previous or contemporary attack on mental disorder." Even Cotton's propensity to seek premature publicity was excused: his work had

> unfortunately caught the eager eye of the press and the public before the trial had run the gauntlet of professional criticism and . . . retrial at the hands of others . . . yet this is not an age in which paternalism is expected to protect the public with Latin passages when only the initiated should be admitted. Hence why should we judge a frank utterance given at the author's and reader's own risks unless we can offer an equally good and convincing array of facts in favor of a more generally satisfying picture of "things as they are."[26]

Those who sought to assess or criticize Cotton's work should "judge only by the results of efforts that have been completely carried out. To pull a few teeth without doing a thorough and reasonably complete job, is not doing justice to the demands of the real cleansing. [Likewise] to say that everybody has these difficulties is a very poor argument."[27] To be sure, "extensive well-controlled trials were desirable," and the attentive reader might have noted the characteristic Meyerian aside, in which he spoke of "somewhat extreme claims which go beyond what I personally believe to be my experience." But he or she was more likely to focus on Meyer's plea to abandon "deplorable and disgraceful halfway measures," and on the grand concluding sentences in which Meyer praised the "important experiment ... being carried out [at] the New Jersey State Hospital at Trenton," and suggested that "if means could be made available to carry out and follow out Dr. Cotton's substantial and not merely speculative work, psychiatry would make another large contribution of importance far beyond its own special sphere."[28]

Buoyed by what he most certainly interpreted as a ringing endorsement, and basking in the afterglow of his successful lecture series, Cotton had further reason for satisfaction later in 1921. Funds from the state had underwritten the construction of two new psychopathic buildings, and on October 21 a festive gathering assembled for the formal opening.[29] The women's building was named after Dorothea Dix, the patron saint of American lunacy reform, and its male counterpart after Stewart Paton. Cotton had invited his other chief patron, Adolf Meyer, to preside over the occasion, but the professor sent his regrets, pleading a prior engagement.[30]

In Meyer's place, the assembled throng was addressed by a series of speakers including Dr. Hubert Work, the president of the American Medical Association, and Albert Barrett, the president of the American Psychiatric Association and head of the Michigan Psychopathic Hospital. Work had spent some time going through the wards at Trenton, and professed himself thoroughly familiar with the pioneering research being done there. His tour of the institution had convinced him that "this is a general hospital, really the first one I ever saw. It excludes nothing. It regards the mental alienation as a symptom, as most physicians regard delirium in a fever . . . It does not make a bit of difference what the name for a condition is, provided the cause of that condition is found and eliminated. This hospital, under Dr. Cotton, is a pioneer in that line of work."[31] Thanks to Cotton, "the treatment of the psychoses is surrounded by medical science and not set apart from any part of it. We no longer mistake the shadow for the substance, treat symptoms only and wait for nature to relieve their cause." The hospital at Trenton numbered among the country's "great institutions." It should be seen as a tribute to "the public mind of the people of New Jersey, a composite picture of their social morals, their charity and Christianity in its broadest sense, and it is as well a monument to the most advanced civilization of her people."[32]

Work's endorsement of Cotton's approach was highly significant, for, already a major figure in American medical politics, he was soon to take a prominent role in national politics. Trained at the University of Pennsylvania Medical School, Work had made his fortune from the private Woodcroft Asylum that he had opened in Pueblo, Colorado, in 1896. Eight years before he became President of the American Medical Association, he had also served as president of the psychiatrists' national organization, the American Medico-Psychological Association. A strong advocate of eugenics, he used his term of office to urge states to institute a nationwide program of sterilization and segregation of the mentally unfit and the "feeble minded." He called for prohibition as part of the war "against the poison of alcohol," and for programs to teach hygiene to children in the public schools, as part of a more general "fight against the adulteration of the human mind, against the poison of vicious inheritance, against the perpetuation of degeneracy, to the economic loss of the average efficiency of the nation."[33]

Work had thus played a prominent role on the national stage for a number of years prior to his speech in Trenton in 1921. His conversion to Cotton's cause came just a few months before he joined Harding's cabinet as Postmaster General, and he was to be highly influential in national Republican politics throughout the twenties. In 1923, he would become Secretary of the Interior, replacing the disgraced Albert Fall, who had resigned in the aftermath of the Teapot Dome scandal, and he would remain in that post under Coolidge, before managing Herbert Hoover's successful campaign for the presidency in 1928. If anything, therefore, the powerful endorsement he made in 1921 of the need for an aggressive assault on focal sepsis gained added weight in the months and years after the Trenton celebrations.

Henry Costill, president of the New Jersey Medical Society, echoed Work's sentiments, and promised his audience that "if you would visit any of the general hospitals [in the state] and see the remarkable amount of work that is being done in the removal of tonsils you would come to the conclusion that the medical profession is following the teachings of our esteemed Dr. Cotton." And well they might, for his endeavors were the product of "hard work and a great deal of research" and constituted "one of the greatest advances in the field of medicine." "Dr. Cotton," he concluded, "has built a foundation for the benefit of the health of the people, of which each succeeding generation will reap the benefit and generations to come will rise up and call him blessed."[34]

It was left only for Stewart Paton to express how "profoundly appreciative" he was to see his name permanently associated with "this great hospital." Expressing his admiration for "the devotion of a pupil and friend, the Medical Director of this Institution, Dr. Henry A. Cotton," he reflected that "if it were

8 *Stewart Paton as a young man. The wealthy Paton, too rich to need a paying academic position, was known to his friends as "Felix" in honor of his good fortune, good looks, and sunny disposition. Author of one of America's leading psychiatric textbooks, he declined the post of professor of psychiatry at Johns Hopkins, serving instead as an honorary faculty member at Princeton University from 1910 onwards, where he instituted the first mental health services for university students. An early mentor to Henry Cotton, he provided influential support as a member of the Trenton State Hospital board of managers in the 1910s. Paton, like many of his psychiatric contemporaries, was a strong proponent of eugenics, differing somewhat with Cotton over the place of hereditary factors in the genesis of mental disorder. Throughout the 1920s, though, he continued to endorse Cotton's assault on focal sepsis.*

possible for Dorothea Dix to be present on this occasion she would rejoice as we do over the increased opportunities now provided for bringing the resources of modern medical science to the assistance of those suffering from nervous and mental diseases." With his dedication to "the actual treatment of disease," Cotton had launched "a more successful campaign than has hitherto been carried on against what had probably become the greatest single manace [*sic*] to the progress of civilization – nervousness."[35]

Puffed up with pride at what was being accomplished under his leadership, Commissioner Lewis now attempted to secure yet more publicity for Cotton's work. At the request of the editor of the *Review of Reviews*, Albert Shaw, who deeply admired Lewis as the very model of the progressive public servant, he wrote an extended encomium to the achievements at Trenton, announcing that his state was leading "The Winning Fight Against Mental Disease."[36] In the breathless prose of a man enamored of modern advertising, Lewis reported in early 1922 on the "epoch-making recoveries of insane patients" produced by Cotton's interventions. "Badly diseased or poorly functioning stomachs, parts of large and small intestines, and other vital organs of the abdomen and pelvic regions have been renovated, rearranged, or, in specific cases, removed entirely" – for, fortunately, "we are so wonderfully made that when one organ fails to do its part another one may be induced to undertake the work." The results were "striking," even "sensational," and recoveries among those afflicted with "functional" mental illness had risen from 37 percent before the new treatments had been adopted, to 65 or even 70 percent of those admitted.

Here was a hospital of a thoroughly modern sort, where the cruel restraints of an earlier era had been abolished and where "vision and kindness win." Its very appearance advertised its virtues, as well as its distance from the gothic horrors of the traditional madhouse (just as Lewis's language conjured up associations of purity, of cleanliness, of asepsis):

The new patient, no matter how disturbed he may be, is ushered into an open modern hospital ward in the charge of young women nurses dressed in immaculate white, which harmonizes with the white interior, the snow-white bedding, the white iron beds and the other equipment. In place of

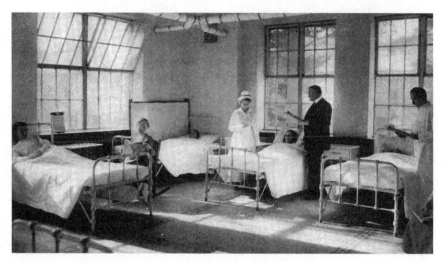

9 *An admission ward at Trenton State Hospital. The hospital's annual report for 1919 used this image to advertise its "modern reception ward for psychopathic patients." (In the Progressive era, the term "psychopathic" did not have its contemporary meaning, but instead was used to refer to recently admitted and potentially curable patients.) Henry Cotton is shown at the bedside of one of the patients, examining her chart.*

the traditional dungeons or strong rooms and burly keepers, these nurses, with the aid of beams of sunlight which burst through the expansive windows, soothe, comfort, and win the excited newcomer back to a semblance of quietude.[37]

Via the skilled, scientifically guided interventions of the physicians, patients would be returned to the world of the sane. With the assistance of his bacteriologist, Cotton had even devised a serum that "has apparently reduced deaths from operations from 30 percent to 12 percent in six months" – a magical potion that might stir up worries about quackery and secret formulae, until one remembered the similar serums that were employed to cure "lockjaw," to end "that terrible scourge, diphtheria, and the vaccines used to prevent small-pox."

Photographs of Cotton and his surgeons at work graphically illustrated the claims about the physical treatment of mental disorder. Here was a picture of

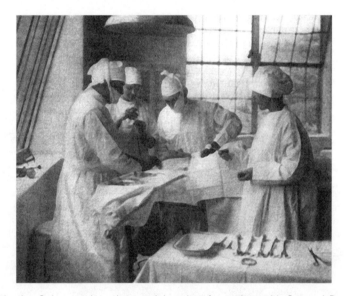

10 *Injecting Salvarsan into the cranial cavity of a patient with General Paralysis of the Insane, or tertiary syphilis. Salvarsan, an arsenic compound, had been developed by Paul Ehrlich as the first "magic bullet" targeted at a specific disease. Whatever its possible value in the early stages of syphilis, its usefulness in the dreadful advanced stages of the disorder had proved quite limited. Cotton used local anesthetic to numb the patient's scalp, before employing an electric drill to make a hole in the patient's skull. Salvarsan was then injected into the meninges in the hope that it would counteract the damage the syphilitic parasite inflicted on the central nervous system. In the caption that originally accompanied this picture in the hospital's annual report, no mention was made of the syphilitic origin of the "insane" patient's psychosis, perhaps because of the stigma attaching to venereal disease.*

an "insane" patient receiving "salvarsanized serum . . . through an opening in the skull (no mention that this was a tertiary syphilitic, lest public sympathy be lost); there of a tonsillectomy, noting that "infected tonsils must be removed in more than 80 percent of the cases at the Trenton, N.J., State Hospital"; and towards the close of Lewis's piece, a portrait of the place "where accuracy triumphs over guesswork – the busy laboratory for the study of specimens." The "generally accepted view" among psychiatrists, Lewis wrote scornfully, was "that insanity is primarily a disease of the mind." Such views were simply "nihilistic so far as stimulating any efforts for the relief of the insane and [their] exponents have signally failed to hold in check the alarming increase in insanity." By contrast, Cotton had "three well-equipped operating services, two for women and one for men, which are busy most of the time" – to say nothing of the dentist's clinic, the X-ray department, and the laboratories. And where other states were experiencing ever greater fiscal strain as they sought to cope with the mounting burdens the insane represented (for they were by some margin the largest line item in most states' budgets), Cotton's pioneering efforts had saved sums that already ran into the hundreds of thousands, attracted "voluntary patients [who] have paid more than $50,000 for treatment this year," and had raised the prospect that "a large part of the asylum section of Trenton Hospital, upon which more than $2,000.000 had been spent in recent years, can be abandoned before long or converted to other uses."[38]

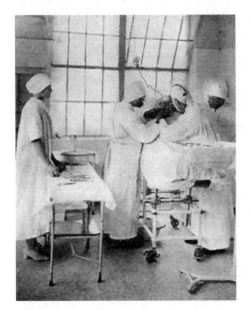

11 *A tonsillectomy.*

12 *The laboratory at Trenton State Hospital. Microscopes and flasks testify to the production of scientific knowledge to aid in the diagnosis of the roots of madness by Trenton's staff.*

Publication in Shaw's *Review of Reviews*, a monthly magazine with a circulation approaching 100,000 that all good Progressive souls regularly read, ensured that Lewis's message would receive a wide and respectful hearing in influential reform circles across the country. Shaw himself had taught at Johns Hopkins in the 1890s, alongside such figures as James Bryce and Woodrow Wilson (with whom he had remained on close terms),[39] lecturing and writing on municipal government, and proselytizing for the management of the city as a form of business enterprise.[40] A quintessential Progressive-era reformer, he used his *Review of Reviews* as a platform to assault the evils of machine politics and the spoils system, and to forward the cause of technocrats and experts as the means to change the world. Cotton and Lewis's work was for him a dramatic demonstration of the benefits that would flow from the application of the principles of science and modern administration to social problems.

At the year's end, Shaw renewed his attempt to publicize the breakthroughs at Trenton, publishing still another lengthy essay on "Physical Treatment for Mental Disorders."[41] Lewis, he informed his readers, "is a notable representative of that new type of technically trained official, the need of which is becoming better recognized every year . . . he is exceptionally qualified, not merely as a trained publicist, but also as a technical expert . . . [Yet] it is as the administrator rather than as the specialist that he serves in his present office. It is his function to see that the experts are supported in the work they are doing in their respective establishments." Prominent among those experts was "a man of singular energy and capacity . . . Dr. Henry A. Cotton" – a man responsible at once for treating patients "so sensibly and wisely that straitjackets, padded cells, and all the old-time horrible paraphernalia of 'insane asylums' have completely disappeared," and for securing what appeared "to be remarkably favorable results in the treatment of insane patients by a somewhat radical policy of thorough and complete attention to their physical condition."[42]

Lewis's discussion of these developments, Shaw remarked with evident satisfaction, had been "very widely read, and it received an unusual amount of attention from members of the medical profession, while it also had a marked effect on public opinion." Shaw's own contribution would be, for the most part, to summarize some of the "numerous letters" he had received in response to the original article, most especially those from medical men, "many of which had come in reply to [my] requests for opinions."[43] There was, however, a prior question, which he acknowledged that some of his correspondents had raised: whether it was appropriate for the laity to intrude upon matters best left to the judgment of professionals.

For Shaw, such criticism was misplaced. Until recently, he argued, the medical profession had concentrated upon "the private treatment of individual cases of disease," but the need for "a systematic attack on ill-health from the social and public standpoint" had become increasing apparent. From efforts "to make sure of pure water and safer milk [through regulation of] tenement houses to prevent conditions that favor the spread of tuberculosis [to] medical inspection in the schools," rational public policy makers were increasingly intervening to secure the community's welfare, and "the old fashioned objections" to such policies "are no longer supported except by ignorance and prejudice." Public discussion of Cotton's work contributed mightily to social progress of this sort, not least by arousing "intelligent laymen," amongst whom Shaw most certainly counted himself, "to demand that in the care of the wards of the State in its hospitals and other institutions there should be medical efficiency and up-to-date management."[44]

Though professing that "we are not partisans of the doctrine that physical maladies produce mental disorder," Shaw's presentation left little doubt of where his sympathies lay. In the words of the first medical man he quoted, the "distinguished authority, Dr. Robert T. Morris, of New York," scientific medicine had been all about shaking off the metaphysical shackles of the past:

Virchow [the widely revered German scientific physician of the late Victorian era] liberated medicine from speculative philosophy. He postulated that illness, including morbid mental states, would always depend upon physical causes. Freud, on the other hand, takes medicine back into mystery. Having given the mind metaphysical position as an entity, he proceeded to draw fanciful pictures upon a small background of fact relating to mental processes. The Virchow position appeals to men of scientific training. The Freud idea appeals to men of literary training. Work at the Trenton, New Jersey, State Hospital for the Insane belongs in category with the Virchow idea.

And Cotton's results were pragmatic proof that "the subject [is] no longer one for discussion in the abstract but is one for recognition of data in the concrete."[45]

Morris's insistence that Cotton's work had the authority of science and real-world results behind it set the tone for most of what followed. Many of those Shaw had written to were themselves in charge of state asylum systems, or were prominent in the emerging field of public health. From New York City, Dr. Royal Copeland, who had recently been elected to the United States Senate after serving for several years as the widely known and popular head of the city's department of health, weighed in "to congratulate this periodical upon publishing Mr. Lewis's article." Copeland had spent considerable time inspecting the wards at Trenton and had been "very favorably impressed with what has been accomplished." The public should be grateful "to these men [for being] brave enough to accept the opportunity to give publicity which will benefit not themselves but the public."[46] From Indiana, from Ohio, from Maryland, came similar letters, some expressing some doubts as to "whether insanity is based entirely upon physical conditions or not," but all acknowledging the country's and the profession's "great obligations to Dr. Cotton for stirring up interest in the use of better methods in our hospitals for the insane," and insisting that "there can be no question as to the necessity of a thorough and exacting analysis and examination of every patient committed to such an institution."[47] Dr. John Oliver of Baltimore dismissed the question of etiology as essentially irrelevant:

> It makes no difference what standpoint one adopts scientifically as to the cause of mental disease, the fact remains that what Dr. Cotton is doing is something definitive and tangible that must appeal to every clear-thinking man . . . At the very least, he is giving to his mentally disturbed patients a surgical treatment that must be of value always, even if one is not absolutely sure that it affects the fundamental causes of mental disease . . . [not least because, in the process,] the public will come . . . gradually, to look upon insanity as it looks upon other diseases that can be benefited by surgical treatment . . . In this indirect way I believe that what Dr. Cotton is doing is of immense value in educating the general public in their conception of mental disease.[48]

Meanwhile, the secretary of the Board of State Charities in Indiana spoke of his admiration for what "Dr. Cotton and his associates" had accomplished, and welcomed public discussion of the issues: "The people should be taught by those who really know about mental health and mental defectiveness, and what our public hospitals are doing and should do. When the people know, they will demand the best for their unfortunate neighbors and relatives, and that is what they should do."[49]

Several of Cotton's fellow state hospital superintendents also lent their support. Charles Page had been Cotton's superior at Danvers in the years immediately before Cotton obtained his position at Trenton, and had now retired, after thirty-six years in the asylum business. Bursting with pride at his one-time subordinate's accomplishments, Page wrote from Hartford to express himself "profoundly interested" in Cotton's work: "after years of scientific investigation," he stressed, "testing each clinical observation by laboratory demonstrations, Dr. Cotton has accumulated a sufficient mass of indisputable facts to . . . establish a positive relationship, as cause and effect, between bacterial toxins and functional insanity . . . and better yet, he has described measures, surgical, bacterial, etc., etc., by the use of which such malign agencies can be eradicated or counteracted."[50] From King's Park State Hospital on Long Island, William C. Garvin wrote that he was "fully in sympathy with [Dr. Cotton] in his desire to eliminate all sorts of focal infection, and for a few years past, in this hospital, every incoming patient receives examination at the hands of a specialist of the eye, ear, nose and throat, and an examination by our resident dentist. Owing to the fact that there are 5,300 patients under our charge and we only possess one dentist, it can readily be seen that we cannot go very far in this branch of medicine."[51] And from Arkansas, Dr. C. C. Kirk noted that his "personal acquaintance with Dr. Cotton" had familiarized him with "the splendid work he is doing at Trenton," and in his deprived rural state he was doing his best to emulate Cotton's achievements. Certainly, the work at Trenton had transformed his own sense of the prognosis for mental illness:

> When I began my work it was in an institution where the superintendent and many of the older members of staff believed that few if any mental cases ever recovered permanently, and not more than 10 percent had remissions. It was an institution where splendid custodial care was given to the patients, but very little scientific treatment administered. The spirit of pessimism affected me and I felt there was not much to be done in the way of treatment. But today I feel optimistic because I have been happily surprised to see the results obtained by scientific, constructive, humane methods.[52]

Shaw had consulted a far wider range of authorities for an assessment of Lewis's claims. Dr. Paul Bowers, "the chief of the Neuropsychiatric Service at the U.S. Veterans' Hospital N. 24, at Palo Alto" reported that "it has been my endeavor to remove all possible focal infections which may undermine the nervous organism of the patients in my charge. To do so we remove infected tonsils and infected teeth and perform surgical operations that may be necessary." He hoped the public might soon start "compelling our hard-hearted legislators to give us the money for our State institutions . . . to carry out the humane and scientific work inaugurated by Pinel in France and Rush in America."[53]

From the private sector came still more praise for "the tireless energy and fearless attitude of Dr. Cotton and Dr. Draper," and a suggestion for multiplying the good effects of their work by intervening still earlier in order to prevent mental illness. As the head of the discreetly named "Idylease Inn" in Newfoundland, New Jersey, "a well-known private institution, [that] has dealt chiefly with patients from well-to-do families," Dr. D. E. Drake spoke forcefully of the need to extend the new forms of treatment to the nervous, the neurasthenic, and the neurotic that flocked to establishments like the one he ran:

> I heartily agree with the rapidly growing group in the medical profession whose members, in accord with the great English school, believe that the so-called 'functional' psychoses, notably dementia praecox and manic depressive insanity, are not in themselves disease entities, but are in reality terminal symptoms resulting from long-continued toxemia; and that in the great majority of cases those patients who go on to this form of insanity have, almost without exception, passed through well-defined periods of 'neurasthenia' and 'nervous breakdown,' due to physical and often removable causes.

His own strong preference, therefore, would be to see Cotton's surgical bacteriology extended to ensure "the recognition and elimination of all focal infections in this great group of the pre-insane, and [I] feel convinced from personal experience that by this removal of the cause there will be even greater success in the *prevention of functional insanity than in its cure*."[54]

Casting his net still more broadly, Shaw managed to obtain further encomiums from entirely outside the ranks of institutional psychiatry. Few Americans would not have heard of the world-renowned Mayo Clinic, where the staff performed the miracles of modern aseptic surgery. A recommendation from this quarter without question would carry great weight, and Shaw reported that "Dr. Mayo, the distinguished surgeon of Rochester, Minnesota, regards the viewpoint of Dr. Cotton and his associates as 'in line with modern investigations as to the origin of disease,' and believes that Mr. Lewis' article will help to bring about an extension of the method to other institutions." From the realm of pure science, the "eminent" Edwin G. Conklin added his voice to the chorus, an opinion Shaw informed his readers was the more valuable since "Dr. Conklin had at one time served on the Hospital Board at Trenton, and his observations . . . therefore represent a mature judgment rather than a casual impression." "I beg to say," Conklin asserted, "that I have no doubt that the methods which are now employed at Trenton in getting rid of focal infections, especially of the teeth and tonsils, will prove of very great value in the treatment of mental disorders and deserve to be widely adopted." And while he was some-what agnostic about its effects on the *numbers* of mental patients, "it is reason-able to expect that it will greatly hasten the recovery of many cases which might otherwise be long protracted or possibly incurable." The redoubtable Stewart Paton, also of Princeton, and also personally familiar with Cotton's accom-plishments, seemed slightly more circumspect, warning of the need not to neg-lect "the psychogenetic factors in mental disease," and emphasizing his own hobby-horse, "the very important role played by mental hygiene." But he, too, spoke of his profound respect for what had been accomplished. "I wish," he concluded, "that what Dr. Cotton is doing at Trenton could be done in every hospital for the insane in this country."[55]

Here was a parade of authorities that might seem calculated to win over the most hardened skeptic. Yet not every expert Shaw had consulted professed himself equally enthusiastic. Several urged caution in assessing Cotton's work. Among them was Frank Billings, one of the principal authorities on focal sepsis, who professed himself "unable to fully evaluate" the work at Trenton, and warned that there was always the danger of a valuable approach being "utilized with poor judgment and discretion by individual medical practition-ers. [Nonetheless] I hope that the work done by Dr. Cotton in behalf of the insane may prove to be of value in the prevention and cure of mental disease."[56]

From within the psychiatric establishment, Richard Hutchings, the superin-tendent of New York State's oldest mental hospital, at Utica, warned that "while Dr. Cotton is doing excellent work, he is only touching one edge of a vast prob-lem, the solution of which is far off." Like other critical voices, though, he con-ceded that "there cannot be two opinions as to the advisability of removing sources of infection, whether located in the tonsils, at the roots of the teeth, or elsewhere" – a stance that hinted at one of the very real difficulties that those who objected to Cotton's work confronted. It was seemingly perverse, after all, to object to measures designed to place "the patient in as perfect physical con-dition as is possible," and hard to argue that bodily health was unconnected to mental status. So those like Hutchings, who insisted that Cotton's monocausal account was overly simple, still found themselves constrained to acknowledge that the psychiatric profession "is indebted to Dr. Cotton for calling attention to sources of infection that might easily be overlooked, which doubtless have some bearing upon the general health of the patient, and secondarily upon his mental condition."[57]

Such caution and qualification were likely to have been lost on many laymen, as in all probability was the characteristically convoluted prose of Cotton's patron, Adolf Meyer, who simultaneously found ways to praise and prevaricate about his protégé's work. While protesting on the one hand that there was a "danger that the public may expect too much in the way of 'solution by just one trick,'" and urging the need for "independent research . . . and not too hasty a jumping at conclusions," Meyer on the other hand once more endorsed the "active and determined work . . . at Trenton" and insisted that "an important experiment is being carried out there."[58]

For Shaw, and presumably for his readers, the implications of all this were clear: the story was one of "progress," "improvements," and "hopeful prospects" – the subheadings he used as signposts throughout his article. And readers were left with what he called "a final note of cheer." Dr. Stanley, the resident physician of the California State Prison at San Quentin had recently visited Trenton. "Personally," said Dr. Stanley, "I feel that the group of doctors [there] are doing a great work," laboring "tirelessly and energetically . . . to do something more for the patients than to give them custodial care." A communication to Shaw from Cotton himself showed with what good effects all this work had been attended: the staff at the hospital had been "tabulating and analyzing the 1,400 cases which have been discharged as recovered in the last four years. Only forty-two of this group," he continued, "have returned to the hospital and are now in the institution. There may be fifty we have lost track of. Of all the others we have very comprehensive reports from the field workers at least twice a year. Thus we have accurate knowledge of their condition."[59]

"The upshot of it all," Shaw concluded, was that the adoption of Cotton's "improved medical methods" was "the crying need of the hour." Quite obviously, "intelligent publicity must be invoked for this great social object," and his *Review of Reviews* was happy to forward the cause.[60]

5

Fighting Focal Infection

Desperate for relief from the demons that tormented them (or their nearest and dearest), and dazzled by the seemingly authoritative reports emanating from Trenton about the extraordinary breakthroughs associated with a bacteriological model of madness, patients (or their families) urgently sought to share in the new miracle cures. Affluent madmen and madwomen flocked to Trenton. Their numbers swelled the ranks of those confined at the state hospital, where their willingness to pay premium rates for the attention of Cotton and his consultants made them a highly desirable commodity. The contribution their presence made to the state treasury was gratefully acknowledged by Commissioner Lewis.

Traditionally, the well-to-do often went to considerable lengths to avoid – or at least to defer – the painful prospect of placing their relatives in an asylum.[1] The malodorous reputation of the madhouse was compounded by the social disgrace that overt acknowledgment that one possessed an insane relative brought in its train, a social stigma that had worsened sharply in the fin-de-siècle era, when madness was routinely portrayed as evidence of degeneracy and hereditary taint. Wealthy families possessed the social standing and financial wherewithal to cope with the unproductive; the ability to employ large numbers of servants to handle their troublesome relatives; the capacity, if need be, to send them off to a quiet and secluded part of the country, or even abroad; and strong motivation to avoid the gossip and scandal that were still the inevitable consequence of having a relative officially certified as mad. In America, a flourishing network of profit-making sanitariums catered to the rich and "nervously prostrated," providing yet another somewhat socially acceptable option for families to consider.

The case of Margaret Fisher, one of the first private patients to be transferred to Trenton, illustrates many of these patterns, and also the eagerness with which wealthy, well-connected, and highly educated people arrived to be treated with Cotton's miraculous new therapies, or brought their relations to receive treatment at his hands. Margaret was the daughter of Irving Fisher, a Yale professor lionized by no less a figure than Joseph Schumpeter as "the greatest economist that America has produced."[2] Fisher was an arrogant, humorless, and domineering man who made (and eventually lost) a fortune exceeding $10 million (more than $40 million in today's terms), enjoyed access to the highest circles of American society, and embraced a host of causes, including Prohibition, eugenics, dietary reform, and the extension of the human life-span – interests that stemmed in part from a temporarily disabling bout of tuberculosis that had laid him low in his early thirties. Developing close ties with John Harvey Kellogg, patriarch of the immensely fashionable Battle Creek Sanitarium in Michigan and founder of the breakfast cereal empire, from the early 1900s, Fisher had begun to take his wife and family there each year to partake of the cure. Hydrotherapy, exercise, a vegetarian diet, close attention to the working of the bowels – all these central elements of Kellogg's regime became a regular part of the Fisher family routine (though at home they abjured a purely vegetarian regimen), and as a dutiful daughter, Margaret embraced these and other "healthy" practices at her father's urging.

Still living at home as she entered her twenties and serving as an unpaid office assistant to her father, Margaret's mental condition seems to have undergone a slow deterioration from about 1916 onwards. The changes were subtle at first, the onset of her symptoms insidious and easy to overlook or rationalize. Only in retrospect did her parents come to see them as signs of incipient pathology.

On April 27, 1918, Margaret became engaged to be married to a young graduate of Yale Law School, George Stewart, who had been inducted into the army and was waiting to be sent to the Western Front. Her parents were delighted, and Margaret's father (having checked the young man's pedigree with one of his oldest friends) urged them to marry as soon as possible. But the prospect seems to have unhinged his daughter. Within days she began to babble "queer things about portents and was afraid her fiancé would not come back [from the war]. She soon began to talk at random about 'God, Christ and immortality,' and reacted to auditory hallucinations. Her conduct was peculiar in many ways. Her condition gradually became worse, and on June 1 she had to be sent to a private hospital."[3]

Thus far, the Fishers had defined her condition as a temporary nervous prostration and kept her out of any sort of psychiatric facility. Unfortunately, however, once hospitalized, "she became much worse, and could not be controlled" – so their hands were forced and Irving Fisher and his wife concluded "it was necessary to send her to the Bloomingdale Asylum" in White Plains, long regarded by America's plutocrats as a suitable institution for those of their social class. Admitted on June 27, Margaret was "pensive and preoccupied, and at times depressed. She responded slowly to questions and when aroused was irrelevant."[4] Her psychiatrists soon despaired of her prospects. Noting the "acute distortion of the patient's personality with marked distortion in thinking, peculiar behavior and disharmony between mood and thought content," they concluded that her psychosis "seems more nearly related to the schizophrenic disorders than to the exhaustive or manic depressive disorders." These were important diagnostic distinctions, since schizophrenia in this era was widely felt to be an essentially incurable condition. Indeed the Fishers were informed that "a recovery without defect symptoms seems improbable."[5] Irving Fisher's response was swift: he arranged to have Margaret released from Bloomingdale on March 29, 1919, and that same day she was spirited out of the state and admitted as a private patient to Trenton State Hospital.[6]

Over the years, Fisher had maintained close contacts with John Harvey Kellogg. In August 1914, for instance, the two men had jointly organized the First International Congress on Racial Betterment in Battle Creek, and Fisher had written for Kellogg's magazine, *Good Health.*[7] Kellogg, like Cotton, emphasized the nefarious influence of decayed teeth and the poisons that lurked in the bowels, so when Fisher learned of Cotton's claims about the etiological connections between focal sepsis and insanity, along with the possibility of intervening to cure the apparently hopeless through a program of surgical bacteriology, he was already primed to accept them.

Neurologically, Cotton reported, Margaret Fisher seemed normal. But there was ominous evidence of "marked retention of fecal matter in the cecal colon with marked enlargement of the colon in this area." To be sure, "because of her resistiveness X-ray studies of the intestinal tract could not be made," but Cotton was convinced that the source of a substantial portion of her problems had been uncovered. Proceeding further, he found evidence that her "cervix was eroded." Deeply suspect as well were two unerupted molars, which Cotton immediately insisted must be extracted. He next approached the Fishers for permission to perform "an exploratory laparotomy . . . based upon the physical examination and the fact of long continued constipation."[8]

Irving Fisher and his wife were obviously eager to embrace this somatic explanation of their daughter's disorder. It provided an etiological account that was in close accord with their own beliefs about human health, and a far more hopeful prognosis than the one the doctors at the Bloomingdale Asylum had delivered. Still, they hesitated to endorse so drastic a remedy as surgery on

Margaret's bowels, announcing that they "preferred to wait till other means such as vaccine and serum should be exhausted." In August, however, they did consent to "a conical plastic enucleation" of Margaret's cervix after being advised of the presence of "pure colon bacillus" in her tissues. The operation was performed by Cotton's assistant, Dr. Stone, on August 15, 1919,[9] and the following day Irving Fisher, George Stewart (Margaret's fiancé), and Cotton himself took the train for Battle Creek to consult with Kellogg. "Speeding to BC," Fisher informed his wife that "Dr. C. brought along a sheet of notes of [Margaret's] records. The cervix was infected with colon bacillus and the blood shows a 'positive reaction to the fixation test for colon bacillus.' These two things fit into each other and (I should say) into the fact that she was so constipated that she went 'off' . . . I suspect that the colon bacillus is the little demon most to blame."[10] Two days later, another letter hinted that his wife had harbored such suspicions long before Margaret had been referred to Trenton for treatment: "I imagine," Irving Fisher wrote, "that you have been as right as anyone that constipation is the key."[11]

At the Battle Creek Sanitarium, Fisher reported that "Dr. Cotton is much impressed with what he sees here," and as for George, he "is 'in love with the place.'" Seizing the opportunity presented by their extended time together, Cotton was clearly doing all he could to overcome Fisher's hesitations about further surgery for his daughter. Fisher noted that "Dr. C. doesn't think M will suffer any pain. The uterus, like the intestines and other internal organs has few nerves. Besides the cervix, you know, there are the bowels. The [indecipherable] which Dr. Draper saw should be removed and perhaps the outer sphincter muscle cut."[12]

Yet still Fisher hesitated. On the return journey, the compulsive correspondent informed his wife that "we had some very satisfactory talks Dr. C., Dr. K. and I re M and Dr. C. is going to use Colax, Tissane, diet, [indecipherable] and get after M's bowels."[13] Back at the hospital, Cotton acknowledged that "the family preferred to wait . . . So in September another course of antistreptococcous [sic] treatment was given."[14] Again, he urged surgery on the bowels. Again Fisher temporized: "As to operating on M," he wrote to his wife in early October, "we'll talk it over with Dr. C. and each other."[15] And then events took the decision out of their hands. Perhaps the crisis was iatrogenic, the result of a failure to kill the streptococci before injecting them into Margaret's body. At all events, in late October she exhibited symptoms of inflammation of the lungs, and a deep-seated abscess developed over the ribs on her left side – an abscess that, when lanced and cultured "gave pure streptococcus . . . the same type found in the teeth and stomach" – and the organism used, though Cotton was

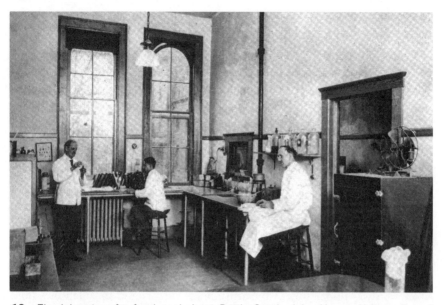

13 *The laboratory for fecal analysis at Battle Creek. John Harvey Kellogg shared Cotton's fascination with excrement. He insisted that frequent defecation was the key to health, since retained feces acted to poison the system. To this end, he emphasized exercise, good posture, fresh air, and hydrotherapy; designed a toilet to ease the process of emptying the bowel; advocated dietary reform and made a fortune by inventing instant breakfast cereals, among many other food products; and repeatedly employed abdominal surgery to correct intestinal stasis when all else failed. Here we see an illustration designed to reassure his wealthy clientele that their treatments were guided by the findings of modern laboratory medicine, their evacuations monitored to ensure that their intestinal tracts were healthy.*

silent on this issue, to create the so-called vaccine with which he had injected her. "The condition of the patient did not improve and her temperature continued to be high. She failed rapidly and died November 7, 1919."[16]

Though devastated by the outcome, Fisher continued to believe in Cotton's theories, and to insist that there had been a "physical cause of Margaret's illness ... Even years later he wrote his friend Will Eliot that some form of toxemia causes a nervous breakdown."[17] Of course, such sustained faith was a natural psychological defense mechanism in the face of the choices he had made and the treatments he had authorized, but it also reflected how stubbornly Fisher held to his beliefs, not just on this front, but on a whole range of issues.[18] And Fisher was clearly not alone. Legions of other well-to-do Americans followed in his footsteps, so many that the number of private patients appearing at Trenton to receive treatment began to exceed the capacity of the state hospital to receive them. As their ranks swelled, Henry Cotton seized the opportunity to open a private hospital in town, an establishment to which the bulk of these paying patients were henceforth referred for treatment.

Across the country, other alienists reported that they found themselves besieged by supplicants seeking the new miracle cure. Frantic families urged that teeth, tonsils, and guts be ransacked for the source of the germs that had prompted hallucinations and delusions, ranting and raving, dolor and depression.[19] For so long, madness had seemed a condition beyond help, a source of stigma and shame. If modern biological science had revealed that it was just another physical affliction, its fearsome and frightening overturning of reason and rationality no more than the effects of bacterial poisoning of the brain, then deliverance might be at hand. What had once been a condition that banished hope and induced the deepest shame and social degradation now appeared in a new guise, as just another form of infectious illness that lent itself to treatment with the wonders of modern medical science.

In a more limited sphere, as Joel Braslow has recently shown, a parallel transformation was under way in the attitude of patients and their families (and their physicians) when confronted with the horrors of tertiary syphilis. Afflicted with a cascading array of ever more awful neurological and psychiatric disasters – seizures, disturbances of balance and gait, paralysis, and incontinence on the one hand, and on the other, mania and increasingly extravagant delusions, often of a singularly grandiose sort, all of which typically culminated in rapid and complete mental decay and an often agonizing death – paretics formed a not insubstantial fraction of most mental hospital populations well into the twentieth century: as much as 20 percent of the male admissions at many institutions across the United States. As we have seen, confirmation of the long-suspected link between venereal infection and so-called general paralysis of the insane had come early in the twentieth century and had added to the miseries of the condition itself the universal moral condemnation meted out to any sexual sinner. Such doomed human derelicts were widely portrayed in the popular press as the very embodiment of a wholly repugnant moral and physical decay. But in the very years when Cotton was experimenting with his surgical bacteriology, a Viennese professor had adopted the practice of treating his tertiary syphilitics by inoculating them with tertian malaria, inducing wracking fevers that by some mysterious alchemy reversed or halted (or so it was alleged) the otherwise relentless degeneration and decay of the afflicted.

Julius Wagner von Jauregg, Freud's contemporary and a notorious anti-Semite who would later become an enthusiastic Nazi, had long argued that fevers might bring about a remission of psychiatric disorders. From the late 1880s onwards, as a relatively obscure junior doctor, he had experimented with a variety of febrile agents, searching for a reliable means of inducing the physiological response he sought. Early on, he made use of *Streptococcus pyogenes*, the organism that produced erysipelas and scarlet fever; then tuberculin, the quack cure for tuberculosis introduced by the famous Robert Koch; and later still typhus vaccine, claiming that the resulting rise in temperature was beneficial in treating a vast array of psychiatric disorders, including "melancholy, manic states and acute mania."[20] But the resulting fevers were slight, and the effects meager and unconvincing to most of his fellow physicians.

Undeterred, von Jauregg pressed forward, increasingly focusing his efforts on the paretic. The years of the Great War saw him installed as professor of psychiatry at the University of Vienna and playing a substantial (and eventually notorious) role in the treatment of the epidemic of shell-shock that afflicted the Austrian army quite as severely as its German ally and French, British, Italian, and American counterparts.[21] In company with many of his fellow medical men on both sides of the "war to end all wars," von Jauregg was incensed by what he saw as the cowardice and malingering of these psychiatric casualties. In common with such men as Lewis Yealland with the British forces, Clovis Vincent with the French, L. de Lisi and E. Foscarini with the Italians, Pearce Bailey with the Americans, and Fritz Kaufmann with the Germans, von Jauregg seized upon the latitude offered by the hostile attitude of the military commanders, and by the demands of the war-machine for more cannon-fodder, as a license to employ brutal therapies to force the recalcitrant human materials that passed into his hands into some semblance of normality. Severe electric shocks, applied repeatedly to the mouth or pharynx, were used to force the deaf to hear, the dumb to speak, the lame and the halt to walk in lengthy sessions that allegedly were so cruel and extreme that they led to deaths and suicides. Indeed, after the war these reports led to an inquiry into whether to prosecute von Jauregg for criminal activities, a fate from which, ironically, he was rescued in part by testimony from Sigmund Freud that he was "personally convinced that Professor Wagner-Jauregg would never have allowed [the electrical stimulus] to be intensified to a cruel pitch."[22]

In the last months of the war, von Jauregg was presented with a shell-shocked patient from the Italian front who was simultaneously suffering from tertian malaria. Finally he had found a reliable source for producing sustained fevers of up to 106 degrees Fahrenheit – fevers that (most of the time) could subsequently be controlled by administering quinine. Immediately, he made use of the source to transfer malaria to first one and then a whole succession of paretics, launching a therapy that he claimed produced near-miraculous results in two-thirds of his patients, and one that, after the war, spread rapidly across

Europe and North America. In the very same year that Cotton's results were lauded in the *Review of Reviews*, von Jauregg published the results of a series of more than two hundred paretics he had inoculated with malaria, claiming a complete remission in fifty cases in what had hitherto been a uniformly fatal disease.[23] Soon, an editorial in the *American Journal of Psychiatry* drew attention to the work, and called for its replication in North America: "It may be that every large hospital for mental disorders may have to maintain one or more malarial patients as sources of infectious material."[24]

As the treatment spread, so it brought in its train a subtle but unmistakable change in the attitude of physicians towards their patients: "No longer seeing them as objects to be manipulated, doctors listened to and acted on their patients' desires," treating them, for perhaps the first time, as human beings fully entitled to the status of "patient." As for the neurosyphilitic and their families, the existence of the new treatment transformed "their attitudes toward state hospitalization and their treatment" in a similarly positive fashion, inducing a number of them, for example, to seek admission voluntarily so as to avail themselves of the new therapy.[25] By shifting the focus, as Braslow puts it, "from disorderly conduct to a disease pathogen" that had invaded "the tissues, blood, and brain," the moral meaning of the paretic's pathology had been decisively altered.

In raising the hopes of patients and their families, in addressing "the desire to heal and be healed," and in presenting the prospect of altering the very meaning of mental disease,[26] Cotton's emphasis on the infectious roots of psychosis held out similar promises of relief to a lay audience. Burdette Lewis had reached much the same conclusion about the appeal of the doctrines of focal sepsis: "The treatment of the physical man appeals more to laymen, because treatment of this kind can be more readily understood by laymen and tested in accordance with the technique of the laboratory, and because present results show it to be more effectual."[27] And Albert Shaw's survey had demonstrated that by no means all medical men were immune to these seductions either.

But the almost uniformly optimistic and positive view of Cotton's activities projected in Shaw's survey suggested a degree of professional consensus that simply did not exist. On the contrary, a number of prominent psychiatrists were privately expressing considerable consternation about developments at Trenton. Meyer had warned Cotton in early 1921 that his stress in the Vanuxem lectures on a monocausal account of mental disorder would unnecessarily antagonize many of his colleagues, and had urged him to concentrate on "a further deepening of the investigation, rather than popularization, which, I think, has been attained very amply in the campaign against teeth that is almost country-wide."[28] It was a reproof that Cotton, characteristically, had spurned.

Mutterings grew in the profession. William Alanson White, the politically well-placed and highly influential superintendent of St. Elizabeth's, the federal mental hospital in Washington, D.C., had been a skeptic from the start. When his counterpart at the Georgia State Sanitarium, intrigued by Cotton's early papers, wrote to solicit White's opinion of the work, he responded tartly that, "my opinion is that the emphasis that has been laid upon infected teeth is a most unfortunate one." And although he acknowledged that "anything that impairs the general health of the individual may be a factor in causing a mental break," he insisted that "this of course does not mean that everybody who is mentally ill ought to have all their teeth pulled."[29] Some months later, when the secretary to US Senator Caraway asked what White thought of the work on focal sepsis, the response was swift: "my very good friend, Dr. Cotton . . . is one of the most enthusiastic and energetic workers in the field of psychiatry in this country," but he is "a man who goes to extremes in his views [and] I myself am not a believer in his theories . . . I would hesitate a long time before I would subject an individual to the serious disfigurement of having all of her [*sic*] teeth pulled or to the dangers of a surgical operation, involving a removal of a considerable portion of the intestinal tract."[30]

White was among the handful of psychiatrists sympathetic to Freud and psychoanalysis, and his objections were perhaps predictable, but hostility was equally evident in other quarters. J. K. Hall, a conservative man who was the most prominent psychiatrist in the South in the 1920s and '30s, and the author of a monthly column in the influential journal *Southern Medicine and Surgery* (in which Cotton was about to publish still another paper on "Focal Infection the Cause of Much Mental Disturbance"), communicated his disquiet to his uncle, Albert Anderson, who was superintendent of the North Carolina State Hospital at Raleigh:

> Cotton's theory and work is doing some good, but, in my opinion, it is doing more harm, because he is having lots of people deprived of their teeth and a portion of their alimentary canal that is probably useful to them. And then the worst feature of his preachment is that he raises hopes in the minds of relatives of insane people that cannot be realized. Cotton is injudicious in his attitude, and unsound in his reasoning . . . The world has been overflowing with lots of damn fool theories, and I think it is important for the welfare of humanity that some of us doctors at least retain what little sense we have and try to keep our feet on the ground.[31]

What particularly rankled, Hall confessed, was Cotton's sharp criticisms of his fellow psychiatrists as do-nothings: "It will be a tragic affair . . . for the citizenship of the state to lose confidence in those men who have charge of their insane relatives in State Hospitals, and this tendency to indulge in unjust criticism of these State Hospitals ought to be combated and corrected."[32] And Hall indicated that he planned to make it his business to do so.

At the New York Psychiatric Institute on Ward's Island, another protégé of Meyer's, George Kirby, had recently assumed control, and, together with two more junior members of his staff, a young bacteriologist, Nicholas Kopeloff, and his assistant director Clarence Cheney, he had begun to cast doubt on Cotton's claims at a number of regional psychiatric meetings. By the time the annual meeting of the American Psychiatric Association was held in Quebec City in June 1922, the stage was set for a fierce debate on the merits of Cotton's approach, an event the official report of the proceedings acknowledged had attracted "probably the greatest interest" of the entire meeting. Kopeloff and Cheney went first, delivering a lengthy paper outlining their preliminary attempts to replicate Cotton's findings. In an effort to provide an independent means of assessing the impact of surgical intervention, they announced that they had attempted to set up a controlled experiment, comparing two groups of patients matched "as to sex, age, duration of psychosis, diagnosis, prognosis, and infective conditions of the teeth and tonsils," one of whom was treated, surgically and otherwise, to eliminate focal sepsis, while the other served as the untreated control.[33] A handful of cases who proved too resistive for surgery were perforce assigned to the control group, a decision Kopeloff and Cheney defended as biasing results, if anything, towards finding an effect for surgical treatment, since it meant that the control group on average was perhaps somewhat sicker.

Reporting on their first series of 60 patients, Kopeloff and Cheney emphasized that their conclusions were "tentative and subject to revision should further facts require it." And they noted that they had not conducted abdominal surgery, considering it too risky, preferring instead to treat chronic constipation with doses of acidophilus milk, an approach they reported had successfully relieved the condition. Otherwise, they had X-rayed and examined, undertaken "comprehensive bacteriological investigation," pulled infected teeth, removed impacted molars, undertaken tonsillectomies, and searched for gynecological sepsis. Even defining improvement among the operative group as generously as possible (counting as "improved," for example, three dementia praecox patients who had persisted in their "delusional ideas, their conduct, and complete lack of insight," but who had been released at their families' request), Kopeloff and Cheney's conclusions were stark: "*We have no evidence on which to base a conclusion that the removal of focal infection has of itself brought about recovery . . .*

There is little evidence to indicate anything more than the most gross relationship between particular species of bacteria and foci which have been considered; and little to suggest that the bacteria found are in any way causally related to the psychoses."[34] Nor, indeed, Kopeloff suggested, were the techniques Cotton's staff used reliable ways to demonstrate bacterial infections in the first place.

Cotton simply brushed these contentions aside. It was Kopeloff's bacteriological work, not that of the Trenton staff, that was inadequate, both with respect to the small number of cases examined in comparison with the New Jersey series, and in its technique. By contrast, his own presentation, Cotton triumphantly asserted, "produced evidence, both clinical and pathological, which should set at rest any doubt as to the accuracy of our deductions . . . The successful treatment of 1,400 cases during the last four years with only 42 return cases now in the hospital must be accepted as evidence that our work is efficient. The fact that our recoveries in the last four years average 80 percent of this group [of functional cases] against an average of 37 percent for a period of ten years prior to 1918 should be convincing."[35] To be sure, "the deplorable lack of adequate laboratory facilities which exists in the majority of the state institutions in the country will necessarily retard the work and greatly hinder those who are conscientiously interested in adopting any methods of treatment which will benefit their patients."[36] But the larger problem was "to overcome the prejudices of traditional psychiatric teaching" which lamentably led many to "a do-nothing policy" – a response he claimed some were now abandoning, though "it is not to be expected that these barriers can be overcome in so short a time."[37] The situation was analogous to paresis, where, within his own professional lifetime, "the question of the relation of syphilis to paresis was doubted in America. Paresis was considered a disease due to overwork and mental strain because it occurred in brokers, bankers, actors, and others who were supposed to be overworked. It was considered purely a mental disease." With the advances in the laboratory, however, "the causation of paresis underwent a complete revolution and no one would dispute the fact today that paresis is an organic brain disease due to destruction of the brain tissue by the spirocheta pallida."[38] So it would eventually prove with psychosis in general, Cotton felt, once a conservative profession looked with unprejudiced eyes at the effects of searching for and eliminating focal sepsis.

When Cotton reached the end of his presentation, a protracted and heated discussion ensued. Most of the first group who spoke from the podium expressed varying degrees of skepticism and criticism of the Trenton work. Among the most vocal of the critics was Edward Brush of Baltimore, superintendent of a private psychiatric hospital on the outskirts of Baltimore and editor of the *American Journal of Psychiatry*. Professing "the highest respect for Dr. Cotton," who was "an old friend," Brush proclaimed that he had "no objection to looking upon focal infections just as one would look upon other conditions which affect the health and comfort of the patient, but I do protest against a tendency which has been the *bête noire* of the profession from earliest times, a tendency to seek for panaceas, specifics, or sure cures, and to become too optimistic when some drug or method is found which appears to produce results, before we have patiently considered every other possible hypothesis." In his view, it was all too obvious that "Dr. Cotton . . . has shown a tendency to blind himself or to shut out views which might modify those he now holds, by permitting the preconceived idea, the theory he has formed, to occupy the whole field of his mental vision."[39]

Adopting a similar tone, Isham Harris, superintendent of the Brooklyn State Hospital, ventured that "Dr. Cotton is sincere in his work, but . . . a little over enthusiastic in his claims,"[40] and Dr. C. C. Kirk, superintendent of the Arkansas State Hospital, noted that, "it is our opinion that many of the women coming to our hospital have had too much surgery instead of not enough surgery. The thorough work of our dentist undoubtedly is of great benefit to the patient, but the mere extraction of a tooth, in my opinion, has never produced a recovery."[41] In other quarters, questions were raised about how thorough Cotton's follow-up work had been, and how permanent his cures had been or would prove to be. With eyebrows raised, the psychoanalyst A. A. Brill then spoke of Cotton's "very remarkable assertion" that he had cured 85 percent of his functional patients. In manic-depressive cases, where the course of the disease was notoriously intermittent, and where the criteria of cure were notoriously slippery, how did Cotton know that he had not mistaken a temporary remission for a cure? And for other forms of psychosis, the type of claims Cotton had advanced stretched beyond what he regarded as the limits of credulity: "I cannot conceive of a real flourishing paranoiac cured by any therapy . . . Nor can I conceive of a dementia praecox who had to be sent to a state hospital who is ever cured in the scientific sense; he is often discharged from the hospital as improved in the sense of social adjustment, but he is always a praecox – surgery or no surgery."[42]

Even these doubting Thomases, however, for the most part did not reject Cotton's work out of hand, or question the wisdom of allowing him to continue to operate. "Personally," C. C. Kirk volunteered, "I believe that the publicity given Dr. Cotton's work will do some harm, but it will also do some good by creating public opinion in certain backward states where the patients are receiving nothing more than custodial care."[43] And Edward Brush ended his lengthy intervention with a plea to his fellow alienists to set "impartial and scientifically trained men" to work to assess "the methods at Trenton, both in the laboratory and the wards . . . We should study this whole matter so carefully and so thoroughly, not being carried away by the enthusiasm of Dr. Cotton, on the one hand, or too much influenced by the more conservative views of men like myself.[44]

Among a number of other psychiatrists, many younger and less senior in rank or from less prestigious institutions, sentiment ran more strongly in Cotton's favor. Among the first to speak, Harvey Clare, the assistant superintendent at the Toronto Hospital for the Insane, confessed that he did "not know how much truth there is in the theory of focal infection." In Canada, however, "there has been in the past an impression gaining ground among the laity that a case of mental illness in the family is a hopeless condition" – an impression, of course, largely congruent with mainstream psychiatric thinking. It was vital to combat such notions: "I believe that if Dr. Cotton's plan of careful investigation is followed up we will have scientific men taking care of our patients . . . we will have patients examined from every standpoint . . . [and] anything that directs the attention of the physician to his patient is bound to react for the benefit of the patient."[45] He was followed to the podium by Armitage Baber, superintendent of the Dayton State Hospital in Ohio, who, while declining "to discuss this matter pathologically," made it clear that on a practical level, "we carry on our procedures in a more limited way than Dr. Cotton does, but our general operating work is along the lines that he has suggested . . . I am certainly in harmony with the opinions that Dr. Cotton has expressed and he has certainly shown that he has been more actively at work and can show greater results than most of us."[46]

Similar sentiments now became the order of the day. Roger Swint, clinical director of the massive Georgia State Sanitarium at Milledgeville, which contained upwards of ten thousand psychotics, granted that Cotton might be "a little too optimistic about his work." For all that,

I think it is undesirable to criticize the procedure that has thus far been developed by Dr. Cotton, but he shares the fate of many other pioneers, of, for example, the inventor of the fever thermometer, who was greatly criticized and looked down upon during the time he was perfecting the instrument, and I might name many others who shared the same fate . . . Dr. Cotton has presented here facts worthy of investigation. If he cures 85 percent of his patients certainly he is doing a lot more than the rest of us are doing. I say let the good work go on.[47]

Arthur Kilbourne, superintendent of the state hospital in Rochester, Minnesota, was equally emphatic. The word of a fellow professional and gentleman ought to be trusted:

> I merely wanted to say that when a man comes before this house and makes a statement I think we feel [*sic*] that it should be accepted as fact until we are in a position to refute it. Dr. Cotton has had four years' experience in this work and unless we have had that, or can come here four years from now and give the results of our own labors in this line, I hardly think we can criticize any statement he has made. Personally, I hope that Dr. Cotton's statistics as to recoveries under his treatment will be duplicated in every institution.

"If we can only get the means to carry on this work," he added, " there will be credit enough for all of us."[48]

In an effort to find some middle ground, suggestions were raised in some quarters that a committee be set up to investigate Cotton's claims, a proposal Cotton himself promptly welcomed: "Our records are open and the work is open and the greatest difficulty has been to get an investigation. It would please me and my co-workers very much if such a committee were appointed. We have always welcomed any man who desired to see our work."[49] But opposition to this idea was widespread. Albert Barrett, the Association's president, questioned the feasibility of the Association undertaking the task, and doubted whether any committee of theirs could provide "a well balanced scientific consideration" of the issues. Others were still more vocal. Howard Gosline, a pathologist from the Rhode Island State Hospital, denounced the whole notion as something that "should be dropped without further discussion": "To my mind there is no doubt these investigations should be continued ... The appointment of a committee for this purpose is to my mind an absurdity. Scientific matters are not being investigated by a committee but by every man interested."[50] Equally firmly, Owen Copp, superintendent of the private Pennsylvania Hospital's Nervous and Mental Diseases department regretted "any spirit of controversy" and forcefully objected to any proposal that might in any way interfere with Cotton's activities:

> I would like to see this ferment go on and work. It is a complaint against us that we do too little in the study and treatment of our patients. Now, will any committee or any investigation settle this matter one way or the other? No! No! Do we want to follow this line of action? No! No! (Applause.) We want this matter to go on. We want Dr. Cotton to proceed

with his investigation; to present facts and not mere opinions. If there is anything in it we want to help him. (Applause.) We do not want to put ourselves in a position of opposition to anything that promises benefit or good to our patients. We are not doing all we might for our patients . . . We need to do more of the work Dr. Cotton is doing, every one working in his own way, in every hospital . . . Give us the facts with which to go to the legislature and secure the money needed for the work: thus we shall make our hospitals real hospitals. God speed Dr. Cotton if he helps us do that. [Granted that] we cannot express final opinions on the subject at this time. I do not know whether it is right or wrong, but I do not want it to stop.[51]

And there the matter rested. Remarkably, Kopeloff and Cheney's findings were simply set to one side and scarcely a murmur was heard about the ethics of experimenting upon involuntarily confined patients, or subjecting them to drastic surgeries with reported mortality rates of 30 percent and more. Edward Brush came closest, noting that "to my mind a colostomy or a colectomy is a somewhat serious operation" and pointing out that "Dr. Cotton speaks of them in a way that would almost lead one to think the operation as simple and devoid of danger as the extraction of a tooth . . . Neither would I regard the amputation or enucleation, to use Dr. Cotton's term, of the uterine cervix as an operation to be performed in support of a theory unless there were indisputable grounds for believing such a procedure necessary or that an infection there had produced one of a more serious nature elsewhere." But even he could not bring himself to call for a halt to the procedures, expressing the hope instead that "the methods at Trenton, both in the laboratory and the wards, can be carefully checked up and tried out in the same detail in other laboratories and other wards."[52] As for the notion of a committee to examine what was happening at Trenton, Dr. Glueck, who had first suggested the idea, protested that there had been a "profound misunderstanding" of his purpose. He had in no way meant his proposal as "putting a check on [Dr. Cotton's] work," and in view of the criticism it had aroused, he sought "to withdraw my motion."[53]

Almost as an afterthought, Clarence Cheney was granted a few minutes to defend his study, and he took the occasion to note that "nobody would be more gratified than ourselves if we had gotten . . . results comparable with Dr. Cotton's." Regrettably, though, they had not. But instead of impressing upon his audience how dramatically he and his co-author's study appeared to undercut Cotton's claims, Cheney's remarks then trailed off into a morass of technical detail that obscured rather than highlighted the force of their findings.[54]

It was Cotton, after all these fireworks, who was given the last word, rising to say he was "very much gratified by the discussion aroused today in our work." He understood that not everyone was yet convinced. "Our statistics, however, speak for themselves and I feel sure that if these methods are adopted as good results will be obtained."[55] No one present ought to have been put off by the apparently contradictory findings his New York critics had presented. To the contrary, "the inadequate unsuccessful attempt of Drs. Cheney and Kopeloff corresponds exactly with our own experience. When we started this work in 1916, in the first 50 cases in which the teeth were extracted no results were noticed. They are undoubtedly going through this period of inadequate treatment. I sincerely hope they will continue the work and follow our technic and not be discouraged by the results in 25 cases." The cleansing, in other words, had to be thorough and complete, and "it requires the combined efforts of the psychiatrists and specialists as co-workers if results are to be obtained." Still, "from the fact that other institutions are getting results comparable to ours I feel that the work is not so difficult as it appears to some."[56]

Ten days later, on his return to Trenton, Cotton wrote to Meyer to report on the confrontation. His enemies in the profession, he wrote, had turned out in numbers. "As usual, they were out for me, especially Ward's Island. Dr. Cheney reported the results . . . [in] twenty-five cases . . . contrasted with twenty-five 'similar' cases not treated. They disagreed with the bacteriology and with the findings in general. It is needless to say the work was very inadequately done and I was not consulted . . . where I might have been of assistance." Fortunately, Cheney and Kopeloff appeared to have made little headway with their critique, and the discussion period, to his great satisfaction, had shown that others were now beginning to follow his example and employ an ever-greater emphasis on surgical intervention. The tide, he recorded triumphantly, was finally turning in his direction.[57]

6

The End of the Affair?

For all Cotton's characteristic bluster, his absolute assurance that he was right, and his equally unshakeable conviction that all his opponents were either ignorant or malevolent, he was well aware that many viewed his activities with disquiet and distaste. To be sure, even his fiercest critics had not sought to block his experiments – indeed, they had urged others to replicate them. But there were clear signs that many of the most influential figures in the discipline were upset with him, above all for his ethical lapses.

"Ethics" here had a peculiarly professional meaning. What troubled Cotton's colleagues, judging from their private and public protestations, was not his decision to experiment on vulnerable human beings, or to proceed with dangerous, disfiguring, or even deadly surgery in the face of objections from his patients. Rather, as we have seen, their concern was with his repeated appeals to a lay audience rather than to his peers, his courting of publicity in the popular press, and his (and his commissioner's) whipping up of public sentiment for a war against "the perils of pus infection."

If the motion to launch a formal investigation into Cotton's clinical practices had drawn widespread opposition from a rank and file convinced that professional gentlemen must be free to follow any course of action they considered to have promise, few were as complaisant when it came to the question of the public advertising of one's wares. The norms governing such conduct were informal and not without their ambiguities, but the medical guild had long railed against actions that imperiled the profession's dignity or that smacked of tradesman-like behavior or quackery. To rein in a fiercely competitive medical marketplace, to reassure the public that mercenary motives were not what actuated "disinterested" professionals, and to retain the illusion of an occupational group that regulated itself, it was vital to police to some degree the boundaries of practitioners' behavior in the marketplace; to take steps to ensure that one's peers, not the public, were anointed as the appropriate court to sit in judgment on disputed matters; and to erect barriers to conduct that too blatantly served as a means of self-promotion. Cotton had already fallen foul of these norms when he consented to the dissemination of claims about his results in the newspapers, complete with his photograph, prior to the publication of one of his earliest papers on focal infection. Despite Meyer's efforts to smooth over the situation, Cotton had on that occasion been forced to seek an alternative venue for his piece, and had faced private reproof from his mentor. Now his stubborn persistence in the same sort of behavior brought the threat of still more trouble from disquieted colleagues.

In the portion of the Quebec meeting devoted to Association business, it was announced that the council, in consultation with the president, had decided to set up two new standing committees. The first of these, on mental health policy, was an uncontroversial move to establish an entity that could provide "guidance of public policy in matters psychiatric" – simply a formalization of an activity the Association had engaged in continuously from its founding in 1844. The second standing committee, however, was put forward to address what was announced as being a novel problem: "In the early days of the Association its ethical standards were high and, with practically no deviation from the standards established by the founders, this condition has continued until now." A serious difficulty had now arisen, however, necessitating the formation of a Committee on Ethics. Somewhat elliptically, it was noted that

> Changing attitudes in professional circles toward methods which a few years ago were considered unethical, a growing interest on the part of the public in medical matters and a tendency on the part of the lay press to discuss subjects which a short time ago were only treated in professional journals, have resulted in a state of affairs wherein it appeared advisable that a standing committee should be empowered to deal with alleged violations of those ethical principles which should, and have, we believe, with rare exceptions, governed the members of the organization."[1]

Lest there be any doubt about the target of this committee's work, a few paragraphs later the editor returned to the subject and made clear whose activities had aroused this heightened concern. The highlight of the Association's gathering, he reported, had been the papers presented by Kopeloff and Cheney, and by Henry Cotton. Having noted that the former "could find no ground of agreement with Dr. Cotton as to the role of focal infections in the etiology of mental disorder" and left his readers to draw their own conclusions from this report, the editor turned to Cotton's work, and the attention it had drawn. There was little in Cotton's presentation, he sniffed, "with which the members of the Association were [not] already familiar, largely, however" – and here the editorial disapproval became overwhelmingly obvious – "through the lay press." Not the least, there was "the somewhat startling assertion that the recovery rate at the Trenton State Hospital, where he has been treating patients for the past four years or more upon the theory that their psychoses were due to focal infections, was 85 percent, with a period of hospital residence about half as long as was the rule at the hospital prior to the inception of the methods now followed."[2]

That the central source of editorial censure was the violation of guild norms became still more apparent in the next paragraph. Though it consisted of a single convoluted sentence, the burden of the criticism being advanced was, nonetheless, transparently clear:

It is no reflection upon the character of Dr. Cotton's paper to say that it was apparent that a considerable degree of the interest that was manifested grew out of a curiosity on the part of many as to any explanation which Dr. Cotton might make concerning the rather remarkable, and in the minds of many, unethical, exploitation of the methods and results claimed at Trenton in a lay periodical; an exploitation made moreover by a layman, Mr. Burdette G. Lewis, and in such a manner as to minimize the value of the work of Dr. Cotton's fellow members and to discredit appeals which are being constantly made for means to relieve the overcrowded condition of many public hospitals for mental disorders, upon the theory that if the methods in vogue at Trenton were followed, such appeals would be unnecessary.[3]

Lewis, as the editor took pains to remind his readers, had previously spoken to the Association itself "two or three years ago," and had spent much of his time criticizing "the business methods pursued in most hospitals and the business ability of most hospital superintendents" – an occasion that obviously still rankled with him, and presumably with others. Worse still was the commissioner's recent disposition to trespass even more boldly on the profession's own turf, presuming to lecture them "on a purely medical subject and one still *sub judice*." Insisting that "no one, least of all, none of Dr. Cotton's associates, desires to place a straw in the way of the general acceptance of the theories which have emanated from Trenton, if they stand the test of critical examination and analysis," the editorial nonetheless objected bitterly to the public campaign in which Cotton was clearly complicit: "The value of Dr. Cotton's work, the soundness of his conclusions, cannot be measured or discussed, with any good either to the public or the profession in lay journals or the daily press."[4]

Predisposed as he was to reject any criticism out of hand, Cotton would have preferred to ignore the whole matter, but found that even Adolf Meyer, who had previously risen to his defense on numerous occasions, was troubled by his actions. In an attempt to mollify his mentor, Cotton proffered a few lines of token and transparently hypocritical contrition: "I realize that you do not approve of the publicity given to the work through Mr. Lewis' article in the *Review of Reviews*. No doubt it is unfavorable to me." But his actions were, he insisted, a violation of professional norms justified by its results: "At the same time I feel the article has had a very good effect in stimulating institutions for it is evident that they cannot go on with the old methods with the public informed as to what can be done."[5]

In response to this truculence, Meyer, whose stiff Germanic manner, sharp tongue, and icy disposition were notorious for emasculating those who worked under him, seemed at something of a loss. Unused to underlings who refused to acknowledge his authority, he contented himself with weakly urging Cotton to moderate his ways: "I just have this feeling, that it is unfortunate that claims of such magnitude should come through the lay press before there is a fair indication that a consensus among the active men in the field has been approached."[6] It was counsel Cotton was determined to ignore.

At his hospital, the attack on focal sepsis was as wide-ranging and aggressive as before. Indeed, 1922 saw a new peak in the number of colectomies undertaken, with the total number of operations rising to 81 from the 63 performed during the preceding twelve months.[7] Teeth, tonsils, sinuses, stomachs, spleens, gall bladders, and cervixes all continued to be the focus of intensive scrutiny and aggressive intervention, and with the assistance of his chief dental surgeon Ferdearle Fischer, oral surgery became more thorough and extensive. Looking back over the preceding four years, they realized that "we can account for many mistakes in our earlier practice by the fact that we were too conservative, so that today we feel that a thorough elimination of oral infection can only be accomplished by radical extraction, or better still, surgical removal of infected teeth." And in deciding what to remove and what to save, the criterion was clear: "If a tooth is at all suspicious, we are of the opinion that it should be extracted and not left as a menace after all other foci of infection have been removed."[8] All bridges, crowns, pivots, and impacted and unerupted teeth were similarly threatening, and must not be left in place to form reservoirs of infection.[9] And because the abscesses and infections at the teeth's roots often extended into the surrounding bony structures of the mouth, extensive oral surgery was essential to excise these further sources of sepsis.

In December, after the busiest year yet in the operating theatre, Cotton responded to a request from Governor Henry J. Fernald by laying out his case for an augmentation to his budget. Funds to permit better follow-up work on his discharged patients, and to expand "the psychiatric clinic for correctional institutions," which he had instituted three years earlier, were now major priorities. Both measures, he assured Fernald, would save the state money, and would provide the data to rebut "criticisms of our work . . . from other hospitals."[10]

For, as Cotton was well aware, such criticisms continued to mount, in both public and private,[11] and had even been voiced by the staff at New Jersey's other state hospital.[12] Edward Brush, the editor of the *American Journal of Psychiatry*, had himself reviewed Cotton's Vanuxem lectures, calling them "enthusiastic propaganda." Cotton's claims, Brush pointed out, had been disputed by Kopeloff and Cheney, but adjudicating their rival claims was difficult, since they "have followed certain aspects of Dr. Cotton's work . . . but no one has followed all aspects of it or presented material which is closely comparable." So, in a sense, Brush was willing to concede that the jury was still out, and he acknowledged that, "while Dr. Cotton emphasizes physical and minimizes mental causes of mental illness, all readers will go a little of the way with him and some will follow to the journey's end." But Brush's skepticism was evident as the review drew to a close. The second part of the published lectures consisted of a "group of 25 clinical cases [and these] will leave many readers cold." All Cotton's peers would have "memories of other recoveries, improvements and deaths which in other hospitals and in private homes have followed many diverse therapeutic agents – or many lucky chances."[13]

Still another major East-Coast psychiatrist, Edward Strecker of Philadelphia's elite Pennsylvania Hospital, made his views clear in the 1923 issue of the *Archives of Neurology and Psychiatry*, which had recently been established as the official organ of the American Neurological Association.[14] The occasion was what purported to be a piece abstracting Cotton's and Kopeloff and Cheney's papers from the preceding year's American Psychiatric Association meeting, but the abstract, in this instance, was accompanied by lengthy editorial commentary. Strecker called Kopeloff and Cheney's work "a carefully controlled therapeutic experiment," and he praised the "care [that] was exercised" in selecting the subjects and following their progress. Cotton's work, he conceded, was "justifiably" a different sort of paper altogether. And to be sure, his "reported results are brilliant." (Strecker's emphasis on the "reported" was implicit but clear.) But Cotton was dealing with large numbers of patients, "and with the limited number of field workers available, it is hardly possible to accumulate a large amount of specific information." More seriously still, "the type and extent of recovery is often a question of medical judgment, and many patients are able to live outside a hospital even though they are far from normal." As all of his readers were aware, insanity could be intermittent, and Cotton's claims might thus be overblown or fallacious. In light of a whole series of concerns – "a clear cut negative experiment, the lack of agreement among competent observers, the possibility of errors in the follow-up work, the insufficient length of time which has elapsed since the detoxication treatment was put into effect on a large known group and the uncertainty of certain aspects of the bacteriological technique" – Strecker concluded that "the majority of neuropsychiatrists rightly prefer to regard the effect of focal infections as problematical." And though he acknowledged that the profession of psychiatry "owes a debt to Cotton and his followers: for emphasizing the importance of locating and removing focal infections," Strecker emphasized that operations should only be undertaken in narrowly defined circumstances. Certainly, he concluded, "any operation which is attended by a mortality rate of 30 percent should not be undertaken unless the indications are clear-cut and definite"; and on a less crucial level, "enthusiasm should not be permitted to outpace judgment, even when the consideration is the removal of a single tooth." Nor should one accept the argument that "death from colectomy is preferable to terminal dementia . . . [since] clinical psychiatry has not yet attained that diagnostic perfection which makes it possible to predict terminal dementia with any degree of surety, at least not until the psychosis has reached a stage in which even colectomy will not avail."[15]

Jelliffe and White, whose *Diseases of the Nervous System* had become one of the most widely used psychiatric textbooks of the era, used their fourth edition to deliver a broadside against Cotton's excesses. These days, they complained, "the neuropsychiater [*sic*] sees . . . patients who have had their teeth pulled, their tonsils gouged out, their eyes refitted, or eye muscles cut, their cervices amputated, their ovaries removed, from nine inches to six feet of gut cut out, all of the endocrine glands dispensed [with], orthopedic appliances applied, weeks of colonic irrigation, with or without electrical rigmaroles" – an orgy of surgical intervention that, so far as they were concerned, accomplished precisely nothing.[17] And at various gatherings of psychiatrists from the fall of 1922 onwards, Nicholas Kopeloff continued to report findings from his research at the New York Psychiatric Institute that directly contradicted Cotton's claims.

Remarkably, Cotton acted as though none of this criticism was of any moment, except for the drumbeat of criticism from New York. Here, as he was well aware, the situation was somewhat delicate. Kirby, from whose institute the relevant research emanated, was a Southerner, just like Cotton, and both men had begun their careers in psychiatry at the same time and at the same institution, as young Turks working under Meyer at the Worcester State Hospital in Massachusetts. Kirby, like Cotton, had gone to Germany in 1906 with Meyer's blessing and support,[17] and he, too, while there had worked with Kraepelin. Meyer and Kirby had remained close. Meyer on one occasion, and quite atypically for him, referred to their "life-long friendship," and their friendship survived even after the older man counseled Kirby not to marry a Polish "girl" working at the Ward's Island facility. Meyer warned him that "racial" differences meant that she was socially impossible to accept in their circle, and that to proceed with the marriage would mean the end of his professional career.[18] Subsequently, it was Meyer who did most to secure Kirby his post at the Psychiatric Institute, and to whom Kirby immediately wrote in triumph when offered the job; and it was to Meyer that Kirby turned when dissatisfaction with the political situation in the New York State hospital system nearly drove him to leave for an appointment at Worcester or to risk entering private practice.[19]

Kirby was thus not only a long-standing professional rival of Cotton's, but he was also every bit as closely connected to Meyer and Meyer's patronage. Knowing all this, Cotton suggested that the attacks on his work were the work of Kirby's underlings, not Kirby himself. The "adverse criticism," he wrote to Meyer, "has come from Kopeloff, of Ward's Island." After the debate at the 1922 American Psychiatric Association meeting, Cotton had apparently asked Meyer to intervene, and to request that Kirby put a stop to his subordinates' denigration of the importance of focal sepsis. Months later, Cotton lamented that, "in spite of your letter to Dr. Kirby and his apparent willingness to listen to reason, in the Fall [of 1922] Kopeloff gave the same paper that he gave at Quebec with same inadequate work and unfair conclusions. This was at the New York Neurological Society meeting . . . I found Kopeloff is a very dangerous individual whose main idea is to refute the work here and I am very sorry that Kirby depends upon him for his information."[20]

But the attempt to drive a wedge between Kirby and his bacteriologist failed miserably. The 1923 meeting of the American Psychiatric Association took place in Detroit in June, in the midst of sweltering weather that produced widespread complaints from the assembled psychiatrists. Clarence Cheney had by now moved on, leaving Ward's Island to serve as the assistant superintendent at Utica State Hospital in upstate New York, and so he was unavailable to report on the further progress of the attempt to assess the validity of Cotton's claims. Nicholas Kopeloff, possessing a PhD rather than an MD, was ineligible to address the Association, and so it was George Kirby himself who rose to report their findings, and whose name appeared as second author when their paper was published in the October issue of the *American Journal of Psychiatry*.

Insisting that their research "was undertaken with no preconceived hypothesis; the object being simply to ascertain facts which might in any way contribute to the better understanding of the relation of focal infection to mental disease,"[21] Kopeloff and Kirby extended their findings to encompass an additional year of experience and 60 additional patients – a total of 120 inmates from the Manhattan State Hospital: 72 women and 48 men, 58 of whom were assigned to the operative group and 62 to the matched control. Prior to commencing work, Kirby made an attempt to assess each patient's prognosis for recovery or improvement, after which all of them were carefully screened to uncover existing sites of sepsis, and their mental illness was diagnosed. For one group, active treatment then commenced; with the other, matched for age, sex, duration, and type of psychosis, prognosis and infective conditions were simply observed to provide a comparative baseline.

When Kopeloff and Cheney had presented results from their first series of patients, their report had been cautious and circumspect. A year later, however, all such inhibitions were cast aside. On every front, Kopeloff and Kirby mounted a frontal assault on Cotton's work. Cotton's technique for diagnosing the presence of infection, his claims for the etiological significance of sepsis, and his assertions about the therapeutic effects of surgical interventions all came in for sustained and withering criticism.

Cotton, they reminded their audience, frequently trumpeted his results with a series of 1,400 patients who had been discharged as recovered or improved over a four-year period; but "the detailed data concerning this . . . group have never been published."[22] In all Cotton's numerous publications, he had failed "to publish complete data on either the psychological or the laboratory side."[23] When it came to documenting the presence of infection, "a careful search through Cotton's numerous publications nowhere reveals the bacteriological technic employed in his work."[24] Internal evidence cast severe doubts on the competence of the work he and his assistants performed. An "amazing feature of Cotton's bacteriological data," for example, was "the simplicity of the flora of the mouth as found in his patients . . . One would be hard put to find anything similar in nature in the entire literature of bacteriology."[25]

Their New Jersey colleague, they complained, "nowhere defines" key terms, relied upon "arbitrary diagnosis" and reviewing his own discussions of his data, "it is patent that gastric infection has not been demonstrated in these psychotic patients and that its influence on the course of the psychosis is sheer speculation."[26] "For example, Cotton considers the presence of bacteria in the stomach contents as a criterion of infection. The mere presence of bacteria we contend does not necessarily imply infection, but it is at least necessary for the bacteria to multiply and probably necessary that they should invade the tissues."[27] For Kopeloff and Kirby, the Rehfuss technique Cotton relied upon to document the presence of bacteria in the stomach was completely inadequate and unreliable for the purpose,[28] and elaborate efforts to culture teeth and tonsils still produced highly dubious findings. As for the alleged infections of "the lower intestinal tract," "we have carried out exactly the same observations on our patients and have failed to find anything which would justify a major operation." Cotton had pointed to "bilious attacks," "delay in the movement of the test meal through the intestine" as shown by "radiographic studies," and, most sinister of all, "a history of habitual constipation" as symptoms of infection. So far from requiring surgery, even "our most stubborn cases of constipation have yielded to therapeutic treatment with *acidophilus* milk," and yet in all cases "in which constipation was relieved there was no improvement in the course of the psychosis."[29] More generally, "focal infections as diagnosed and operated upon at Trenton State Hospital are not consonant with the procedures employed by other well-established clinics and hospitals" and "one is forced to conclude that Cotton's interpretations are at variance with his facts."[30]

As if this barrage of criticism were not damning enough, Kopeloff and Kirby proceeded to detail the results of their own experiments. Whereas the first year's results from the Psychiatric Institute had rested upon only dental extractions and tonsillectomies, over the ensuing twelve months they had broadened the range of interventions they had undertaken, and had intervened aggressively: "So far as operations on teeth, tonsils, sinuses, and generative organs were concerned, we did not hesitate to resort to surgical measures if there was the least suspicion of infection – in many of our operated cases our consultants stated that they would not have advised operative treatment in similar conditions in ordinary practice."[31] Their 58 operative cases had sacrificed 253 teeth to the experiment. Tonsils were removed, even in cases where a prior tonsillectomy had left only "a small amount of tonsilar tissue . . . and really no local indications for operation . . . in order to fulfill our radical requirements and remove all possible sources of infection."[32] They were equally diligent in attacking other possible sites of trouble, making use of "the Sturmdorf conic plastic enucleation of the cervix" and paying "particular attention to the gastrointestinal tract."[33] (As a further warrant for the soundness of their conclusions, Kirby pointed out in the discussion period, they had consulted broadly with leading experts: "We were fortunate in having the help of some of the ablest specialists in New York so that we feel that the diagnostic and operative work was carefully and thoroughly done.")[34] Cotton, they acknowledged, might object that they had not performed any surgeries on their patients' colons, but, "since no colectomies were advised in our cases by Dr. Jerome Lynch, who performed such operations at the Trenton State Hospital in 1918–1919, none was undertaken."[35] Besides, on Cotton's own account in the March issue of the *Archives of Neurology and Psychiatry*, "colon resections [at Trenton] now number over one hundred and fifty. As a result of this work, at least 25 patients owe their recovery to his [Draper's] skill."[36] At best, these 25 cases amounted to a tiny fraction, less than 2 or 3 percent of the more than a thousand cures Cotton claimed to have made in this period, and could do little to account for the "wide discrepancy between his recoveries which average 85 percent, and ours which are below 15 percent."[37]

And here, of course, was the heart of the matter, so far as Kirby and Kopeloff were concerned. All their diligent efforts to search for sepsis and to operate to remove it wherever it might be found had proved fruitless. Among manic-depressive cases, the proportion of recoveries among the operative and the control groups were identical, and in the dementia praecox series, "there is a slightly lower percentage of improvement in the . . . operated group than in the control group; that is, 18 percent as compared with 25 percent."[38] Moreover, "our observations demonstrate that in every case that recovered, a recovery had been forecast before treatment was started; that no case recovered in which a poor prognosis had been given, and that in only one case did any improvement occur."[39] Convinced by now that "*there is no relation of cause and effect between specific bacterial toxins coming from focal infection and the functional psychoses,*" the two men announced that they were "terminating this investigation."[40]

By comparison with the lengthy and animated discussion that had roiled the Quebec meeting, Kirby's presentation aroused remarkably little controversy. Only a small handful of the audience ventured to speak, and they were almost all of one mind. Clarence Cheney, not surprisingly, congratulated his erstwhile colleagues on bringing the study he had commenced to such a convincing conclusion. Two pathologists, one from Rhode Island, and the other from the Essex County Hospital for the Insane in New Jersey, rose to endorse Kopeloff and Kirby's findings based upon their separate experiences, though both added that their own work had been far less rigorous and definitive. The second of them, Harold Gosline from Rhode Island, did stress the difference between treatment and etiology, and noted that, "the fact that a patient does not recover when you remove an infection is no sign that the focus removed was not the cause of the mental disease," since he might already "be so far injured that he will never get well again."[41] But that was the closest anyone came to dissenting from what they had heard.

Edward Strecker from Philadelphia was particularly lavish in his praise. He had followed Dr. Kopeloff's work closely, and "I am not surprised at the conclusions he arrives at today." The work was especially "timely because I presume that scarcely a day has passed during the past year when neuro-psychiatrists both in hospital practice and in consultation practice have not been approached as to the desirability and advisability of using a method of treatment, removing alleged foci of infections, in the attempt to cure patients who had psychoses. Also the work had acquired considerable publicity, so that it was no longer sufficient to say simply that one did not believe in it." With a palpable air of relief, he hailed the end of the enthusiasm for focal sepsis: "I think Dr. Kopeloff's and Dr. Kirby's presentation has for us, all the interest which attaches to the last chapter of a thrilling serial story."[42]

It would prove to be a spectacularly mistaken assessment.

7

An American Abroad

Henry Cotton was not among the throng of psychiatrists sweltering in the heat-wave in Detroit in late June 1923. Without him, those who, in his words, were "out to get me"[1] were spared the noisy objections he would undoubtedly have made to their findings, but his absence made the whole session much more low key, and may have contributed to the diminished attention Kopeloff and Kirby's paper received. Where the preliminary report on the New York research had been the centerpiece of the 1922 meeting of the American Psychiatric Association, the potentially more devastating follow-up drew a lesser crowd and spawned far less wide-ranging discussion. Nor did it merit any special mention in the summary of the annual conference that subsequently appeared in the pages of the *American Journal of Psychiatry*. Like a performance of *Hamlet* without the ghost, the whole episode was somewhat anticlimactic without the catalyst of Cotton's belligerent personality and truculent demeanor to provide some fireworks.

Cotton's absence, to be sure, did not reflect any disposition on his part to avoid confrontation. He simply had another, more pressing engagement before an audience more disposed to recognize his stellar accomplishments. While his North American colleagues endured "weather [that] ... was hot and ... humid, conditions which detracted from the comfort of those in attendance,"[2] and looked forward longingly to the 1924 meeting, which was to take place in the ocean air of Atlantic City, Cotton was aboard an ocean liner steaming towards England.

An official invitation had arrived at Trenton that spring for Cotton to travel to London to deliver a plenary address to the Medico-Psychological Association of Great Britain and Ireland on his breakthroughs in the discovery and treatment of focal sepsis. He had accepted with alacrity. A number of British physicians and surgeons had, he knew, speculated on the connections of infections and psychosis, and the prospect of seeking more converts across the Atlantic provided a welcome respite from the barrage of criticism he had recently confronted at home. Young Adolph Meyer Cotton had reported on their preparations for the trip to his namesake in late May, and father and son had set sail on June 23, hoping to see the great man himself once they arrived in London.[3]

The prime mover behind the invitation to Cotton was Thomas Chivers Graves, superintendent of the Rubery Hill and Hollymoor mental hospitals in Birmingham, England's second city.[4] The son of an itinerant and impoverished Plymouth Brethren minister, Graves had wanted to become a surgeon, but at first had been forced to settle for operating on animals because his straightened circumstances had dictated veterinary rather than medical training. His considerable talents, however, had subsequently won him a scholarship to medical school, and briefly it had appeared that his childhood ambition might be realized. But the Great War had derailed his plans to specialize in surgery, stealing his early thirties from him. Once he had compounded the difficulties by marrying his commanding officer's daughter, he could scarcely contemplate the years of uncertain and fluctuating income that even the most talented had to endure while building a surgical practice.

The war years, in any event, exposed him to a new set of realities that dramatically transformed his career choices. As an army doctor during the First World War, like so many of his fellow physicians, he had had to cope with the epidemic of shell-shock. The prejudices and predilections of early twentieth-century British psychiatry for organic accounts of mental disorder had been shaken in some instances by the experience of seeing fighting men reduced to mental wrecks – hallucinating, paralysed, mute, psychosomatically blind, emotionally distraught – by the horrors of trench warfare. But the willingness to countenance psychodynamic etiologies of mental breakdown was by no means universal. For many, the separate and combined effects of defective heredity, physical concussion, and neurological damage were at the root of the problem.[5] In this account, just like their civilian counterparts, psychotic soldiers were somatically sick or biologically degenerate specimens whose mental weaknesses were but a reflection of their deeper physical flaws. Certainly, these were views Graves found more palatable than their psychological rivals, convinced as he was that all disease was rooted in the body and that the only "real" medicine was surgery.[6]

In electing a career in psychiatry, Graves was undoubtedly influenced by his wartime experiences, but also by the realization that in this specialty, at least, there were prospects of secure pay and accommodation.[7] Despite the paucity of his prior experience in the field, his exemplary medical credentials,[8] coupled with his wartime clinical duties, enabled him to move into the psychiatric service at its highest levels, entirely avoiding the years of drudgery and sub-servience as an assistant medical officer that were ordinarily the precondition for a superintendency.[9] On leaving the army, Graves immediately secured a position as superintendent of the Hereford County Asylum, and less than a year later, a still more prominent and lucrative post as head of the Rubery Hill and Hollymoor hospitals in Birmingham – glittering prizes in the psychiatric pantheon, in search of which assistant physicians in the psychiatric service toiled for decades. For a man of Graves's energy and ambition, however, there were also the distinct drawbacks of being consigned to a specialty widely viewed as a professional backwater, and of the prospect of a career devoted to overseeing the asylum farm, supervising the management of its sewer system, and presiding over the day-to-day routines of a warehouse of the unwanted. It was not an enterprise a man of his appetites and enthusiasms could view with equanimity, and he was not content for long with the dubious pleasures of ruling like a displaced squire over his peculiar Potemkin village.

Into the world of the asylum, Graves brought with him reservoirs of energy and enthusiasm, and "a determination to bring the study of pathology and the basic principles of medicine into the practice of psychiatry."[10] Like other super-intendents of the period, he possessed considerable latitude to implement his ideas and enthusiasms. If not quite the monarch of all he surveyed, a superin-tendent nonetheless possessed near autocratic powers in the artificial, closed community over which he presided, and Graves's imposing physical stature (he stood over six feet and one inch tall) and his domineering and charismatic per-sonality allowed him to exercise his nominal authority to its full extent.[11]

Graves's early months at Rubery Hill were occupied with the task of re-transforming the institution back from the war hospital it had been to the mental hospital it was once again to become, and renovation and expansion of the physical infrastructure were to occupy a substantial part of his time through the mid-1920s. The almost uninhabitable set of buildings he had inherited, bereft of any residents, had by early 1921 been refitted to house 560 patients, and by 1925 he had added new day rooms and a number of bungalow wards at both Hollymoor and Rubery Hill.[12] A larger-than-life figure who pos-sessed considerable talents as an administrator, Graves revelled in his position, dominating both his colleagues and his patients, and seizing opportunities to secure the spotlight – whether in lectures to fellow psychiatrists, illustrated with copious slides and statistics; or in taking the leading role in asylum pro-ductions of Gilbert and Sullivan, and annually in "the part of Pooh-Ba at the hospitals' Christmas show, where the applause stopped the performance at sev-eral points."[13] He even had the opportunity to play the gentleman-farmer: like

14 *Thomas Chivers Graves, superintendent of the Rubery Hill and Hollymoor Asylums, dressed as the Duke of Plaza Toro, and starring in a hospital Gilbert and Sullivan production. Graves reveled in the limelight, strutting before the captive audience of staff and patients in a variety of theatrical roles during the course of his long career.*

most hospitals of its era, his had a farm attached, whose milk, butter, meat, and eggs were worth more than £7,500 in 1922. Indirectly, therefore, Graves's veterinary training was eminently useful on a regular basis.

It was, however, his background as a surgeon that was to place a more distinctive mark on his psychiatric practice during the next three decades. Though a psychodynamically orientated psychiatry had made notable advances during and immediately after the war and was rather less often the target of open hostility and intemperate criticism than it had once been, the long-standing disdain and distrust felt by the mainstream of the profession still lingered only barely beneath the surface.[14] Graves's refusal to place much stock in a "childhood history of frustration" as the source of mental disorder thus made him very much a part of mainstream professional opinion.[15] In 1922, in more direct opposition to psychodynamic explanations, he began to advance, both in print and in person, a very different account of the sources of mental illness, one which from the outset found a sympathetic audience among leading figures in the medical profession at large, as well as among many of his fellow specialists, and one that made his surgical training and predilections directly relevant to his practice in the asylum.

First articulating his views in a short paper published in the *Lancet* in 1922,[16] Graves advanced with increasing aggressiveness the same basic thesis as Henry Cotton: that mental disorder was the product of auto-toxicity, caused in turn by the presence in a variety of organs of chronic, untreated reservoirs of infection. The hypothesis, as he acknowledged from the outset, was by no means a novel one, with speculations to this effect appearing in the literature as early as the late 1860s. And in July 1922, at the annual meeting of the Medico-Psychological Association in Edinburgh, Graves's views on the importance of bacterial poisoning of the brain in the genesis of mental disorder received a powerful endorsement from Chalmers Watson, an influential physician at the Edinburgh Royal Infirmary.[17] Graves's own work in this early period emphasized that "clinically an important relationship can be demonstrated to exist between prolonged emotional disturbance and chronic septic processes, occurring in hard tissues, especially in connection with the jaws."[18] Watson, in contrast, placed at least as much stress on "excessive putrefaction in the bowel" as on decay in the mouth, and had invoked the sainted Lister in urging his audience to recognize "the urgent need at the present time to all cases of mental disorder being studied by alienists more from the standpoint of the general physician, full use being made of the routine modern methods of investigation as carried out by physicians with a modern outlook and knowledge."[19] But both men shared the sense that insanity had a straightforward physical cause and a comparably straightforward therapeusis. And if Watson, as a general physician, was entirely without formal ties to psychiatry, Graves was in many ways equally marginal to the profession, someone (as his obituarist would put it more than four decades later) whose own primary "ambition was to bring the study of pathology and the basic principles of modern medicine [as he understood them] into the practice of psychiatry."[20]

Graves welcomed Chalmers Watson's backing for the experimental work he was conducting, but he was still more emboldened by reading Henry Cotton's striking claims for the potency of a more thorough-going assault on pus infection. Well ahead of the gathering of his colleagues in London for their annual conference in July 1923, Graves had secured an invitation for the American visitor to give the major address, and had also made plans to give a paper of his own on the results to date of dental surgery in his own hospital. Learning of the program, Chalmers Watson made it a point to attend, as did the surgeon William Hunter, who as early as 1900 had urged the application of the principles of "Listerism" to general medicine, and had suggested a role for focal infection in the etiology of a wide range of diseases, including psychiatric disorders.[21] Since the sitting president of the Medico-Psychological Association,

Professor George Robertson of Edinburgh University, was already known to be broadly in sympathy with the focal sepsis hypothesis, Cotton faced a far more receptive audience when he rose in the crowded assembly room of the Medical Society of London just off Cavendish Square on the morning of July 11 to deliver a lengthy address outlining his etiological findings and his dramatic therapeutic successes.

Founded three years before the American Declaration of Independence, the Medical Society's meeting rooms lay just to the north of one of the most elegant Palladian squares in London, at that time lined with the palatial town houses of a still-wealthy landed aristocracy. Lettsom House was a more modest but still classically styled three-storey building where the Medico-Pychological Association, still lacking a home of its own, regularly held its meetings, its borrowed and somewhat faded grandeur a subtle reminder of psychiatry's status as the step-child of British medicine. For Henry Cotton, though, the aristocratic, old-world setting and the assembled throng of immaculately dressed British alienists provided a splendid platform from which to proselytize on behalf of the scientific breakthrough he brought with him from the colonies, an opportunity for which he fulsomely thanked his hosts.

Oddly enough, in one wholly unexpected respect, the surroundings were reminiscent of the meeting in Detroit that Cotton had missed. London was still in the grip of an extraordinary heat wave that had begun on July 6, with temperatures advancing daily into the nineties.[22] To make matters worse, it was almost unbearably humid. The night of July 9/10 had witnessed the most violent and the longest thunderstorm of the century, with torrential rain and lightning keeping the sky constantly illuminated over a six-hour period, beginning just before midnight. By one count, there were as many as 6,294 lightning strikes just to the west in Chelsea, an average of 18 flashes a minute. And on the night before Cotton's speech, there were more violent storms, accompanied by vivid and prolonged lightning.[23] Accustomed to the heat and humidity of New Jersey summers, Cotton was doubtless less enervated by the conditions than his hosts. The Society's meeting room did not help matters, however. Entered through a single door at the top of a rather grand curved staircase, it was handsome enough. Its walls were covered with Victorian portraits of medical notables and their wives, and an impressive raised oak lectern ran across the width of the room, the whole arrangement set off by a high curved and embossed gilded ceiling that was supported by a series of ornate Corinthian columns. The only ventilation, though, came from a half-dozen small arched windows arranged high up on the two side walls, an inadequate arrangement at the best of times, and particularly so in the sweltering weather that had laid siege to London. Still, even though the report

15 *The auditorium at Lettsom House, headquarters of the Medical Society of London, where Henry Cotton delivered his lecture on focal sepsis and psychiatry on a sweltering day in July 1923. Note the arches high up on the walls, where small windows provided the only ventilation for the assembled throng who gathered to hear him speak.*

on the day's proceedings bemoaned the "intense heat" the participants had to endure, curiosity about the work of a man who claimed to have the key to curing madness drew a great crowd to hear him.[24]

Cotton did not disappoint his listeners, speaking at length with the aid of charts and slides about the revolutionary findings that, so he informed the rapt crowd, had transformed the prospects for the mentally ill and for those who claimed to minister to minds diseased. Over the hour and more for which he spoke, fascinating photographs of radiographs of diseased colons and entire gastro-intestinal tracts flashed on to the screen in front of his audience, a display of visual pyrotechnics quite routine in medical meetings three-quarters of a century later, but then quite novel. Pictures of decaying teeth and charts documenting the presence of harmful bacteria in the gut provided vivid evidence of the technology and laboratory analysis that lent scientific substance to the tale of triumph that Cotton unfolded for them. And to cap it all, there was a poster-sized female torso, her body adorned with a map of the various possible crevices and corners of her anatomy where "foci of infection" might lurk to transform her into a lunatic.

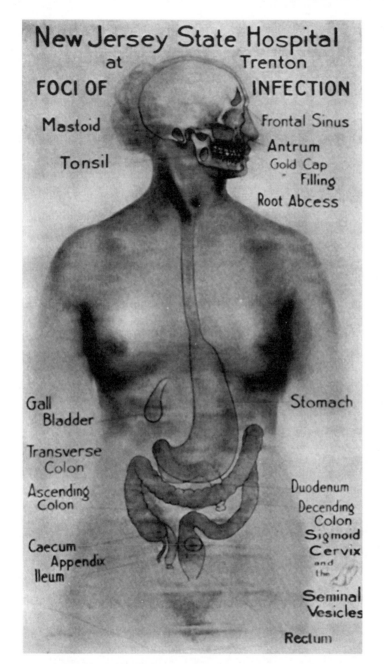

16 *The sites of focal sepsis. Cotton used a version of this diagram on multiple occasions – at the American Medical Association meeting in New Orleans, at his London lecture in 1923, and in a series of articles – to illustrate the often obscure nooks and crannies of the body where focal sepsis could lurk undetected, spreading its poisons into the system and prompting a descent into madness.*

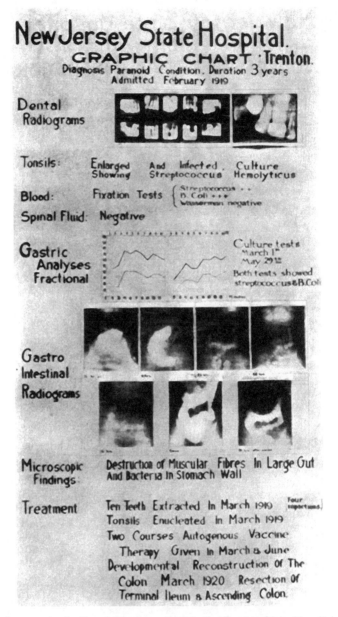

New Jersey State Hospital.
GRAPHIC CHART · Trenton.
Diagnosis Paranoid Condition. Duration 3 years
Admitted February 1919

Dental
Radiograms

Tonsils: Enlarged And Infected. Culture
Showing Streptococcus Hemolyticus

Blood: Fixation Tests { Streptococcus · ·
B. Coli · · ·
Wassermann negative }

Spinal Fluid: Negative

Gastric
Analyses
Fractional

Culture tests
March 1st
May 29th
Both tests showed
streptococcus & B.Coli

Gastro
Intestinal
Radiograms

Microscopic Destruction of Muscular Fibres In Large Gut
Findings: And Bacteria In Stomach Wall

Treatment Ten Teeth Extracted In March 1919 [Four importans.]
Tonsils Enucleated In March 1919
Two Courses Autogenous Vaccine
Therapy Given In March & June
Developmental Reconstruction Of The
Colon March 1920 Resection Of
Terminal Ileum & Ascending Colon.

17 *Treating psychosis: the chart of a patient in the Trenton State Hospital who had been diagnosed as suffering from paranoia. The search for sepsis had involved dental X-rays, culture of the tonsils, lumbar puncture to examine the spinal fluid, blood tests for syphilis and infection with e coli, fractional analyses of the spinal fluid, radiograms (or X-rays) of the intestines using barium enemas, and microscopic examination of the large intestine and the stomach wall. Such a mass of text and images, listing as well the extracting of teeth, tonsils, and colon, drove home to the lay reader just how wide-ranging the investigations of patients were, and how extensive the "surgical bacteriology" that followed.*

Given the chance to address a new and receptive audience, Cotton's self-confidence and showmanship knew no bounds. Flattering his listeners by first stressing the British origins of the doctrine of focal infection, he then launched upon a panegyric to the effects of mounting a full-blooded assault on its presence in the mentally ill, urging them to join in "the fight against sepsis in medicine" and for "antiseptic medicine" – a term he credited to William Hunter. In 1910, he reminded them, the prophetic Hunter had predicted that "the time . . . is fast approaching when the title of 'antiseptic physician' will become equally distinctive of a good doctor; when it will be equally honoured and honourable as that of 'antiseptic surgeon'; when the knowledge and outlook which it implies with regard to the importance of sepsis in medicine will be deemed one of the highest qualifications which a good doctor can possess." The moment had arrived, he was convinced, for the psychiatric profession to embrace "this declaration of principles."[25]

Turning to his own work in the field, Cotton credited his training in Germany for reinforcing his conviction that "the causation of mental disorders" was to be searched for "from the standpoint of an organic rather than a functional viewpoint. In this work [the writer] stood somewhat isolated, as his views were contrary to all psychiatric teaching at that time." Indeed, in his native land, resistance to the truth remained high, as "the majority of psychiatrists" still clung to outmoded ideas and theories, which "has prevented the acceptance of the practice and principle outlined by the writer in many contributions in the last five years." Switching to the first person to emphasize his point, he concluded his introductory remarks by commenting that, "needless to say, I was much gratified in learning that many of the English psychiatrists had no such prejudices, and that our theories were being given an honest hearing in England."[26]

Between 1907 and 1916, Cotton informed them, he had sought to link lesions in the cortex to underlying bodily processes, eventually searching for a "disturbance of the endocrine system . . . but unfortunately, after five years of work in this field, we were unable to produce any decisive result. Glandular therapy was a failure." At last, in 1916, "we became interested in chronic sepsis as a possible causative factor." Like Graves, Cotton proclaimed that "our first work was naturally confined to infected teeth." Though initial results were unpromising – "in the first fifty cases in which extractions were done, no results were obtained" – Cotton refused to be discouraged. Beginning with tonsils in 1917, the battle had soon extended to a variety of other fronts in what amounted to a thorough-going assault designed "to literally 'clean up' our patients of all foci of chronic sepsis."[27] Sinuses, tonsils, stomachs, gall bladders, colons, cervixes, and seminal vesicles, all these and more might be potential sites of silent chronic infections leaching toxins into the lymphatic system and the blood-stream and poisoning the brain; and any or all might require excision by the surgeon's knife.

Such ruthless pursuit and elimination of sepsis, however, was blessed with the happiest of outcomes: an increase in "our recoveries in this group from 37 percent to 85 percent."[28] All of these efforts, Cotton insisted, were dependent upon the most recent scientific advances of modern medicine: gastric analyses and serology, bacteriological work and X-rays, serums and vaccines, and above all the miracles of modern aseptic surgery – for only the surgeon's knife and the dentist's forceps could in the last analysis ensure successful "detoxification." His audience were perhaps made somewhat uncomfortable by the scorn he poured upon what had long been British psychiatry's preferred explanation of mental disorder, defective heredity ("this doctrine was more or less fatalistic, and simply served as a cloak to hide our ignorance of other factors" and it "has had the most unhappy result of stifling investigation, and retarding constructive work");[29] but most found themselves nodding in agreement when he turned to a far more savage assault on psychoanalysis ("the extravagant claims made by its advocates are without foundation or justification. Freudism has proven to be a tremendous handicap to psychiatry").[30] And, as he promptly reminded them, both approaches led to a therapeutic impasse: heredity was "a fixed quantity in the equation" and "a factor which cannot be influenced by discussion or treatment"; and "no one connected with hospitals for the insane would delude himself that mental treatment of any character has been successful when applied to the so-called functional group."[31]

Making the obligatory bow towards a multi-factorial origin of "the so-called functional psychoses,"[32] Cotton insisted that instead "the most constant [cause], and, from the standpoint of treatment, the most important one, is the intra-cerebral, bio-chemical cellular disturbance arising from circulating toxins originating from chronic foci of infection ... [To be sure, t]he psychogenic factors should not be ignored, as they have an important *role* in precipitating the mental disturbance in an individual literally saturated with infection, and the resulting toxaemia."[33] But they were purely secondary, at best, neither necessary nor sufficient to account for the emergence of insanity.

There was a further implication of the discoveries that had been made at Trenton: instead of considering psychosis as a disease entity, Cotton pointed out that logically it should rather be considered "a *symptom*, and often a *terminal symptom* of a long-continued chronic sepsis or masked infection, the accumulating toxaemia of which acts directly or indirectly on the brain-cells."[34] Americans had apparently made the mistake of swallowing Kraepelin's classification of mental diseases *in toto*, and therefore assumed that there were a whole array of different disease entities making up the category of insanity. On the contrary, Cotton truculently asserted that "as a result of our work, I do not believe there is any fundamental difference in the functional psychoses. The more we study our cases, [the more] we are forced to conclude that distinct disease entities in the functional group . . . do not exist. The aetiological factors are the same . . . [in] the whole so-called functional group, such as manic-depressive insanity, dementia praecox, paranoid condition, the psychoneuroses, etc."[35] What appeared to be different diseases were in fact simply the reflections of the ways "the psychosis is modified by several factors: first, the duration of the sepsis, the severity of the toxaemia produced, plus the patient's resistance, or lack of resistance, to septic processes."[36] Perhaps it was because "in England you were not so credulous" that it had proved easier for many of them to swallow the idea of a unitary psychosis and to embrace the results he had produced by eliminating focal sepsis.[37]

The attentive listener would have heard Cotton confess to certain unfortunate side effects that sadly were the inevitable accompaniment of this massive advance. There were, for example, the patients whose "serious lesions of the colon" necessitated remedial action – amounting to "about 20 percent of the 'functional' group." As with other kinds of sepsis, the only remedy in his view was "elimination," a term that here turned out to have an unfortunate double meaning: "In our early operations the caecum and ascending colon were resected only . . . Further examination of the unsuccessful cases proved that the splenic fixture and descending colon were also involved. Consequently, in the last two years total colectomy has been performed in practically every case. This operation was done in 133 cases, with 33 recoveries and 44 deaths. Partial resection at the right side was done in 148 cases, with 44 recoveries and 59 deaths" – mortality statistics that, he explained, could be tolerated since they were "largely due to the very poor physical condition of most of the patients."[38]

But it was the extraordinary therapeutic success that Cotton claimed, and the degree to which his approach seemed to call up the most "scientific" features of modern medicine, that his audience chose to focus upon. A series of prominent figures took advantage of the discussion session that followed to lavish praise on their American visitor, never uttering a word of dissent or serious criticism, and ignoring completely the mortality figures with which Cotton had provided them.

Chalmers Watson, speaking, as he took pains to emphasize, as a general physician, and not as a psychiatrist, pronounced the American's work "wholly admirable," though he suggested, based on his own experience, that the proportion of mental patients with diseased colons would prove to be "definitely higher" than the 20 percent Cotton had estimated. Presumably, therefore, more rather than less abdominal surgery would turn out to be necessary to cure eight or nine out of ten patients. For psychiatry, Cotton's approach had the admirable effect of re-emphasizing that "mental medicine was only a branch of general medicine." But once the lessons of Cotton's work had been applied in psychiatry, "it should spread [back] into the realm of general medicine. And the application of those principles to general medicine was bound, he thought, to yield a harvest no less fruitful than that which Dr. Cotton had suggested in connection with the study of mental symptoms."[39]

Watson was followed to the podium by Sir Frederick Mott, the head of the London County Asylums' Pathological Laboratory, a fellow of the Royal Society, and an enormously influential figure within British psychiatry. Mott had been primarily responsible for persuading Henry Maudsley to endow the acute-treatment mental hospital that bears his name, and in 1923, after wartime delays, the Maudsley was just beginning to establish its pre-eminence in the training of British psychiatrists. A neurophysiologist who earlier in his career had, like Cotton, visited German laboratories to further his scientific training, Mott had long exhibited an unwavering commitment to a somaticist model of mental illness, and had persistently sought, following the German example, to link psychiatry with the universities.[40] His political skills and his public standing as one of the few "intellectuals" in the field of psychiatry made him a formidable figure, and Cotton was thus fully conscious of the significance of the moment when Mott offered extravagant praise for the American's accomplishments in the war on sepsis: "He was particularly struck with the specimens of bowel which Dr. Cotton showed because they so closely resembled those which he, Sir Frederick, had seen in his own experience ... Dr. Cotton's work showed emphatically the importance of the bowel as a source of chronic infection" and it was vital that all asylums take steps "to prevent ... bowel disease – ulceration of the bowel – from typhoid, paratyphoid, and dysentery – infectious diseases which many of the subjects of them acquired in the asylum." Dr. Cotton's address had been notable for its "beautiful pictures and photographs. The illustrations he had given were most convincing. He referred especially to the beautiful radiograms of teeth and of the bowel conditions." All in all, they had been fortunate to hear a "very valuable contribution, which would be most stimulating to everybody in this country."[41]

Speaking at still greater length, William Hunter, the surgeon to whom Cotton attributed the original hypothesis connecting mental illness and focal infection, declared they had just listened to "one of the greatest accomplishments connected with the subject of mental disease." He was "not qualified to speak of it from the experience of a mental specialist, but from his knowledge of the lesions with which Dr. Cotton was dealing and from the effects known by him to be produced by these lesions, he recognized that the results which Dr. Cotton was receiving were utterly sound, and were of a character likely to be produced."[42] What was still more remarkable and fortunate was that Dr. Cotton's work appeared to demonstrate that "it was disordered action, not actual degeneration, that underlay many mental disorders even of the severest character . . . [so that] on removal of the septic infective foci present in such cases, the whole mental disorder was profoundly affected, and might in cases be made to disappear in as many weeks as it had been years in existence." Skepticism had no place any more. "The striking individual and statistical results described by Dr. Cotton placed the matter beyond all reasonable doubt. It only remained to put measures against sepsis into routine operation not merely in isolated cases, but in all cases of insanity."[43]

It was now time for the president to close the morning's proceedings. Newly inaugurated, Edwin Goodall was full of praise for "this valuable lecture."[44] Sharing the belief of most of the British psychiatric establishment that Freud was a quack and an unscientific charlatan, and clearly stung by the popularity of Freudian notions among some segments of the educated elite, Goodall enthusiastically embraced an approach that re-biologized mental disorder. Cotton's new therapeutic and etiological ideas "should have served to draw members from the alluring and tempting pastures of psychogenesis back to the narrower, steeper, more rugged and arduous, yet straighter paths, of general medicine . . . Before seeking to summon spirits from the vasty deep and one's subliminal consciousness, let members remember that they were brought up as materialists and biologists; let them, before plunging into those depths, exhaust every material means for dealing with and curing their mental patients."[45] As Goodall had stressed when introducing the discussion session, "here, presented today, were results which no one could deny; seeing was believing, and he was sure all were greatly impressed and instructed."[46]

With some considerable relief, the assembled throng now moved from the crowded and stifling meeting room and traveled south of the Thames to the Bethlem Royal Hospital, the ancient Bedlam. Here they were welcomed by the medical superintendent Porter Phillips and spent the afternoon at one of those peculiarly British rituals, the garden party. And "notwithstanding the intense heat a most enjoyable afternoon was spent," some of it on a sort of busman's holiday, going "though the wards of this ancient yet still virile and up-to-date institution."[47] Then on to still another ritual occasion, the Association's annual dinner, held at the New Hotel Metropole on Northumberland Avenue, where Cotton was seated at the head table as one of the honoured guests, alongside Sir Humphry Rolleston, the president of the Royal College of Physicians, for an evening that stretched well into the night: an occasion replete with lengthy speeches and toasts, beginning with "His Majesty the King," and extending on and on, as a variety of politicians and professional luminaries rose in turn to display their wit and congratulate the assembled body on their wisdom. Meantime, the assembled black-tie audience steadily slipped into an alcoholic stupor that cast a benevolent glow over the interminable verbiage.

Late on in the proceedings, Cotton struggled to his feet to thank his hosts. "I come," he reminded them, "from the land of the brave and the home of the once-free. (Applause.) Naturally, since our small minority . . . have legislated for the great majority, we have had the unfavourable legislation of prohibition. When our Society [the American Psychiatric Association] wishes to hold a successful meeting we now go to Quebec. (Laughter.)" Turning more serious for a moment, he once again sought to flatter his British colleagues:

> I feel somewhat in the same way as the Prodigal Son, who left his home and travelled to far lands, and for some years subsisted on the husks of other nationalities, especially the German. We were imbued with German philosophy and German psychiatry, much to our own detriment. And this meeting has shown me particularly that we should be in the position of the Prodigal Son returning to the source of real science . . . When we get away from that metaphysical, fantastical and otherwise objectionable theory of psychoanalysis, we come down to the facts . . . In our own institution we have a recovery rate of 37 percent up to 1918; but when we put into our work the clearing up of focal sepsis we have, in the last 5 years, increased that to 85 percent recovery rate. (Applause.) These figures are based on very conservative facts, and are not due to enthusiasm . . . I shall be taking to America a great deal of stimulus to further work, and I feel that a great chapter in the treatment of mental diseases now will come from England . . . and I feel that our work in America has been merely the application of the research work carried on by the English psychiatrists. I thank you. (Applause.)[48]

Back in the United States, Cotton basked in the memory of his London triumph. A more extended printed version of his address appeared in the October issue of the *Journal of Mental Science,* complete with the bouquets from the luminaries of British psychiatry and medicine. Seizing the occasion to pen a separate editorial on "Chronic Sepsis and Mental Disease," the editors of the journal complimented Cotton on his "remarkable courage and tenacity" and expressed the hope that his work "will herald the dawn of a brighter day for those afflicted with mental disease and for the practice of psychiatry." Certainly, they added, "the idea that there may be one basic morbid condition underlying all these psychoses will not come as a matter of surprise to many psychiatrists." The prospects were simply revolutionary: "If, by eliminating chronic sepsis in cases of manic-depressive insanity, dementia praecox, paranoid conditions, the psychoneuroses, and toxic psychoses, between 80 and 90 percent recover, what a jettisoning of cherished theories, beliefs, and writings there will be!"[49] *If,* indeed.

The editors acknowledged that the breakthrough, Dr. Cotton's kind gestures towards British antecedents notwithstanding, was essentially American. However, thanks to Dr. Graves, "a beginning has been made in Birmingham. It is now up to London and other great cities . . . not to lag behind."[50] The editors insisted that they were "not prepared to accept in their entirety the theoretical consideration he places before us." But they hastened to add that "we cannot fail to be impressed with the practical results, and we feel that he has pointed to an avenue of treatment well worthy of extended exploration."[51] To add the necessary operating facilities, and, more importantly, to bring in teams of outside consultants would necessarily add considerably to the expense of treating the mentally ill. But "the Government and local authorities [must be] persuaded that the cost, though at first considerable, will in the end be cheaper than maintaining chronic lunatics."[52]

When, by December, these encomiums and Cotton's reiterated claims to have solved the mystery of psychosis made it across the Atlantic and began to circulate in the United States, his fiercest critics could scarcely contain themselves. Having perused the latest version of Cotton's claims, William Alanson White wrote angrily to Smith Ely Jelliffe: "Of all the thoroughly 'Gottmensch' productions that have passed over my desk recently, the communications from New Jersey have certainly snatched the bun. I am expecting momentarily to hear a tremendous explosion from that direction. If I do I shall know what it is. Have you by any chance noticed any bulgings, baloonings [*sic*], or extrusions indicating compensatory activities? Apparently our friend has an aneurism of the personality and I tremble for the future."[53]

White was no happier by the early spring, when the Canadian psychiatrist A. T. Hobbs solicited his opinion of the research on focal sepsis. "Dr. Cotton's work," he sniffed, "as it has appeared to us in the literature . . . I consider most profoundly unfortunate for psychiatry." Not least, were it to be accepted, "psychiatry becomes but an adjunct or the handmaiden of the gasteroenterologist, the genito-urinary surgeon and the dentist, and man's crowning glory, his mind, receives no further consideration than this." So far as he and his staff were concerned,

> the exclusive centering of attention upon either the body or the mind of a sick individual is . . . a serious scientific error, and whether or not Dr. Cotton believes that all the problems of psychiatry can be solved from a somatic approach the implications of his work as it appears in print clearly warrant that assumption . . . We cannot believe that the removal of focal infection, no matter how carefully or thoroughly it be done, can affect the constitutional organic make-up of the individual . . . and I confess it is quite difficult for me to see how some of the confessedly or at least apparently very inconsiderable infections which are dealt with by Dr. Cotton can have any very material effect upon the gross output of the individual. I do not understand the figures which Dr. Cotton gives. I cannot fit his extraordinary percentage of recoveries with my concept of what is going on in these patients . . . I cannot conceive from my own point of view how such results can be accepted by the scientifically trained mind."[54]

Cotton had anticipated such criticism, and had already dismissed it as the ravings of willfully blind psychiatrists who were so prejudiced on the psychoanalytic side that they "are not willing to consider any other factors, no matter what results have been shown."[55] But his critics came from a much broader spectrum than he was willing to acknowledge, as A. T. Hobbs's unofficial survey of professional opinion revealed. Hobbs was a Canadian psychiatrist who himself had a history of employing dubious somatic therapies for mental illness. (At the turn of the century, as superintendent of Homewood Sanitarium in Ontario, he had been an enthusiast for removing his female patients' ovaries to cure their insanity.)[56] Quite what prompted him to solicit the opinions of various medical men about Cotton's work is unclear, as are the criteria by which he chose his informants. The published version of Hobbs's findings, however, appearing in the October 1924 edition of the *Journal of Mental Science*, was, with few exceptions, highly critical of the Trenton approach. Cotton himself, for example, had repeatedly cited Llewellys Barker of Johns Hopkins as an inspiration for his work, and a prominent supporter of the focal sepsis doctrine. But when Barker had been approached about the interventions at Trenton, his reaction was fiercely negative: "The indiscriminate pulling of teeth simply because the nerves in them are dead seems to me to be unwise, as does the radical operation on quiescent sinus residuals. Moreover, excision of the colon in the hope that it will cut short the course of a manic-depressive psychosis or a schizophrenic process seems to me the height of absurdity."[57]

Two of Hobbs's informants expressed cautious interest in Cotton's approach. Franklin Wilcox, superintendent of the Norwich State Hospital in Connecticut, indicated that, "we have been using a form of treatment somewhat similar to Dr. Cotton's for the past three or four years. We have done work on tonsils, teeth, uterus, cervix, rectum, and anus, and in general have followed out the ideas expressed by Cotton and others, with the exception of the intestinal resections . . . I am not in a position to cite the great records that Dr. Cotton does, but I am entirely willing to take the stand in evidence that these things which tend to increase the physical condition do improve the mental standing of many of our patients."[58] And Frankwood Williams, medical director of the National Committee for Mental Hygiene, while expressing agnosticism about the theory, and insisting that regardless of "whether Dr. Cotton would quite agree with us . . . the whole subject is in the experimental stage," was quick to add that "we say this without desire to detract in any way from the great importance of the work which Dr. Cotton is doing."[59]

In other quarters, however, criticism was severe. Albert Barrett, past president of the American Psychiatric Association, insisted that Cotton's "viewpoint is extremely narrow, and has had a bad influence upon psychiatric development in America and Canada." William Russell, superintendent of Bloomingdale Hospital, an elite private establishment in New York, claimed that his staff had investigated his patients' teeth, pelvic organs, and gastrointestinal tract, and could report "no remarkable nor specific results can be demonstrated to be effects of this treatment, except in cases of delirium, due to sepsis."[60] Macfie Campbell of the Boston Psychopathic Hospital accused Cotton of "an over-optimistic estimate of what can be done along surgical and bacteriological lines";[61] and Edwin Brush, the editor of the *American Journal of Psychiatry*, objected that "to my mind a colostomy or colectomy is a somewhat serious operation, but Dr. Cotton speaks of them in a way that would encourage one to think that the operation is as simple and as devoid of danger as the extraction of the tooth."[62] C. K. Mills summed up the prevailing sentiment with the warning that "we seem to be passing through another of the periods of fad and fallacy which so often has misled the profession and the public. If the craze for violent removal goes on, it will come to pass that we will have a gutless, glandless, toothless, and I am not sure that we may not have, thanks to false psychology and surgery, a witless race."[63]

But Cotton was heedless of such complaints, and his aggressive surgical therapeutics continued to keep Trenton's laboratories, dental facilities, and operating theater fully engaged in the assault on sepsis. Meanwhile, he made sure to seize upon any and all public occasions to trumpet the splendid results he and his staff were attaining. To be sure, during 1924 the number of cases in which he felt compelled to remove patients' colons fell sharply to only 4 cases, the first decline since he had come to understand the dangers of intestinal stasis. In no sense, however, did this reflect any loss of faith in the importance of eliminating fecal poisoning. Instead, the change reflected some novel approaches he had brought back with him from England. Sir Arbuthnot Lane, whose lectures on the dangers posed by the clogging up of the cloacal regions of the body had drawn widespread attention among the general public, had for years been removing troublesome lengths of gut to forestall the perils of constipation and intestinal toxaemia. But, as Henry had learned during his London visit, "recently Sir Arbuthnot Lane has devised a method of releasing adhesions to correct intestinal stasis and . . . we have [now] substituted this operation for resection wherever possible . . . We have gradually improved the technique so that mortality is still decreasing [dipping, he claimed, below 10 percent] and we are now able to determine which case should be resected and which should not."[64]

The first 19 of these so-called "pericolic membranotomies" were undertaken in the fall of 1923. Following Arbuthnot Lane's lead, Cotton sought to ensure "releasing of adhesions found around the appendix, terminal ileum, ascending colon, hepatic flexure, splenic flexure and descending colon,"[65] and during the following twelve month period, 99 patients were recorded as "benefiting" from the new surgery. By all accounts, fewer of those treated by this modified approach died: a subsequent outside review of the hospital records suggests a mortality of 19 percent among the membranotomy cases, as compared with an overall rate of 44.7 percent of the colectomies.[66] Cotton was evidently not entirely satisfied, though, that the new operation got at the root of the problem, and in 1925 there was a slight decline in the number of operations of this sort, to 76, and a renewed emphasis on colectomy, 27 patients undergoing the more drastic form of abdominal surgery. Some of these were patients whose membranotomies had left them mentally unchanged, and for whom Cotton decided a renewed assault on their sepsis was warranted, just as, in 17 other cases, a right partial colectomy that failed to produce a cure had been followed up by a left partial colectomy.[67] In one significant respect, not much changed with regard to the selection of patients for these major operations: 77.9 percent of those subjected to colectomies were female, and that disproportion became, if anything still more marked with the membranotomies, where, remarkably enough, 83.6 percent of those treated were women.[68]

The substantial mortality associated with the operations might well seem "rather alarming" to surgeons outside institutional work, though Cotton insisted that even with "30 percent succumbing to the operation," surgery "was justified in chronic insane patients who would never leave the institution."[69] In any event, there was simply no acceptable alternative to the knife: "We would emphasize one very important point that these lesions are mechanical. The adhesions cause a mechanical constriction of the colon at various points, and no method has as yet been devised which will correct this condition except surgery. Drugs, diet, and other medical procedures, while they may have some effect on the condition, do not correct the underlying trouble. Surgery, whether resection or release of adhesions, is the only method which gives permanent results."[70]

Of course, surgery on the gut was only one part, and in many ways the smallest part, of the treatment regime at the hospital. As before, dental extractions and tonsillectomies were the order of the day for virtually every patient admitted to Trenton. Gall bladders, stomachs, and spleens continued to draw attention, as did the genito-urinary tract – occasionally in men, but routinely in women, whose cervices Cotton continued to find were very frequently infected and required amputation.

With the enthusiastic support of Commissioner Lewis, whose empire at the Department of Institutions and Agencies included the state prisons and juvenile reformatories, Cotton continued to expand the activities of the Psychiatric Clinic for Correctional Institutions that he had established in 1918, adding staff psychologists to the three psychiatrists seconded from the Trenton State Hospital, and systematically screening inmates at "the Jamesburg Reformatory for Boys, the Rahway Reformatory for juvenile delinquents, and the State Home for Girls and the State Prison. Every newly admitted individual receives a thorough psychological, psychiatric and physical examination," as does "any person in the institution showing any abnormal conduct."[71] Suspicious cases – and Cotton noted a total of "274 individuals" who had been identified by early 1925[72] – were then transferred to the state hospital for further investigation and treatment. The program of aggressive intervention outlined in his Princeton lectures on "The Defective Delinquent and Insane" thus seemed ever closer to being realized, and Cotton had plans afoot to extend his reach even further, to encompass "the abnormal school-child."

Addressing the American Association for the Study of the Feeble-Minded in May 1925, he spoke eloquently of the dangers facing America: "The problem of the abnormal child during the early school years has assumed alarming proportions in the last twenty-five years. In every educational system it has been necessary to make provisions for this rapidly increasing group . . . Such discipline as was administered in the last generation is entirely inadequate to meet the situation as it exists today . . . Hardly a week passes that I am not called upon to examine a child who has exhibited abnormal behavior, and frequently to a point of definite psychosis."[73] What (as a contemporary of Cotton's had asked in a rather different context) was to be done?

There were, to be sure, some attempts being made to provide a degree of "medical inspection in the public schools," but these were limited, and hampered by the fact that "many of these cases fail to receive what we consider an adequate physical examination by means of laboratory and X-ray studies . . . When a child has become so incorrigible that it is necessary to have him or her committed to a correctional institution, then and only then, are the proper studies made of both the mental and physical defects."[74] Obviously, a more proactive response needed to be adopted instead, one that emphasized prevention and early intervention. To be sure, among "the younger generation, most of the children have had their tonsils removed . . . the defective and delinquent group, have not had their tonsils removed."[75] But the difficulty only began there. Infected and unerupted teeth were another source of trouble, as were infected stomachs and genito-urinary systems. "More serious, however, are the abnormalities of the lower intestinal tract, especially the colon or large intestine . . . Over fifty percent of our mental cases with pronounced psychoses show disturbance in the colon and this percentage would also apply to the defective and delinquent classes."[76]

"Stasis and toxemia" were no respecters of age: "We have found this condition in children as young as three and a half years of age and have operated on many cases from seven to fifteen years of age."[77] To make the point still more forcefully, Cotton then proceeded to detail two representative cases, of a six- and and eight-year-old, where "chronic constipation" was associated with a variety of anti-social activities – "uncontrollable rage," "destructive" actions, "moody, sulky and depressed," even "suicidal" behavior. One was a child who "made no effort to learn and could not be made to obey," the other "tried to shoot his father with an air gun." Both had surgery on their colons, following which the six-year-old "acted in a normal manner, showed no peculiar conduct, attended school regularly and . . . had no difficulty in learning"; and the eight-year-old displayed "temper, appetite and general behavior [like] that of a normal child."[78]

Cotton could, he asserted, "go on citing cases indefinitely, but these illustrate the principle we are trying to establish."[79] In these respects, the "emotionally unstable" and "defective" children, often exhibiting "hyperactivity of a purposeless type," closely resembled "frank mental cases," which should occasion no surprise given their common origin in chronic sepsis. Furthermore, were these children left untreated, psychotic and/or physical breakdown would be their likely future fate.[80] "One thing is certain [therefore] and that is that these conditions should be recognized and treated long before the patient develops a psychosis"[81] – as should another sizeable group, children who were guilty of "abnormal sex practices." Cotton noted that, "I am constantly consulted by the parents of young children who have already developed abnormal sexual habits . . . In a number of these cases we have found that the cause was an underlying chronic sepsis and toxemia and in a number of these cases the colon has been resected with improvement of the individual and cessation of the abnormal sex practices, such as masturbation."[82]

Even such an extended sphere for potential intervention did not satisfy Cotton. On the contrary, he urged that careful screening be undertaken of *all* "school children between the age of 10 and 18, not alone those who show abnormal mental symptoms, but those who are apparently normal." Only such an aggressive program could hope to uncover the hidden reservoirs of trouble that lurked unseen in the community. Once implemented, however, such proactive measures could be expected to have dramatic effects: "First, we will undoubtedly limit the number of abnormal children who have to be treated in special classes, and second, probably the most important, we will prevent a later occurrence of serious mental disorder."[83]

To the consternation of his critics, therefore, Cotton showed no signs of retreat. On the contrary, he remained as convinced as ever of the righteousness of his cause, and resolutely committed to eliminating all vestiges of chronic sepsis. As he looked towards the future, he envisioned an ever-wider sphere of relevance for a reformed psychiatry, a veritable revolution in public health that waited only upon a broad adoption of a properly physical perspective on the roots of madness, crime, and delinquency.

Part Two

8

Making a Medical Career

Passing the great clock tower on the corner of Harrison and Wells Streets, the cab turned through the first of the three arches that gave access to the covered carriage court of Chicago's aptly named Grand Central Station. Dr. Greenacre had arrived in good time for the express to Baltimore. She had brought her luggage with her: two large trunks and assorted suitcases addressed to the Johns Hopkins Medical School.

After tipping the driver and porter for their trouble, Phyllis Greenacre took up her small travel bag and made her way into the massive waiting room, ornately decorated with expensive materials that produced anything but a harmonious effect: red and white marble floors from Vermont, pink marble wainscotting from Tennessee, and florid false marble columns reaching up some twenty-five feet to the elaborate ceiling above. The interior was, truth to tell, somewhat gloomy. The enormous stained-glass windows admitted only a muffled light and even the new Edison light fixtures suspended some twenty feet above her head cast only a dim illumination on the seating area below. With its arched windows, its sepulchral atmosphere, and its serried ranks of oak benches arranged like pews, Grand Central Station was a shrine to American mobility.

Dr. Greenacre, a tall, elegantly dressed woman of reserved demeanor, was naturally preoccupied with her own emotions and thoughts as she prepared, at only 22 years of age, to leave behind the city of her birth and face the formidable challenge of building a career as an independent professional woman, in surroundings wholly unfamiliar to her, and in competition with the most talented men of her era. In the hour or so before her departure, she could have been forgiven for casting her mind back to the obstacles she had already overcome.

By the standards of most, hers had been a privileged upbringing. Her father was not one of the merchant princes whose lakeshore palaces defined the meaning of success for the Chicago plutocracy. He was not a Potter Palmer, a

18 *Phyllis Greenacre as a young woman, a picture probably taken while she was in medical school. Throughout her life, Greenacre shunned the camera, and few images of her survive. I am grateful to Dr. Peter Richter for providing this one.*

Rockefeller-McCormick, a MacVeagh, or a Borden. Still, he was successful and prominent, a valued advisor to Chicago's moneyed classes, and an important figure in Progressive politics. He provided handsomely for his sizeable late Victorian family – or rather families.

For Dr. Greenacre's father had an embarrassing secret. He maintained two households simultaneously: the publicly acknowledged and "legitimate" one in which she and her six siblings had been raised, and the shadowy parallel underground establishment, where Isaiah Greenacre's mistress and their offspring resided. Perhaps her mother's tendency to lapse into periods of profound depression (a trait Phyllis already showed disturbing signs of sharing) offered some explanation or excuse for her father's behavior. Perhaps not. Regardless, the powerful strains produced by his unacknowledged but scarcely hidden double life profoundly affected Phyllis Greenacre's childhood. Adding to the turmoil, she had lost her twin sibling in infancy, and nearly died herself from scarlet fever a few years later.[1] Until the age of seven, a speech impediment had prevented her from communicating intelligibly, so instead she taught herself to read and write by the age of four, and passed notes to her parents when she needed to say something.[2] At sixteen, when she sought to escape the confines of the flawed domesticity she had somehow survived, her father had absolutely refused to underwrite her education. Only her own determination and single-mindedness, her willingness and ability to borrow the funds she needed to pay for the University of Chicago and the Chicago-Rush Medical School, allowed her to come in sight of the alluring future that now opened before her.[3]

It had certainly been a struggle. For all her great intellectual gifts and strength of purpose, Phyllis was painfully shy. In the raucously male atmosphere of medical student life, an environment actively hostile to female intruders, she found herself as one of a bare handful of women, often treated rudely and with scarcely concealed disdain. Rush had begun to admit women to its programs only in 1901, shortly after it had cemented its alliance with Harper's University of Chicago. Though technically co-educational, it never permitted more than a handful of the weaker sex to register – Greenacre was one of only a half-dozen women in her year, and fewer than sixty women had received a Rush MD by the time she graduated in 1916. Along the way, in 1913 she had obtained an SB (bachelor of science degree), with honors for excellence for general scholarship, and had been elected to the Phi Beta Kappa honors society.[4] Much of her medical school instruction had been in large lecture classes, and she had for the most part gratefully hidden herself in the back rows of the amphitheater. Only when she submitted her written work had her talents become obvious to some of her instructors, and yet so superior was her performance that she had won a prize that made her the envy of all her classmates, male and female alike.

For Greenacre was now en route to take up a staff appointment at what was undoubtedly the most prestigious medical school in the country. She had applied "for an internship at the Phipps Clinic"[5] the previous November, and had written an anxious follow-up letter when she heard nothing more about her application, reminding Meyer that if she was not to obtain the Hopkins post, she needed to approach other institutions. In the event, her glittering résumé, and Dean Dodson's report on her talents, were more than sufficient to secure her the post. She was, the dean wrote to Meyer, "one of our most brilliant students in the matter of scholarship," and he regarded her as "exceptionally well qualified" for a position at Hopkins.[6]

Suitably impressed, Meyer wrote back to Greenacre informing her that "I have reserved a place for you for the year beginning September 1, 1916," adding, "if there would be any prospect of your coming East before that I should be very glad to see you and to talk over the plans of work more specifically."[7] She accepted with alacrity.[8] Her achievement was the more remarkable since Johns Hopkins was notoriously disinclined to make junior appointments from amongst any but its own graduates. Hopkins, too, was no more disposed to appoint women physicians to its staff than other medical schools of the era. In every respect, her new post, as assistant to the redoubtable Adolf Meyer, was testimony to the extraordinary abilities she had displayed in the course of her training.

Her new position promised much. Not least, it offered the prospect of decisively leaving behind all vestiges of her unhappy upbringing – or so, at that moment, she naively assured herself. How glad she was finally to bid adieu to a father whose hypocrisy she found hateful, whose failure to support her ambitions she naturally resented, whose egotistical and extroverted character was so foreign to her own sensibilities. She recalled with a shudder his frequent boasts that he had never lost a case in his career, an only too typical exaggeration; and if it *were* true, she told herself tartly, it was only because he never took a case he was not sure of winning. She would not miss his cold and distant demeanor, or her mother's passive–aggressive response to his philandering – a retreat into invalidism and depression. Only once she had gained some physical and emotional distance from the whole miserable situation did it occur to her that the very conditions she so detested may have had one very positive effect as well. They may well have nurtured her desperate desire to secure her independence, to make something of herself, to flee.

The ornate clock above the waiting-room door struck the hour. It was time to board the train. Picking up her travel bag, she joined the passengers who were moving through the wrought-iron gates. Overhead soared the immense barrel vaulting of the train shed, its intricate latticework of iron and steel girders stretching off into the distance.

On all sides, crowds of relatives and well-wishers were gathered to see their loved ones off. Amidst the swirl of activity and emotion, Dr. Greenacre stood alone. Not even one of her family – mother or father, sisters or brothers – had turned out to wish her well. Apparently, her departure would occur unmarked and unmourned.

It came as a shock, therefore, as she moved down the length of the train searching for the sleeper car, to hear footsteps behind her, and a man's voice anxiously calling out, "Dr. Greenacre, Dr. Greenacre." Turning, she found an assistant from the Chicago morgue. He was rushing along the platform, carrying what looked suspiciously like two buckets.

Buckets indeed they were, covered and sealed, a present, he proudly told her, from Dean Dodson, one each for Popsy Welch and Adolf Meyer at Hopkins. As he stood before her, a whiff of formalin assaulted her nostrils. The unmistakable, peculiarly penetrating odor of the fixative made plain the nature of the gifts hidden within those two anonymous and innocent-looking pails. A curious cargo indeed.

Thus it was that her intimate companions on the journey to Baltimore came to consist of two containers of pickled human brains – prize specimens she was contracted to deliver on arrival at the university for the assistance of Welch's and Meyer's anatomical researches. The fussy little man from the morgue helped to stow them safely on board, and then rushed away – a memorable episode to mark her last moments in Chicago.

Fortunately, Phyllis had the compartment to herself. The strange, oddly unpleasant and slightly sickly smell of the preservative was only faintly evident, and besides, she had grown used to it during her own time in the morgue. Still, she had little doubt that anyone in the adjacent accommodations would have been horrified had they only been aware of what she had brought with her. It would remain her secret.

Crossing to the window, she lowered it and took a last look at the station. She would seldom see it again. Ahead, the locomotive that would speed them to Baltimore stood waiting for the signal to depart. The characteristic odor of sulphur, soot, and steam mingled with the acrid smell of the brakes holding the locomotive in check. The whistle sounded. Amidst hissings and clouds of vapor, there was a sudden shudder as massive engine sprang to life, a quick burst of noise as the pistons engaged, the squealing of metal on metal, and with a jolt, the train gathered itself and moved majestically out of the station. Gaining momentum, it inched across the drawbridge that allowed it passage over the Chicago River and headed south and east, out of the city, towards the Appalachians and the still distant East Coast, carrying Phyllis to a new life.

As the sun set behind them, Phyllis Greenacre left the confines of her compartment and found her way to the Pullman dining car. Though it was already crowded with hungry passengers feasting on one or another of the more than two hundred items on the menu, she was able to secure a table for herself, and seated in a high leather-backed chair before a table covered with starched white linen and laid with gleaming silver and glassware, ate simply but well. Beneath the gilded and painted ceiling, the hanging lamps swayed back and forth as the train sped on its way. As twilight fell, a glance through the elegantly curved windows revealed that they had left the flat and featureless prairie behind and had begun their steady climb through the foothills of the Appalachians.

Back in her compartment, Dr. Greenacre found that her sleeping berth had been made up in her absence. The buckets had been moved over to one side by an attendant obviously oblivious to their contents. At the end of a long and emotionally draining day, she gratefully settled down for the night.

By the time she woke the next morning, the train was well into its pictur-esque descent of the valley of the Potomac, hugging the path of the winding river in the shadow of hills that rose abruptly on each side. The spectacularly beautiful mountain scenery, wholly unfamiliar to someone raised in the flat environs of Chicago, held her entranced for a time, but she was impatient for the journey to be over, and to begin her new life. Breakfast occupied her briefly, and then there was the hustle and bustle of their arrival in Washington, the dis-embarkation of many of her fellow passengers, and her first glimpse of the Capitol.

But seeing Washington would have to wait, still forty miles and another hour to go. As her anticipation grew, it seemed to take much longer than that. At length, though, the train entered the city, and, plunging through the tunnel that burrowed under Howard Street, emerged at her destination, the Mount Royal Station.

Even on first acquaintance, Baltimore was quite unlike the booming metro-polis she had left behind. To begin with, it was barely a quarter of Chicago's size. Then, too, it was so much older, its Victorian row houses, its brick man-sions, and its small corner shops contrasting sharply with the skyscrapers, the ostentatious pastiche palaces, the grand public buildings, and garish empori-ums of commerce that dominated the Chicago skyline. The great fire of 1871 had ensured that little or nothing of the older frontier Chicago remained, but on the ashes of that shattering calamity, a great modern city had constituted itself, unabashedly gaudy and vulgar, flaunting its new-found wealth and power for all to see and marvel at. Its self-confidence and swagger, its splendor and magnificence, even the sheer unbridled foulness and squalor of its stock-yards and slaughterhouses, whose stench periodically drifted east and blan-keted the city, found few echoes in the staid old seaport in which she now found herself.

Baltimore was, besides, an essentially Southern town, moving at a very dif-ferent pace from the frantic and frenetic hustle and bustle of life in America's second city. It had had its own fires, in 1873 and again on a larger scale in 1904, but though these destroyed a variety of colonial and Victorian structures, and though the latter fire devastated the downtown business area, they did not alter the basic character of the city – what its inhabitants liked to think of as its charm and stateliness (adjectives no one would have thought to apply to turn-of-the-century Chicago). Baltimore's manners and customs remained those of the South, its first families thought of themselves as aristocrats. Deeply conservative and provincial, their fetish for tradition and hierarchy created an atmosphere that could scarcely have been more different from the raucous city of her birth, stately and unhurried, and more than a trifle smug and stuffy.

For all that it had taken its place at the very pinnacle of American medicine, she could not help noticing that, architecturally speaking, Johns Hopkins also contrasted highly unfavorably with the handsome neo-Gothic buildings that Rockefeller's money had purchased for the University of Chicago. John Shaw Billings's university hospital might embody the most modern notions of the pavilion design and contain within its walls the cream of American medical talent, but it was a plain and utilitarian structure, graceless and entirely lacking in aesthetic appeal: sprawling one-, two-, and three-storey brick buildings linked together by a single covered corridor. And as she was reminded every day, the medical school stood in one of the more dismal and unfashionable areas of the city, surrounded by a maze of narrow streets and alleys, badly lit and worse maintained, a squalid neighborhood filled with the fetid odors of sewage and decay, with cheap brick row houses providing inadequate shelter for poor whites and Negroes, and lodging houses for the medical students.

19 *Meyer's staff at Johns Hopkins: a group portrait taken just after Phyllis Greenacre arrived to join the faculty in 1916. Meyer is the figure in the front row with a pointed beard. A tall and attractive Phyllis Greenacre stands on the extreme right of the front row, half stepping down on to the step below to minimize the height advantage she enjoyed over Professor Meyer.*

But for intellectual vitality, arrogance, and self-assurance, Hopkins and the Hopkins staff took second place to no one. Once arrived, Dr. Greenacre immediately found herself plunged into a world of brash self-confidence, fierce ambition, and grinding hard work. Quite understandably, she had a difficult time of it. Certainly her sex did not help matters. To be sure, Hopkins had opened its doors to women from the very outset – but only with the very greatest reluctance. Just as the medical school was on the brink of opening its doors in 1888, the railroad that had brought Greenacre from Chicago – the Baltimore and Ohio – had run into fiscal trouble and suspended its dividend. Disaster loomed for the fledging school, since virtually its entire endowment consisted of B&O stock. Only the gift of half-a-million dollars from an unlikely group of financial angels – four independent-minded and wealthy daughters of men on the original university board of trustees – had given the administration the wherewithal to proceed. But the money had only been forthcoming on condition that women would be admitted on equal terms with men – a condition that roused fierce opposition among the faculty, but one the trustees ultimately felt constrained to accept.

"Equal terms" had turned out to mean only a token handful of female entrants, less than 10 percent of each class. Moreover, just because the male faculty had found themselves forced to accept the presence of the lesser sex did not mean they had to like it. Nor did it preclude the more bitterly opposed from exhibiting their displeasure and doing all they could to embarrass and harass the intruders. Greenacre heard the stories. There was the notorious occasion, for instance, when the professor of otolaryngology had delivered a lecture comparing the cavernous tissues of the nose with the corpus spongiosum of the penis, spicing his presentation with an array of smutty stories that had the male students rolling in the aisles, and their deliberately humiliated handful of female counterparts, beet-red with embarrassment, on the brink of reconsidering their choice of career.[9] Then there was the time that Dorothy Reed and Florence Sabin had the audacity to earn appointments in medicine, the most prestigious of all Hopkins internships, by graduating at the top of their class. The superintendent of the university hospital, Henry Hurd, had immediately attempted to persuade at least one of them to relinquish her appointment in favor of a man. He assigned Reed to the charge of a male Negro ward, certain that any young lady could not possibly accept such a post, and finally, when she still proved obdurate, informed her that "he understood that [she] wanted the colored wards" and assumed it reflected "her abnormal sex perversions . . . [since] only [her] desire to gratify sexual curiosity would allow [her] or any woman to take charge of a male ward." To his evident astonishment, not even this sort of deliberate humiliation produced the desired result.[10]

Such episodes had become part of Hopkins lore, and on a more mundane level, the hostility in many quarters towards women who refused to remain within their proper sphere was almost palpable. Yet psychiatry, like pediatrics, represented something of an exception to the rule. Perhaps because of the specialty's lowly status in the medical hierarchy, a female physician was less of an anomaly here. Indeed, on reporting to duty, Greenacre had found herself one of three new women associates in the department and was soon working alongside Ruth Fairbank and the formidable Esther Richards (who was later to be appointed Meyer's principal clinical associate).

It hardly helped, though in truth her first six months went reasonably well. She was assigned to the pathology department and then to the neurological service, both areas in which she had some prior background from her coursework at Chicago. Spending long hours in the morgue, she worked on an article on brain hemorrhages, which afterwards became her first professional publication.

Soon, however, she moved to take up her Phipps internship, and now problems emerged. Though she had come to Hopkins determined to become a psychiatrist, the background training she brought with her was woefully inadequate. However solid some of her schooling at Chicago had been, the fact was that psychiatry was accorded little space in the curriculum there. Now she was called upon to work in a setting where even the third and fourth year medical students seemed to know more than she did.

While she threw herself into her work, she felt desperately alone and increasingly unhappy in this strange environment. She felt unsure of herself, and for the first time began to question her own abilities. Oddly enough, the presence of other women seemed to make things worse. *They* seemed to cope, and their apparent success made it harder for her to persuade herself that her troubles stemmed from the fact that she was a woman. That, perverse as it might seem, would have been a relief, for it would have provided reassurance that her despondency was rooted in the real difficulties of her situation, rather than, as she increasingly feared, a sign that she shared her mother's disabling and near pathological emotional lability.

She sought to console herself with the notion that her anxieties all stemmed from her status as an outsider.[11] She was not, after all, one of the charmed circle of Hopkins graduates, but to her evident disadvantage, the product of a mid-Western institution that had only recently shaken off the stigma of being a proprietary school. For Rush had been owned for years by its faculty and, as she had discovered to her dismay, its new-found excellence and the prestige it had sought from its affiliation with Rockefeller's university were only gradually and grudgingly being acknowledged in snobbish East-Coast medical circles.

That might be so, but emotionally, she discovered, such rationalizations provided no relief whatsoever. Her sense of isolation deepened, and she felt vulnerable and frightened, a trainee psychiatrist wrestling with her own psychological demons and steadily losing the battle. To make matters worse, Adolf Meyer, the head of her department and the man under whom she had come to work, turned out to be a forbidding figure, an authoritarian Swiss German with rigid European ideas of hierarchy, obsessed with detail, cautious to a fault, determined to control all aspects of his service. Despite his modest stature, even his appearance was intimidating: his piercing eyes, his sharp features, his pointed black beard, his Old-World mannerisms, and the Teutonic accent that made him all but impossible to understand.

She had found him a terrifying figure on first acquaintance, and in this she found she was not alone. People seemed either to worship or despise him. There was no middle ground. All the new members of his service, eager enough to make one another's acquaintance and to make an impression, seemed to be struck dumb in his presence, and at the first staff meeting of the year an awful silence reigned. Even in his absence, she subsequently learned, no one would risk incurring his displeasure, so that when Meyer left each summer to take his vacation, the business at the Phipps Clinic slowly ground to a halt – no one, not

20 _Adolf Meyer in 1916._

even the most senior of his associates, daring to order the admission of a patient in his absence.[12] In years to come, when Greenacre heard of Smith Ely Jelliffe's harsh assessment of Meyer's influence on his staff – the accusation that he had "put partly castrated pupils in professional chairs"[13] – she knew just what was meant.

In time, Dr. Greenacre would lose some of her initial fright, and develop a more complex relationship with an authority figure she eventually viewed with a mixture of frustration and admiration. Yet her earliest months working under him were traumatic and unbearably difficult. He seemed so remote, so unapproachable, his standards so hard to meet, and his ideas so enigmatic that she despaired of her future. In less than a year after her arrival at Hopkins, she had fallen into a depression so deep, a mental collapse so profound and disabling, that she could no longer continue to work. Meyer himself diagnosed her as psychotic.

Months passed before her mental state began slowly to improve. She was unable even to begin to resume her duties until the spring of 1918. But for some reason, Meyer kept her on his staff. Perhaps it was her talent; perhaps what she came to perceive as his Messiah complex and his associated propensity to engage in "rescue fantasies"; perhaps his undoubted loyalty to his subordinates, or simply that so many of his male assistants were away on military service; perhaps – a dark personal secret that he kept hidden from everyone – his sense of guilt about the depression his own mother had irretrievably fallen into when he left Switzerland to pursue his professional fortune in America; or perhaps it was for all these reasons. In the end, from Greenacre's point of view, it scarcely mattered: her career in academic medicine might yet be salvaged.

Within eighteen months, her life was turned upside down once more. Her shyness notwithstanding, her striking appearance and remarkable qualities of mind had at last attracted a male admirer. In January 1919, John Watson, the founder of behaviorism and head of the psychological laboratory at Hopkins, recruited a brilliant young assistant, Curt Richter, to his staff. Meyer soon invited the new associate to attend his staff rounds and to give some lectures,[14] and in the process inadvertently introduced the two young scientists to each other.

It was no wonder that when they met, Greenacre was swept off her feet. Curt was a handsome former high-school athlete from Colorado. He had spent three years in Germany, ostensibly to train as an engineer, but in fact developing a taste for theater, the opera, and literature. Back in America, a year and a half after the outbreak of the Great War, he enrolled at Harvard, casting about for a new career now that his earlier interest in engineering had waned. Diplomacy, economics, and philosophy all caught his interest in turn, and all were soon discarded. But a growing acquaintance with the psychoanalytic literature, and a spell working with L. J. Henderson and with Robert Yerkes on animal behavior, increasingly led him towards what became a lifelong interest in the biological bases of behavior, and that brought him finally to Baltimore. With his cosmopolitan polish, his immense intellectual curiosity and range, and his physical charms, here was someone Phyllis found irresistible.

A romantic entanglement was no unmixed blessing, however, for amidst her new-found happiness, Phyllis could not escape the nagging realization that any attempt to marry would constitute yet another grave threat to her professional ambitions – and very possibly to Curt's as well, given that their financial resources would be so meager. Such doubts did not restrain her for very long. On June 24, just before Meyer left for California, she broke the news: "I want to tell you of my engagement to Curt Richter. We want to marry as soon as possible, probably in the fall." She was, she assured him, "extremely anxious to go on with my work in the laboratory . . . I cannot think of relinquishing it with equanimity. I do not believe I should be less efficient but more so, under the altered circumstances."[15]

Meyer's approval was clearly of great importance to her. Practically, it could make an enormous difference, because under the terms of Curt and Phyllis's contracts, neither could marry without the consent of the Hopkins trustees, which was seldom given.[16] At least as significantly, she needed his support emotionally, since Meyer had by now become something of a surrogate father-figure for her. Surprisingly, beneath the formal veneer that still marked his relationships with all his subordinates, her once distant superior turned out to harbor reciprocal feelings towards her, to welcome her confidences, and to be anxious to provide advice. "Above all things," he reminded her, "do not forget that hard as it may have been in the past to get help and a chance for free discussion with yr [sic] own family, you can count on an absolutely frank and thoughtful and yet not meddlesome hearing and discussion with your more neutral but none the less keenly interested 'chief' who has always felt himself to be, as far as this can be accepted, in loco parentis (and I hope without suggesting paternalism)."[17]

Characteristically, Meyer was both cautious and ambivalent in responding to the news of Greenacre's proposed marriage. Caught off-guard by the hastiness of her decision, he worried that her marriage plans might in part be the product of her past emotional turmoil, and, to use her own words, that she had been "more or less swept away this Spring." She hastened to assure him that, on the contrary, "I have never looked upon marriage as an attempt at a therapeutic adjustment as promising of any success or stability. It has always seemed to me that the half-digested problems are bound to be augmented by the new complexities." She insisted that, "I have been more at ease this past year . . . Certainly less energy has gone into the vague states of tense depression which used to swamp me; and my thinking has, I believe, become more purposeful, with less of the depressive musing."[18]

Separately from his concerns about her emotional state, however, many of the misgivings Meyer felt were of a more practical sort. In his first response (and later in several more long letters written between July and September), he worried openly about the stresses Greenacre and Richter would face as both sought to build professional careers: "I have seen a few happy student marriages, but also [know] how important it is to be free during the hard period during which one is tested out by the hard world for one's final career."[19] Her career, he pointed out, was developing well, but Richter's had scarcely begun, and seemed far less defined and secure. The uncertainty worried him: "He is a man whose potentialities I find difficult to evaluate," in part because he appeared to have "a certain difficulty about getting focused . . . I have had the feeling that whenever I thought Richter had focused on a point he was off on a tangent without having finished the starting point."[20] Before taking precipitate action, he urged his protégée to try to weigh things rationally and carefully: "If the practical balance proves promising, there is no reason why your two careers could not blend to a reasonable extent. And the question in my mind is whether this balance cannot be gaged [sic] within a reasonable time and that without interfering with the frankness and sincerity of your relationship, but also without engaging *first* in the life-contract of marriage before the balance of *facts* is reasonably clear."[21] Her work, he noted approvingly, mattered enormously to her, and she should take care not to jeopardize it:

> I remember so well your sensitiveness and reaction to the appearance of a slight in promotion a year ago when I had planned to lead you towards the laboratory and Dr. Fairbank took the line of work for which she seemed better fitted, not than you, but better than for the other type of work. That type of preferences and deferments will be very larger with a married couple, and I should feel it very wrong that you should be exposed to all of that instead of having a chance to become the vigorous and capable person you give every promise to become if at least you are not swamped by incidental difficulties and especially difficulties accruing to Mr. Richter.[22]

To Meyer's dismay, Greenacre's initial response ignored his strictures about the possible "complications which go with premature marriages" and focused only on his promise that "whatever you may decide I shall try to be helpful."[23] Instead of taking more time to reflect on the situation, she wrote back that she and Richter had decided to marry on September 1, before the academic year began.[24] Clearly hurt, he responded that "your decision seems to leave no room for what I had hoped for," and he tried once more to urge her to be more circumspect. Yet, "if the course of things *must* be so . . . I accept the situation . . . You can count on the 'presumptions' being in your favor of your own plans *whatever* they may be."[25]

Brought up short by this letter, Greenacre acknowledged that "I apparently did not realize the content of your fears." Appearances to the contrary notwithstanding, she valued "the advice of a 'neutral' person who had a better opportunity to interpret my inadequacies than I am able to do for myself." And she hastened to reassure him that "our plans are by no means rigid."[26] Indeed it turned out that they were not, for three weeks later she sent a cryptic note to Meyer informing him that "the plans of which I first wrote you have been entirely disrupted. I shall write you – or better, talk with you of whatever new plans unfold."[27]

Quite what had happened to bring about this abrupt change remains unclear. Whatever it was, however, it led to a delay, not a permanent alteration in the couple's intentions. Meyer's reiterated warnings to Greenacre that, "it is not your mutual affections but the complications which go with premature marriage that I fear might be apt to create perplexities which may hinder the one or the other or both [of you], and especially also Mr. Richter and possibly in ways in which you may have to suffer without being able to help,"[28] could not dissuade her from proceeding. By the spring of 1920, she and Richter were married, and within weeks, Phyllis found herself pregnant.

To the outside world, and soon enough even to Meyer himself, Curt and Phyllis seemed an ideal couple. Earlier worries that the former would remain a dilettante, with insufficient commitment to the rigors of a professional career were soon set aside, and the young Richter quickly became one of the professor's personal favorites. Far less dogmatic than his superior John Watson, Richter's European training and catholic intellectual interests made him an infinitely more congenial member of Meyer's team. Watson, of course, had his own intellectual agenda to pursue, and once installed at Hopkins he had quickly made it clear to Meyer that he had no time for windy philosophizing about human consciousness and similar "mythical" entities. If the eminent Swiss professor wanted others to help lend some substance to his grandiose claims to build psychiatry on a foundation of "psychobiology" (whatever that peculiar creature might be), Watson had made it clear that no assistance could be expected or would be forthcoming from him. Richter, however, might prove more pliable. Certainly, his expressed interest in psychoanalysis, his biological bent, and his talent for laboratory experiments formed an intriguing starting point for the sort of researches Meyer hoped to foster.

The appearance of some such scientifically respectable original research from within his domain was becoming an increasingly urgent necessity. Meyer's appointment at Hopkins, and much of his prestige in the medical world beyond the confines of psychiatry, derived from his rigorous European training and his early anatomical researches on the brain and the central nervous system. Here was science as the elite of the medical profession understood it, a research program that promised to lift some of the fog of etiological ignorance and therapeutic impotence that shrouded institutional psychiatry and rendered it a growing professional embarrassment. Yet the truth was that by the time Meyer arrived at Hopkins, whatever limited contributions he personally planned to make along these lines were, to all intents and purposes, already at an end.

To be sure, Meyer's eclectic emphasis on the multiple determinants of behavior – environment, hereditary make-up, habits, and individual psychology, as well as organic factors – provided an almost limitless field for investigation. Psychology, physiology, neuropathology, even sociology, all might plausibly contribute to unravelling the mysteries of madness. But a decade of work had produced remarkably little beyond a succession of increasingly obscure programmatic statements from the master himself. Keeping his staff busy was no problem. With everything potentially relevant to understanding what he called "the dynamic biological processes of the whole individual" and nothing excluded, and with an emphasis on gathering and recording as many of "the facts" as possible, his students and associates could spend endless time tracing in excruciating detail all the factors possibly relevant to what Meyer referred to as "the unhealthy reaction of the individual mind to its environment."[29]

But what did it all amount to? Meyer insisted that his was a "commonsense psychiatry," but it was a peculiarly impenetrable commonsense, often couched in language so obscure that few could discern just what he had in mind. Perhaps he was on to something, or perhaps he was just spounting empty verbiage? Certainly, many of his Hopkins colleagues seemed increasingly skeptical of the value of what he was up to at the Phipps Clinic.[30] And when the medical students had the opportunity to poke fun at the faculty, they made their scorn for what they saw as psychobabble equally clear. At the play they put on one year, a bearded "Meyer" appeared on stage and gave his lecture in Chinese, interspersed with a handful of favorite bits of Meyerian jargon – integration concept, family formation, experiment of nature, the ergasias, and so forth.[31] The great man was not amused, and his fury induced the Medical Board to ban all future performances of the kind. It would not do to hold part of the Hopkins enterprise up to ridicule, particularly when it was evident that many of the faculty shared the students' stance.

Meyer's young protégé was of potentially inestimable value in combatting such sentiments. Richter's technical wizardry, his intellectual curiosity, and his skill at designing and conducting experiments were already evident. So too was his remarkable talent for making friends among the Hopkins science faculty. His early work on the endocrine glands and their influence on animal behavior had unquestionably impressed them, and if it could only be linked up to the mysterious periodicity of certain psychiatric disturbances, psychobiology might seem more than an appealing slogan.

For the moment, the talented young Richter remained subordinate to the uncooperative, even actively hostile John Watson, with whom Meyer's exchanges had become increasingly vitriolic over the years.[32] Not for long,

21 *Curt Richter and Phyllis Greenacre, pictured collaborating on an experiment testing the grasp reflex of an unidentified infant, possibly their own child. Richter's investigations along these lines were controversial, and he was soon compelled to substitute sloths for human infants.*

though. Richter's chief had secured his original appointment as the director of the psychological laboratory in 1909 when his predecessor, James Baldwin, was caught in a police raid on a Baltimore brothel and subsequently forced to resign. Now Watson in his turn became trapped in the coils of what became an even more scandalous affair. Richter and Greenacre were to be the unwitting beneficiaries of his arrogant presumption that his eminence in the emerging world of professional psychology would protect him from similar public disgrace.

Not for the first time, in the fall of 1919 Watson had been unfaithful to his wife. His previous affairs had been handled with a modicum of discretion, but on this occasion, his choice of partner proved astonishingly self-destructive. Rosalie Rayner was the strikingly beautiful grand-daughter of a Maryland tycoon and the niece of a United States senator. Barely nineteen, and a Vassar graduate, she had come to Hopkins in the autumn of 1919 as a graduate student in Watson's laboratory. Within a matter of weeks, despite or because of the near quarter-century difference in their ages, they were lovers, and careless lovers at that. Their stolen weekends in New York were risky enough, but soon in their passion to be together, Rosalie persuaded a college friend to loan them her Baltimore apartment, where Watson promised that "everything will be lovely and we ought to play safe. Still, play we will."[33]

Play they did. Watson acknowledged he was "an awful sinner," then threw himself into the joys of sinning more. "Could you," he demanded of Rosalie, "kiss me for two hours right now without ever growing weary? I want you all 24 of the hours and then I'd quarrel with the universe because the days are not longer. Let's go to the North Pole where the days and nights are 6 mo. each."[34] As their mutual infatuation grew, all remaining caution was thrown to the wind. Complaining that the hours they spent together daily in the laboratory only whetted the appetite for more, the two lovers were soon foolishly exchanging billets-doux, Watson avowing, in his own inimitable jargon, that "every cell I have is yours, individually and collectively. My total reactions are positive and towards you. So likewise each and every heart reaction. I can't be any more yours than I am even if a surgical operation made us one."[35]

Rosalie reciprocated. On one occasion, her middle-aged lover teased her that he "had made enough love for one day to so young a girl!" But in the next breath, he sounded like a heart-sick adolescent: "I just think I'll die if I don't hear from you. If I thought you were in, I'd call you, dangerous as it is. Every time the phone rings I know I'll jump from my chair. My heart will be in my throat but I can listen anyway . . . do write to me that . . . your heart and body will still be mine."

Their hunger for one another seemed insatiable. Nothing could stand in their way. Evenings spent apart were a torture, so Rosalie brazenly induced her parents to invite John and his wife Mary to dine with them at their mansion, on Eutaw Place. The experiment was repeated. Watson was on his best behavior and charmed his hosts. Soon enough, the two families were dining together several times a week, Rosalie's parents somehow managing to remain oblivious to the deliciously dangerous sexual by-play taking place under and across the table between their daughter and her lover.

Not so John's long-suffering spouse. For months, she had suspected that he had embarked on another affair. The signs were everywhere. Now, as he and Rosalie chose to flirt so blatantly in front of her, she could no longer doubt her rival's identity. Yet she had no proof of her husband's infidelity. In late February, however, Watson left one of Rosalie's love letters in his pocket, and she found it while putting his clothes away. Such a slip-up had become almost inevitable – indeed, Watson's increasingly reckless behavior seemed positively designed to court discovery. But a single letter might be explained away. Determined to secure yet more evidence, Mary resorted to a clever ruse. When next they dined at the Rayners', she pleaded a headache, and, urging the two lovers to continue their conversation about events at the Phipps Clinic, retreated to Rosalie's bedroom, ostensibly to lie down and recover. The door locked, the room searched, a whole packet of damning letters from her husband discovered and pocketed, she resumed her place at table, acting as though nothing were amiss.

Her sangfroid was short-lived. Having read the letters, she paid a return visit to the Rayners, this time *sans* husband. In the presence of an unrepentant Rosalie, she proceeded to reveal the sordid details of the affair, urging the Rayners to avoid the otherwise inevitable scandal by sending the young woman to Europe for a year – more than enough time, she assured them, for her husband's passing fancy to evaporate. But Rosalie would not budge, and Mary's subsequent efforts to induce her husband to break off the liaison were equally unsuccessful. By April, the Watsons had separated, and news of the affair was circulating busily in the incestuous world of the Hopkins faculty.

With supreme self-confidence, Watson assumed he could ride the scandal out. He proved a poor prophet. Adolf Meyer's ruthless intervention sealed his fate. Consulted by President Goodnow as the divorce hearing loomed, Meyer's advice was blunt and uncompromising. Watson had scorned his earlier admonition to end the affair. Now he must pay the price for his immorality. Notoriously puritanical about sexual matters, Meyer proclaimed himself shocked, positively shocked, by Watson's betrayal of his colleagues' trust.

The potential damage to the institution was great: "Without clean-cut and outspoken principles on these matters, we could not run a coeducational institution." Hence, the "severance" of Watson's relationship with Hopkins was "inevitable."[36] His career in academia was at an end.

Having intervened decisively to remove Watson from the scene, Meyer promptly secured Richter's appointment to replace him as head of the psychobiology laboratory on the third floor of the Phipps Clinic. The unexpected reward for Meyer's approbation was more than welcome to the young couple, already worrying about how to provide for the baby they expected on the paltry salaries of junior academics. But the financial relief was short-lived. Not one, but two children arrived on the scene within two years of their marriage: Ann in February 1921, and Peter, in May 1922. Even after Richter's promotion, with their scant resources feeding so many mouths, things were difficult, and as a result they could afford only a modest and quite tiny apartment at 731 Reservoir Street, near the railroad station.

Richter responded to their cramped and difficult domestic circumstances by throwing himself into his research, spending endless hours in the laboratory on the work that formed the basis of his doctoral thesis: a study of levels of physical activity in the caged rat, documenting the rhythms of its behavior and the existence of an inherent "biological clock."[37] Not to be outdone, Greenacre had somehow stretched their budget and hired a black nanny to look after the

22 *The Phipps Clinic at Johns Hopkins University, where Meyer, Richter, and Greenacre all worked during the 1910s and '20s, c. 1920.*

children. To general astonishment, she still insisted on maintaining her own professional career on a full-time basis.

Hopkins had certainly not made it easy to do so. When Ann was born in February 1921, Greenacre explained to Meyer that "the hospital was unwilling to grant me any extra time [off]" and she had had to use her vacation allowance instead. In January of the following year, she appealed to Meyer to support her request for "a month or six weeks of vacation this summer. I shall have my second baby in May which will of necessity absorb three weeks of the usual allotment of four weeks." She professed herself undeterred by the prospect of a further rebuff. Much as she would appreciate the time to recuperate, "if that is not possible next summer either, I shall accept the time in May as a good enough investment and let it go at that."[38]

Always shy and reserved, Greenacre was quite diffident about pushing herself forward, but increasingly her own lack of advancement under Meyer rankled, and the intensified financial worries associated with the imminent arrival of her second baby emboldened her to speak openly of her concerns. She justified her presumption by turning the professor's own teachings against him: "My years at the clinic have taught me the necessity of getting dissatisfactions cleared up and talked out rather than storing up for a cumulative explosion."[39] Meyer, she could not help recalling, had assured her in the course of their correspondence concerning her marriage plans that, "I am much less prejudiced than most organizers against favoring women and married couples,"[40] and she knew that to an extent this was so. And yet, as she pointed out, "I think I am alone in the clinic in maintaining in the sixth year the same official rank that I achieved automatically when I was accepted as an interne" – a situation that, as the "only available index [of her standing available] to strangers and students," she perforce found "occasionally embarrassing." The spectacle of others advancing "by flattery, glittering talk, obsequiousness, and insincerity, too often with deliberate falsifications and distortions of facts" had intensified her "present discomfort and revulsion." So far from enjoying an advance in rank commensurate with her growing responsibilities, "I find myself right now in a situation where I am neither consulted nor usually even informed of those few clinic arrangements which do concern me and my work." Her position as head of the laboratory needed clarification, and she wanted to expand her role in working with students in this setting. As for clinical practice, she would welcome an expansion of her opportunities in this sphere, though she admitted quite frankly that she proposed this as "a means to increas[e] my income rather than [from] any deeply rooted ambition. But as a practical means of easing urgent financial needs, I should welcome it." And here was the nub of the matter, for an increased salary "is an urgent need for me, and which must have just now a governing influence on my plans. The present struggle is one which I cannot keep up and [I] must find some way of relieving." Listing her income since arriving at Hopkins in 1916, she pointed out that "the apparent increase in salary during the last 2–3 years has not been a real one, amounting to no gain in actual cash at all over the year 1919–1920."[41]

Despite feeling both under-appreciated and under-rewarded, Greenacre maintained a punishing schedule. She continued some earlier research on the effects of syphilis on the central nervous system, and kept up her clinical work with patients, absorbing Meyer's insistence on the close scrutiny of the individual case. She supervised his laboratory for him, and sought opportunities for "developing further work with students to include the relation of the laboratory examinations to the clinical material" and supervising "the rotation of internes [*sic*] in the laboratory." "Follow-up work [with clinic patients] is now absorbing all of the spare time I can manage during the day, and 2 or 3 evenings a week spent in abstracting old histories at home. The unavoidable evening interviews [with patients] could be simplified if I were able to establish an office [nearby] . . . rather than making the extra night trips to the clinic. This, however, is quite out of the question on my present income which is limited strictly to the clinic salary."[42] Unlike one of the other pioneering women at Hopkins, Dorothy Reed (who had also had the temerity to marry), Greenacre, at least, would not retire to the sidelines until her children were grown.

Repeatedly, in an attempt to bring her work on syphilis to closure and to begin to make a name for herself via publication, she wrote up her laboratory findings. Each time, however, Meyer raised some new objection or suggested another line of investigation she should pursue. Some days, he would agree that the piece was now ready for publication, only to call her in a few days later to demur, and urge her to invest yet more time in what she was coming to see as a Sisyphean task.

When he suggested that she get in touch with his protégé Henry Cotton at Trenton State Hospital in order to compare her results with his, she responded with enthusiasm, real or feigned: "I've been wanting to go over someone else's g.p. [general paresis] material, and that with so optimistic an outlook is especially enticing."[43] To prepare herself for a visit, she read Cotton's Princeton lectures, *The Defective, Delinquent, and Insane,* and confessed she was taken aback by Cotton's "sweeping claims and equally sweeping, though casual, way of dealing with psychogenesis and related problems." Still, "I suppose we should be concerned chiefly with . . . a survey of his positive results . . . – the question whether they justify the rather heroic procedures, rather than with the fallacies of some of his claims."[44] During the late summer, she also encountered Cotton himself: "I got a curious impression of him at the Bloomingdale [Asylum 125th anniversary] celebration, where he was withdrawn and a bit aloof in an informal group, but he must be a person of intense energy and hopefulness. I find myself very eager for the work."[45]

Yet once again, she met with disappointment, for nothing came of Meyer's preliminary proposal. Beneath the calm exterior her dependent position forced her to exhibit, Greenacre was furious about these repeated delays. Professionally, she needed to publish, and she was convinced that her research was sound. Yet without Meyer's permission, she could not possibly proceed.[46]

Meanwhile, in the clinical arena, still other sources of tension lurked only just beneath the surface. Like all Meyer's assistants, Greenacre had been compelled to spend three months on rotation in the local state mental hospital – a dismal experience dealing with hopeless, chronic cases on overcrowded wards where she could scarcely supply even a semblance of medical attention. It was sobering to realize that only her own professional status, and the remission of her depression, had saved her from sharing their miserable fate.

Working back at the Phipps Clinic was a relief at first. What ambitious young psychiatrist could fail to be stimulated by the sheer variety of the case material, by the fact that all the patients eventually left (either restored to sanity or shipped off to the state hospital system), by the excitement of being able to work with the individual patient, of learning to use Meyer's life-chart technique, of working as part of a team? It was exhausting and exhilarating by turns.

But disenchantment soon set in. Where was all this effort leading? Why did so much of the work seem so pointless, so disconnected from any advance in understanding or treatment? More and more, she came to see Meyer's approach as masking "an obsessional and probably futile search for accuracy." Privately, she was convinced that "the emphasis on recording all possible phenomenological details sometimes reached fantastic proportions" and she found she was not alone. One exasperated colleague turned to her in disgust and suggested that "in the pressure to note *all* details of the patient's environment, we would presently have to record the colors and patterns of the wallpaper of his home, as these might be considered of possible significance in contributing to the patient's state of mind." Unconvincingly, Greenacre tried to reassure herself that "the situation was never as bad as this."[47] But in essence it was, a mindless tabulation of all the events of a person's life, arranged in chronological sequence: birth order, childhood diseases, school experiences and performances, changes in height and weight, relationships with parents and peers, sexual experiences, mental state, employment history, injuries and disabilities, courtship and marriage, intelligence, hobbies, politics, life experiences, and on and on. Nothing was too trivial or insignificant to note. As the great man himself constantly assured her, "a fact is anything which makes a difference."[48]

But what *did* make a difference? How could one tell? In the end, Greenacre grew dissatisfied with the lack of clear answers to such questions. Honesty compelled her to acknowledge that "the training to observe has been of incalculable benefit to me and I owe a debt of gratitude for it." But she told herself that quite as important as anything Meyer had taught her about how positively to proceed was what implicitly she had learned *not* to do: "not the least part of [my experience] has been the warning not to drive recording observation to a stage of the infinite and the absurd in the effort to cover everything"[49] – a heretical conclusion she perforce kept to herself.

But if work had its dissatisfactions, so too did what passed for domestic bliss. To the outside world, Curt and Phyllis seemed a marriage of equals: two extraordinarily talented young scientists, each launched on careers of exceptional promise. Among the handful of women at Hopkins, only Greenacre had successfully combined work, marriage, and motherhood. Meyer's initial doubts about their union seemed to have faded and, for a time, his two subordinates enjoyed the most convincing mark of his favor, frequent invitations to dine at his house. In private, however, all was not well.

Perhaps it was the strains of managing the complications of household and careers on incomes that barely sufficed to keep themselves fed and clothed, let alone providing enough to maintain the semblance of professional respectability. Perhaps it was that they were both too committed to their work to spare sufficient time for one another. Or perhaps it was Greenacre's recurring bouts of depression, never quite sufficient to disable her, but a constant source of strain nonetheless. At all events, within a few months of their son Peter's arrival on the scene, their marriage began to deteriorate. Phyllis responded by overeating and had soon gained some forty or fifty pounds; but though the change in her appearance was dramatic, none of their co-workers appeared to realize what it signified.[50] Which was, of course, just as well. Though Curt and Phyllis could ill-afford to be married, still less could they afford a separation. Financially, but more importantly professionally, such a step might well spell ruin.

A move to an even smaller and cheaper first-floor apartment on Dukeland Street in early 1924 was symptomatic of just how straightened their finances had become. As the children grew beyond infancy, the expenses of maintaining the

23 *The staff of the Phipps Clinic in the mid-1920s. A visibly heavier Phyllis Greenacre is on the front step, positioned next to Meyer, while her estranged husband Curt Richter has chosen to stand almost as far from her as possible. (Richter is the second figure from the left in the picture, one row behind Meyer and Greenacre.)*

household increased, yet their incomes remained stubbornly static. The piling up of worries and the constant sense of being on top of one another only worsened their mood. Externally, they had to maintain appearances, but behind closed doors, their fights escalated. Both responded by immersing themselves still more thoroughly in their work, avoiding being thrown together as much as possible. As tensions increased, Greenacre grew close to despair. Surely it would be a matter of weeks rather than months before another black depression overcame her, and then what would become of her career, her life, and her children?

A further appeal to Meyer asking for his intervention to secure a salary increase for her from Hopkins met with several weeks of ominous silence. Finally, just days before he left for his summer break in Santa Barbara, California, Meyer responded: "I certainly owe you an apology for this long delay in answering your letter. If I had anything pleasant or favorable to report to you, I should feel better about it." But the word from the treasurer's office was "to the effect that the University owed you nothing . . . I hardly know what the next step should be."[51]

Briefly, Greenacre flirted with the idea of taking a "position offered me by the National Committee for Mental Hygiene," but in the end she could not bring herself to abandon her work at Hopkins: "There are certain concrete problems which I have started which I feel I *must finish*." Again her frustrations boiled to the surface: "I *should not wish to continue*, however, *unless* I can foresee *greater development* and more *contacts through publication and* especially through *teaching*, than have yet come to me." And once more she returned to the issue of her inadequate salary: "I have just received the annual appointment notice from the President's office, and find myself officially reappointed as an associate in psychiatry with a salary of *$2,500* [$700 more than she had made in 1921–2]. I did not know whether in the event of my return to the clinic, this was intended to constitute the whole of the salary. I should find that *extremely difficult*, as I think you will understand."[52]

From a response to this powerful litany of grievances and complaints that Meyer drafted at the Hotel St. Francis in San Francisco, it is clear that he *did* understand the sub-text – that he was at risk of losing one of his most valued associates unless he did something credible to meet her demands. The document makes clear his plans to accommodate her on a variety of fronts. So far as teaching was concerned, he had immediately begun to make it possible to take "every other Thursday for a topic of clinical discussion, or a series of Thursdays if you prefer," and would "arrange with Dr. Richards a certain amount of group teaching." He promised a "readjustment . . . in which the aims of research and teaching of both yourself and the clinic come to best fruition." And he acknowledged the need to ensure that "the problem of publication is adjusted (which is my first concern)." As a result, "there should be a cause of grievance out of the way which I regret very much."[53]

All in all, this constituted a remarkable series of concessions to one of his juniors by the hierarchically minded Meyer. On the question of her financial rewards, he was in a more difficult bind. The Hopkins administration were unwilling to pay her more, so the question remained of how he could address this, the most pressing of her concerns. He assured her that in the first instance, "concerning the sex studies, the same amount of money will be available as last year."[54] A more important possible source of supplementary income was a project he had broached to her just before he left for the West Coast. Joseph Raycroft, a Princeton faculty member who was one of two medical men on the Trenton State Hospital board had approached him about conducting a study of Cotton's work on focal infection and insanity, and he reminded her that there were plans afoot for her to conduct the research, assuming she were willing, under his broad supervision. Here was still another potential source of supplementary income.

As she knew, he had first suggested that she look at some of Cotton's work in connection with her studies of tertiary syphilis, but this present project was on a much broader scale, with the promise of financial funding from the State of New Jersey and the hospital authorities. The idea was for an intensive and systematic study of the results of Cotton's controversial surgical interventions to combat focal infection, and thus, purportedly, to cure psychosis – a project that would necessitate extensive fieldwork at the hospital and perhaps elsewhere. Over the course of the first part of the summer, Raycroft had drafted "a provisional and confidential" plan for the study, and Meyer indicated that he planned to seek her advice on this, and to discuss the situation with her on his return to Baltimore in September.[55] In the meantime, he would attend to the matter of her financial recompense for the work.

Meyer was aware – indeed had discussed with her when he first broached the subject – of the fact that the work would require great personal sacrifices on her part. It would entail spending at least several days of each week for an extended period in Trenton, and that meant, of course, being separated from both her husband and her children. He indicated that the amount of information to be gathered was considerable, but then so was the potential importance of her findings for the profession. If there was any substance to Cotton's claims (and Meyer had acknowledged that he found the basic notion of focal sepsis as a major cause of psychosis an intriguing one, and fully compatible with his own theories), then the therapeutics of mental illness and the standing of psychiatry in the medical profession and among the public at large would be absolutely transformed.

By September, he was in a position to inform Greenacre that taking on the work would be financially quite advantageous to her. She would remain on salary at Hopkins in return for the Trenton hospital's agreement to forward him duplicates of all her materials. In addition, the asylum board in New Jersey had agreed to supplement her existing pay with a further $300 a month, and to pay all her expenses. Greenacre was thus to receive the equivalent of $6,000 a year plus expenses, more than half Meyer's salary, and more than twice the amount she was already making.[56] Her complaints about being under-appreciated and under-rewarded seemed no longer so legitimate, and her pressing financial worries at the very least considerably abated.

9

Cotton Under the Microscope

The decision to commission an outside assessment of Henry Cotton's work at Trenton had been the subject of considerable internal controversy and debate among members of the hospital's board of managers.[1] The board, and Commissioner Lewis himself, had long been among Cotton's most devoted admirers, and for weeks after the suggestion first surfaced, some of them resisted the idea of such a study, fearing that it "would be unsatisfactory [and] it might give the Hospital a lot of undesirable notoriety." If they were not careful, "the reports might even get into the public press," and besides, as one of them told Joseph Raycroft when lobbied on the subject, "the work is too new and I just don't think the thing is feasible."[2]

Yet Raycroft, perhaps Cotton's strongest supporter on the board, would not be dissuaded, and he quickly won the support of both Commissioner Lewis and of Cotton himself. Politically astute, Raycroft knew that the authorities at New Jersey's other state hospital, Greystone Park, had long chafed at Trenton's higher public and professional profile, and – he was convinced it was either from jealousy or sheer bloody-mindedness – they had resolutely refused to even consider adopting Cotton's innovations. He was aware, too, that Cotton's work was controversial among many of his fellow psychiatrists in the profession at large. But their objections, he felt certain, were once again testament to the sort of envy and inertia that always bedeviled genuine innovators. Cotton's achievements rested on an unimpeachable scientific foundation, and besides, as the board well knew, they paid off in dollars and cents. Most of the objections from other psychiatrists came from "stand-patters" who exhibited "a general distrust of anything new" and a culpable "unwillingness or inability to consider any change from the traditional custodial care of insane patients in favor of a more modern medical and surgical treatment." And as for those who claimed to have tried treating focal sepsis without obtaining comparable results, it was apparent they had only treated a handful of cases, and then "on a different basis from that used by Dr. Cotton."[3]

Still, this rag-tag opposition was far more dangerous than his fellow board members appeared to realize. Raycroft insisted that he had "no desire to be classed with those who are running around looking for avoidable trouble." But "the fact of the matter is, as I see the situation, that some sort of a study of this work by Dr. Cotton is going to be made." Unless the board pre-empted them, Cotton's critics might well manage to set up a hostile investigation, seeking to discredit the greatest advance in the treatment of the mentally ill that Raycroft thought had occurred in his lifetime. Far better to anticipate such a move and set up their own study run by those "neutral or at least not unfriendly to the plan of work under consideration."[4]

Together with Cotton and Lewis, Raycroft worked through February to design a suitable scheme.[5] But when he tried to recruit Paul Mecray, the other medical man on the Trenton board, he ran into unexpected resistance. Mecray remained unconverted for more than a month, resisting even when Raycroft warned him that the State Board of Institutions and Agencies was itself on the brink of setting up its own investigation, "independent of our Board."[6] Finally, however, Mecray capitulated in the face of his colleague's entreaties, and thereafter the lay board members quickly fell into line.

There remained the delicate question of who should be entrusted with the organization of the study. It must be someone of real stature, or the whole exercise would be pointless. But whom could they trust with such a sensitive task? It was at this juncture that Raycroft revealed his master-stroke: he suggested that they should approach Adolf Meyer at Hopkins to oversee the study. They knew Meyer was well disposed towards Cotton's work. After all, he had written a glowing foreword to the published version of Cotton's Vanuxem lectures at Princeton just a few years before. And Cotton, of course, was his long-time protégé. Given Meyer's standing among his fellow psychiatrists, and the prestige his Hopkins appointment gave him with the medical profession at large, his endorsement would surely stifle even the most vociferous of critics.

There was, indeed, concern among some of Raycroft's colleagues that Meyer's rigid Swiss sense of propriety might lead him to reject the invitation. Oddly enough, though, Meyer never raised the issue. Instead, he complained repeatedly about his overloaded schedule. Still, the professor seemed to recognize the importance of the study, and after some further correspondence and a meeting, agreement was finally reached: he would appoint one of his assistants to conduct the study itself and personally oversee the work, which would allow him to lend his name and prestige to the final report.[7] Raycroft was delighted. On June 30, he wrote to Meyer assuring him that "we want to help you in every way possible," and promising a free hand in the design and conduct of the study. He enclosed "a copy of the memorandum outlining the general features of this study revised along the lines that you suggested in our conference about a month ago," together with "a copy of the resolution presented to the Board of Managers in connection with this project. I remember your suggestion that the Board should not take formal action on this matter, but . . . it seemed wise . . . to formulate a resolution to present the matter in its proper light, and to prevent the likelihood of anybody saying that Cotton was being 'investigated.'" Cotton, Raycroft hastened to assure Meyer, had promised his cooperation, feeling that the work was now far enough along to allow the study to reach "conclusions of authoritative character and of permanent value." As for funding the costs associated with the work, "I think it is quite possible that we can take care of Dr. Greenacre, and any extra clerical help by putting them on our regular pay-roll. Expenses in addition to those mentioned could be provided for from other sources. I will take this matter up just as soon as you can give me some idea of the amount needed for yourself and for others."[8]

Ten days later, Meyer replied from "Riven Rock," that the planned investigation "looks like smooth sailing, but I do not know whether the plan can be arranged before my return Sept. 15." He would place the day-to-day inquiry in the hands of "Dr. Phyllis Greenacre (a graduate of Chicago and Rush and with me since 1916)." By an odd coincidence, Greenacre had studied with Raycroft when he taught biology at Chicago and "remembers you well." Meyer was sure they would all be pleased with her, and closed with the admonition that he thought the hospital authorities should set up a special fund to support her work, because then it would "not be a matter of public pay role [*sic*] which would be open to employees."[9]

Meyer's presence at this then-remote Californian outpost reflected his continued involvement in the care and treatment of the enormously wealthy Stanley McCormick, heir to the McCormick Harvest Machine Company (later International Harvester) fortune, a man who for four decades served as a one-man gravy train for the psychiatric profession, notwithstanding their collective inability to do anything for him. Meyer had first been brought into McCormick's case in 1906 when Stanley's wife and his blood relatives for once agreed on something, and turned to America's most eminent psychiatrist to diagnose the pugnacious and delusional man, by then confined in the McLean Asylum just outside Boston. Despite a nine-month honeymoon following his marriage to Katherine Dexter (the strong-minded daughter of a wealthy Chicago lawyer, whom he had single-mindedly pursued across the Atlantic to her family's Swiss chateau), poor Stanley had been unable to consummate their relationship. Separated from her for some months before his institutionalization, Stanley had begun to masturbate openly and, what was worse, to speak of giving his fortune away to the socialists.

24 *Riven Rock, the McCormick mansion in Santa Barbara, where the mad Stanley McCormick was housed for much of his adult life.*

Asked for his professional opinion about the young man's prognosis, Meyer from the outset issued the bleakest of diagnoses – catatonic schizophrenia. In typically convoluted Meyerian prose, he commented that Stanley had an early center of trouble in the excessive development of frustrated sex functions. He had an extreme sensitivity in his adjustment to his mother, worried endlessly about his business responsibilities, and tortured himself about rather abstract standards of an all-encompassing socialist and moral–religious system. Under the strain of these conflicts, the patient went through courtship and marriage only to find himself utterly unable to cope with the new problems, not at all sexually, and socially only with an excessive expenditure of energy. Thereafter, allying himself with the McCormicks, and in opposition to Stanley's wife Katherine, Meyer had remained for years a consultant on the case – a highly lucrative sinecure not to be abandoned because it occasionally required a transcontinental railroad journey. (While not as handsomely rewarded as the New York psychoanalyst Edward J. Kempf, who was paid the princely sum of $150,000 a year not three years later to devote his entire attention to "mad McCormick," with the usual lack of success, Meyer was paid handsomely for his services, perhaps as much as the $2,000 a week plus expenses the family had paid Emil Kraepelin in 1908 when it summoned the great man from Germany to confirm Meyer's diagnosis – as he duly did.) That the disagreeable task substituted the balmy Santa Barbara summer for the heat and humidity of an East-Coast July and August was an unlooked-for bonus, even if it did complicate, on this occasion, the start of the Trenton study.

Because of Meyer's absence, Greenacre did not commence her study until the fall.[10] Three weeks before she first arrived in Trenton, Meyer himself paid a two-day visit to the hospital. He found it a sobering experience. In his private notes recording his first-hand impressions, he confessed plaintively that "the cases I saw this forenoon leave me rather troubled and uncertain." Uncertainty, however, was certainly not his protégé's problem: "when I hear Dr. Cotton discuss his cases the problem seems to be absolutely nothing but one of focal infection . . . Re colon: Dr. Cotton considers any retention of more than 24 hours pathological" and had informed him that "headaches are a 'sure' indication of trouble." Cotton had, moreover, the statistics to back up his claims – or so he asserted. One of his former patients, a Mrs. Rue, a manic depressive who exhibited a touching enthusiasm for Cotton's work, had been placed in charge of the statistical work and proudly displayed the results. Meyer in response murmured something about the general uncertainties of psychiatric statistics, but otherwise made no comment, even when shown statistical tables displaying the results of Cotton's operations on the colon. Of the 133 total colectomies Cotton and his staff had performed, Mrs. Rue recorded 33 recoveries and 44 deaths; and out of 148 "developmental reconstructions" of the colon, 44 cases had recovered or improved, while 59 had died.[11]

But if results like these were somehow passed over in silence, Meyer had certainly already seen enough to start worrying about the task he had assigned his young assistant. Seemingly as much to reassure himself as Cotton, he twice wrote to promise him that he could "depend thoroughly on Dr. Greenacre's attitude and training." "I feel certain," he continued, that "you will find her a very capable and judicious worker and a thoroughly cooperative personality."[12] Cotton by contrast seemed blithely sure of his position, and at once wrote back that "I feel sure that Dr. Greenacre is the one to do this work and everything possible will be put at her disposal for a complete survey."[13]

When Dr. Greenacre finally arrived, however, she was greeted none too warmly. She had travelled up on the early morning New York train, and after she had breakfasted in town, a cab dropped her at the hospital gates just after nine thirty. Cotton's attitude was reasonably welcoming, but underneath a surface calm, she detected considerable uneasiness. He struck her, too, as a singularly peculiar man, so much so that she privately wondered about his own

25 *The ornate entrance to the main building at Trenton State Hospital, where Phyllis Greenacre arrived to commence her study of Cotton's methods and their results in September 1924.*

mental stability. She pushed such thoughts aside. She had not even begun her work yet, and she reminded herself of how important it was that she should keep an open mind.[14]

Cotton himself gave her a brief tour in order to orient her to the hospital, introducing her along the way to various members of his staff. It was an old institution, the central portion dating from 1848. Cotton stopped to show her the room in which the sainted Dorothea Dix had died – the famous crusader who had to her credit (or on her conscience) the construction of so many museums of madness. There was her travel bag and the portable desk on which she had penned a lengthy series of emotional and effective memorials to state legislatures, appealing for funds to construct a whole network of public asylums: a shrine Cotton himself had constructed early in his tenure at the hospital. The childless Dix had always referred to Trenton as her "first born child" – and to that child she had repaired to spend her declining years, when advancing age had dulled her own mental powers.

As usual, the buildings gave off that sour, fetid odor so characteristic of mental hospitals – a scent of dirt and decay compounded of an ugly amalgam of the stale urine that had impregnated the floor boards over the years, the sweaty bodies of hundreds of patients crammed together in overcrowded wards, the thousands of unpalatable and overcooked institutional meals the hospital kitchens disgorged every day, the stench of the paraldehyde used to sedate the inmates, and the fecal smells that no amount of attention to the drains ever seemed to eliminate. She shuddered inwardly. It brought to mind the months she had spent in a Maryland state hospital, at Meyer's insistence, at the very outset of her training. It had been a dismal barracks of a place, filled with chronic, long-stay patients lolling about in a state approximating suspended animation – not the raving madmen that haunted the popular imagination, but burned-out wrecks of human beings, locked up and herded about in a cemetery for the still breathing. After that experience, the Phipps Clinic had seemed a paradise – and perhaps that was just the impression Meyer had sought to create.

But there was something subtly different about the patients at Trenton. She could not put her finger on it at first. Something about their faces and their conversation struck her as odd and vaguely disquieting. She slowed the rapid pace through one of the wards to observe more carefully, and then she understood: the old joke about Trenton as "the Mecca of exodontia" no longer struck her as the least bit amusing. These patients were all devoid of teeth, and they had not been given dentures. *That* was why their speech was slurred and so difficult to comprehend – and why their sunken faces gave even the youngest among them the appearance of premature age. One of them unexpectedly grinned at the elegant young woman who had stopped to inspect him. She saw only his gums, and recoiled in shock. Like others on the ward, he seemed thin and malnourished. Small wonder, she thought, for how on earth did they manage to eat?

Having completed their tour of the main buildings, Cotton next escorted Greenacre across the grounds to another structure, isolated behind its own barbed-wire fence, and with iron gratings over the windows. If the rest of the hospital had been gloomy and oppressive, this portion seemed even more self-consciously prison-like. Not surprisingly so, for it turned out that this building contained the wards for the criminally insane – including some of the most murderous and violent human beings one might ever hope not to set eyes on. It was here, Cotton informed her, with just a trace of a smile, that her own sleeping accommodations were to be found, in a converted broom closet located in what by any measure was the most forbidding wing of the hospital. It was too overcrowded elsewhere, he told her, and smiled thinly once more.[15]

It was a grim prospect, since Greenacre could look forward to spending three nights of each week there for the foreseeable future. But if Cotton thought this sort of thing would discourage her or induce her to take short cuts in her work, he was in for a surprise. It was, however, a curious move on his part. He surely could have found her some more satisfactory accommodation than this, and one might have expected him to be anxious not to offend her.

By the time Cotton and Greenacre got back to the superintendent's house, her old Chicago professor Joseph Raycroft was waiting for them. Now installed just up the road as professor of hygiene and head of student health services at Princeton University, Raycroft greeted her more warmly than Cotton had. He was delighted, quite delighted to see her. The hospital was the site of some great and wonderful breakthroughs in the treatment of the mentally ill, and he was sure her report would prove invaluable in winning over the skeptics. The hospital staff had, of course, been hard at work in anticipation of her arrival, doing some of the preliminary work in accordance with the plan they had agreed upon with Meyer. Mrs. Rue, the statistician, had prepared the information on a series of 100 cases, and he was confident that she would find this an invaluable starting point. It was all neatly typed up and bound in blue covers, tied with ribbon. Somewhat ceremoniously, Raycroft handed it over to her.

Cotton had brightened up on seeing Raycroft, and he now graciously showed her across to the office they had set aside for her. To facilitate her follow-up studies, he told her, he had assigned two of his best social workers to work on the study. Their assistance should certainly make her task much easier. And, of course, both Cotton and Raycroft assured her once more, they would do everything in their power to help her work along. Finally, they left her alone. Phyllis looked around the cramped office they had given her. At least it had a desk and a typewriter, and the view from the window was pleasant enough. Just as well – she would be spending a good deal of time there.

The statistical report the hospital authorities had prepared seemed as good a place to start as any. She untied the ribbon and began to read. Immediately, she was struck by its legalistic tone. Far more disturbing, though, were the numbers the statistician had provided: they simply did not add up. There were elementary mistakes in the very first tables. As she looked more closely, she found several instances in which multiple admissions of the same patient were counted as though they were new cases each time. In general, the statistics just did not tally, and her suspicions were further aroused when she saw that virtually all the discharges were classified as cures. The whole document was so sloppy and unprofessional that she was appalled. How could the hospital's board possibly accept this sort of thing? Obviously, it was no use to her. She would have to start from scratch.

The next three months were a period of absolute drudgery. She and Meyer had agreed that she needed to examine a large series of cases if her findings were to carry the necessary weight, including a group of older cases, so as to explore the long-term effects of the treatment; a group currently under treatment, to show the immediate effects of the treatment and take account of any improvements Cotton had made since he first began to treat focal infections; and a selection of cases Cotton himself regarded as having the best outcomes among those that had passed through his hands. The composition of the two latter groups was determined easily enough: she would look at all those admitted during the first few months of her study, and Cotton would supply the names of the specially chosen cases for her to look at. As for the older cases, she asked Mrs. Rue to supply her with three consecutive series of patients from among those admitted in 1920 and 1921: the first hundred cases, regardless of diagnosis; the first hundred functional cases; and a final group composed of those patients admitted during the same period of time who had received all phases of treatment for focal sepsis, which turned out to be some sixty-two men and women.

Greenacre's first task was to examine the clinical records on each of these patients in order to determine what was known of their histories, diagnoses, treatment, and fate. On the surface, this seemed a straightforward process, but in reality, the haphazard way in which the records were kept meant that securing even basic information on each case often took hours of effort. She had assumed that she would be able to assign this sort of work to the two social workers Cotton had assigned to help her, but once she had met and talked with them, she quickly revised her plans. Both were eager and enthusiastic – unfortunately, only too much so, for like Mrs. Rue, they also were among Cotton's former patients, and they proudly displayed complete sets of dentures to prove it. Pathetically grateful for his ministrations, and for the jobs he had subsequently provided for them, they were obviously not assistants she could rely upon. She thus saw no alternative but to undertake the whole tiresome task herself.

Though the patient records were a shambles, through hard work she eventually managed to assemble the necessary information on each of the cases, one by one, using the principles Meyer had taught her to organize and record the data. Even at this stage, and without independently checking the outcomes recorded for the patients, Greenacre had already acquired sufficient information to know that Cotton's published claims for his interventions were sharply at variance with what a close scrutiny of the case records revealed. As she proceeded, she wrote up each case promptly, making two carbon copies, one for Meyer and one for Cotton. Early on, Cotton had looked at a handful of these, and once or twice commented that she was being too harsh in her assessment of a particular outcome. In general, however, he kept himself aloof, and she had the impression that he had somehow persuaded himself that her findings generally supported his published assertions.[16]

Back in Baltimore, Meyer was under no such illusions. As the reports piled up, he recognized that her careful work amounted to a devastating commentary on Cotton's claims. By early December, he had seen enough, informing his brother Hermann that "the investigation of the material of Dr. Cotton discloses a rather sad harvest. His claims and statistics are preposterously out of accord with the facts."[17] Later that same day, he was therefore somewhat startled to receive a brief note from his former student recounting his pleasure with the progress of the study to date: "We have given Doctor Greenacre every opportunity to get the information desired," Cotton informed him, "and I personally have been very much pleased with her interest and attitude toward the work. She has said very little, but I am confident that she will view the work impartially and will be interested in the facts. I want to tell you how much I appreciate your selecting her for the work."[18] Meyer must have privately wondered how long Cotton would continue to feel that way.

The professor nonetheless seemed content to wait for the six to nine months Greenacre estimated it would still take her to complete the remainder of her study. Such caution was entirely in character, and it therefore did not surprise her; but still, as she privately admitted to herself, she could not help feeling somewhat resentful, and more than a little dismayed. Meyer, after all, was comfortably ensconced in his study more than a hundred miles away, and unlike her, he did not have to deal with the oppressive atmosphere of the hospital. Emotionally, despite her best efforts to remain detached and professionally neutral, she found that, as her research made her certain that Cotton's interventions were misguided and even positively harmful, it became more and more difficult to return to Trenton each week.

In her review of the clinical records, she had deliberately left until last her survey of the group of patients who had received the most thorough "cleansing" at the hands of Cotton and his staff. Going through those sixty-two cases turned out to be a particularly harrowing experience, for even the flat, bureaucratic prose typical of clinical records laid bare a chronicle of terrible suffering and a litany of quite astonishingly bad outcomes. Even Cotton conceded that seventeen of the patients in this group had rapidly succumbed to peritonitis or post-operative shock, and her own assessment suggested there were others, not counted in these mortality statistics because they had lingered for some months post-operatively, whose demise could most plausibly be attributed to the long-term effects of the surgery.

There was Stella Norris, for example, a manic-depressive woman who had never really recovered from the colectomy performed on her on October 20, 1921. Post-operatively, she complained of abdominal pain and diarrhoea for some weeks, then temporarily rallied, before steadily losing weight after her surgical wound re-opened. Cotton professed to find her something of a success story, claiming that, "mentally there is some improvement – she can be made to smile, – conversation is less irrelevant. She does not dwell on her condition to such an extent as formerly." Her wound nonetheless continued to granulate and separate, and three days before Christmas, she died – officially of a combination of "pulmonary tuberculosis, myocarditis, and tuberculous peritonitis."[19]

Still more upsetting were cases such as Julia Thompson's, a young woman who had suffered from recurrent manic depression. Admitted on September 11, 1922, she was subjected to be a particularly aggressive therapeutic regime. Two days after arriving at Trenton, her tonsils were removed. Nine days later, she underwent "the usual total colectomy," following which "she ran a fever of 100–102 for a month or six weeks, without cause being discovered." During that same six-week period, she had sixteen teeth extracted, and was injected with vaccines derived from "streptococcus mitis and stock colon streptococcus." When, in the aftermath of all these interventions, she "showed some more interest in her surroundings," she was discharged to the care of her relatives, "her mental condition considerably improved." Eight months later, however, following her mother's death, she had a relapse accompanied by stomach pains and vomiting. This time, there would be no reprieve. In the face of her protests, the family had returned her to Trenton, where the ward staff recorded that she "was confused but tried to conceal her pain, fearing operation." Her fear was well-founded. Her attempts at concealment and pathetic gestures of resistance were in vain, and within hours of her arrival, she was being wheeled into the operating theater, where a laparotomy and colostomy were performed. Eight days later, she was dead – from post-operative peritonitis. Recalling her own bout with depression, Greenacre found it easy to empathize with this sad creature, sucked back into a nightmare world from which she must have thought she had escaped, fearful and frightened, and destined to linger for days in agonizing pain before dying a horrible death.

Sorting through the written records was intended to be, of course, only the preliminary foundation for the still more difficult and time-consuming job that then confronted Greenacre. Leaving aside those patients who had died during the course of their treatment, she knew that each and every patient in her sample must now be traced, and if possible, interviewed at length in order to allow her to reach an informed judgment about the outcomes in each case. By the second half of December, she was ready to begin this mammoth task. For most of those who had moved out of state, she relied primarily on correspondence to locate them and gain a sense of their current mental status. Some she simply could not find, though she did subsequently locate four of these such hidden away on Trenton's own back wards. (It was a measure of how poorly kept the hospital records were that their presence back in the institution apparently came as news to the staff.) But for the much larger group still resident in New Jersey, she set about conducting a personal tour of inspection, spending two days of each week driving round the state to interview the ex-patients, their families, and neighbors to develop a first-hand assessment of how they were coping. Cotton might be satisfied with desultory reports from relatives that all was well with his former patients, but she would make her own assessment of their mental state. Jersey City and Fort Lee, Rahway and Haddonfield, Hoboken and Newark, and a host of rural, out-of-the-way communities became part of her itinerary, as for months she criss-crossed the state, determined to leave no one with any room to question the validity of her findings.

It was a thankless chore, one that on occasion landed her in some rather difficult situations. At least it got her out of the hospital, though, where the atmosphere and the hostility of many of the staff (particularly Cotton's assistant physicians) had made her life quite miserable. From the very first day, she had been disturbed by the hordes of malnourished, edentulous patients, pathetic creatures whom the attendants treated with indifference and worse. Within weeks, as even her preliminary findings showed how delusory Cotton's claimed cure rates were, she had become still more distressed by the parade of patients into the operating theater. She was uncomfortably aware that all this abdominal surgery seemed to be doing little good, and alarmed by the quantities of physical damage and death that followed in its wake. The nightmarish quality of the whole experience was only intensified by the serene conviction Cotton and his assistant Robert Stone displayed in the merits of their approach, and by her conviction that others on the medical staff were only too aware of the realities of the situation and were shutting their eyes to what was going on for purely careerist motives.

Cotton might somehow have persuaded himself that her work was providing definitive support for his claims. Several of his lieutenants clearly knew better, and the hostility they directed her way was palpable. At night, locked into her cell in the criminal wing, listening to the animal-like howls and shrieks of the most disturbed inmates down the hallway, she sometimes had to repress paranoid fears for her own safety. She agonized incessantly about the surreal quality of the events she was now irretrievably a part of, consoling herself only with the knowledge that her report, once completed, would certainly put an end to this awfulness. But she had to be sure of her ground, and that inevitably meant delays while she completed her follow-up work, analyzed her data, and wrote her report.

Though preferable to more days and nights in the hospital, by no means were her forays into the community without their own threatening and disturbing moments. She never knew what to expect when she tracked down released patients and arrived to interview them. Some welcomed her, and spoke gratefully of what Cotton had done for them. Others reacted with suspicion or outright hostility. For many, the hospital experience was obviously a bitter memory, one of which they were anxious not to be reminded, and even encounters with ex-patients who appeared to have recovered and were willing to talk to her could prove harrowing.

There was Mrs. Anita Ludwig, for example, whom she visited at her farm near Crosswicke, New Jersey, on March 26, 1925. On her arrival, Mrs. Ludwig

> came to the window of the house in response to my knock, and while she talked she held the curtains round her so that only her face was visible. After a few minutes, however, she relented and invited me in. The house is an old-fashioned farm house with large rooms. These were crowded with a profusion of half-broken furniture. The two rooms through which we first passed, – those most used by the family as living rooms were exceedingly dirty, the other two rooms – evidently parlors, were only disordered. Mrs. L[udwig] is an enormously obese woman, with irregularly bobbed hair which appears unwashed and uncombed. Her face is dirty and there are coffee marks around her lips. Her costume is a striking affair of one piece of rough brown material, with a hole cut out for the neck. The frayed edges around the neck are not hemmed, and the whole dress is appallingly dirty. She wears no shoes and the toes of one foot protrude conspicuously through a hole in one stocking.

All of this surely prepared Greenacre to discover, once the interview began, that here was still another of Cotton's patients who, discharged from Trenton or not, remained as mentally unstable as ever. To her surprise, however, reality

turned out to be rather different, though on some levels no less disturbing:
Mrs. Ludwig

> makes no apologies, and on the whole shows considerable poise through-
> out the interview. She tells me now that she herself is quite well, and that
> things would be going very well with her except for her husband's
> drunken fighting and abuse. She bares her arms and shows bruise marks
> and other tangible evidence of abuse. She now suffers from headaches
> which she believes to have followed a blow on the head from her husband.
> She shows the scar where the skin is actually adherent to the underlying
> bone. She pours forth her difficulties, telling of how her husband comes
> home drunk and she has to go out driving with him because she fears to
> have him drive alone. She feels quite superior to him in general, in that he
> can neither read nor write, while she prides herself on her ability to speak
> three languages, Russian, German, and English. Her talk is perfectly clear,
> coherent, and relevant. She complains of no mood disturbances, worries;
> and has no longer vomiting or dizziness.

Leaving poor Mrs. Ludwig to her dismal fate, Greenacre recorded that in her
judgment, "she has probably recovered from her psychosis; and the dirty, disordered state of her person and house probably represents standard of living
rather than deterioration."

Then there were the even more bizarre visits, where she found herself
trapped in the presence of the clinically crazy. There was the time in early
March, for instance, when Greenacre arrived at an isolated cottage on a farm
outside Haddonfield to interview Alice Stephens, a middle-aged woman the
hospital records indicated had been released and subsequently found
"improved" after a tonsillectomy and an extensive course of vaccine therapy.
Much knocking eventually brought a white-haired, amply built woman to the
door in an old and very dirty dress that gaped badly, disclosing unpleasant
glimpses of filthy underwear. After some delay, Alice (for it was she) admitted
her to a disorderly and dirty living room, whose other occupant, a peculiar-
appearing, angular, gaunt woman promptly fled upstairs. Minutes later, still
another figure stole downstairs, a tall girl with irregularly shorn hair and
a hopelessly delapidated appearance – shoes unlaced, clothing soiled, and a
stocking hanging loosely round one ankle. Alice grimaced and introduced her
daughter Rebecca, a Swarthmore graduate, and another former Trenton
patient. The girl grinned repulsively, and went silently back upstairs.

By this time, a few minutes of conversation had convinced Greenacre that
both women were still actively hallucinating and quite thoroughly mad, and

given the oppressive atmosphere of the place, she longed desperately to leave. Alice, however, would have none of it, insisting on showing her the rest of the house. Everywhere, there was dirt and disorder – dirty dishes, dirty tablecloth, filthy floors, piles of discarded clothes – and upstairs, they once more encountered the gaunt, awkward woman who had fled when Greenacre first arrived. Introduced by Alice on this occasion as "my boarder, Mrs. Wilson," who slept in the upstairs hallway, she, too, was evidently psychotic.

Now somewhat alarmed, Greenacre steered her peculiar hostess back downstairs, and sought somewhat desperately to make her exit. Alice Stephens was visibly distressed by the thought. Couldn't she stay? They could talk about books, or about her son, a Rhodes scholar who was off at Oxford. Greenacre could share their supper. Surely, she did not have to leave just yet. Making her excuses as best she could, and edging towards the door, Greenacre grew still more alarmed when she discovered that it was bolted and barred from the outside. Mr. Stephens, who had apparently still been home when she arrived, had chosen to use their time upstairs to leave for his job across the Delaware, and, as was his custom, had locked the three lunatic ladies in for the day.

Once she realized what had happened, even Greenacre began to lose her equanimity. Recalling the scene some six decades later, she remembered some panic-stricken moments as she wondered whether she was destined to remain trapped in this house of pathology for several hours more. Was she personally at risk, locked up with these three seriously psychotic women? On the contrary, it turned out that her hostess found the whole situation rather amusing, and after vainly trying herself to open the door, offered to help Greenacre effect her escape. Her first plan was to push a chair out of the kitchen window and for the doctor to lower herself out on to it – but contemplating the six- to eight-foot drop that still remained, her guest suggested an exit via the cellar might be preferable. Treating the whole thing as an elaborate game, Alice gravely escorted her downstairs and watched while her elegantly dressed visitor clambered over the pile of coal and squeezed through a narrow opening, emerging on all fours with a blackened and somewhat torn dress and dented dignity, but otherwise safe and sound. Afterwards, Greenacre could laugh about the experience, but at the time, it left her deeply shaken and questioning whether she had done well to accept Meyer's invitation to undertake the study in the first place.[20]

Luckily, such alarms and excursions were the exception rather than the rule, and by July, after ten months of exceptionally hard work, the bulk of the study was complete. There remained only the task of reducing the mass of information she had gathered to a systematic statistical form, analyzing its implications for the theory of focal sepsis, and setting down her conclusions in clear and convincing prose. For Greenacre had long since realized that the large-scale experimentation on the Trenton patients she had witnessed and recorded was hopelessly wrong headed and profoundly damaging, and she was determined to leave no room for debate on the subject.

Though Greenacre had continued to provide Cotton with copies of her findings on each case as she completed it, he seemed to remain oblivious to the damning conclusions to which they ever more insistently pointed. It was as though he could not believe that this self-effacing young woman, more than a decade and a half his junior, could possibly pose any threat to a psychiatrist as established and important as he. Besides, she reflected wryly, not even the most grossly delusional patient in the Trenton asylum possessed a greater capacity for self-deception than he.

In any event, by this point in the summer, Cotton had become wholly preoccupied by the looming political threat to his position posed by the runaway Bright Committee. Ordinarily, the New Jersey legislators transacted their business during three or four months in the winter and early spring, making sure to spare themselves the discomfort of the statehouse and the state capital in July and August. Ordinarily, too, few outside the borders of the Garden State either noticed or cared what occupied their time and energies. In the present case, however, normal expectations were cast aside. What had begun as a routine and humdrum political exercise, an attempt to embarrass the Democratic administration of Governor Silzer by exposing waste and extravagance in state government, had unexpectedly yielded much richer political dividends.

Yet it had all begun so innocently. The news that Senator William Bright, leader of the Republican majority in the New Jersey legislature, had formed a committee to investigate waste and fraud in state government, drew only the most glancing notice beyond the boundaries of the state. Even locally, it seemed little more at first than the typical grandstanding of an ambitious politician, anxious to use the convenient stick of fiscal responsibility to embarrass an incumbent governor of the opposite party. Before six months had elapsed, however, events from Cotton's point of view had taken a much uglier turn.

Politicians of both parties had long resented Burdette Lewis, the arrogant Commissioner of Institutions and Agencies, whose department ran both prisons and mental hospitals. During his six years in office, Lewis had doubled his department's budget, and he ran what was by far the largest state agency. Along the way, his new-fangled New York notions, his constant hogging of favorable publicity, and his contempt for politicians seeking patronage appointments had won him few friends in the legislature, and the rapid escalation of his department's expenditures now drew vigorous scrutiny. Bright wanted his scalp.

As a major part of Lewis's empire, both state mental hospitals could expect to receive their share of scrutiny. In early July, however, Cotton must have thought he had successfully deflected the committee's attention elsewhere. Ostensibly, he had been summoned to testify about the Quackenbush case, a dreadful incident in which an elderly woman, discharged from Trenton State Hospital only days before, had hacked her feeble-minded daughter to bits with an axe. As Cotton must have anticipated, however, his appearance quickly became the occasion for a broader inquiry about conditions in the hospital, including a series of questions about the innovative treatments he had intro-duced and the mortality associated with them.[21]

On the whole, this portion of his testimony seemed to have gone rather well. Not that there were no awkward moments, most notably after he sought to deflect some of the questions about his surgical interventions by revealing that they were the subject of a detailed on-going investigation directed by Adolf Meyer and conducted by his assistant, Dr. Greenacre. Recalling the long-standing ties between the two men, one of the senators had the temerity to challenge the independence of the investigation and the appropriateness of using state funds in support of such an enterprise. Characteristically, Cotton bristled at the criticism. Meyer's integrity, he icily informed them, was beyond reproach – and if they were unwilling to continue funding the study, he would meet the remainder of Dr. Greenacre's expenses from his own pocket.

Cotton's self-belief appeared to carry the day. Bright's committee included some of his most faithful supporters in the legislature, and when he gave his standard presentation on the enormous prestige New Jersey had accrued from adapting the most recent advances in scientific medicine to the treatment of the mentally ill, he could see their criticisms melting away. Indeed, so far from dis-puting the value of his surgical approach to mental illness, a number of his interrogators seemed disposed to criticize him for not following through on the logic of his own position, by failing to remove Mrs. Quackenbush's teeth and tonsils before discharging her. And they made no serious effort to dispute Cotton's claim that "the cures in the last seven years averaged 87 percent, which in terms of dollars and cents, represented a savings to the State . . . of about a million dollars."[22]

Having so effectively reassured politicians ostensibly concerned to expose waste and unnecessary expenditures in state government, Cotton must have thought that they would now turn their attention elsewhere. But then, out of the blue, over a series of sessions that seemed to stretch indefinitely into the future, came the parade of disgruntled employees, malicious ex-patients, and their families, testifying in damning detail about brutality, forced and botched surgery, debility, and death. Quite suddenly and wholly unexpectedly, Henry Cotton found himself fighting first for his professional life, and then for his very sanity.

The first of his adversaries to take the stand, some two weeks after his own appearance before the committee, was a Miss Edith Strong, a disaffected nurse with more than twenty years' experience who had recently been discharged from the hospital. Once sworn in, she proceeded to make a series of charges so electrifying that they drew the attention even of the august *New York Times.* From that moment forward, the hospital moved to the forefront of the committee's concerns, and weeks of lurid headlines ensued.

At the very outset, the journalists were presented with "a sensational story of deaths, following operations on patients . . . In nearly every case, Miss Strong testified, patients fought against the operations, but, she declared, "they were rushed in a room 'like cattle,' given a hypodermic injection and operated upon. She said that one patient had begged her to save her from the operating table." Cotton, she asserted, was "experimenting on patients with the knife," and with quite disastrous results. To her own knowledge, "five women patients in her ward upon whom operations had been performed died and 'only two or three got well.'"[23]

Adding to the force of her testimony, Miss Strong claimed that her charges would be corroborated by another former Trenton nurse, Mrs. Helen Bernard, who was now working at the Charles Private Hospital in Trenton, an establishment where Cotton treated some of his many private patients. Investigators for the Bright Committee at once served Mrs. Bernard with a subpoena, and just as promptly the matron at Cotton's private hospital dismissed her, claiming, when reporters showed up seeking comment, that "her services had not been satisfactory." Cotton, meanwhile, had avoided his own encounter with the press, sending word that he was "busy in the operating room" – perhaps not the most diplomatic of excuses under the circumstances. At the short-run cost of some further bad publicity in the newspapers, however, Mrs. Bernard's firing appeared to have had the desired effect, since, subpoena notwithstanding, she declined to appear before the Bright Committee.[24]

But if one witness had been intimidated into silence, there proved to be no shortage of others to take her place. Senator Bright had adopted the clever tactic of scheduling his hearings once a week on a Wednesday, and for nearly two months, the committee's hearings dominated the headlines in the New Jersey newspapers. At the session on July 29, Cotton was briefly back on the witness stand, reluctantly confirming that half a dozen patients on Miss Strong's ward had died following surgery, and briefly addressing the issue of surgical mortality rates in the institution. The bulk of the several hours of testimony, however, took a somewhat different tack, focusing on the issue of attendants abusing patients.

The first witness, Henry Graby, a Philadelphia chiropodist who had previously worked as an attendant at Trenton, informed the committee that a subculture of violence existed at the hospital. "It was a common occurrence for attendants to beat up patients" and "the guards . . . ruled by brute force," gambling with patients, stealing their money, and on occasion taking bribes to allow an inmate to escape. His protestations that his criticisms were in no sense directed at his former superior, who was "doing wonderful work" and should properly be seen "as the miracle man of the ages,"[25] were soon forgotten as more dramatic evidence of patient abuse surfaced.

Leah Bloom was a woman in her sixties who had been in and out of the hospital on at least a dozen occasions since 1895. In the aftermath of her penultimate admission in December 1924, she had had her teeth and tonsils removed, and had been discharged three months later. Now her daughters appeared, punctuating their testimony with tears and self-reproaches, and insisted that these operations had been undertaken without the consent of the family or the patient herself. They vividly recalled their mother's vociferous, panic-stricken protests when she learned of their decision to seek to return her to the mental hospital once more in early July. Pleading with her children in a vain attempt to escape her fate, she had spoken despairingly of the asylum as a place where "they operate, do anything to you." Her guilt-ridden relations had nonetheless proceeded with their plans, and now confronted the consequences of their decision.[26]

A few days after Mrs. Bloom's most recent arrival in the hospital, her son, son-in-law, and daughters had visited her. They found her in a frightful state. In the words of her older daughter, Mrs. Parent, "she was lying on a bed in a corner of the room . . . One eye was closed and dreadfully swollen. I hardly knew her. Her arms were dug out and flies swarmed about her. I pulled down the covers and she was a mass of bruises. The side of her face was in a terrible condition. There were nail marks on her throat as if she had been choked . . . she looked as though she had been dragged by her hair."

"'She was a sight,' her other daughter, Bessie Ross, confirmed, trembling with emotion. 'Her arm had been dug out and it looked as though she had proud flesh. There were scratches on her back and breast . . . There was a big lump on her neck and she tried to call for my eldest sister and her mother and father.

I could hardly distinguish what she said.'" In words that acquired immensely greater force and resonance a week later, Bessie wept as she recalled her parent's greatest fear. "During [her final] stay at her mother's bedside, the woman had raised her arms and whispered 'Take me – take me.'" Even before her admission, the distraught daughter continued, "Mother [had] said 'If I'm ever taken back to the State Hospital, I'll never get out alive.'" "And," Bessie added, "I don't think she will."[27]

Two weeks of these goings on had left Cotton a deeply worried man. To be sure, his convictions about the vital importance of his fight against focal sepsis remained unshaken and, characteristically, he was inclined to attribute the spate of unfavorable publicity to the machinations of his enemies. Yet the scandals now swirling about him were eerily reminiscent of the ones that had brought down his predecessor and allowed Cotton himself to secure the superintendency of the Trenton hospital. Lewis, too, was fighting for his future, and Cotton found it ominous that in the aftermath of Edith Strong's testimony, the commissioner had demanded that he prepare a written response to her charges.

He had counterattacked fiercely, telling Lewis that "at no time was this woman on the surgical ward during the daytime and she could have no knowledge of operative procedures or preparation of patients . . . she either grossly misrepresented the facts, or her statements are those of a person suffering from delusions." At least for the moment, Lewis seemed satisfied, and inclined to accept his claim that "she was not mentally competent."[28] Yet the awkward part was that all the patients she had named had indeed died of complications following abdominal surgery, and all of them within the four months immediately preceding the Bright Committee hearings.

If the barrage of criticism and negative publicity had raised Cotton's blood pressure, events over the course of the next few days were to drive him to the verge of panic. Over the weekend, within the space of forty-eight hours, two women patients were found dead, their bodies a mass of contusions – a situation that prompted their relatives to call loudly for an investigation of alleged brutality on the part of the hospital staff. Worse yet, one of them was the very same Leah Bloom who had been the focus of the committee's most recent hearings, her premonitions of meeting a violent end all too soon proved prescient.

Cotton was beside himself. Panic stricken and close to despair about his future, he summoned the county prosecutor and asked for an inquiry into the deaths. Geraghty was an old ally, and Cotton hoped that somehow such an investigation would keep the politicians at bay and ultimately clear the hospital of any wrong-doing.[29] It was a desperate and probably futile gesture. If last

Wednesday's hearing had been a nightmare, this week's promised to be even worse.

Worse indeed it was – so bad that the mad-doctor himself was driven mad. His behavior before the Bright Committee's Wednesday session grew more erratic and embarrassing by the minute, until he stalked from the room and lost all semblance of contact with reality. In the weeks and months that followed, the Trenton hospital board arranged for its deranged superintendent to remain safely hidden away, first in southern New Jersey and then in Arkansas, and strove, in his absence, to defuse the scandal that threatened to engulf the institution. Cotton's staff, left behind to cope and keep the machinery ticking over, continued pulling teeth, removing tonsils, and extracting the occasional colon. It was obvious, however, that the survival of Cotton's more extensive war on sepsis hung in the balance.

10

Averting a Scandal

As the 1924–5 academic year drew to a close, Adolf Meyer, with considerable relief, was able to leave behind the East-Coast heat and humidity. In late June, he boarded the transcontinental express, and traveled once more to Santa Barbara, where he had been asked to undertake yet another lucrative assessment of the mental state and prospects of Stanley McCormick. His expectations of a pleasant stay at the Riven Rock mansion in Montecito overlooking the Pacific Ocean were rudely interrupted, however, for on June 28 an earthquake hit Santa Barbara, and on his arrival he found the main house badly damaged. Stanley's entourage had been forced to relocate to one of the smaller buildings in the grounds, Meadow House.

Meyer's 1907 diagnosis of Stanley's illness as a form of catatonic schizophrenia had implied an almost hopeless prognosis, and developments over almost two decades seemed amply to have vindicated his judgment. Though at times Stanley had brief periods of lucidity, there were long spells where he was inaccessible, inactive, stuporous, mute. Then there were the episodes when he masturbated openly in front of his nurses, and reacted violently when any attempt was made to stop him; or the occasions when he put his plate on the ground and lapped up his food like a dog. His violent rages and propensity to attack women had led his regular medical attendants to bar all contact with the female of the species. For all the opulence of Riven Rock, with its Moorish architecture and eighty-seven acres of grounds, the mansion and its dependent structures served as no more than a luxurious prison devoted to housing one of the world's great plutocrats. Confined during his worst periods in a room with iron bars on the windows and a metal cage over the balcony, Stanley was a hopeless case. By way of compensation for the long journey to see him, however, Meyer could console himself with fees running into the thousands of dollars from at least one branch of the feuding family.[1]

Leaving behind the Montecito estate in mid-July, Meyer joined his wife in Silver Lake, New Hampshire. Here he had the first inkling of the trouble that the Bright Committee had been stirring up in Trenton. Waiting for him was a letter of July 25 that Phyllis Greenacre had sent from the summer resort where she was staying with her children, at a lake in Clinton County, New York. Enclosed with it was a clipping from the *New York World*. The story acquainted Meyer with perhaps the most explosive allegations the committee had heard, the testimony of Edith Strong, who had spoken of patients being dragged kicking and screaming into the operating theatre, and of the massive mortality associated with abdominal surgery at the hospital. While Greenacre told Meyer that "I do not recall Miss Strong – the nurse referred to, nor anything of the situation involved in her discharge," she confessed that the whole episode "has made me a little uneasy, – and rather relieved that I am not now in Trenton." As for her own report, it "will be quite ready, I think, by the first of September, being practically finished now. When I talked with Dr. Cotton last at the end of June, I told him I should finish the working up of the findings during the summer and he seemed to feel that was quite satisfactory." Her departure from Trenton had thus been "somewhat tentative but entirely pleasant," and she hoped it would not "be necessary for me to go back." "Just at present," she confided, "I should of course prefer not to, unless the need should be urgent."[2]

In mid-August, Meyer replied. Following some pleasantries about her news of "Lake Chautauqua life," he got down to business. "Things at Trenton," he confessed, "look like a cloud threatening to disturb one's peace of mind. I am glad to hear," he continued, "that you intend to travel *around* N.J.!" Under the circumstances, he assured her, "the report will have my first attention so that we may be ready to confer with Dr. Cotton possibly by having him come down to B[altimore]."[3]

By the time Meyer arrived back at Johns Hopkins in September, however, events had taken a distinct turn for the worse. With considerable alarm, he discovered that the Bright Committee had become aware of Greenacre's study – indeed, he was astonished to hear that Cotton himself had revealed its existence in his testimony in early July. Equally bizarrely, immediately after his return, Meyer received a letter from Raycroft asking "whether the study made by Dr. Greenacre is in such shape as to be available for our use in meeting some of [the] baseless charges" emanating from the Bright Committee.[4] As had been arranged at the outset of the study, the hospital authorities had copies of all of Greenacre's findings to date, but, remarkable as it seemed, they had obviously not fully grasped their import.

Meyer, however, was astute enough to realize that at any moment the New Jersey politicians might summon his assistant to testify. If Greenacre revealed what she had uncovered about the therapeutic bankruptcy of Cotton's treatments, he knew the result would be little short of explosive. And if there was one thing he loathed more than scandal,[5] it was politicians poking about in professional matters that did not concern them. Besides, what would become of Cotton, and of the experiment in the treatment of focal sepsis itself, if the politicians got wind of Greenacre's findings? For Meyer remained convinced that the elimination of focal sepsis was an approach that, setting aside Cotton's excesses, might yet prove to have some value.

Meyer's mind was made up. When Greenacre herself returned to Baltimore, she received an urgent summons to his house, where Meyer proceeded to coach her in what to say if and when she was subpoenaed to the witness stand. Somewhat reluctantly, she concurred.

The next day Meyer sent a letter to Raycroft suggesting that the public discussion of Greenacre's findings would not be helpful to his cause. The matter was extremely delicate, and recognizing this reality, Meyer continued, "I went very carefully over the situation with Dr. Greenacre. I feel that our investigation and the investigations of this committee have to be kept apart." Raycroft noted in the margin his approval of this strategy. "Dr. Greenacre," Meyer continued, "has had intimate contact with everything, and tells me she can say that she has not seen any cruelty or neglect of the principle of getting permission for operation from the responsible relatives." Again, Raycroft noted his relief in the margin. "The question whether the operations would have been justified in the light of critical scrutiny of the results is a different matter." This was the crux of the affair, of course, and Raycroft must have by now been concerned. Meyer's next two sentences immediately put his mind at ease, on this front at least: "We can say," Meyer continued, "that neither the time was right nor was the investigation made." Moreover, he and Greenacre had agreed that, if questioned about her findings, she would say that her report "could not be considered finished" – a literally true, if disingenuous, response that Meyer excused by saying that "indeed it could not be considered finished until Dr. Cotton shall have had the opportunity to go over the report with us so as to draw our attention to any points that may have been overlooked."[6] With evident relief, Raycroft scribbled his final "OK" in the margin. Now the hospital authorities could concentrate on undermining the testimony of that parade of mad folk and disgruntled ex-employees without worrying that Greenacre's findings would create a new political explosion.

Raycroft at once wrote back to Meyer to express his gratitude: "I agree that the report of your study of the methods and results of the treatment at the State Hospital should not be involved in the present investigation by the Bright (?) committee. Your suggestion as to Dr. Greenacre's observations on the charges of cruelty and neglect meets all that I had hoped for at this time. I have wired her that I will be glad to meet her at the Trenton Station tomorrow before the Board meeting"[7] – as, indeed, he most assuredly was.

Travelling back to Trenton, Greenacre had a very different reaction to the interview with Meyer.[8] She felt strangely troubled about what she had just been asked to do. Naturally, she did not relish the prospect of being at the center of a storm of publicity in the newspapers. Still, she could not forget all those broken and maimed bodies she was about to mingle with once more, along with the hundreds of deaths that her inquiries had uncovered, the direct result of Cotton's radical and ruthless surgical interventions.

For the first time, too, she had the uneasy sense that Meyer's attitude to her work in New Jersey was somewhat ambivalent. He seemed extraordinarily concerned about preserving Cotton's reputation, and while she could not exactly say that he was indifferent to the fate of the patients, he certainly had not been as appalled as she was about what was going on. If anything, assuming she had understood him properly (and, as usual, she could not be sure, given his characteristically elliptical and apparently contradictory remarks), it was as though Meyer felt that on occasion one should welcome Cotton's sort of fanaticism, since it allowed a more thorough test of the value of a particular approach.[9]

Angrily, she pushed such worries and concerns aside. Her anxieties were surely overdone. And yet, she could not help remembering that Meyer was notorious for protecting his inept associates, even at the expense of the more able. She herself had long felt herself victimized by that foible of his. How else to explain his continued attachment to such people as Ruth Fairbank and Esther Richards?[10] And his abhorrence of scandal, and of washing dirty professional laundry in public was proverbial in Baltimore. Certainly, though, there could be no doubt that when the time came, he would be on her side, and would act decisively to suppress what was clearly a case of medical experimentation run amok. Or so she thought.

Whatever Phyllis Greenacre's worries on this front were, they would have escalated enormously had she been privy to Meyer's correspondence with the principals at Trenton over the following days and weeks. Meyer's letter of reassurance to Raycroft had contained no overt criticism of the massive program of surgical intervention at the hospital, and the operations and dental extractions continued unabated even with the superintendent temporarily *hors de combat*. But if Meyer voiced no apprehensions for the fate of the patients, for his protégé he expressed the most sincere concern: "I am naturally very much distressed over Dr. Cotton's condition. I have not written to him, but shall do so."[11]

The professor was as good as his word. Later that same day, he sent Cotton a solicitous note, expressing his dismay and disgust at how badly the politicians had treated him:

"My dear Dr. Cotton:

On my return from my long absence I heard with great distress and regret the report of your illness and of the great strain that has been put upon you. I hope most sincerely that you are allowing sufficient time for recuperation, and that this terrible habit of our official America to institute public hearings of irresponsible people will in one way or another be handled so that a reasonable perspective and sense of justice gets injected.

In his concluding paragraph, Meyer sought to allay any concerns Cotton might have about Greenacre's investigations: "Dr. Greenacre has nearly finished her report. It will be necessary for us to get together and go over the data before any final conclusion is formulated and offered. I am determined not to let it be mixed together with this public hearing business."[12]

When Greenacre was finally summoned to testify before Bright's committee, her appearance turned out to be thoroughly anticlimactic. The legislators were apparently under the impression that her investigation had reached conclusions generally supportive of Cotton's work (and who could blame them after Cotton himself had offered to pay to complete it?). After she had answered a few perfunctory questions about whether she had personally witnessed cruel treatment of patients or operations undertaken without prior consent, carefully following the instructions Meyer had given her to be as brief and noncommittal as possible, she was quickly excused from the stand.[13]

At this point, Raycroft and his allies finally attempted to strike back against their critics. The Trenton board had spent some weeks feverishly reviewing the assorted charges from former patients, their families, and discharged employees, and putting together a detailed rebuttal of their evidence. Before a packed hearing in the Senate Chamber, Raycroft now sought to place the managers' report before the Bright Committee, only to encounter considerable initial resistance.[14] Bright himself indicated that he and his colleagues objected to receiving written documents in place of oral testimony, and to what he saw as an argumentative rather than a factual response to the charges that had been made.[15] Briefly, it appeared that Raycroft's strategy had failed, and that the committee would resume hearing testimony from yet more hostile witnesses – this time three shackled inmates from the hospital's wing for the criminally insane.

First, however, the legislators adjourned for lunch at the nearby Stacy-Trent Hotel. Out of the public eye, a furious row erupted, as for the first time the committee split on how to proceed. Clifford Powell, the speaker of the House and a longtime Cotton ally, argued that his colleagues were committing "a fatal blunder" by refusing to hear the hospital's side of the case. If they stuck by their earlier decision, "the public would feel that the committee was acting in a highly prejudicial manner." After considerable debate, this view carried the day, though some members of the committee were so angry at the reversal of their previous decision that they boycotted the afternoon session.[16]

Raycroft and his allies now took full advantage of the committee's disarray, and, as he later boasted to Adolf Meyer, succeeded in putting up "so aggressive a defense" that the investigation of the hospital seemed to have been brought to an abrupt conclusion. They had even, "with the aid of Dr. Costill, head of the State Board of Health and Dr. Cotton's physician, succeeded in keeping Dr. Cotton out of the stand without leaving room for suspicion that he was avoiding investigation."[17] The Princeton professor had prepared the ground carefully. First, he had provided a series of detailed sworn affidavits refuting the various charges that had been made, and impugning the motives and competence of the witnesses who had testified.

Some witnesses were former patients, "their testimony characterized by an exaggeration and lack of truthfulness, which is one of the characteristics of the form of insanity from which they suffered." Others who had made allegations against the hospital were apparently well-meaning people, "who had no first-hand information, and whose testimony is unreliable because of their lack of information and understanding of necessary institutional conditions." As for the discharged employees, they were just disgruntled and failed people seeking to take revenge, and consequently were wholly unreliable.[18]

Raycroft claimed that the board's own independent inquiries had demonstrated the fallaciousness of the criticisms that had been advanced. (In reality, here, as elsewhere in their rebuttal, the managers relied almost entirely on documents Cotton had prepared before his breakdown, accepting at face value every claim he made.)[19] Patients, Raycroft insisted, had emphatically *not* been operated on without either their own or their relatives' consent. Nor were the forms of surgery practiced in the hospital in any sense experimental. And as for claims of excessive mortality in the aftermath of the operations, the board had traced all surgeries performed over a seven-year period, July 1918 to July 1925, and could report that "the death rate for all operations was 3.7 percent, and for major operations 8 percent." Such figures reflected some clever juggling of the statistics – the inclusion in the demoninator of 2,957 tonsillectomies, for instance, and of hundreds of enucleations of the cervix and what were delicately referred to as "removals of the seminal vesicles" – and Raycroft's presentation deliberately served to obfuscate the fact that mortality rates from the total and partial colectomies ranged between 30 and 44 percent. But the numbers nonetheless served their purpose, reassuring the Bright Committee that Cotton's interventions were good medical practice, with mortality rates that "would make as good a showing as in any general hospital in the country."[20]

All of this therapeutic activity, moreover, had resulted, Raycroft pointed out, in real economies to the state through the discharge of at least a thousand patients who would have still been confined under the standard regime of custodial care, savings running into the hundreds of thousands if not over a million dollars on the maintenance account alone – and such calculations took no account of the fact that higher discharge rates had obviated the need to construct still more expensive hospital beds. So, far from joining in the chorus of criticism of Cotton, "the Board wishes to go on record with an expression of complete confidence in the Medical Director and his Staff and a sense of pride and satisfaction in the valuable and progressive work that has characterized the transition of this Hospital from a custodial institution to the status of an active, scientific, and effective treatment of insane patients."[21]

Shrewdly, alongside this refutation of the criticisms and accusations levelled at Cotton and the hospital, offered on the board's own authority, Raycroft had also marshalled an impressive battery of medical authorities to speak out on Cotton's behalf. As the *New York Times* informed its readers the next morning, these "eminent physicians and surgeons testified that the New Jersey State Hospital for the Insane was the most progressive institution in the world for the care of the insane, and that the newer method of treating the insane by the removal of focal infection placed the institution in a unique position with respect to hospitals for the mentally ill." Most prominently, Emelius Dudley, for forty years the professor of gynecology at Northwestern University and one of the best-known surgeons in the United States, praised the hospital's pioneering therapeutic regime, and subsequently told reporters that "when the detoxication method was better understood, it would revolutionize 50 percent of the treatment of the insane and that ultimately every hospital in the civilized world would adopt the method of treatment." And Senator Royal Copeland, formerly commissioner of health for New York City, and famous across the United States for his syndicated health advice column "Your Health" (which was published daily in scores of newspapers across the country), then spoke at length of his enormous regard for Cotton's accomplishments.[22]

Long convinced of the merits of the doctrine of focal infection, Copeland had frequently used his advice column to warn of "the perils of pus infection."[23] He now made an impressive witness on the hospital's behalf, claiming to have first-hand acquaintance with its procedures, having observed operations, inspected the wards, and talked with patients, and being thoroughly impressed with the technique of the surgeons, the efficiency of the nurses, and the meticulous care given to all insane patients. Strenuously denying that the surgical work done in the hospital was in any sense experimental, he asserted that no surgical work was performed at Trenton that would not be conducted if the inmate were sane.

Under questioning from the committee, he conceded that in other institutions for the insane, it was not the custom to perform so large a percentage of operations. Immediately, however, he turned the tables on his interrogators: that was precisely what so commended the New Jersey Hospital to him. Whereas in other institutions, patients were admitted and that was generally the end of the active treatment they received, at Trenton the inmates were treated as patients, were the beneficiaries of an exhaustive inquiry into their mental and physical health, and modern treatment was prescribed. Again, when Senator Simpson raised the question of possible brutality in the hospital, he found the witness able to reframe the issue to the hospital's advantage. Where attendants were underpaid, Copeland promptly informed him, a certain amount of harsh treatment was inevitable. In that sense, brutal attendants were not a reflection on the hospital management at all, but rather on parsimonious politicians who did not provide the money needed to recruit suitable staff.

Licking their wounds, the committee ceased trying to challenge Copeland's testimony, and allowed him to finish with a ringing endorsement of Cotton's regime. "The State may well be proud of the hospital," he told them. "I have never seen an institution conducted in a better way. There is every consideration given through the latest medical methods, and we should commend its work in every way possible."[24]

The previous unity of the Bright Committee was now shattered when it came to deciding whether to continue their investigation of the events at the Trenton State Hospital. Raycroft's beautifully orchestrated counterattack had succeeded in virtually every respect. The assault on the motives, qualifications, and character of the witnesses who had provided such lurid testimony about events at the hospital appeared to have reduced the critics' case to rubble, ex-mental patients, unemployed nurses, and vengeful family members weighing lightly in the balance when set against forceful testimony from the head of the student health department at Princeton University and a parade of nationally renowned medical authorities.

As the *Newark Evening News* put it in its editorial on the day following the hearing, "the evidence presented by the board of managers was clear and convincing" and New Jersey "should be proud of what is being accomplished."[25] Its Trenton counterpart was still more emphatic: "Professor Raycroft's statement seems to amply meet and refute the unfortunate revelations of disgruntled former employees and insane witnesses, whose outpourings were given currency by the Bright Committee. Legislative committees should be held accountable for these unwarranted attacks on the good name of those who are honestly endeavoring to serve the people. The usefulness of the Bright Committee seems to be at an end."[26]

Scrambling to distance themselves from what now appeared to be a political embarrassment of major proportions, members of the Bright Committee let the journalists in attendance know that they would go no further into the affairs of the state hospital. The reporter for the *New York Times*, after speaking to some evidently chastened politicians, informed his readers that "most members of the committee are said to be convinced that it was a mistake to permit unsifted charges to go into the record" and planned to direct the inquiry as far away from the topic of mental health as possible, possibly taking up the much safer subject of fire insurance at their next weekly session.[27] So indeed they did, with Senator Simpson, who had previously been in the vanguard of the hospital's critics, using the occasion to extend a standing invitation to Trenton's superintendent to complete the inquiry with his own testimony, "whenever his physical health permitted," and simultaneously rushing to remind the audience that "Dr. Cotton is a friend of mine and I am not prepared at this time to say that there is any room for improvement at the State Hospital."[28]

Cotton had remained holed up in the hospital for more than a month after his breakdown, before being sent off to Spring Lake on September 10 to continue his convalescence. His mental state still precluded any public appearances, though the hospital authorities in their period bulletins about his illness now mentioned only his physical ailments. On September 25, Raycroft wrote to Meyer indicating that Cotton was "greatly improved but he is still far from well" and in need of "an extended vacation."[29] And five days later, the patient himself belatedly responded to his mentor's two-week-old letter.

Clearly relieved at the knowledge that the Bright Committee's investigation was virtually at an end, Cotton spoke bitterly of the whole experience. There had been a monstrous conspiracy among those anxious to discredit him and his work. He had learned that one of his fellow psychiatrists, a man named O'Gorman, formerly of the Bloomingdale Hospital in White Plains, "was the chief conspirator, or at least he informed the Committee that our work was no good – that our statistics were all wrong." In that connection, Cotton continued, he had wished that at some stage during the whole nightmare the report

Greenacre and Meyer were preparing had been available to him: "it would have been quite helpful to have had it; at the same time I knew you were not ready." (Meyer must have winced on reading this. Cotton really *was* out of touch, if that was what he expected from Greenacre's report.) For weeks, Cotton continued, in the absence of such an authoritative endorsement of his work, "they were after me and were using any means to get me. But they have been discredited. The board and Mr. Lewis came to the rescue while I was down and out." As for his health, he spoke only of his physical symptoms: "my heart is acting OK. But it has borne a shock that will always have residuals." In closing, Cotton thanked Meyer profusely for his letter and support ("I appreciate it very much as I have had so few letters from my friends since the trouble began"), and sent "kind regards to you, Mrs. Meyer, and Dr. Greenacre."[30]

However peculiar Cotton's perceptions remained, Meyer hastened to reiterate his support. "Your letter," he informed him, "is a great relief to me. We are glad for you and your family that you are recuperating from your illness and from the strain you have undergone." His protégé had suffered, and had suffered, in Meyer's view, quite unjustly: "It is a terrible way this country has to have . . . legislative investigations that allow the most indiscriminate standards to be thrown out before the public in the most irresponsible and damaging manner." Cotton should concentrate all his energies on ensuring "a complete recuperation." Some time after that, Meyer reiterated, he and Cotton would have "an opportunity to go over the data . . . which Dr. Greenacre has put together, so that you can look into the facts yourself and add your own observations and impressions. But as I say, I do not want any discussion until we shall be able to make it a conjoint report. I shall absolutely refuse to give it to any committee or board before a mutual going over . . . The result has to be constructive and instructive or nothing at all."[31]

It was an assurance that Cotton welcomed. Yet in still another indication that he had not read, or else had not grasped the import of, the reports she had sent him, Cotton informed Meyer that "Dr. Greenacre has certainly been conscientious and capable in her work and we are all perfectly satisfied with what she did." And he rejoiced that "we have triumphed over [the investigating committee]" and should expect no more trouble from that quarter. Still, his tentative attempts to return to work had raised some anxieties, and, "at the Board meeting last night it was decided to send me away for another month as it was not thought wise for me to continue to work in my present condition."[32] It was a decision Meyer heartily endorsed, and only now did he provide a gentle hint that Cotton had misconstrued the nature of Greenacre's findings. Once Cotton was fully better, he wrote, "it will, I feel, be necessary to approach the whole problem without any foregone conclusions, as if it were a totally new issue." Any discrepancies, he hastened to add, were not at all Cotton's fault: "I can readily see that the statistics that were offered you were worked up by someone not rigorously trained, since the foundations for the statistics are not always well-defined and adhered to." Fortunately, though, Dr. Greenacre "has all the data here and put together in such a way that it will be easy to go over it," and for that purpose, Cotton should plan eventually on spending "a full week in our neighborhood."[33]

Gradually, over the next two to three months, Cotton's condition improved, though into the new year he remained unable to resume his hospital duties. Periodically, as autumn turned to winter, he wrote to Meyer about the state of his health, always exuding optimism about his prospects for a full recovery. In late October, he announced, "I am feeling very much better, but still a little overweight." But he had a new reason to be confident about the outlook for the future: he thought the true source of his malady had finally been uncovered, and once the focal point of his troubles was treated, he was certain his recovery would soon be complete: "I found three teeth dead and badly infected. I have had one out and today will have two more extracted."[34]

For some weeks, there was no further communication between the two men. Then, just before Christmas, Cotton wrote again. "I am," he assured Meyer, "very anxious to go over the material with you and get your opinion of the work." At present, however, there was no prospect of fixing a date for the meeting, since despite the fact that "I am getting better all the time, and I am losing weight – which I need to do very much," he was not yet in a position to resume his duties at Trenton, or to review Greenacre's draft report. On the contrary, Cotton informed him, for the past three weeks he had been under the care of Dr. William Turnor Wootton at an establishment for nervous invalids in Hot Springs, Arkansas, where he likely would have to remain until some time after the first of January.[35]

Meyer hastened to reply. "Your letter is a great relief to me. I wondered why I had not heard from you. You were no doubt wise to go where you could have both leisure and opportunity to train down your weight. You owe it to yourself and your family and the rest of us to get yourself in the best possible trim again." As for meeting to discuss the work on focal sepsis, "I hope you will work out your material at your leisure and I wish very much it could be done in conjunction with Dr. Greenacre, whose study and follow-up of a number of cases might be of considerable value. I trust [when you come to Baltimore] you will be able to spend a few days with us so that we may go over Dr. Greenacre's material with some leisure."[36]

It was a prospect Cotton professed to welcome: "I am looking forward to my stay in Baltimore with much pleasure. I shall be very glad to work in conjunction with Dr. Greenacre, whose help I realize will be very beneficial. Mrs. Cotton" – who had remained behind at Trenton to be with the children – "expects to meet me in Baltimore some time next week."[37]

It actually would take a little longer than that. On January 6, en route from Arkansas, Cotton wired Meyer from Chattanooga, Tennessee, "TRIP TO BALTIMORE NECESSARILY DELAYED TILL NEXT WEEK."[38] After seemingly endless delays, however, the meeting between Cotton, Greenacre, and Meyer at last did take place.

11

Showdown

Inevitably, the meeting between Cotton, Meyer, and Greenacre promised to be a fraught affair, for even if Cotton had hitherto managed to misconstrue Greenacre's findings, at Johns Hopkins he would inevitably be forced to confront them. As it turned out, though, in the final weeks before the meeting, it seems finally to have dawned on Cotton that Greenacre's report was profoundly critical of his work. The first indication that his view of situation had changed came when he refused his mentor's hospitality: Meyer had invited his old student to stay with him and Mrs. Meyer while he was in Baltimore, but Cotton would have none of it. Signalling his intentions from the outset, "Dr. Cotton had not let me know definitely of his arrival on Tuesday and had gone to the Emerson Hotel instead of notifying me and coming to the house. Under the circumstances," Meyer acknowledged, "it may have been for the best."[1] Evidently prepared for battle, Cotton had brought his wife along for emotional support.

After all the delays and postponements, the lack of forewarning that Cotton would actually show up meant that Meyer initially had some difficulty freeing up time for the three of them to meet. Cotton, as Meyer reported to Raycroft, "came to my rounds Wednesday forenoon. In the afternoon all my time was taken up and I asked him to come and see me Thursday forenoon."[2] It was then, on January 14, that the two sides eventually managed to begin their discussion of the impact of Cotton's assault on focal sepsis. After months of delay, it appeared that a final reckoning was at hand.

It was Meyer, oddly enough, who seemed the most nervous and ill-at-ease at the prospect. Decades after the event, Phyllis Greenacre recalled with some bitterness that he uncharacteristically seemed unable to control the proceedings.[3] Where Meyer's Hopkins associates were invariably deferential, clearly cowed by his icy demeanour, afraid even to speak unless spoken to, Cotton's belligerence was evident from the outset. Faced by an aggressive and angry younger man, Meyer visibly recoiled and seemed at something of a loss. Unwilling to confront

Cotton directly, he instead turned the proceedings over to his female assistant, asking Greenacre to summarize her findings.

Greenacre began to do so, describing how she had gone about selecting her cases, and detailing how she had generated the data on which her report was based. Cotton glared and began to interrupt, bluster and fume, and take issue with even the most minor detail. And Meyer, for the most part, sat passively taking notes, occasionally intervening feebly to urge Cotton to deal with "facts," not statistics – a request Cotton contemptuously brushed aside. His normally courtly Southern manners in the presence of a lady vanished as he turned upon a young woman he now saw as his enemy, someone seeking to undermine his life's work.

But if Cotton thought he could intimidate Greenacre into silence, he was badly mistaken. Early on in her career at Hopkins, a young hot-shot prosecutor had made a similar mistake. Greenacre had been called upon to testify in a trial about the mental status of the defendant. Seeing a seemingly shy and diffident young woman, and playing to the prejudices of a conservative Baltimore jury suspicious of the very notion of a female physician, the lawyer had sought to humiliate and discredit her claims to expertise. Could she, he asked scornfully, tell him how many bones made up the human skeleton? Indeed she could not, came the swift response, but she could name them all. And so she began to do, moving from head to toe. The tables turned, it was the overbearing lawyer who found himself humiliated, and he was forced to ask her to stop.[4] So, too, with Cotton. If Meyer was nonplussed, his younger assistant refused to be intimidated.

Relentlessly, and despite all attempts to throw her off stride, she began to review her findings, beginning with a sequence of a hundred consecutive cases selected from the Trenton records from July 1920 onwards. As Meyer subsequently informed Raycroft,

> To my regret we became at once confronted with this attitude: that our 100 cases would not be representative and that our statistics were not to be compared with his, which were based on admissions and discharges; that to be fair we should have to compare our series with a similar series of 10 years ago giving us the rate of 'spontaneous recoveries without treatment.' Any suggestions that there might have been any difficulty in the statistical material furnished him [by his staff], yielding the 85% [cure rate], where we had but 20 . . . was peremptorily turned down.[5]

Several confrontational hours later, the meeting broke off, and the participants adjourned until Friday afternoon. Again, when they reassembled, Cotton challenged Greenacre's statistics: "Dr. Cotton said he knew now where our mistake lay. It was the calculation by admissions and discharges which was the only way that could be used in comparing the work of different hospitals." Greenacre sought to force him to see the fallaciousness of his arguments by presenting him with a re-analysis of the data in his own publications, and by showing him "that the figures given in one of his papers did not yield" the sorts of cure rates he claimed. Cotton refused to acknowledge her point, and off they went again, arguing fiercely over minutiae. Cotton insisted that certain cases had been misclassified, and that he knew of instances where her assessment of individual cases was unduly pessimistic. At one point, Greenacre confessed that "she had made a slight error in about five cases and had figured out 59.6% rec[overed] and imp[roved]. Dr. Cotton immediately tried to raise it to 65% and then said 'well figure it out!' It yielded about 60.1%." Still, he insisted that such small acknowledged errors and corrections vitiated the value of her conclusions.[6]

Meyer, meanwhile, sat making pencil notes of the proceedings on index cards in his compulsively neat script. Greenacre remembered him only occasionally intervening to remonstrate or ineffectually to urge Cotton to recognize that he was in error. At one point, he pointed out that Cotton's means of calculating his statistics were "quite different from the practice at other hospitals" and added that "I feel I was able to make him recognize that." But only for a moment – soon Cotton was off on a different tangent, "and [he] always comes back to the 85% figure."[7] Later still, "Dr. Greenacre showed him that the figures given in one of his papers did not yield that amount."[8] But again, he immediately raised a different set of issues. Whatever Greenacre and Meyer tried, nothing seemed to get resolved. Finally, after a long and fruitless session, Meyer confessed that "when I had to leave we had practically not got any further, and adjourned till Saturday at 10, when we had a brief interview, since I had to go to a committee meeting in Washington."[9]

Cotton appeared as truculent and unyielding as ever. At one point, pressed to acknowledge discrepancies in his data, he "remarked 'You are not going to get me on these statistics' etc. To us both he had said he would have to look up his material at Trenton." At times, in his anger, he seemed incoherent and verging on the irrational. When Meyer suggested that changes in "administrative policy" might have increased discharges without an underlying increase in the cure rate, he shot back that administrative policy "meant nothing, because there were among the patients in the hospital many that they *cured* by simple extractions and tonsillectomies."[10] With Meyer anxious to leave, "Dr. Cotton then was shown that the figures given the National Committee for Mental

Hygiene for 1922 only yielded 60% [cured and improved]. But there again we were met with an explanation: that his figures represented the data as obtained in 1925 from the social workers' reports. When I said this would be alright but did not make the figures comparable any longer with the other hospital reports . . . and did not explain the discrepancies, we evidently came to the end of the discussion."[11] Realizing that matters were close to an impasse, Meyer "appealed to him to put things more in the form of questions, that he had always taken that attitude before, and that we both wanted to be guided by facts."[12]

But Cotton continued to be obdurate, and the normally intimidating Meyer found that on this occasion he was on the receiving end of the intimidation. Curiously, his response was to act as though he was the supplicant. Unmoved by all Meyer's efforts at diplomacy, "[Dr. Cotton] left the clinic without saying goodbye. I took him to the Emerson [Hotel] in my taxi, almost against his will and left obviously very preoccupied."[13]

With Meyer in Washington and unavailable to meet on the Sunday, it seemed that both sides would have a day's respite. In his private notes, Meyer recorded that ,"we adjourned to Monday at 2 P.M., because Dr. G[reenacre] did not wish to have the interview alone"[14] – a refusal he ought surely to have understood. In the event, though, the Monday meeting never took place. Having pondered the situation overnight, the furious Cotton decided to bring matters to an

26 *Adolf Meyer, displaying the gaze that emasculated so many of his students.*

immediate halt. As Meyer informed Raycroft some hours later, "Dr. Cotton just telephoned (Sunday morning) that on account of Mrs. Cotton's not feeling well, they had decided not to return, and that he would let me know what the Board would request him to do."[15]

In his own account of the three days of confrontation, Cotton made clear that his wife's "illness" was purely diplomatic. Reflecting on the Saturday night about what had occurred, "I became convinced that it was futile for me alone to combat the unfavorable impression that Dr. Greenacre had given Dr. Meyer . . . I considered it futile to argue these matters and notified Dr. Meyer that I was coming home to take the matter up with the Board and any further conferences would be decided according to their wishes."[16]

Meyer's reaction to the transparent snub was remarkably complaisant. In his account of the proceedings written to Raycroft, when one might have expected that the insult and the refusal to confront the implications of Greenacre's findings should have been foremost in his mind, he instead sought to explain, or explain away, Cotton's behavior: "A combination of human limitations with a tremendous conviction of the achievement of the work done, and the feeling that nobody should 'get him'! He needs some time now, and I hope my appeals to take an inquiring attitude since no defense was needed may yet take root." In the meantime, the professor felt impotent and unable to see any clear way forward: "I can think of various possibilities but of nothing specific to do until I shall learn more definitely what Dr. Cotton's attitude is." But he confessed he had no clue when that might be, given the terms on which he and his protégé had parted. Plaintively, he implored Raycroft to keep him informed: "Since I may not hear from [Dr. Cotton], would you kindly let me know his reaction and what would seem to you the best next steps? How," he wondered feebly, "can I help?"[17]

To this paralysis of will there was only a single exception, an absolute insistence that no word of Greenacre's findings should reach the outside world: "One thing is certain. The report has to be kept out of the Legislative Committee. It is 'not yet finished' until it will be signed by both Dr. Cotton and ourselves."[18]

And it was not just the politicians and the laity from whom Meyer was determined to keep Greenacre's findings a secret, unless and until agreement could be reached with Cotton. A few weeks after the confrontation in Baltimore, Meyer received a letter from Dr. Augustus Knight. Knight was the medical director of the Metropolitan Life Insurance Company in New York, but he also served on the board of managers of the New Jersey's other state mental hospital at Greystone Park. The Greystone authorities had long been skeptical of

Cotton's claims, and resented the favored status their southern rival enjoyed with the state's politicians. Having heard of Greenacre's study, and got wind that it was critical of Trenton, Knight wanted to know of Meyer,

> if you do not think it fair and best to let us see Dr. Greenacre's report at this time. I can tell you already what we may more than suspect the reactions in Trenton will be [among the legislature and the state bureaucracy], for when I was talking with the Department of Institutions and Agencies about a different matter and said something about Dr. Meyer's [*sic*] report, the immediate reply was, 'Well, Dr. Knight, it is too bad that they sent the wrong person to do that work.' I asked why, and the answer was, 'Well she doesn't know anything about figures anyway. We have already had our statistician at work on it and have proven that the figures and the tabulations are all wrong and that she doesn't know anything about figuring.[19]

Such comments, of course, only served in Knight's eyes to confirm the rumors that the report was highly critical of Cotton, and he reported that "I immediately told the Acting Commissioner that this matter should be handled in as kindly a way as possible for Doctor Cotton but that we must all do what was fair and right. I do feel, however, that if we could see the report or if we knew just what is in it, we could then be sure of being correct in our own conclusions and in our own actions which might be guided by Dr. Greenacre's findings – especially in view of the adverse criticism that they are beginning to raise about her report in advance of its publication."[20] Already rebuffed by Commissioner Ellis, Knight obviously hoped that Meyer would be more willing to share what he had learned.

But he found himself promptly turned aside for a second time. Clearly angry about the leaks, Meyer responded testily that, "I regret most sincerely that there should be any consideration of the study of Dr. Cotton's material until there shall be a reasonable agreement and understanding concerning the actual cases that have been studied, and after that a discussion of the statistical methods to be used." Such consensus had not yet been reached. "I am grateful to you," Meyer continued icily, "for the light thrown on the attitude of the acting commissioner, but I feel sure that it would be exceedingly unwise to let such a difficult task get out of our own hands before the foundations are adequately taken care of. I do not see anything gained in hurrying beyond our facts." And lest Knight have any notion of making a public issue of the report, Meyer warned him that, "I cannot say anything further until I hear again from Dr. Cotton, and I should appreciate your keeping our communications *confidential*; because I know that any discussion thereof would only complicate things, although there is really absolutely nothing to be hidden about it."[21]

Days later, Meyer heard from D. M. Baillie, a Canadian physician based in Victoria, British Columbia, who was seeking to lobby the Provincial government about "the close relation of focal, and particularly of oral sepsis to mental derangements in various forms." Baillie had been impressed by Meyer's foreword to Cotton's lectures on *The Defective Delinquent and Insane*, and sought "to amplify and corroborate the evidence of my personal experience by reference to the valuable work you have carried on in this connection over a long period, if you are good enough to assist me thus to intensify the weight of the material I shall present."[22] Meyer's response was, to be sure, distinctly tepid:

> I am afraid I cannot give you as encouraging a statement with regard to focal infections and their importance as the book of Dr. Cotton promises. I am not in a position to give you a full account of our own investigations on this question as yet, but should certainly insist that while it is always wise to make provision for the best possible care of the physical conditions of the patients, it is also eminently important to have competent students of human problems of adaptation and provisions for adjustment and re-education, and a thorough study and care of the patients . . . My own impression, is that the great increase of attention to the patients brought about by the surgical interests is to a large extent responsible for the favorable results of Dr. Cotton, and the direct and immediate advantage of the operations has to be evaluated at a more moderate figure than he puts forth.

None of which, he hastened to add, should be interpreted as a shot at Cotton, for "I have a great deal of respect for his energy and determination and outlook."[23]

Only someone fully acquainted with the details of Greenacre's meticulous work could understand the full extent to which Meyer's remarks were economical with the truth. Cotton's constant interruptions, his bullying, his attempts to challenge Greenacre at every turn, had kept the three-day conference on her findings from examining her detailed conclusions about the effects of his treatment. But her typed report, of which both Meyer and Cotton possessed copies, was uncompromising and unambiguous in its findings, and supported by voluminous case records and other supporting documentation. Alongside forty-six pages of data analysis and conclusions, Greenacre supplied four bound volumes of case notes, and a number of detailed appendices. Taken together, these materials amounted to a devastating commentary on Cotton's activities.

Greenacre's analysis began with a close look at three overlapping groups of patients admitted in the period from July 1, 1920, to November 20, 1920. In choosing when to initiate her study, she had decided "to select a period allowing the longest possible time to elapse since treatment. The work on focal infections was begun in 1917–1918, but was not then generally enough applied and had not reached a stage of development of technique so that the first material was thoroughly representative. By 1920, however, the work was well under way, and the recovery rate for functional cases was figured [by Cotton] at 85%."[24] The three groups of patients from 1920 consisted (or were supposed to consist) of the first 100 consecutive admissions from July 1, regardless of diagnosis; the first 100 cases of "functional" psychosis, as Cotton defined the term ("to include all patients diagnosed with manic-depressive insanity, dementia praecox, paranoid conditions, schizophrenia, toxic psychosis – confused state, all depressions, psychasthenia, hysteria"); and all patients admitted in this period who had received the full range of detoxification therapies their individual conditions were thought to require (which amounted to some 62 patients).[25]

In the course of her work, but too late to revert to her original plan, Greenacre realized that the hospital statistician, Mrs. Rue, had attempted to load the dice in her former psychiatrist and superior's favor by manipulating the composition of the second of these groups. What was supposed to be the first 100 consecutive admissions of functional cases was in fact a carefully selected subset, chosen from a total of 220 admissions. "That in this selection of functional cases there has been a tendency toward the selection of favorable cases is indicated by a comparison of the death percentage and the percentage of patients still remaining at Trenton [State Hospital] in the selected group with similar percentages in the *first* 100 functional cases admitted after July 1, 1920 . . . In the latter, the death percentage is 26 instead of 15, and the percentage remaining at Trenton is 17 instead of 10."[26] Analysis of results in this group therefore needed to proceed cautiously, bearing in mind this deliberate bias that had been introduced into the study.

Looking at the first group of 100 admissions, Greenacre found that 60 of these were "functional" psychotics, the remaining 40 being "organic" cases of various sorts – alcoholics, those suffering from tertiary syphilis, epileptics, and the like. Though she provided data on both groups of patients, it was the functional cases Cotton claimed to cure with his surgical interventions, so for the most part she focused on them. Only 7, or 11.67 percent could be classified as recovered, with a further 5 "improved." Most were either dead (16, or 26.67

percent) or unimproved and still in a mental hospital (18, or 30 percent). Moreover, among the handful of recoveries, most had had either minimal or no treatment for possible focal sepsis – only two patients having "a full quota of treatment, all desired therapeutic measures being carried out," and both of these having a prior history of psychosis and spontaneous recovery. On the other hand, among these 60 patients, "there was one death from suicide . . .; six deaths due directly to operative procedure . . .; two deaths . . . where operation was a contributing but not immediate cause of death; and seven deaths from unrelated causes."[27]

Among the second group (the biased selection of 100 functional cases produced by the hospital statistician), results were somewhat better, with 32 of the patients "recovered and living normal, active lives." Even adding the eight patients Greenacre was unable to locate, and presuming they had all recovered, the results were a far cry from the 85 percent cure rate Cotton repeatedly advertised that he had achieved. Half of the patients even in this select group were either unimproved (35) or dead (15). And further analysis of the data revealed yet more problems for Cotton's claims, for when the patterns of treatment and recovery were examined more closely, "*the results in the selected 'functional' group appear somewhat paradoxical in that among the recovered patients there is the highest proportion of untreated and incompletely treated patients, while among the unimproved patients there is the highest proportion (9/35) of completely treated patients, except among the dead, – where the proportion of thoroughly treated rises to 7/15 or nearly 50%.*"[28]

Turning in the last part of this section of her report to the 62 patients "who have had complete treatment including abdominal operation, irrespective of the diagnostic grouping," Greenacre documented only 5 recoveries (8 percent), with a further "three patients [who] are improved but still show psychotic symptoms." There were 26 unimproved (41.9 percent) and 27 (43.5 percent) dead, one patient not being located. Across all three groups, she concluded, "*the lowest recovery rate and the highest death rate occurs among the functional cases who have been thoroughly treated . . . the least treatment was found in the recovered cases and the most thorough treatment in the unimproved and dead groups.*"[29]

Death was indeed not just more common among those operated upon, but all too often the direct sequel of the surgery. Of the 62 patients subjected to abdominal surgery, 7 died from post-operative shock, 8 from post-operative peritonitis, 3 others from immediate post-operative complications, and 5 more from conditions associated with "post-operative diarrhea, and rapidly progressing to death." In 2 cases, the cause of death was unknown, and in 2 more, death came some months after the operation from apparently unrelated causes.[30]

Determined to examine every possibility, Greenacre argued that, even given these negative results,

> it might be possible that a drastic treatment entailing a high death rate, might still be very effective in the case of the patients who survive, – in which case the treatment should not be wholly condemned, but every effort made to reduce the mortality. When, however, we analyze the recovery rate among the survivors of the thoroughly treated functional group . . . we find that of the 31 surviving patients with functional psychoses, five (16.1%) recovered; three (9.7%) improved; three (9.7%) are unimproved but at large, and nineteen (61.2%) are unimproved and in hospitals. Consequently, it must be concluded that *thorough treatment, including abdominal operation, is not only dangerous to life, but ineffective in the cases of those who survive.*"[31]

The surgery had continued, of course, during the many months that Greenacre had worked at Trenton. Indeed, she noted that, "the vast extent of the operative work undertaken is apparent in the facts that during the period October 1, 1924, to January 1, 1925, fifty-four different patients were operated on." Greenacre had seized the opportunity to observe the surgery and its sequelae. These fifty-four patients had a wide variety of operations, many of them being subjected to several different interventions. There were 45 appendectomies and 45 underwent Lane's operation, designed to release adhesions in the colon; 27 operations on the small intestine and stomach; 9 removals of ovaries and fallopian tubes; 3 hysterectomies; 4 colectomies; and a variety of other operations, from the removal of the spleen to the removal of hemorrhoids.[32] In these cases, she was able to observe the patients in the aftermath of the surgery, and she noted that,

> The immediate effect of the operation is often very startling, in that a patient who has previously been excited, resistive or even combative often becomes quiet and relatively cooperative. The appearance and atmosphere of the ward for the convalescent operative patients really resembled much more closely the ward of a general hospital than that of a psychiatric institution. The patients appeared remarkably alert and answered questions which were limited to facts concerning their recent operations, usually relevantly and quite promptly. Only occasionally I saw post-operative patients so disturbed and excited that I felt the combination of excitement and operation was a serious menace to the patient.[33]

Obviously, this "almost instantaneously quieting effect" of the surgery might encourage a positive assessment of the results of the treatment, but the data on outcomes 5 to 8 months later should have proved quite sobering: 1 in 6 of the patients operated upon died (a lower death rate than that characteristic of the early 1920s, but still extremely high); and a further 40 percent remained hospitalized.[34] Once again, detailed examination of each individual case led to the stark conclusion that, "*there is practically no evidence of positive results obtained by detoxication methods.*"[35]

With massive documentation to back her findings, and nearly 18 months of meticulous work providing the basis for her assessment, Greenacre felt that she had decisively shown the fallacy of Cotton's claims. Not only were his published data wholly incompatible with what her own analysis had shown to be the case, but it was also clear that his interventions were associated with appallingly high (if recently diminished) mortality rates, and left the survivors mangled and disfigured without any offsetting therapeutic advantages. As Meyer's trusted assistant for a decade, and having consulted closely with him on the study as it progressed, she naturally expected that such unambiguously negative findings would produce a swift and decisive response from her superior. Eight years of experimentation that had produced hundreds of deaths and thousands of mangled bodies ought surely now to be at an end.

12

Playing for Time

For Meyer, during the days and weeks immediately following the disastrous Baltimore meeting, the hope persisted that Cotton could somehow be brought to see the error of his ways. The pressing issue was how to accomplish this delicate task. Casting about for some means of breaching Cotton's defenses, he made the odd decision to attempt to enlist Cotton's wife to the cause.

The day after Henry and Delha Cotton had abruptly departed for Trenton, Meyer sent Mrs. Cotton a long letter imploring her to use her influence with her husband to reconsider his position. He was "exceedingly sorry," he began, that "Dr. Cotton did not inform me when you would arrive" and that "on Thursday it was evidently too late to win you to stay at the house. It soon became clear to me that Dr. Cotton found it difficult to accept the facts we had to discuss and even more so on Friday and Saturday. I was all the more sorry then that my desire to see you both on Sunday [evening] came to naught. I do feel that you could have helped us greatly and it might have been easier to explain the situation *together.*" As it was, he was forced to confess that "unfortunately I have been wholly unable to reconcile Dr. Cotton to a mutual consideration of the facts as found."

Before trying to enlist Mrs. Cotton's help, he hastened to assure her that Greenacre's findings would, for the time being, remain under wraps: "our report will be treated as 'not finished' as long as the Bright Committee is in existence and as long as there is any hope that it can become helpful to Dr. Cotton." For the latter to happen, her husband must somehow be coaxed "to take an inquiring attitude and not one of defense" – though Meyer freely confessed that his own efforts to this end had been a miserable failure. For him, this outcome was a puzzle: "It is inconceivable to me that I ever should get into a situation where I would not rather submit my case to the fair judgment of true and thoughtful friends than stick to a conclusion of my own. If I have to modify a claim I made, and explain a statement, I should infinitely rather take the opportunity myself than have it done by others." Perhaps, he implied, Mrs. Cotton might have more success than he.

The problem, it went without saying, was not a lack of good faith on Cotton's part.

> No one who knows him could possibly doubt his integrity and sincerity. The discrepancies are due to his tremendous energy and zeal but insufficient scrutiny given to the statistics handed to him, and inadequate time and attention to the criticisms and suggestions of his friends. When Dr. Cotton put me to the difficult task of writing the preface to his book – which I feared would be misinterpreted as a testimonial of unconditional approval –, he should have heeded the spirit of it and should have taken pains to inquire and to look at the facts from all sides. Now what can we do?

Still Meyer sought to put the best possible face on the situation. "Dr. Cotton's enthusiasm was a great risk but also a great *boon* to his patients." (Quite how this might have been so was left unanalyzed. Instead, he hurried on.) "The problem now is to take stock and to review the facts, and to use the most critical but also the most constructively minded methods in doing so. I doubt there will ever again be such a crusade against focal infections because the risks are too great and the results only to a small extent due to surgery. That small extent we will have to learn to pick out. It was all done in good faith and it must not pass without thorough study . . . This is," he reminded her, "such a vital matter. It means the life of many a patient, and it means the neglect of many other methods." Though her husband refused as yet to acknowledge it, "the statistics [he relied upon] are misleading; there is no reason to be sensitive about that; much of it [*sic*] was done by others and it is the method used in many state hospitals and one that should be replaced by a correct scheme." In closing, Meyer hoped "that you are not being taxed too much by this inevitable strain" and urged her to help Cotton to "feel the worthwhileness and also the fairness and sincerity and the necessity of doing all that is possible in teaming on this issue. I remember what he said of his father's firmness. I also know Dr. Cotton's own devotion to the best ideals. It is a hard pull. But it is so important!"[1]

If Meyer harbored hopes that his appeal would fall upon receptive ears, they must have been dashed by the letter he soon received in reply. Seeking to excuse their refusal of the professor's hospitality, Delha Cotton begged to reassure him that it reflected not an implied hostility or a determination to do battle, but a settled refusal on her own part not to allow "myself the pleasure of staying one night in the home of any friend where there were small children," as well as "the feeling on Dr. Cotton's part that were we with you he would be taking too much of your time, at a time when you were particularly busy." It is thus "unfortunate that we may have seemed unfriendly when we mean only to be friendly in the truest sense."

The social niceties observed, she moved directly to "the work of going over the report," and immediately reproached Meyer for the way he had proceeded. "I believe," she informed him, "that [the situation] would have progressed and something good would have been accomplished had the conference been alone between you and my husband. It was the presence of a third person that made the situation what it was, I think." Her rebuke now grew fiercer: "After his years of experience and tremendous labors – you could not expect him to be told by a young woman of limited experience that his work was all wrong – and that he did his patients more harm than good – without developing on his part an atti-tude of defense. You – by yourself," she continued "– would never have made such a statement."

Unwilling to endure such an obviously unsatisfactory situation, "we came home – not with any idea of being unwilling to go farther or of closing the matter but because he thought he would like to talk it over with Dr. Raycroft and I thought a little recess would be for the best. I do not think you feel in a hurry and time does so much – bit by bit progress may be made."

As now became apparent, for Delha quite as much as Henry, it was unlikely that that "progress" would involve any substantial reassessment of long-held beliefs. "Dr. Cotton's work is the most important thing in life to him. Who knows that as well as I? It is his *misfortune* that it has been so. Looking over it all and knowing the price paid – it has been a big price in more ways than one, still – I see the gain to the cause. On many sides and from many sources one sees that the physical care of the patient being given more attention and whether he gets the credit for it or not – that has been brought about by his work."

Resolutely, Mrs. Cotton testified to her own continued faith, a faith that had been tested, and for which she had made direct and major sacrifices. "Though he and I differ many times as to ways and means – even to the point of bitter-ness – I do believe in the value to the patient of detoxication. I cannot help believing – having followed every step of the way and having seen in myself – my children and my friends – aside from patients – the happy results." (Her allusion here, whether Meyer realized it or not, was to the prophylactic sacrifice of her own and her children's teeth, to secure their own mental stability.)

There was, she confessed, one aspect of her husband's work from which even she had at times shrunk in horror: "In regards to the colon removals – you know that this was long a source of great distress to me and a topic on which my husband and I were unable to speak." (Left unspoken was the matter of whether her dissent on this point reflected the massive patient mortality from this surgery, or a more specific reaction centering around Henry's insistence on subjecting his younger son, Adolph Meyer Cotton, to one of these operations, a surgery he had survived.) "But," she continued, I respected his attitude and lived in hope and now my hopes have been rewarded and I see him learning new methods and ways of treating the colon – by physiotherapy etc. – so that only in extreme cases will he in future resort to its removal. His eagerness to go always on and try new ways wins my admiration. For this reason it seems to me any report made could not be final. There is still so much to be done."

As to the silly squabble over "statistics – the discrepancy it seems," she blithely commented, "was due to the fact that they were not made by the same method and therefore should not be compared. He would be perfectly willing to accept the figures obtained by your method provided they were compared with figures computed on the same basis." And to that end, since his return to Trenton, Cotton had been busy consulting with "a statistician from the State House ... [and] with Dean Eisenhart, assistant head of the Mathematics department of Princeton. Dr. Cotton will himself write you of all this – I only speak of it to show you that he also desires facts." Sending "warm regards from us both to you and Mrs. Meyer" and assuring him that "things do work out,"Delha Cotton left Meyer to contemplate what further steps were now open to him.[2]

Remarkably, given what was ordinarily Meyer's strong sense of hierarchy and of the respect due his rank, along with Delha Cotton's lack of any semblance of medical background or qualifications to comment on the issues at hand, neither the tone nor the content of her letter seems to have provoked him. To the contrary, he wrote back to her that, "your good letter expresses what I hoped it would" and criticized only her "overscrupulous[ness] in not accepting Mrs. Meyer's sincere invitation" to stay with them. Moreover, so far from objecting to being drawn into a debate over the merits of Cotton's work with a lay person, Meyer was immediately on the defensive: "You ... put your finger on a point that complicated matters. I know Dr. Greenacre so well with over nine years of working together that I may well be forgiven" for inviting her to such a meeting. Apologetically, he explained that "her presence carried no other meaning but that I wanted her to be there to explain her findings which she did without any derogatory comments. She has no doubt," he continued soothingly,

> about Dr. Cotton's earnestness and devotion to his work. If her data led to
> bad results she was and is quite ready to be shown. The unfortunate part

came through the fact that we could not accept the basis of the calculation of statistics by discharge and admissions which Dr. Cotton claimed was calculated in all hospitals but which in reality he calculated with the records secured by 1925 which *we* also did for our 100 cases, but which no other hospital does. Anyhow the point is not comparisons of statistics but a dispassionate study of a definite series of cases accepted from Mrs. Rue as consecutive whereas they proved really to be selected according to an unintelligible principle probably a special way of record-keeping that was unfortunately not discovered till later in the inquiry otherwise it would have been corrected.[3]

Delha Cotton's letter had referred to a new series of cases dating back to 1912, which her husband had already assembled to provide a baseline cure rate prior to the decision to excise focal sepsis surgically. Meyer, referring to them in passing, saw them as "really showing a high rate of results in harmony with Dr. Cotton's keen interest in his patients even before the operative period." He was, he assured her,

intensely eager to know which cases are toxic and how. I deplore that there is in the main a very conservative attitude at Hopkins. It was for this reason that I felt the question should be studied only with Dr. Cotton's patients with their full quota of work. If we both can get a basis for our inquiry without any feeling of need of defense or comparisons before we have controlled the facts and their weight, I know we can get a far-reaching agreement. We may then take up comparisons with other methods and times and places. I cannot disregard the greatly increased attention all the patients get since operations are performed. We shall therefore have to be very particular about our interpretations. However it be, nobody will gainsay Dr. Cotton's merits and nobody will fail to admire his devotion.[4]

Just as Meyer had been largely passive in person in the face of Henry Cotton's bluster and blunt refusal to accept Phyllis Greenacre's findings, so too his response to Delha Cotton's insistence on her husband's rectitude and the value of his work was to hedge and apologize, to prevaricate and to present himself as sympathetic to Henry and his work. Greenacre had been deeply unhappy at how little overt support Meyer had offered her in what had been a tense and thoroughly unpleasant three-day confrontation. Unbeknownst to her, the professor showed himself equally unable or unwilling to provide an unambiguous and forthright endorsement of her work in private correspondence. And within days, encouraged by his disingenuous words, Delha Cotton had contacted Greenacre with the extraordinary suggestion that she alter her report, removing the material that was critical of Cotton's surgical work. Astonished at what she regarded as a bizarre and wildly unethical notion, Greenacre by contrast did not hesitate to reject the approach on the spot, making clear to a woman she saw as blinded by ambition to see her husband famous just how improper her request had been. Not that Delha Cotton seemed abashed by her frosty reproof: for years afterwards, she would send her friendly greetings and notes, as though they had parted on the best of terms.[5]

If Meyer was unable or unwilling to confront either of the Cottons directly about the appalling state of affairs revealed by Greenacre's meticulous work, in his correspondence with Raycroft, he was episodically more inclined to press the issue. Raycroft wrote to him from Princeton on January 25, just over a week after Cotton had stormed out of the Baltimore meetings, to give Meyer some sense of the superintendent's state of mind. Cotton, he informed Meyer, had, in the course of their brief conversation, supplied him with his own typewritten account of the confrontation.[6] One complication had vanished: "the Bright Committee is no longer in existence so that we need not concern ourselves further with that phase of the situation." But on other fronts, Raycroft confessed, "I have not been able to find an answer to the situation."[7]

Raycroft, like Meyer, aimed "to find a formula which will harmonize two positions that seem now to be pretty divergent. In the meantime I have told Dr. Cotton that the matter was in no shape to present to the Board, and for that matter to anyone else, until we have had an opportunity to consider further a basis for agreement between Dr. Greenacre's report and Dr. Cottons [*sic*] position."[8] It was, though neither man seemed willing to acknowledge as much, a formula that guaranteed stalemate.

Cotton's account of the Baltimore meetings, which Raycroft claimed he had "looked . . . over with a good deal of care,"[9] would have struck most neutral observers as at once incoherent and unambiguous. No one who read it could have any doubt that Cotton utterly rejected all criticism of his work and remained as convinced as ever of the link between focal sepsis and madness. Greenacre's report, he insisted repeatedly, was "very unfair, illogical, and prejudiced," full of "erroneous, illogical reasoning."[10] Repeatedly, he attacked her statistics. When she reported that only 20 percent of the 60 "functional" cases in her first group of 100 patients had recovered, a percentage she and Meyer "considered to be very low," Cotton observed that this result "would be expected by the method adopted."[11] Quite what was meant by this statement, he left to the reader's imagination. As for her complaint that, in compiling a second group of 100 patients, the hospital statistician had not given her 100 consecutive cases to examine, as promised, but had carefully selected that number from a larger group of 220 admissions, "my comment was that if Dr. Greenacre had not received proper cases the time to mention that fact was at the beginning of the survey so this matter could be corrected at once"[12] – a response that conveniently overlooked the fact that the subterfuge had not come to light until months after she had begun her work.

Throughout the pages that followed, Cotton unselfconsciously placed on view his peculiar means of calculating his results, reiterating again and again that the recovery rate from his treatments demonstrated their value. If Greenacre's follow-up work showed that only "32 [of her second group of 100 functional cases] had recovered, 8 had improved, and 8 were not located," Cotton insisted (and claimed that he had received Meyer's agreement) that 4 of the 8 patients who could not be found "could be put in the recovered list," and then by adding in a further 8 patients who were listed as "improved," he claimed that "48 cases or 48% of the 100 cases" should now be counted as recovered. Even these results were apparently a far cry from the rates he repeatedly claimed in print that he had achieved. But, on this point, Cotton took umbrage at the idea that "our alleged 85% recovery rate . . . would mean that 85 out of every 100 cases admitted [were] recovered or improved" (another elision of the distinction between recovery and a wholly undefined "improvement"). He conceded that when initially confronted on the issue, "this statement seemed plausible and logical," but "only after I reached home and considered the matter more carefully did I see that 48 recovered and improved cases out of 100 consecutive ones could not be compared with the 85% rate which was merely the ratio of discharged recoveries to admissions for a year and that therefore they [Greenacre and Meyer] had not proved that 85% was erroneous."[13]

By his own account, Cotton had resolutely adhered to this position throughout the three days of meetings with Greenacre and Meyer. Doubtless with some degree of understatement, he noted that "the question was argued with some feeling as I felt . . . that if the 85% could be eliminated, then it could easily be shown that we were entirely wrong in our assumption that treatment of cases was beneficial."[14] Round and round they had gone. Meyer had attempted to compare Cotton's results at Trenton with statistics from Massachusetts, which appeared to show a 10 percent higher recovery rate in that state, only for his protégé to insist on "the absurdity of such comparison" and to ask "if he would be willing to state that the work of Trenton was one-third less efficient than that of Massachusetts . . . I continued to protest that I would not consent to such comparisons and insinuations that this comparison proved that our statistics were in error 100% . . . [and] that if our figures of 85% were to be questioned, this work would have to be done at Trenton where the material was available."[15] "Eventually," he informed Raycroft, "I became convinced that it was futile for me alone to combat the unfavorable impression that Dr. Greenacre had given Dr. Meyer . . . and notified Dr. Meyer that I was coming home to take the matter up with the Board and any further conferences would be decided according to their wishes."[16]

Quite how Raycroft or Meyer thought they could harmonize the two viewpoints was never clear. Writing to his Princeton colleague on January 27, Meyer insisted that, "I am not hopeless. Our series of cases cannot be brushed aside. Dr. Cotton will have to show how he gets his figures for each year, and we shall be glad to review them. I do hope something constructive can come of all this. It must. Please tell me what difficulties you see in the comparison of the two statements. They cannot be insuperable."[17] And later the same day, he wrote a second letter to Raycroft indicating that he was "very anxious to get the statement that Dr. Cotton has worked out, and to see where the common ground can be reached." In doing so, "the first thing to be thought about is not the *figures* but the *facts*. It is the deplorable use of figures before the facts have received any consideration that has created the whole chance for a misguided policy, and it is just this point that seems again to be disregarded at present by Dr. Cotton."[18]

Raycroft's response was immediate. He assured Meyer that he had already met with Cotton, and had refused to allow him to deflect the discussion on to the two sets of statistics "because it seems to me that they are based upon different grounds and are not comparable." He had urged instead that Cotton refocus on a longitudinal study of the fate of his patients from 1908 onwards, an approach that "will, I think, help to bring Dr. Cotton to a realization of the fact, if it is a fact, that the bases of his comparisons are in need of revision." Here was a hint, notwithstanding Raycroft's assurance to Meyer that "I am greatly impressed with Dr. Greenacre's report and the facts that appear to be made clear by her study," that he had not necessarily concluded that the whole line of approach at Trenton rested upon a fatally mistaken set of assumptions. In closing, however, he sought to reassure Meyer that, "while Dr. Cotton is somewhat excited and intense over the whole matter . . . he really is in a mood to face the facts and to accept the conclusions that are indicated by them. I believe," he reiterated, "that the affair is capable of being straightened out harmoniously and satisfactorily."[19]

So there for a time the matter rested. Meyer made it clear that, "I should be glad to get Dr. Cotton's line of approach and his criticisms of Dr. Greenacre's report. But," he continued, "it will be best to give him all the time needed."[20]

With that assurance in mind, Raycroft seems to have done very little over the following weeks and months to move matters towards a conclusion. Toward the end of the year, he would excuse his inaction as a concession to the superintendent's doubtful mental stability: "during the winter and spring Cotton's condition was such that I felt it unwise to put pressure on him in connection with the cleaning up of the questions relating to the hospital study."[21] As for Meyer, though it was more than a year since he had concluded that Cotton's "claims and statistics are preposterously out of accord" with reality, he simply sat on his hands.

Cotton meanwhile spent some of his free time working up a new series of cases designed to refute Greenacre's report, informing Raycroft in early March that,

> the study and investigation of five hundred cases has shown much better results than by our old method. For instance, the conditions at the end of five years would show the following. In 1907–1911 [prior to the adoption of measures against focal infection], the untreated cases show at the end of five years 140 recoveries or 28%, 37 unimproved, 67 died, or 13.4%, and 256 still in the hospital or 51% of the five hundred. In the five hundred treated

27 *Henry Cotton at work at his desk in his office at the Trenton State Hospital.*

cases [1918–20] 328 are out as recovered or 66%, discharged unimproved 27, died 65, or 13%. In the hospital 80 or 16% . . . I will try to come over on Wednesday to the Club for luncheon. I want to have a chat with you and will bring the figures along so we can go over them.[22]

Periodically, too, he received encouraging letters from other physicians praising his work. John Harvey Kellogg wrote from his Battle Creek Sanitarium to thank him for "the courtesies I received when I visited your institution," and to say that in his opinion, "your work in Trenton in relation to the therapeutics of mental and nervous troubles has created a greater stir than anything which has developed within my memory. You have set a multitude of people to thinking and I believe the result will be a radical change in the management of our insane asylums throughout the United States and the world."[23] And Dr. Baillie wrote from Victoria, British Columbia, to thank Cotton for the several valuable reprints he had sent, and to reiterate his admiration for the work being accomplished at Trenton: "My long and increasing belief that the work which you have done so much to pioneer is absolutely on the right track gains strength . . . and it is a measure of encouragement also to read the endorsement of your methods so cordially given by such men as Dr. William Hunter and Dr. Chalmers Watson in Great Britain."[24] Baillie added an invitation to attend the upcoming meeting of the Canadian Medical Association in June, an invitation Cotton regretted he had to decline.

During all this time, of course, the program of tooth-pulling, tonsillectomies, and a whole variety of abdominal surgeries proceeded apace. It was not until early June that Meyer and Cotton finally encountered one another at a medical conference. They chatted briefly, and Cotton provided some details about his attempts to re-examine the hospital records to refute Greenacre's report. Prompted to renew his contacts with Raycroft, and to press once more for a resolution, Meyer insisted that, "the fact that he selects 500 cases out of a period of nearly two years preceding the series of investigations by Dr. Greenacre may have some value, but Dr. Cotton certainly should go over the cases that Dr. Greenacre has actually studied." He added that through the professional grapevine, "Dr. Greenacre understands that Dr. Cotton has occasionally made the remark that it was unfortunate that there was not somebody else sent, and she naturally feels very much embarrassed" to hear such a thing. It had made her particularly "anxious that there should be an early understanding," not least because that would mean "releasing her from the silence that is imposed upon her." For his own part, Meyer professed, "I am naturally anxious to get at the facts and also to save all the feelings, but I wonder what can be expected."[25]

If Meyer preferred to spare Cotton's feelings rather than unknown patients' teeth, innards, and lives, Raycroft was no less inclined to move circumspectly. "I know," he responded, "how Dr. Greenacre must feel about the matter, and I sympathize with her, but I don't see how I could have done any more than I have attempted to do, unsatisfactory as the results have been up to the present . . . I have been trying for some time," he assured Meyer, "in fact ever since Dr. Cotton got back to working condition, to get this matter of the question studied by Dr. Greenacre into such shape that the various views on the situation could be harmonized, and we could come to some final conclusions. I have not succeeded so far in bringing this about for reasons that I need not go into in writing to you, and I am afraid it will be impossible for me to go any further this summer, because I am leaving for the University of California within the next couple of days."[26]

Summer passed into fall, and still there was no further response from either Princeton or Trenton. Finally, perhaps prompted by further complaints from Greenacre, Meyer wrote to Cotton directly. "I wonder," he inquired, "whether you have had the time to go over the series of cases that were examined and made the topic of Dr. Greenacre's review. It will, I feel, be most valuable if the further discussion of the problem can be based on these specific cases. I fully appreciate the value of the other material that you have gone over for comparison, but with these cases and the differences of opinion that may occur in connection with them it will be much easier to trace the validity or lack of validity of the conclusions."[27]

Cotton, it transpired, had made no such attempt, and rather than write back directly, he approached Raycroft, who intervened on his behalf. "The delay," Raycroft once more assured Meyer, "has been in large part due to my unwillingness last winter to put pressure on Dr. Cotton to do the work which he must do on the cases mentioned by Dr. Greenacre, because of his poor physical and mental condition." Then there had been his absence on the West Coast over the summer, and a busy beginning to the fall semester at Princeton. Quite why this should have prevented Cotton from proceeding was left unspecified. At all events, Raycroft blandly assured Meyer that the matter was now in hand: "I urged [Dr. Cotton] yesterday to start immediately on his own study of the cases which Dr. Greenacre considered in her report as that was the only way in which to start from a common basis . . . so that the whole matter can be talked through . . . would Friday the 19th [November] be convenient to you and Dr. Greenacre for a conference in Baltimore if Dr. Cotton can get his material into shape and can arrange to meet at that time?"[28]

In the event, Cotton and Raycroft showed up in Baltimore on November 17, bringing with them two new series of statistics, each encompassing 500 cases, which Cotton contended decisively disproved Greenacre's findings. They met with Meyer over two days, in sessions that were intended to be a prelude to a three-way meeting with Greenacre on the 19th – an encounter that never materialized. Meyer kept extensive penciled notes of his discussions with Cotton, in a wide-ranging memorandum that also contained a record of his own efforts to get his protégé to rethink his position, and he subsequently wrote up an assessment of where the matter stood for his files. The atmosphere was far friendlier and less tense than at the meeting in January. Cotton and Raycroft were invited back to Meyer's house, and at the end of the two days, in a downpour, it was Mrs. Meyer who drove them both to the station.[29]

As he had previously, Cotton began the meeting by trying to focus Meyer's attention on his own statistics, which closely resembled the ones he had shared with Raycroft back in March. Once again, he insisted that these data showed a massive increase in cure rates among the 1918–20 patients, as compared with those he had treated in 1907–10, well before he had recognized the significance of focal sepsis. At length, the discussion took up Greenacre's work, and Cotton accused her of omitting 37 cases from one of her series. When Meyer demurred, and pointed out that "this figure could nowhere be found," he next responded with "a fault-finding refusal of the idea of any error" and an insistence that "the cases . . . not found by Dr. G. should be counted as recovered" – only to be met by Meyer's reminder that "as a matter of fact only 6 cases of her series could not be found." As the meeting wore on, Meyer's penciled notes appear to show him becoming somewhat disenchanted with Cotton's stance: part way through the proceedings, he observed to himself that, "what has happened to Dr. Cotton is that his admirable capacity for action and his energy have passed into the service of advocacy instead of inquiry. One asks with wonderment how is it possible that something can seem so true and final and yet meet such flat contradiction?" On at least one occasion, Meyer broke in to warn of the dangers posed by a failure "to scrutinize one's methods and facts . . . We have to learn to think in terms of our critics and opponents as well as our own . . . lest we might be misled by our zeal. I am staggered," he went on,

> by the way your statistician has in one way or another misled you and how you have misled yourself by not wanting to have anything to do with anyone who did not see things as you do . . . you were guided by success or the appearance of success and by a form of reasoning that led you around in a circle. Instead of asking those who doubted to come into your laboratory to work, you surrounded yourself with persons who think too conclusively as you do . . . and under the pressure of success you mistook

the results of any kind of arduous and devoted work with patients as the results of your special work and reasoning . . . it is easier to work with a simple or coercive principle, that of operative work. It is easier to talk in terms of colons and toxins – and to be in an attitude of bloody warfare, to keep the spirit of the personnel at the highest pitch.

But, Meyer implied, only at a considerable cost.[30]

And yet, as always, in the final analysis Meyer was ambivalent and unable to reach any definitive conclusions. Reflecting back on the session of November 18, he seemed in a much more positive frame of mind, commenting that Cotton's "statistics are indeed remarkable: 85, 82, 85 and 92% of recoveries. Of the colectomized 30% died." (This last statistic drew no special comment.) "What I want," he continued, "is the review of the rank and file of the admissions without arbitrary decision as to functional and non-functional, the admissions of two localities, of 1911–15 and then 1919–23. It should be possible to see some non-objectionable parallels." Cotton's enthusiasm and conviction seem ultimately to have worn Meyer down. "There is something about these claims," he later confessed privately, "that sounds quite irrefutable. And when C. says that in years past he always had to add to the list of terminal dementia, but not now – one has to ask how and why? There is evidently an indisputable fact" – and "facts" were Meyer's favorite things – "and I have to make my mind up by actual study through one or more of our people and not by waiting and 'thinking.'" They ended with a discussion of colectomies, and Cotton boasted that, "this year he had 16 consecutive women without a death, then after a death 6 more successful. The men are more active to develop peritonitis. I pointed out the differences among animals (horses very sensitive). Possibly women *are* more satisfactorily protected by nature." And Meyer then professed himself "convinced that . . . with a little more time it would become clear what standards should be required to make the current work an adequate test and fruitful research."[31]

Cotton promptly retreated back to Trenton, confidence in his theory and methods apparently completely intact, and his determination to root out focal sepsis as strong as ever. Months passed before Meyer received another missive from Joseph Raycroft. "This long silence on my part," the Princeton professor assured him, "does not mean that we have lost sight of the matter. The delay has been due to the difficulty which I have met in attempting to get Dr. Cotton to do the necessary work to review the Hospital records of the cases which were studied by Dr. Greenacre, and to get his ideas into shape as a basis for a conference with you." He acknowledged that, "the delay in coming to some conclusion in this matter has been most exasperating," but contended that it was "apparently under the circumstances unavoidable." At last, he had good news, though: Cotton's "work is now near enough to completion so that I am in a position for you to have us come down to Baltimore to discuss the matter." Recognizing that, with the academic year almost over, and Meyer due to leave in June for Britain, his schedule was full, "I am writing to say an appointment almost any time from the 21st of May to the 11th of June would be convenient for us."[32]

Two days later, Meyer responded that he "expect[ed] to see Dr. Cotton next week at the Atlantic City meeting, and we shall then be able to determine what time would be most suitable. I am anxious for him to let me have the summary of his review of the data so I can orient myself in a useful manner."[33]

That summary was forthcoming in a letter from Cotton written on May 28 and hand-delivered to Meyer two days later. With the help of his assistant physician Robert Stone and, he assured Meyer, in close consultation with both Joseph Raycroft, president of the hospital's board of managers, and with Commissioner William J. Ellis, the head of all New Jersey's mental hospitals, prisons, and reformatories, he had reviewed Greenacre's "preliminary report" and made "a very careful check upon the individual case records which constituted [its foundation]." Based upon that work, "we find that Dr. Greenacre's study is an inaccurate, inadequate, and misleading picture of the work which we have been doing for a period of the last nine years. We have tried," he continued, "to make the report as impersonal and objective as possible" and to that end, they had prepared tables contrasting their own view of the individual cases with hers. They had retained their worksheets giving their reasons for regrouping patients, and would make "this material available for study by yourself or any other impartial investigator."[34]

Having generated their own set of "data," Cotton (and implicitly the commissioner and Raycroft) announced that "we feel that the conclusions and generalizations [in Greenacre's report] are found to be inaccurate and unfair particularly as they are based on inaccurate and disputed statistics." Greenacre had argued that the fact that minimally treated patients had recovered when the Trenton staff themselves claimed that many of their infections had remained untreated should count against Cotton's theory, as should the fact that the most thoroughly treated patients had yielded the worst results. Not so, Cotton and Stone insisted: "The error here is in confusing sufficient and thorough treatment with minimum and maximum treatment. We have often noticed the fact that patients who had the minimum of treatment have had sufficient treatment to eliminate the overload of toxemia which was producing the persistence of the mental symptoms, recovery therefore occurred when this overload was relieved and the resistance raised; even with a persistence of sources of infections untreated." As for the most thoroughly treated patients, the explanation for apparent failures in these instances was equally simple: it was the most chronic, desperately ill patients who required the most treatment, and their "physical and mental debilitation and dilapidation" ensured that "they are less responsive to treatment, even to the extent that the proportion of deaths is necessarily higher."[35]

Finally, Cotton focused on two particular cases, which he insisted were representative of "many" others, as examples of the inaccuracies and bias in Greenacre's report. One young patient,

> the Corman child is the daughter of a physician of sound training and broad experience who has kept us fully informed of his daughter's progress and who will be glad to write to you, as he has written us, a complete refutation of Dr. Greenacre's statements regarding the history of his child following treatment at the Trenton State Hospital. Dr. Corman personally approved and witnessed the operative procedures carried out in respect to his daughter and has kept the most careful clinical records of her later progress, and assures us of his confidence that her present improvement is directly due to treatment given by the hospital.

If Greenacre's statements on this case were "entirely unjustified and inaccurate," so too were her conclusions about a Mrs. McGregor, a patient "well known to the staff who have kept very close and intimate touch with her progress [and know that she has made] a complete recovery . . . so that she is now self-supporting."[36]

A man with a more highly developed sense of irony than the self-important Meyer might have appreciated the coincidence that "Cotton's visit coincides with the removal of a jaw abscess by Brun." Meyer had come down with a sore bicuspid on the Friday night, which "led me to urge that Dr. Lewis and Dr. Street should sanction its removal." But these men were evidently not devotees of focal sepsis. "When I came to Dr. Brun I found him persuaded by Dr. Street to let the tooth alone. He again put some gauze in the hole and to-day Sunday I woke up with much pain . . . [and] an uncomfortable crick in the back."[37] Not in the best of moods, he then had to deal with Cotton.

Cotton had made a special trip "to bring the report, unfortunately without the corrected case material, only with a letter impeaching Dr. Greenacre and berating her with adjectives." This was scarcely an auspicious beginning, and "when I asked for the materials, he said he did not know what Dr. Raycroft's decision would be on this point, and that he would confer with Dr. R. and Mr. Ellis." Not best pleased by this news, Meyer then had to listen to a further litany of complaints. "Dr. C. complains that Dr. Greenacre spent more time in the office trying to find out something on him than in the actual work that was going on" – something Meyer knew was untrue, and whose untruth was quite manifest in the lengthy reports and case notes she had presented to the two of them; he "emphasized that Dr. Gjessing" – an eminent Norwegian psychiatrist who had recently visited and praised the work at Trenton – "would have a different report, etc."[38]

Lest Meyer should somehow have forgotten what was going on at Trenton while he dithered about what to do, Cotton then launched into a panegyric to "the [colonic] irrigations and their effect, based on the observation of 300 colons." Meyer noted "the impressionistic encouragement [Cotton] gets from ... certain outstanding cases." And when Cotton insisted that "a certain amount of toxicity can be coped with, but a relative overflow causes the outbreak [of insanity]," Meyer privately confessed: "My own feeling is in harmony with such a principle; but I want to replace plausibility by actual evidence." As for Cotton's own statistics, their value was vitiated by the fact that "practically any discharge is counted as a recovery," and "if the refutation of Dr. Greenacre's report is throughout of a 'manner and degree' of that in the McGee and Coleman cases it would be misleading"[39] – a revealing choice of words, since Meyer had checked and knew that Greenacre's judgments in both cases were carefully justified with meticulously gathered evidence.

In the end, Meyer's musings trail off in a display of petulance. "My attitude just now," he laments privately, "is of intense regret and revolt against the impossibility to carry through any really controlled work." He lapses into a self-pitying aside: "Why can I not get a strictly thorough bacteriological job on my teeth?" And then he launches back into more complaints: "Why can we not carry more than one hypothesis? Why can we not get several persons to work on a problem?"[40]

Phyllis Greenacre was now dispatched once more to Trenton, to meet with Cotton, Stone, and Raycroft, and to review the "pink sheets" that had been compiled with data that allegedly refuted her findings. The meeting was as tense and unpleasant as might be expected, dissolving into bitter squabbling about the details of individual cases, where Greenacre's own detailed follow-up work, based on her extensive travels through New Jersey and the neighboring states was "refuted" by what even Raycroft subsequently called "discursive" data from the two Trenton doctors. Writing to Meyer on June 3, Raycroft professed to be encouraged by "the interesting conference we had last night" and claimed he was "very anxious to keep the job moving now that it is started, and overcome the tendency to avoid the issue and to let the matter rest where it is."[41] Greenacre, however, had left Trenton thoroughly discouraged, sensing that Cotton's nominal superiors had no intention of acting on her findings or of reining in his activities.[42]

Meyer wrote back to Raycroft on June 4 accepting the idea of a further conference with him and with Cotton on the following Monday, shortly before a scheduled departure for New York to take the ocean liner to England. But he appeared to have few illusions left. "The account Dr. Greenacre gave me makes me exceedingly doubtful as to whether any benefit from Dr. Greenacre's work and report was desired on the part of the hospital and whether any discussion is at all possible. After all we deal with an attitude based on the manipulation of large figures, and in the light of the experience with the material that has actually been studied, I am unwilling to draw any inferences from uncontrolled material . . . There are too many obvious questions I would have to raise with regard to the new series of 500."[43] (Cotton had evidently once more sought to deflect attention away from the cases Greenacre had studied to his own chosen series.)

Yet instead of standing firm and demanding a change of attitude on Raycroft's part, or insisting that Raycroft must mobilize the hospital board to curtail belatedly the mutilating and often deadly treatments being performed at the institution they oversaw, Meyer characteristically began to prevaricate, to soften his comments, and to minimize the harm that had been done. "I have not the slightest inclination," he hastened to add, "to question the fact that the devoted and hard work and the spirit of activity in the hospital must have done a considerable amount of good; but the actual scrutiny of the claims," and here there was almost a tone of wistful regret, "is far from being reassuring with regard to the extreme claims and the tendency to lump together the improved cases with the recovered when as a matter of fact there is a strong tendency always to speak of 50% 'recoveries.' Personal friendly feelings and the fundamental appreciation of the actual spirit of the work has [sic] never been shaken on my part, but this is a problem of facts."[44]

As it turned out, there was no time for any further meetings before Meyer sailed for London. Instead, there was a flurry of last-minute correspondence, beginning with a June 8 letter from Meyer addressed to "My dear Dr. Cotton." Once more, Meyer could scarcely bring himself to utter direct criticism or to state clearly what the issues at stake were. He had learned from Greenacre that Cotton's attempt to refute her work had consisted of little more than vague and unsubstantiated complaints about her conclusions, coupled with statistics whose provenance was completely mysterious. Here those defects were alluded to in the most anodyne language: "My brief 'phone conversation with Dr. Raycroft and what Dr. Greenacre told me of your conjoint interview made me feel that it was very essential that modifications of Dr. Greenacre's findings should be much more specifically justified and that without that and perhaps a reexamination of some of the cases no conclusions should be drawn . . . it simply will not do to let the matter be left in a state of mere impressions concerning any of the cases used."[45]

Repeatedly, Meyer pleaded with Cotton to stop accusing Greenacre of bad faith or malevolence.

> Please do not allow yourself to get under the impression of any ill-will on anyone's part . . . One thing I feel great solicitude about and that is this: You should be willing to dismiss once and for all any feeling that Dr. Greenacre would want to plead for any preconceived idea and that she had intentionally changed the original agreement of the material to be studied. She is as willing as I am to let the cases speak, and to modify her summary if the cases demand it . . . She feels, and I should say justly, that she had investigated more directly than you or Dr. Stone could have done [and again Meyer was impelled to soften the implied criticism] considering the great amount of work you are doing and considering her putting most of a year on the specific visits and studies.

Moreover, contrary to Cotton's assertions, "she *did* interview Dr. Corman, and a teacher of the girl and failed to get an answer to two letters to Dr. Hallowell." Cotton's insinuations about the case, like his general attempt to cast aspersions on her motives, were thus simply wrong. Closing with a typical Meyerian appeal that they be guided by "the facts" (as though he had not been in possession of the necessary "facts" for nearly two years at this point), he once more acted like someone who needed to placate rather than be placated: "I refuse to be discouraged and I hope you feel that way too."[46]

Cotton replied at once by special-delivery letter, sent to Meyer at the Hotel Pennsylvania in New York where he was waiting with Mrs. Meyer and his daughter Julia to sail on the *Lapland* of the Red Star Line to England. If Meyer thought his desperate efforts to avoid conflict might have some effect, the letter's opening paragraph swiftly disabused him. While thanking him for his "kind letter," Cotton insisted that it was Greenacre, not he, who was "quibbling over one or two cases." She had, he complained, just as he had first done in January 1926, amended the original plan of study, and had throughout displayed a hostile attitude to him and to his work. Again he brought up the Corman case, essentially accusing her of lying when she claimed to have interviewed the patient's father, and adding that Dr. Corman and he "would like to know when and where the interview took place." For the sake of Meyer's feelings, he pretended to "hesitate to think that there has been any ill-will on the part of anyone," but immediately protested that "I do feel that Dr. Greenacre has not presented the facts adequately or accurately and I think that opinion is shared by Dr. Raycroft, Mr. Ellis, and my own staff . . . I also feel that Dr. Greenacre was not frank while here." The belligerent and accusatory tone continued all the way to the end of the letter. "You will admit," he wrote in a characteristic passage, "that when Dr. Greenacre makes such sweeping statements [about our work being dangerous and useless] without any basis as far as we can see, that necessarily I cannot feel she is impartial in her deductions . . . Fortunately, we have others who, after studying our work in every way as adequately as Dr. Greenacre, would not subscribe to these conclusions."[47]

Cotton had closed his letter almost jauntily: "Mrs. Cotton joins me in wishing you and Mrs. Meyer and Julia a pleasant voyage and a happy summer."[48] But the immediate effect of its arrival in Meyer's hotel room was to throw the older man into a funk. The intimidating professor in whose presence young associates barely dared to speak, and in whose absence none dared act, the dominant figure who put castrated students into almost all the major chairs of psychiatry in America, turned out to be, as on every previous occasion when Cotton had challenged him, unwilling or unable to stand his ground.

On several occasions, he sat down to write to his protégé. Successive drafts fell incomplete, were scratched through, and never sent. None, however, was consigned to the wastebasket, and so the spectacle of his indecision and lack of courage was preserved, albeit in the deep recesses of his filing system. For the obsessive Meyer seems to have kept every piece of paper he had written on – indeed had done so from his very earliest childhood, so that his files in Baltimore contain even his kindergarten scribbles.

In draft after draft, he appealed to his former pupil once again to "dismiss the idea of attack and confrontation and replace it with curiosity and eagerness for facts." That, he assured Cotton, was the way to reach "a final common ground and freedom from appearances of quibbling or unfortunate extremes of statement." It was all, he kept insisting, a matter of "facts," and all that was necessary was to "just give these facts for anyone to judge for himself. Let us get the facts quite dispassionately, otherwise we cause mistakes just like those of Dr. Corman and inject matters which obscure." He complained of "no doubt truthful in intention but erroneous statements," and objected that "to assume that Dr. G. was 'not frank' is I feel misleading." After all, he wrote, "she gave you the case reports as she went along, and certainly had no intention to conceal." As for Cotton's new series of cases, which were supposed to refute Greenacre's work decisively, "I shall have to abstain from any critical statement because I shall have to overcome some questions such as the length of time covered by getting a 'series of 500 consecutive cases.'"

In another draft, he asked plaintively, "can we not suspend the emphasis on the deductions until the points for and against the statements on the specific cases in the series are quite objectively stated, case by case – absolutely free of any quibbling and any other spirit by that of search for facts?" Casting that version aside, he wrote, "your special delivery letter just reached me. I should feel very much at ease about the matter if you could see one good point in Dr. Greenacre's statements. I am absolutely convinced of the trustworthiness of her *attitude.*" Implicitly, of course, this passage represented a less than whole-hearted defense of his subordinate, and in yet another draft, Meyer took a still more passive tack: "Somehow I have to leave it to Dr. Raycroft and to you and to Dr. Stone whether Dr. Greenacre was quibbling. She certainly was discouraged and could be even more discouraged by this comment."[49] One might well imagine, with "support" like this, why she might feel that way.

If Meyer was about to leave for Britain, so too was Cotton. Both were to attend the joint meeting of the British Medical Association and the Medico-Psychological Association in Edinburgh, and Cotton had written of how much he was looking forward to the plenary session that was to be devoted to the role of focal sepsis in the production of mental disorder. Cotton was to be one of the major speakers, and he clearly remembered with pleasure the triumphant reception he had received on his prior visit in 1923. "I think," he had told Meyer,

> the meeting in Edinburgh is going to be very interesting. Dr. William Hunter will open the discussion and he will be followed by Sir Berkeley Moynihan, President of the Royal College of Surgeons. Dr. Chalmers Watson will also speak. These three men I know will support the work based on their own experiences as well as what they know of our work at Trenton. While I think Dr. Goodall is sympathetic, I do not know whether he has any definite experience. Dr. Bond, Secretary to the Lunacy Commission, may raise objections based on technical points, but not upon actual work.[50]

The prospect of attending this session, and perhaps being called upon to speak, clearly petrified Meyer. He was unwilling to comment on Cotton's work, and yet if he did not do so, given Greenacre's findings, his silence might be construed as assent to Cotton's claims. Privately, in one of his unsent draft letters

28 *Adolf Meyer (left), with an unidentified companion, on an ocean liner bound for Europe.*

to Cotton, he confessed his discomfort: "I cannot help wavering about the Edinburgh meeting but I prefer not to speak until the series of Dr. Greenacre is cleared up on both sides beyond reproach, and until I shall have had an opportunity to read the reports of the others you [Cotton] mention as having studied cases in every way as adequately as Greenacre."[51] He must surely have suspected that no such reports existed. They would have required enormous amounts of labor on someone's part, and surely he would have learned of such extensive follow-up work. More importantly, if these documents existed, Cotton would naturally have produced them. But anything that allowed him to rationalize further inaction was preferable, it would appear, to having to grasp the nettle and act on what he knew.

In the end, Meyer simply could not come up with a response to Cotton's letter that satisfied him and, instead, he sent no more than a brief and somewhat curt acknowledgment of Cotton's missive: "Thank you for your letter. I assure you of my sincerity and of my determination to let the facts speak and of the determination to avoid any quibbling. A patient and unbiased collecting of the facts of the series studied; a simple statement of all the facts and complete elimination of personal feelings."[52] In the face of the need to fight, to speak up in the face of months and years of obstructionism, and notwithstanding Greenacre's pleas to be released from the silence he had imposed upon her, Meyer chose yet again to rationalize a complete failure to act.

13

The New Lister

Within days of Meyer's departure for London, Cotton himself set sail for Europe on the SS *Carmania*, docking at Le Havre "after a pleasant voyage," and then taking the train to Paris, where he arrived on the night of July 3. From a professional point of view, he found Paris a disappointment. "As there was very little of psychiatric interest . . . very little important work was attempted," though he did indulge in some sightseeing: "we visited the Salpetrie [*sic*], the old insane asylum, and saw the oil painting of Pinel striking the shackles off the insane, somewhere about the year 1780 . . . We also visited the Charcot Museum."[1] Having seen these sacred shrines of modern psychiatry and apparently finding little else in the city worthy of remark or notice, a week later he and his wife left for London, where they arrived on the evening of Sunday July 10.

The next three weeks were a whirlwind of activity, and for Cotton, emerging from months and months of feeling beleaguered and stressed, they came as a great relief. Everywhere he traveled – in England, in Scotland, and even on a side-trip to Norway – he found himself among friends, medical men who hailed his contributions to modern medicine, who shared his commitment to the need to tackle the perils of pus infection, and who looked upon him as the great man he had always assumed he was. As on his previous visit to Europe some four years earlier, the great and the good of British medicine hastened to praise him as a brave pioneer, embraced his theories of the origins of madness, and lauded his breakthroughs in the treatment and cure of the insane.

On the Monday after his arrival in England, he met briefly with Dr. White Robertson, and then spent five hours with William Hunter. Hunter had first suggested a connection between sepsis and insanity in 1900, and he was to be one of the featured speakers at the symposium on focal sepsis that was planned for the joint meeting of the British Medical Association and the Medico-Psychological Association in Edinburgh in two weeks' time. He and Cotton "had a five-hour conference over the paper he was to give in Edinburgh two weeks later," and then the Cottons attempted to leave London to travel to Birmingham.[2]

On Cotton's previous visit to England in 1923, he had experienced London's biggest thunderstorm of the twentieth century, and his luck with the English weather continued. The journey to the Midlands "ordinarily is a two hour ride, but because of a severe storm we were delayed. [At one point in the journey,] it was necessary to change cars and go another way, because of the floods, finally reaching Birmingham two hours late." The travails that stemmed from the weather-induced chaos were not yet over, though the Cottons were now within a few miles of their destination. "My objective was to visit Rubery Hill [mental hospital], which is in the charge of Dr. T. C. Graves, whom I had visited in 1923. It was impossible to get him over the telephone and a telegram failed to reach him." The day was rapidly drawing to a close, and prospects for a night's sleep looked increasingly bleak. "At Birmingham we were unable to get hotel accommodations and the taxi-cab driver refused to take us out to Rubery Hill, a distance of six miles, because of the flooded condition of the roads." It was thus a considerable relief when "finally Dr. Graves managed to reach the hotel and took us to the hospital."[3]

His host was a man with whom Cotton felt thoroughly at home. Physically imposing, Graves had no truck with compromise or with those who focused on the psychological dimensions of mental disorders. Rather than lament, as others had, that "psychiatry has failed to keep pace with progress to the same

29 *Thomas Chivers Graves, Cotton's most enthusiastic British supporter.*

extent as other branches of medicine," he sought, like Cotton, to assimilate the two, and to break down that "regrettable isolation [that saw] . . . psychiatry occupying a position in relation to medicine as a whole analogous to that of a certified [and confined psychiatric] patient to the life of the community."[4] Graves had made great progress since Cotton's first visit in 1923, adding a visiting gynecologist and an ear, nose, and throat specialist to his staff, as well as establishing a new research laboratory at the second mental hospital he simultaneously headed, at nearby Hollymoor. By 1926, his aggressive advocacy had secured a whole new set of buildings to which patients could be brought for the most advanced forms of treatment: an operating theater, rooms for hydrotherapy, apparatus to administer ultraviolet light treatment, and a room devoted to colonic lavage. With full-time pathologist F. A. Pickworth on staff, as well as bacteriological laboratories, X-ray facilities, and the like, he could boast that he had moved decisively to introduce the latest scientific advances into the treatment of mental disorder.

Inspecting all this activity and comparing notes about the war on sepsis, the two men enjoyed a busy and productive week. "We spent our mornings on the wards, and most afternoons . . . This visit was really the most important of my trip and several important things were learned."[5]

To begin with, Cotton discovered that Graves had found a new method of "diagnosing infections of the sphenoid and ethmoid sinuses" and was able to watch the "visiting nose and throat man, Dr. W. S. Adams . . . diagnose and treat some sixteen cases. While we had recognized the importance of these sinuses in our work and had had several cases recover as result of treating the sinuses, still we had missed many cases because of the difficulty of making such a diagnosis. Inspection of the nose and X-ray of the sinuses are of very little help unless the infection is very severe." Cotton was delighted to discover, therefore, that his British counterpart had discovered a way around the problem, a method, moreover, that "is a very simple one and easily learned. It consists principally of pushing a cannula through the nose, puncturing the sinus, withdrawing the contents and actually seeing the pus. Where there was any doubt about the fluid being pus a culture was made." Graves then showed him "many cases which had recovered as result of this treatment."[6]

Nor was this the only technical innovation Cotton observed. During his visit to the operating theater, he was "much impressed by the method of removing tonsils. The operator tied off the vessels before cutting, thus preventing any hemorrhage, which occurs in a certain number of cases and is rather difficult to arrest. While this is not a dangerous situation, at the same time it is more or less bothersome and it seems to me the method of preventing the hemorrhage was an admirable one." As for the dental work, one difference struck him forcibly: "It was rather astonishing to see them extract teeth without any local or general anaesthetic." So far as he could tell, however, "the patients did not seem to object to this method of extraction." Perhaps, he speculated, "pyorrhea has so infected the teeth that they are almost ready to fall out."[7] Or perhaps, another observer might have concluded, it was the formidable presence of Thomas Chivers Graves, a notoriously intimidating man.

Graves was still using malaria as a treatment for his syphilitic patients, where Cotton had substituted "anti-typhoid vaccine given intravenously," but Cotton found that his Birmingham host had developed a new use for the typhoid vaccine: "This is given about once a week. It produces a chill and a sharp rise of temperature, 103 to 105, which in an hour subsides and there is no further discomfort on the part of the patient." So "remarkably satisfactory" were the results, "that I wrote to Dr. Stone at once and in a short time after the method was introduced at the State Hospital."[8]

The two men also found that they were in agreement regarding the "septic nature of epilepsy." Their therapeutic responses, however, differed in some key respects. While acknowledging "the influence of gastro-intestinal toxaemia," Graves and his staff "were paying special attention to the infection of the sphenoid and ethmoid sinuses." Shown "several interesting cases which had recovered entirely after the employment of anti-septic measures to eliminate sinus infection," Cotton concluded that "the neglect on our part of the infection in these sinuses may account for the fact that we did not get good recoveries in all cases treated."[9]

Cotton had "long maintained that . . . parents infected the child's mouth by contact (kissing, drinking from the same glass, eating out of the same spoon, etc.) . . . [and] that this was the principal route by which the child obtained oral infection of both teeth and tonsils." He was delighted to find that Graves fully concurred with his views, and had even coined a useful phrase to sum up the problem, "transmissible familial infection." And as their wide-ranging discussions continued, Graves suggested another arresting concept, "septic heredity," by which he referred to "the effect of maternal toxemia upon the child in utero." Cotton found this to be "a very important point," for it suggested that "in all probability the child is sensitized against these various toxemias, so that he is more easily affected later on in life."[10]

Finally, "many discussions were also had over 'over-load' of toxemia." Critics of both men had taken some delight in pointing out the temporary nature of some of their patients' recoveries, and had noted that some patients had recovered after only some of their infections had been treated, presumably casting doubt on the etiological relationship of sepsis and psychosis. For Cotton and Graves, the concept of toxic overload proved just how misguided their critics were. In any individual case,

> the patient may be carrying a certain amount of infection which he is able to counteract by his own immunity. Add to that another infection or increase the severity of the original infection and soon symptoms supervene. This goes far to explain the technique which has been a stumbling block to many who did not understand the mechanism of the infectious process, namely that by removing one infection, say 'infected teeth,' even if other foci of infection had not been removed, the patient will temporarily recover. This is a phenomenon we have observed in many of our cases, but if other infections are not removed, sooner or later there will be another breakdown. Consequently many of our patients, after having infected teeth and tonsils eliminated, would recover, although they still had infection in the genito-urinary tract or colon.

All of which made still more manifest "the importance of cleaning up all infections before the patient is allowed to leave the hospital and so prevent any further attacks." Here again, "we found we were in perfect accord in our interpretations of these various phenomena."[11]

Their busy week completed, the two men left on Monday July 11 for Scotland. Unusually, the British Medical Association and the Medico-Psychological Association, renamed the Royal Medico-Psychological Association since Cotton had last addressed it, were to meet in joint session in the ancient capital of Edinburgh. Here was a splendid opportunity to advance the cause of waging war on sepsis and to encourage a rapprochement between psychiatry and general medicine. With the influx of medical men, all the hotels were full, and Cotton and Graves found themselves "quartered in a very comfortable private house. We found Edinburgh delightful in every particular and began to experience some of their well-known hospitality."[12]

On Wednesday, they assembled before a large crowd of professionals and journalists for the promised session on focal sepsis. The morning's proceedings opened with a lengthy address from William Hunter, the London physician with whom Cotton had met when he first arrived from Paris. The year 1927 was, as Hunter reminded his audience, the centenary of the birth of the sainted Lister, and they could best commemorate the great man's achievements by "inaugurating a new campaign against sepsis in one of the greatest domains of medical diseases – that which bears the ill-omened title of insanity."[13] For more than a quarter of a century, he noted, he had been calling for a broadening of

Lister's ideas and for an attack on "sepsis in the realm of nervous disorders, as presented in ordinary general practice, its neuritis, its neurasthenias, its mental depressions," or its more severe so-called "nervous attacks" or "nervous break-downs." For years, he confessed, his had been a voice crying in the wilderness, but finally, at first "from the American side at the hands of Dr. Cotton, the director of the New Jersey State Hospital, Trenton,"[14] and more recently among a handful of British psychiatrists, the approach had finally begun to obtain its due attention. Meanwhile, in the profession at large, there had been a recognition among some of the most eminent figures on both sides of the Atlantic – men like Frank Billings, Llewellys Barker, and Charles Mayo in America, and Chalmers Watson and Sir Berkeley Moynihan in Britain – of "the apparently negligible character, but nevertheless supreme importance of the foci of sepsis with which medicine as distinct from surgery is specially concerned."[15]

It was to Cotton's work at Trenton that Hunter then gave most of his attention, citing his successes at length, and suggesting that in view of the scope and scale of his work, it was time to coin a new term that captured the promise of a "new era of antisepsis in mental disorders . . . 'septic psychosis.'"[16] Faced with the graver varieties of psychosis, the medical profession had been tempted to throw up its hands and confess defeat:

> The degree of disorder may be of such a character and duration – for example, that presented in dementia praecox, or in manic-depressive insanity – as to suggest permanent damage to the higher brain centers, and to appear, therefore, incapable of being influenced by the removal of slight septic foci. But the clinical facts show that this is not the case, and the extent to which the degree of sepsis present in each case is affecting the character and degree of the mental features of the case in causing a 'septic psychosis' can only be determined by the removal of that sepsis.[17]

Cotton, in Hunter's view, was the hero of the hour. For while he himself had argued *theoretically* for the significance of sepsis, it was the New Jersey psychiatrist who had had the courage to demonstrate *practically* what its removal could achieve.

> Dissatisfied after some fifteen years' experience of mental work with the results obtained, he began from 1918 onwards a desperate frontal attack with horse, foot, and artillery – namely, medical recognition of the importance of oral and focal sepsis, surgical help for its removal, and bacteriological support for both – on the whole field of the sepsis presented by his cases (1,400 in number), in the teeth, the tonsils, nasal sinuses, stomach,

intestine and colon, and the genito-urinary tract, with the result of doubling the number of his discharges, and reducing the average stay in hospital from ten months to three months.[18]

It was a lesson they all should heed. For, "however much ordinary people in health may be able to resist, and do successfully resist, the deleterious action of the varying degrees of similar sepsis which they carry, the sufferer from mental disorder *cannot afford to have any such sepsis unregarded.* He is playing for the highest stakes – the preservation of his brain-power and his sanity. He can run no risks. And . . . in his own interests, it is all the more incumbent that every possible measure of treatment should be available and should be applied for his benefit."[19] A still-greater role for antiseptic psychiatry loomed, for "it is in the realm of prevention that this new application of antisepsis will find its greatest triumphs – namely, the cutting short of all sorts and degrees of nervous and mental disturbances that in most cases precede and herald the onset of the graver mental disorders."[20]

Graves and then Cotton himself followed Hunter to the podium. It was an opportunity both men reveled in, and they spoke persuasively to an apparently approving audience about what Graves called "the possibilities of thorough disinfection."[21] But it was in the remarks of many of the great and good in British medicine that Cotton could take the greatest satisfaction. Sir Berkeley Moynihan, president of the Royal College of Surgeons, spoke first. Cotton in his private notes called him hyperbolically "perhaps the most outstanding figure in medicine and surgery in England," and noted with gratitude that he was "a firm believer in the theory of focal sepsis and mental disorder."[22] Sir Berkeley quoted "many cases of mental disorder which had recovered after surgical relief" and complained that "frequently psychiatrists would not allow a mental case to be operated upon until he showed better mental condition." He emphasized the fallacy of such a doctrine because the surgical procedure used in removing foci of infection undoubtedly relieved the patient of the mental symptoms. He said further, "it is no use for the alienist to say that this story is incredible and consequently untrue. Many things that are incredible are profoundly true. Nor is there any use to say that everyone has dental infection but is not insane, for there you run up against the problem of immunity. Looking back over thirty years of practice I am able to say that the removal of an organic disease had often meant the removal of a neuro-psychosis." Lister himself had received "outrageous treatment . . . from his contemporaries." In ignoring Hunter's achievements, "[his own] contemporaries were just as guilty as Lister's contemporaries of that numbing and sterile vice, – apathy."[23] By way of peroration,

Sir Berkeley concluded his remarks with a bow towards two alienists who had not remained apathetic: "The work of Cotton . . . in New York [*sic*] . . . and of Graves in this country seems to set a new standard of inquiry in this branch of medicine, and to show that no mental hospital will in future be considered as adequately equipped unless it has an X-ray laboratory, a skilled bacteriologist, and can command the services of an enlightened surgeon."[24]

All this was stirring stuff, especially as Moynihan was far from alone in lavishing praise on those who aggressively sought to eliminate sepsis among the mad. Only one dissenting voice seriously marred the harmony of the occasion: D. K. Henderson, who had returned to Scotland after some years assisting Adolf Meyer and then George Kirby in New York, rose to challenge the consensus. Hunter's talk of "septic psychosis," he suggested, threatened "to make British psychiatry the laughing-stock of the world . . . It is," he continued, "a very dangerous leap in imagination to suggest that because something exists in a given mental case, that that something is the specific agent." And while Hunter had praised Cotton extravagantly, he noted that, "he passes over, very lightly, the work of Kopeloff, Kirby and Cheney. The work of the latter group of observers has been infinitely better controlled than the work of Cotton, and is much more in accord with the opinions of psychiatrists generally."[25]

The scattered applause that interrupted portions of Henderson's commentary suggested that at least some of the audience sympathized with his point of view.[26] That many did not was reflected in the skeptical laughter that greeted his suggestion that the case of Cotton's that Hunter had referred to might have recovered, not because she had "eleven bad teeth extracted [but] due to the building up of her strength during two years in the hospital ward."[27] And certainly most of those who followed Henderson to the podium were of a quite different mind. The ear, nose, and throat surgeon Eric Watson Williams recounted, for instance, a series of "mental cases who recovered sanity after an operation on the ear. Still," he pointed out with an elaborate air of seriousness, "that might, in the opinion of many, be a coincidence" – a sally that drew renewed laughter from the audience.[28]

Hunter himself spoke towards the end of the proceedings, noting with his own touch of sarcasm that he was "particularly grateful to Dr. Henderson for his criticism," and for reminding the audience about the work of Kopeloff and his collaborators. He himself had read their work with interest. "Yet, while paying his tribute to it, he did not think that psychiatrists need worry unduly about the negative results of this particular work." Kopeloff, after all, was a bacteriologist, not a physician, and for the most part he and his collaborators had removed only a token tooth or three. "One could not expect to modify a whole clinical picture by such a limited removal of sepsis . . . The removal of sepsis must be thorough and detailed." It was significant, surely, that "the only case of complete success which the Americans had mentioned was one in which 30 teeth were removed, ensuring that at least that patient's oral sepsis was taken away." Small wonder that, while objecting to Cotton's work, these men had conceded that, "we are whole-heartedly in favour of removing all septic foci."[29]

There remained only for George M. Robertson, professor of psychiatry at the University of Edinburgh and himself a past president of the Medico-Psychological Association, to bring the day's discussion to a close, remarking on the "deep impression" it had made on everyone, and chiding Dr. Henderson for objecting to the term "septic psychosis" when he himself, "every day of his life, talked about 'toxic psychoses', which was the condition Dr. Hunter meant . . . He was sure," he added, "that in the future no one attending clinical cases would overlook septic foci."[30]

With great satisfaction, Cotton noted that two of his greatest supporters, William Hunter and Sir Berkeley Moynihan, were the recipients of honorary degrees from Edinburgh University that same evening. Moynihan's fame had ensured considerable coverage of the proceedings in the daily press,[31] and with some glee, Cotton recorded that some of the reports had even been reprinted in America.[32] "It is to be hoped," he wrote in his private account of the day's events, "that recognition of this work by the British Medical Association will do much to overcome the apathy and opposition that has been so evident in this country."[33]

Cotton marveled at the extreme formality of the social events that formed a large part of the medical meeting: men dressed like peacocks in their academic regalia, their wives resplendent in their own evening dress. There was the ceremonial piping in of "the Haggis" at the association's annual dinner (the chef downing his Scotch and tossing the glass over his shoulder), and a further elaborate meal at the dinner of the Royal Society of Medicine, to which Professor Robertson had invited him. Then there were "the usual garden parties . . . without which no English [sic] gathering is complete. And Cotton even participated in the golf tournament "at Muirfield, about ten miles from Edinburgh . . . We left Edinburgh in a downpour of rain at eight o'clock Thursday morning and were a somewhat bedraggled lot as we emerged from the bus . . . This was a very picturesque course, but very difficult. It bordered on the open water, the North Sea. Here the water and sky were exactly the same shade, dark drab, so one could not see the horizon. Ships in the distance seemed to be sailing in the air."[34]

And so, after an eventful week, his spirits revived by the praise he had received on almost all sides, Cotton boarded the Flying Scotsman for his return journey to London. Here his mentor Adolf Meyer had remained, skulking at a safe distance from the Edinburgh symposium, and thus making sure that he was not drawn into the debate on the merits of treating focal sepsis to cure madness. Together, the two men attended the joint meeting of the British and American Neurological Societies, held at the Royal Society of Medicine, and enjoyed yet more lavish hospitality from their British hosts.[35]

Time was now running short, but Cotton still squeezed in a brief excursion to Norway before his return to New York. In 1926, the Norwegian government had sent Rolf Gjessing from the Dikemark Asylum in the Oslo area to work alongside Cotton in Trenton and to learn his methods. Now they arranged for a visit by the great man himself to the Norwegian capital. Sailing from Newcastle on Saturday July 30 on a small steamer, the *Bessheim*, Cotton spent three busy days consulting and sightseeing with his Norwegian hosts. Gjessing took his American guest to the asylum where he served as assistant superintendent, and "exhibited a number of patients who had been in America and while there had become victims of our American dentistry; many gold caps, Richmond crowns and fixed bridge work were noticed." He noted ruefully, however, that since he "had only returned from America last October he had not had the time to put into effect [all] the methods studied at Trenton." Still, Gjessing had thrown himself into the study of his patients' metabolism, and "the work of removing focal infection had progressed fairly well, especially in regard to the teeth." Regrettably, from Cotton's point of view, "as yet very little work had been done in removing tonsils because of the general aversion throughout the country to removing tonsils. I had heard of this from several sources and Dr. Gjessing spoke of the great difficulty he had in getting his nose and throat man to remove tonsils. It was very clearly brought out [though] that the same foci of infection existed in the patients in this country, even including intestinal toxemia, and they were fully cognizant of the importance of these facts."[36]

Fêted for his work at a series of elaborate dinners and lunches attended by leading Norwegian psychiatrists and politicians, it was naturally with some reluctance that Cotton finally boarded the train for Bergen and made the return trip to England. Exhausted, but buoyed by his uniformly positive reception, he barely had time to make his connections to Southampton, where he boarded the same ship that had brought him to Britain, the SS *Carminia*, for his return to the United States. Seven weeks and a day after he had first begun his travels, on August 14, he reached New York. At once, he set out for Trenton, newly invigorated, and ready once more to lead the assault on the perils of pus infection. He was, he recorded privately, "positive that what I have learned will be of immense benefit in the future treatment of our infected cases."[37]

14

Betrayals

The fall of 1927 marked the twentieth anniversary of Henry Cotton's appointment as the superintendent of Trenton State Hospital. In celebration of this auspicious occasion, the grateful state legislature passed a concurrent resolution lauding the "great humane and economic value to the State" of his work, and expressed the hope that, "he will continue for many years in the field of activity which he has so nobly graced for so long."[1] The troubles spawned by the Bright Committee's hearings in the summer of 1925, and Cotton's own mental breakdown and recovery, had been safely buried by now. The press had forgotten the lurid tales of evisceration and death that disaffected patients' families had stirred up, and Cotton's mental equilibrium had apparently been restored. In place of scandal, there had been reports in the New York papers in August of the triumphant reception accorded Cotton and his ideas by the assembled luminaries of British surgery, medicine, and psychiatry, and such ringing endorsements of their superintendent were a source of enormous pride to a state often seen as a provincial appendage of that great metropolis.

To be sure, Cotton had scarcely succeeded in converting most American psychiatrists to his way of thinking, and periodic expressions of disquiet surfaced in the professional literature about his claims for focal sepsis. Sanger Brown, for instance, the assistant commissioner of the New York State Department of Mental Hygiene, had used the occasion of his presidential address to the American Psychopathological Association to denounce Cotton's work:

> This form of treatment is supposed, by some, to be applicable to most forms of mental disease and mental disturbance, and often is accompanied by one form or another of surgical procedure. Now, no one would be so unwise as to minimize the need to remove focal infections in the maintenance of health; but on the other hand the treatment of nearly all forms of mental disease and mental disturbance through surgical procedures by

the removal of focal infection is unwarranted. This type of treatment takes on the nature of a cure-all. This treatment seems attractive to the laity, because it is so simple, but that fact does not make it scientifically sound.[2]

Criticisms of this sort, however, in no way inhibited Cotton's ability to extend his program of surgical bacteriology, and patients of means continued to find their way to Trenton in search of the promised cures. Only the damning report written by Phyllis Greenacre still lurked in the background as a potential problem, and the combination of obfuscation and obstruction by his allies on the hospital board, Cotton's own truculence, his aggressive assault on Greenacre's findings, and Adolf Meyer's decision to grant his protégé veto power over the release of her report seemed to have contained that difficulty, for the time being at least. Even the flurry of meetings before Cotton and Meyer had left for their visits to Europe had ended in stalemate, and far from pursuing the issue of the value or otherwise of defocalization when he had the chance to do so before a broad professional audience, Meyer had shied away from even attending the meeting, ignominiously preferring to avoid venturing an opinion in the debate over focal sepsis.[3]

Though Phyllis Greenacre may not initially have been aware of Meyer's decision to avoid traveling north to Edinburgh, his diplomatic silence, his refusal to speak of what he knew of Cotton's claims, even before his professional peers, could not long remain a secret. The fall numbers of both the *British Medical Journal* and the *Journal of Mental Science* included extensive and prominent coverage of the joint session of the British Medical Association and the Medico-Psychological Association devoted to focal sepsis, reprinting the formal papers presented and the lengthy discussions that had ensued. On reading these reports, which were full of extravagant praise for Cotton's work and extolled the virtues of removing focal sepsis among the psychotic, Greenacre inevitably felt a deep sense of betrayal. For she knew full well that Meyer had sailed for Britain intending to attend the conference. Yet where was his voice in the debate? Why had he once more remained silent, even in the face of claims he knew were false, even while patients continued to be maimed and to die at the hands of Henry Cotton and his associates?

Greenacre was not alone in feeling betrayed by Meyer's silence in this matter, and in being astonished by Cotton's reception in Britain. In New York, Nicholas Kopeloff, whose experimental work with George Kirby had been central to American doubts about Cotton's claims, also read the reports in the British medical press with something approaching incredulity. In early January of 1928, he wrote to Meyer regretting that, "when last in Baltimore I found that you had left for New York and therefore had no opportunity to discuss this matter with you." Still, "you have doubtless seen in the *British Medical Journal* for November 5, 1927, that Dr. H. A. Cotton's ideas are being ardently championed in England by Drs. Hunter, Moynihan, Graves, and others. I am particularly anxious," he continued, "to ascertain your opinion as to the present status of the relation of focal infection to the functional psychoses." Kopeloff revealed that during his Baltimore visit, "I learned that Dr. Greenacre had spent considerable time at Trenton going over Dr. Cotton's material. It was my hope that the results of her study would be published; but since this has not been the case, may I take the liberty of inquiring into the general nature of Dr. Greenacre's conclusions?"[4]

Kopeloff might take that liberty, but Meyer insisted that he was not *at* liberty to respond. Once again, as on previous occasions when others had attempted to learn what Greenacre had found, Meyer was obdurate: "I regret to say that the investigation of Dr. Greenacre is still under discussion, and I am not in a position to give the details until the whole matter will be thoroughly reviewed by Dr. Cotton and myself." Disingenuously, he insisted that, "in the discussion of the English group Dr. Henderson represented very effectively the critical attitude" – though Meyer knew full well that Henderson, another of his former assistants, had been isolated and scorned when he raised his skeptical points, an isolation to which he himself had directly contributed by opting to stay away from the session. And then Meyer took matters a step further: "today," he continued, "clinicians seem to be in a rather weak position when they have to determine whether an individual is or is not reacting unfavorably to any existing focal infection." There was a need "to determine what is reasonable and plausible in that which led Cotton rather unhappily to think of his having discovered *the* cause of functional psychoses" – for with respect to the possible role of sepsis in the genesis of psychosis, "I personally still feel that the question cannot be considered as disposed of. There should be pretty thorough work done on the *share* of infections, and that evidently would require methods that are not at present dependable."[5] The implication so far as Kopeloff was concerned, of course, was that neither his own research, nor Greenacre's as yet unpublished findings constituted such sufficiently thorough work, and that the question of the value of Cotton's interventions remained an open one, at least in the Hopkins professor's eyes.

It had been Greenacre's promptings, and her periodic requests to be allowed to publish some of her Trenton findings, that in the eighteen months before he sailed to Southampton had led to Meyer's half-hearted private attempts to pressure the Trenton authorities into some sort of response to her detailed critique. Those efforts had unquestionably grown more feeble over time. Yet even after his triumph in Edinburgh, Cotton had to be concerned that this meddlesome – and, as he saw it, misguided and malevolent – woman might yet derail his plans. Instead, unbeknownst to him, unrelated events in Baltimore would soon permanently remove that threat. For within a short period, Meyer's professional betrayal and cowardice would soon seem of quite minor personal significance to Greenacre, when placed alongside a deeper personal betrayal, one that would threaten, not just her career, but her own sanity.

Virtually alone among her contemporaries, Greenacre had sought to combine a full-time career in academic medicine with marriage and children. Ann and Peter, now aged six and five respectively, had been looked after by a nanny for much of the time while their mother pursued her professional ambitions. Even the eighteen months of fieldwork at Trenton had not dissuaded her from continuing her career, and so far as the outside world was concerned, as Adolf Meyer commented to his brother Hermann, "everybody had thought she was one of the few who had succeeded in combining scientific and professional work with homemaking."[6]

It was, however, an illusion. Greenacre's marriage to Curt Richter had been fraught and unhappy for some years now. Her depression, which Meyer himself had diagnosed as a "psychosis" in 1918,[7] had resurfaced periodically, most notably after Peter's arrival, when her emotional turmoil had led to rapid weight gain. And beneath the surface, it turned out that Curt Richter deeply resented her decision to continue her academic career. In the months to come, he would bitterly accuse her of "a lack of affection for the children as shown by her continuing in medicine," and complain of "her inability to create a home that would have attracted him."[8]

One suspects that these harsh and wounding attacks were *post hoc* rationalizations, for the truth was that Richter had for some time been having an affair with a Hopkins laboratory assistant, just like John Watson before him. For months, with her marriage increasingly in tatters, Greenacre sought desperately to keep up appearances, but the emotional toll was enormous, and it was compounded by a growing inability to sleep. Enduring months of what, even a year later, "still stands out as such vivid pain,"[9] she was nonetheless devastated when she finally became aware of the identity of her husband's inamorata, a young woman with whom both she and the children had been on friendly terms.

It was a crushing blow to her self-esteem. "I did care very deeply; and the disruption of all that feeling and of all the ideals involved, seems to have shaken me very fundamentally."[10] Almost without thinking, she rushed to inform

Meyer, who subsequently confessed to his brother that, "I was absolutely bowled over when Dr. Greenacre came to tell me the tale of disaster."[11] Richter, he confided, would have to go – the parallel with the Watson case, when Meyer had played a major role in forcing his philandering colleague's dismissal, was clear to them both. On the other hand, "I do not know whether Dr. Greenacre will or can stay."[12] Three weeks later, matters were clearer on that front, and he lamented that, "these are rather hard days. Dr. Greenacre is going to leave" – adding, as an aside, that "Dr. Richter no doubt will have to do so too."[13]

Selfishly, Meyer's first instinct was to complain about the difficulties *he* confronted as a consequence of these developments: "Dr. Greenacre leaves at a time when I should have had all her help." But he was also sensible of the emotional and practical difficulties his long-time colleague now confronted: "I am afraid she is not going to have an easy road. She may get into the depressive condition again which she had in 1917 and 1918."[14]

So indeed it proved. Leaving her children briefly with Mrs. Meyer while she sought an apartment in White Plains, New York,[15] Greenacre chose the week between Christmas and New Year's Eve to flee Baltimore, securing, with Meyer's assistance, a position as staff psychiatrist with the juvenile court and department of child welfare. Her children and their nanny soon joined her, and she just barely managed to keep functioning on the job while for two bitter years negotiations over a divorce dragged out. Profoundly depressed and deeply unhappy with the constricted intellectual horizons her new job provided,[16] Greenacre sought emotional relief from courses of psychoanalytic therapy, first with a Jungian analyst, Beatrice Hinkle, and then, in the early '30s, with two Freudians, Fritz Wittels and Edith Jacobson.[17] And though Meyer invited her back for a Phipps reunion in May 1928, and then (perhaps partially out of a sense of guilt) offered her a position as head of a new unit conducting research on schizophrenia,[18] he can scarcely have been surprised when she rejected both invitations.[19]

Meyer's puritanical instincts notwithstanding, Curt Richter had proved too valuable to dismiss. Meyer's wordy and convoluted proclamations about grounding psychiatry in "psychobiology" had turned out to be largely devoid of substance. The obscurity of his prose barely disguised – and in many quarters seemed increasingly insufficient to disguise – the emptiness of his claims, and to an increasing extent, too, many of his Hopkins colleagues seemed disposed to believe that his department was unworthy of their respect. Richter's skills as an experimentalist, his talents in devising new laboratory instruments, and his ability to link physiology with mental and emotional life, as in his discovery of the biological clock that deeply affected the quotidian reality of every human being, would in the future prompt his election to the National Academy of Science. Already, his research provided what little seeming substance there was to Meyer's psychobiological rhetoric, providing systematic evidence of some of the links between biology and behavior. Richter's friendship with many of the leading Hopkins scientists, and the respect with which they viewed his work, with its clever instrumentation and meticulous data collection, further complicated any decision to seek his dismissal.[20] Not long after Greenacre's departure for New York, Meyer had even suggested – and to her, no less – that Richter's contributions in the classroom, long a source of contention between the two men, were now so valuable as to make it difficult to contemplate his departure.[21]

The contrast with Meyer's behavior on an earlier occasion is instructive. He had clashed repeatedly with John B. Watson, Richter's predecessor, in the 1910s and early '20s, and when Watson was caught conducting his affair with an underling, Meyer had played a decisive role behind the scenes in ensuring his rival's ejection from his university post. Ever the sexual prude,[22] he had repeatedly pressured the Hopkins president to insist that Watson must resign, and he rejoiced in his departure. Almost incredibly (for it was the third time an occupant of Richter's position had been caught up in a sexual scandal in the space of a decade and a half), Meyer now confronted a parallel set of circumstances.

In some ways, on this occasion he was drawn even more deeply into the emotional maelstrom. Phyllis Greenacre had been his close associate for more than a decade now. She had grown to professional maturity under his guidance, and her estrangement from her own parents in Chicago had meant that she had come to regard Meyer as something of a substitute father figure,[23] seeking his advice on personal as well as professional matters, depending upon him when she had experienced two mental breakdowns, and sharing with him quite intimate details of her personal life. In the aftermath of her discovery of her husband's affair, it was to Meyer that she repeatedly turned for advice and support, and it was with him that she shared a blow-by-blow account of the disintegration of her marriage.

The shock of her husband's unfaithfulness, and the humiliation that flowed from the increasingly public knowledge of the collapse of her marriage, were only the beginning of Greenacre's troubles. Richter refused to enter discussions with her; objected at first to providing support for his children; suggested that since she had chosen to leave Baltimore, taking the children with her, and had her own professional career and income, she should provide for their support; and in general behaved in ways that magnified the pain that she suffered.

Bewildered, hurt almost beyond endurance, financially strapped, and her personal and professional life in ruins, Greenacre confided all these details to Meyer, going so far as to send him copies of both sides of her correspondence with Richter, and continually soliciting advice from her paternal substitute.[24] Characteristically, Meyer procrastinated and dissembled, wrung his hands over Richter's behavior, and expressed his sympathy to Greenacre, recognizing that were her husband's infidelity to become public knowledge he would be condemned, as the English would say, as a cad.[25] But when it came to acting upon what he knew, Meyer did essentially nothing,[26] though he was well aware that Richter's continued presence in Baltimore and as a member of the Hopkins faculty ensured that Greenacre would not return.[27] It was, of course, but the last in a series of personal and professional betrayals she felt that she had suffered at various hands.

Greenacre's permanent departure from the scene removed the last chance that Meyer might make any further attempt to confront the impact of Cotton's continued human experimentation. Even as she was packing to leave for New York, the Trenton board of governors had sent Meyer a formal invitation to join them for an elaborate celebration of the twenty years of progress at their hospital under Cotton's guidance. Though Meyer declined "because of another engagement," he did so "with very great regret . . . It is," he wrote back to Joseph Raycroft, "a splendid and well-deserved thing to celebrate the 20th anniversary of what has been a most creditable and noteworthy period in psychiatric activity. I remember with great satisfaction having had an opportunity to encourage Dr. Cotton to accept his position, and following step by step the many valuable innovations he had brought about . . . hence my pleasure in conveying my expressions of highest appreciation through you."[28]

The celebration of those "valuable innovations" drew more than 450 guests to the dinner to mark the occasion, notable among them New Jersey's governor,[29] and with the congratulations still ringing in their ears, Cotton and his associates turned once more to the seemingly endless task of elimination. Wealthy patients, many from out of state, continued to flock to Trenton, as their families sought his services. And to meet the urgent demand from the importunate, and to augment his state salary, Cotton maintained a private hospital in town, where he could operate on his private patients as needed.[30]

If the rich often volunteered for detoxification, the poorer patients who thronged the wards of the state hospital were not always so eager. Martha Hurwitz, for example, was brought to the asylum on December 28, 1928, from her parents' house at 24 New Street in Trenton. She had been born in Russia in 1902 and had arrived in America in 1921, marrying some four years later. But her

30 *Dr. Joseph Raycroft was, like Phyllis Greenacre, a graduate of Chicago-Rush Medical College. He was recruited to Princeton, where he served as the founding chairman of the Department of Health and Physical Education. President of the Trenton State Hospital board of managers from the late 1920s onwards, he was for many years a key supporter of Cotton's therapeutic approach.*

husband turned out to be a drunk and a ne'er do well. He was "a gambler and did not want to make a living for the patient. He even wanted to sell the furniture for money when they were pressed."[31] Within two months he had deserted her, and within a few months more had stopped paying her court-ordered maintenance. A bright young woman who had attended night school and who, her parents proudly reported, could read and write in "Polish, Jewish [*sic*], and English," Martha sought employment as a dressmaker in Philadelphia. But soon she fell into a depression, ceased to work, and became intermittently violent. Short spells in a private mental hospital in Philadelphia and then at Byberry State Hospital produced a temporary improvement, and she was released back to her parents' care. For a time, "she was quiet and gave no trouble," but she had a fall and broke her ankle on the day she was admitted to Trenton, and became talkative and restless, prompting her family to bring her to the state hospital. Provisionally diagnosed as a case of "Septic Psychosis, Schizophrenic Type" by the admitting physician, she was subjected to a searching physical examination. Nine gold fillings were found in her mouth. Her other teeth appeared to be sound, however, and "constipation is denied by patient." "Defocalization, institutional and symptomatic treatment" was ordered, and on January 4 she received the first of a series of three doses of typhoid vaccine, had a tonsillectomy, and several teeth were extracted. Following these interventions, Martha "was quiet and gave no trouble," and within a few months she was released as "recovered" – yet another success story for Cotton to boast of.

Unluckily for Martha, however, her mental improvement did not last. In the late summer of 1929, while she was in the midst of divorcing her husband, she fell and broke a leg, severely enough to require surgery. Together, these events seem to have precipitated another crisis, and on October 23 her mother and brother brought her back to the hospital, complaining that in the aftermath of her accident she was "very nervous and excitable," depressed and occasionally violent. Martha was evidently in a state of panic over the prospect of being re-admitted to Trenton, crying, fighting with her mother, insisting that "she would rather be dead than to be returned to this hospital" and running outside in an attempt to escape – a hopeless effort, since the cast on her leg allowed for her easy recapture. On admission, J. B. Spradley, one of Cotton's assistants, indicated that she "appeared depressed. Very neat in appearance. Cooperative. Irrational conduct at home indicated mental disorder."[32]

The hospital's case notes indicate that Martha's cooperation did not persist long after her admission. Later that same day, she was reported to be "resistive and uncooperative and stated she was not going to stay here." Three days later, she again "insists on going home. Will not stay in bed, has to be forced to take her food. Is resistive and uncooperative." When her physician attempted a gynecological examination, she resisted so fiercely that she had to be held down by four or five nurses, and then was placed in seclusion. On November 13, the ward notes indicated that she "is mildly agitated, wants to go home. Fairly well oriented to time and place . . . Shows considerable spontaneity . . . Resistive, but not assaultive." Her case was presented at a clinical conference by another of Cotton's assistants, Harold Magee, on December 12, and the poor woman, speaking only broken English, was briefly interviewed before the assembled psychiatrists:

Q. Come here, have a seat, you know me.
A. I don't want to stay here. I come for a couple of days.
Q. You remember me, don't you?
A. I don't know. I have to get out.

Q. Let me see your mouth.

A. I have false teeth, they used to take it out. This dress came from someone else and I couldn't stay here fight, my brother comes for me . . .

Q. How old are you?

A. I am thirty years old,

Q. You were twenty-six when you were here in twenty-eight. All right,
that is all, we will excuse you.

And she was led out.

Septic psychosis, schizophrenic. Confused type. That was the verdict, and
a week later, the clinical consequences of the diagnosis began to manifest
themselves. On that date, December 19, 1929, her case file simply records,
"Extraction – complete." All her remaining teeth, fourteen of them, had now
been removed, rendering her edentulous. Next, her doctors turned their attention to her "Gastro-Intestinal Tract, although the barium plate shows some
improvement over the plate taken when she was here before." Perhaps sensing
her fate, Martha spent the following days desperately trying to take the cast off
her leg, crying and irritable. "She seems to live in a world all by herself. Is restless
and walks about the ward aimlessly at times. Has been extremely resistive and
uncooperative, assaultive and ugly [*sic*] to all examinations and treatments. Will
not answer questions . . . Shrugs her shoulders and says she wants to go home."

Efforts by the staff to document continuing mental problems during this
period were largely fruitless. In December, her case notes indicate that, "no
delusions or paranoid trends have been elicited. Hallucinations and Illusions –
Are not elicited." Her charge nurse recorded that "P[atien]t answers questions
spontaneously. Quiet at all times, likes to read, rational." A few days later, an
apparently contradictory note claimed that "Patient is disoriented for time and
space." Yet the only evidence cited in support of this judgment was Martha's
sarcastic retort when she was asked when she had come into the hospital – "says
that she did not bother to look at the calendar." And at that same interview,
when she was asked where she lived and how many times she had been in the
hospital, her answers were acknowledged to be correct. Later still, a note in the
file that "she has absolutely no insight into her condition" sits uneasily alongside another that records that "due to the patient's extreme uncooperativeness
and resistiveness it was nearly impossible to obtain very much insight into her
mental organization, insight and judgment."

With her resistance defined as pathology, and her refusal to share her cap-
tors' diagnosis of her problems interpreted as a lack of insight, more vigorous
efforts were now directed at Martha's mysterious mental state. She found

herself subjected to a series of twenty colonic irrigations, and when she remained recalcitrant, a second series was ordered. Calcium therapy was tried, along with coagulation of her cervix. Her sinuses were punctured in the search for yet more sepsis, but on this occasion, the laboratory results were negative, so further invasion of her nasal passages was called off. The colonic irrigations, likewise, were adjudged to have been a failure, so more serious surgery was now in store: "She had an X ray study [of her abdomen] which showed pathology and [on February 20th] Lane's operation was performed." (Named after the British surgeon Sir Arbuthnot Lane, this was an operation designed to relieve "adhesions" in the bowel wall, thus accelerating the passage of potentially poisonous fecal matter through her system.)

Perhaps this series of surgical assaults taught Martha Hurwitz a lesson, for subsequent notes record that "she is now improving and the prognosis is considered good." And, sure enough, offering renewed testimony to the value of defocalization, she left the hospital with her father on June 16, 1930. In the eyes of her psychiatrists, she had recovered once more.

In many respects, Martha Hurwitz's experience mirrored that of other Trenton patients in the late 1920s. For, spurred on in part "by a personal experience," Henry Cotton had become more, not less aggressive in his approach to the necessary work of "elimination." In early summer of 1928, Cotton himself was diagnosed with "a heart condition and angina," and "on the advice of [his good friend] Dr. Thomas C. Graves of Birmingham [, England]" he had "a number of vital teeth extracted in August 1928. Twenty-four hours following the extraction of the teeth, the so-called vital teeth which were supposed not to be infected, the extra systoles" – or skipping of the pulse every second or third beat – "disappeared and have not been in evidence since." All was not completely well, however, because "the angina symptoms persisted . . . Finally in July 1929, the last four vital teeth were extracted . . . The blood pressure which was below 100 has reached normal and the condition of the heart was so good that he was accepted for life insurance during this summer."[33] What was good for Cotton would surely be good for his patients. Henceforth, he announced, "in the treatment of oral infection . . . one must be radical"[34] – even more radical, that is, than he had previously been. There was a critical need, he insisted once more, to educate doctors and dentists, but also the public, about the dangers of root canals, crowns, and the like. Defocalization directed at other hidden reservoirs of infection in the deeper recesses of the body would do no good at all if infected teeth remained in place.[35] In determining which teeth were infected, he had now concluded that both X-rays and direct inspections of the mouth were "unreliable," and the Trenton staff consequently felt that an elevated white blood cell count provided sufficient grounds to pull out teeth. Similarly, direct evidence that unerupted wisdom teeth were infected was lacking, so "we have to depend largely on our experience for justification in extracting these teeth." That presented few problems, since "we could cite many mental cases which recovered within twenty-four hours after the extraction of impacted third molars."[36]

In parallel fashion, Cotton announced that "the degree of infection is not a reliable indication in determining whether the tonsils should be removed. From our experience we are convinced that tonsils showing any infection whatever need to be enucleated."[37] And yet, regrettably, even such radical measures as these did not always suffice to produce recovery. So far from discrediting his approach, however, "from the fact that elimination of infected teeth and tonsils in some cases produces marvelous results and in other cases no results whatever it is logical to conclude that infection is brought to other parts of the body" and to operate accordingly.[38]

Temporary improvements, followed by a relapse, as exemplified by Martha Hurwitz's rehospitalization, provided, in Cotton's eyes, yet further support for his approach: "Possibly every person is subject to a certain amount of systemic toxemia which he is able to neutralize through his own immunity. However, when the toxemia becomes excessive the patient breaks down." Cutting down on some, but only some, of the sources of trouble could provide temporary relief and a brief but deceptively incomplete recovery. As the underlying infection built up again, however, relapse was apparently all-too-likely.[39] While his opponents might cite these relapses as a disconfirmation of his claims, for Cotton they were precisely the reverse: only a complete cleansing would suffice, and it was precisely the failure of his critics to obliterate every vestige of sepsis, their failure to be as persistent and thorough as he was, that explained their inability to replicate his success.

Cotton cited three other cases to exemplify what happened when surgical treatment was insufficiently radical. One of his patients, for example, had had no fewer than five separate attacks of insanity between the ages of 15 and 22, and had recovered from all of them. A sixth breakdown was treated with a series of colonic irrigations, designed to wash out toxic materials from the intestines, but the family of the patient had refused to allow any dental work to be done. The upshot was that recovery proved only temporary, and the patient was soon back. Extraction of six lower molars in July 1929 produced a modicum of improvement, but it was only after a course of typhoid vaccine and the extraction of all remaining teeth in November that Cotton felt able to pronounce the patient cured – just days before composing the paper in which he announced these findings.

An eighteen-year-old Italian girl with "agitated depression" provided another valuable illustration of the underlying principle. Successively, the hospital staff extracted upper and lower molars, undertook a tonsillectomy, drained her sinuses, treated her infected cervix, and removed her intestinal adhesions via abdominal surgery, all without effecting any improvement. Some months later, Cotton insisted that all her remaining teeth be extracted, and the consequence was a rapid recovery. Her case was paralleled by their experience with treating a fifty-year-old married female who had been admitted on July 14, 1928, with an agitated depression of some three months' standing. Her tonsils were removed, her colon was regularly irrigated, she was given serums and vaccines, prescribed a course of calcium therapy, had her cervix coagulated, was given three blood transfusions, and placed under ultra-violet lights, all to no avail. Eight months of treatment and no apparent improvement, until on March 8, 1929, the dentist extracted thirteen more teeth (all she apparently had left) and her sinuses were drained of pus. The following month, she was sent home recovered.[40]

In fact, more than a decade of experience, and the beneficial effects of radical treatment in his own case, had convinced Henry Cotton that it was time to address problems more aggressively still. "The dental profession," he complained, "still have a horror of extracting teeth and its conservativism is deplorable from many standpoints."[41] Foolishly, as he somewhat shamefacedly conceded, he too for a time had not had the courage of his convictions. Now he knew better:

> Many dentists would hesitate to extract vital [in other words healthy] teeth and for some years we followed this practice. But we have found within the last year that many of our failures were due to the fact that we allowed vital teeth to remain in the mouth although we had extracted a large number of devitalized teeth, which were infected. It has become the rule now that if a patient is found to have a considerable number of infected teeth complete extraction must be done in order to eradicate all infection in the mouth . . . we have by necessity become more radical.[42]

Some might complain that such measures went too far. On the contrary, "we have yet to have any regrets when we have ordered complete extraction in our patients and no patients when they have recovered have ever blamed us for extracting the teeth . . . [Better yet,] it is a source of satisfaction to know that the infection has been entirely eliminated and there is no prospect of any further trouble." And bearing this rationale in mind, a further extension of their work suggested itself: the screening of all children between the ages of twelve and fifteen for dental trouble, an approach by which a whole generation might escape the scourge of mental disorders. "Of course, infection of the tonsils is pretty well recognized," he commented, "and very few children today escape having the tonsils enucleated. However, the dental work leaves much to be desired . . . Here is a condition which is menacing the health of the nation . . . It is our duty to educate the public as to the seriousness of oral infection," and perhaps to launch a campaign of prophylactic extractions – a sensible precautionary move he had already pressed upon his own two sons and his wife. "Often," to be sure, "the removal of impacted molars at an early age would conserve the rest of the teeth, but if these impacted and unerupted molars remain in the mouth infection is very apt to spread to other teeth and sooner or later it will mean complete extraction."[43]

If wholesale removal of the teeth was now seen as the precondition to an effective assault on the perils of pus infection, it most certainly would not always suffice by itself. As a new decade dawned, Cotton reiterated his insistence that, "we do not depend on any single method to produce results," and proclaimed that "our success has been due to a combination of methods, all directed to the elimination of all sources of infection."[44] In a recent survey of 500 consecutive admissions at Trenton, "there were found 3,550 pathological conditions, or an average of 7 pathological conditions per patient."[45] Just as he had had to adopt a more aggressive approach to the pathologies of the mouth, so, too, a more invasive approach to other regions of the body now appeared to be mandatory, "for there can be no question that infection originating in the mouth, especially in the teeth and tonsils, migrates to other parts of the body setting up secondary foci of infection."[46]

Searching more scrupulously than before, his staff had uncovered "infections of the cervix . . . in about 76% of the female patients" and innovative measures had been adopted to attack the problem – the diathermy treatment to which Martha Hurwitz had been subjected was, it seemed, "a successful measure producing recoveries."[47] Problems involving "the lower intestinal tract, especially the colon," were, it now transpired, even more common. With "sluggishness and delay due to the toxic effects of chronic infections on the musculature of the colon . . . at least 86%" of both male and female patients "will be found to have intestinal stasis and toxemia," making these pathologies a far more frequent source of insanity than even he had hitherto thought. Removal of teeth and tonsils, and aggressive treatment with vaccines derived from the contents of the stomach could be expected to produce a degree of improvement, but the underlying difficulties often persisted. Even where patients reported no problems with constipation, further investigations were warranted, since quite commonly, even in these cases, "X-ray studies showed very serious abnormalities."[48]

Fortunately, in a "large proportion" of cases, the putrefactive processes and the mental illness to which they gave rise could be eliminated "by means of physiotherapy which consists of massive colonic irrigations, 15–20 gallons in a treatment, and diathermy and Morse Sine Wave."[49] As Cotton had come to realize how crucial these treatments were to his success, he had reassigned twelve nurses to the unit where they could be administered, and he boasted that utilizing a King–Scheerer Table and two way stop-cock, diathermy, and Morse sine wave on alternate days, they were able, in many cases, "to restore the muscular tone of the colon." Irrigating patients' colons for as many as six to eight hours a day, these dozen nurses had managed to give almost ten thousand such treatments in the preceding year, "and while this work may be very uninteresting and laborious, the results which they obtain are so marked that they show an extreme interest in the work." Even patients with a history of years of constipation yielded to the treatment, and they now, he contended, recovered with alacrity.[50] Hence, "the procedure has come to the point of each case right after admission being given colonic irrigations as soon as possible."[51]

Two courses of this treatment, extending over four or five months, usually sufficed to produce positive results. However, if, after all this sustained effort, improvement was still lacking, then more extreme surgical measures were called for. The issue was a complicated one. Cotton recalled that the colectomies he had relied upon between 1918 and 1925 had produced a mortality rate of some 30 percent, though "then it seemed to be the only method to be used." To be sure, as he hastened to add, the surgery had also produced a 30 percent recovery rate. Still, "we had to admit that the mortality was of sufficient importance for us to limit the surgery as far as possible," even though another criticism that had been leveled at the time, "that on removing the colon the patient would become a chronic invalid . . . we have found not to be the case."[52] Further experience had now convinced him that in non-responsive cases, a conservative approach was misplaced. Not that resecting the colon guaranteed a cure, "but even patients who did not recover their mental trouble [*sic*] following resection" could console themselves with the thought that they were "in perfect physical condition as far as the intestinal condition is concerned."[53]

Abdominal surgery was thus once more a central part of Trenton's treatment program, and the hospital's operating theater, its dentist's chair, and its laboratories were again hives of activity. For Henry Cotton, the confrontations in Baltimore over Phyllis Greenacre's report were now little more than a bitter memory. Adolf Meyer showed no disposition to press him or the Trenton board of managers any further. And free of any anxieties from that quarter, Cotton's grand experiment moved forward with even greater vigor than before.

15

Death in the Trenches

Like most psychiatrists who headed state hospitals, Henry Cotton enjoyed near-autocratic powers over the day-to-day affairs of his institution. After more than twenty years as the medical director at Trenton, he had in place a compliant staff, a group of medical men who evidently shared his enthusiasm for the campaign to root out sepsis, and his authority at the beginning of 1930 must have seemed stronger than ever. Yet within months, a threat from a wholly unexpected direction sharply curtailed his powers and led to his being shunted sideways into a newly created position, as "medical director emeritus, and director of research."

Ironically, it was the very success of his efforts to educate the general public about the dangers of pus infection, and the widespread publicity given to his claims to have a surgical cure for madness, that had prompted his problems. Early on, following his recognition of the significance of focal sepsis, news of his claims to have produced a therapeutic breakthrough had drawn affluent patients from well beyond New Jersey's borders in search of a miracle cure. At first, these out-of-state patients had been accommodated at Trenton State Hospital itself, the state charging a healthy premium over what it cost to house and treat them, and Cotton boasting of the financial windfall that thereby accrued to New Jersey's coffers. Soon, however, the sheer numbers seeking his ministrations outgrew the available space to house them. Besides, Cotton had sensed an opportunity to add to his own state salary. By the time the Bright Committee had begun its inquiry into the hospital's affairs, Cotton had long been diverting many of his most affluent patients to a private nursing facility in town, where he could supervise the extraction of teeth, the enucleation of tonsils, and perform abdominal surgery, pocketing handsome fees in the process.

But if his private practice was not novel, and was scarcely a secret from his board of managers, it was nonetheless a source of vulnerability. Cotton was, after all, a full-time, salaried state employee, paid quite handsomely (and given a house and maintenance into the bargain) for overseeing a state hospital that housed hundreds and hundreds of patients. In the roaring twenties, the fact that he simultaneously profited from a growing private practice had passed without comment, but in the new environment brought about by the Great Depression, such double-dipping provoked growing resentment among private-sector physicians. Complaints were made to the New Jersey State Medical Society, and then to state politicians, that Cotton's actions were unethical and an affront to the taxpayers. Cotton tried to dismiss it all as so much sour grapes, "a question of financial and professional jealousy."[1] But the issue would not go away.

The Trenton hospital board came under mounting pressure to act. At its July 10 meeting, it noted that the state had recently promulgated regulations about "outside private practice" by medical men in state employment, and its medical sub-committee, composed of Drs. Raycroft, Mecray, and Gill, were instructed to speak with Cotton and with New Jersey's commissioner of institutions and agencies, about the situation. The upshot, at a special board meeting held on July 31, 1930, was a decision to remove Cotton as medical director after twenty-three years: "Whereas," their resolution read, "it is the desire of the Board of Managers and Dr. Cotton to make arrangements whereby he can pursue the research and preventative phases of psychiatric services to the State, therefore, in order to make it possible for Dr. Cotton to give more attention to these activities to the exclusion of administrative details," they now elected to appoint him as "Medical Director Emeritus . . . to serve as consultant for psychiatric clinics and to conduct clinical research at the institution, at his present salary without maintenance." The administrative change was to be phased in, and was fully operational by October 1, 1930.[2]

Though this compromise offered a face-saving way out of a difficult dilemma, the hospital authorities' action did not appear likely to bring any drastic change of therapeutic regime. In truth, Cotton lost his autocratic control over the hospital, but the managers had appointed his enthusiastic deputy, Robert Stone, to replace him as medical director, and they gave no public evidence that they had retreated from their long-standing endorsement of Cotton's therapeutic regime.[3] Thus, though no longer resident on the hospital grounds, and stripped of direct authority over the hospital's day-to-day operations, Cotton had every reason to expect that his therapeutic program would survive essentially unscathed.

To Meyer, Cotton presented the change in his circumstances as the product of his own initiative. He announced to his mentor that he had "retired from the active executive work of the State Hospital after 23 years. The Board of

Managers made me Medical Director Emeritus and appointed me Director of Research Work. I had contemplated this change for sometime [*sic*] as I found it almost impossible to get any time for writing or reviewing my material while actively at the head of the hospital." There were other reasons he had embraced the change. He and Mrs. Cotton had bought a house in Princeton and planned to move in November. "After 31 years spent in institutions I thought I was entitled to have a few years outside of hospitals." There was also the issue of his health: while it is "very much better than it was a year or two ago, at the same time I found that I was hardly equal to carrying on the work as I had been doing in the past." All things considered, it seemed "an appropriate time to retire from the executive work."[4]

Not having responsibility for the day-to-day administrative chores, however, would allow him to focus his energies more intensively on what really mattered to him: "I have moved my office to the laboratory and now I am back to my first love. I shall devote my time to both clinical and pathological research and in the work of prevention." He was particularly keen, he informed Meyer, to expand his therapeutic activities because, "we have been able to locate and correct some of our serious mistakes and now I think the work can go on without hindrance."[5]

Those "mistakes," though, were errors of omission, not commission, as Cotton immediately made clear. His experience at Trenton since his return from Britain in the fall of 1927 had simply served to confirm "that we were not being radical enough in extracting teeth and the principal error was in failing to extract teeth which were infected although no evidence of infection could be demonstrated by X-ray or inspection." Once more he cited his own case as a clear demonstration of his basic point: "After the extraction of the last four lower teeth a year ago, my heart symptoms entirely disappeared and I have had no recurrence. As I probably told you, I had a very serious angina and was somewhat incapacitated for a year or so but I have had no return of the symptoms and each examination shows a steady improvement." The more ruthless pursuit of sepsis had had equally salutary results when applied to the patients: "In going over our cases we have turned many failures into success by extracting the remaining teeth. We also found the necessity for correcting the colon conditions, not necessarily by colectomy but by releasing the adhesions and in some cases this has to be done twice in order to produce results."[6]

Meyer hastened "to congratulate you on the well-earned change from administration to the undisturbed devotion to study," expressing not the slightest qualm about Cotton's plans for a more aggressive surgical program. Plaintively, if disingenuously (for Meyer would cling desperately to his Hopkins position well past the normal retirement age), he added that, "I wish I could do the same. But I have not quite the upper staff to do it."[7]

Months earlier, at Cotton's request, Meyer had spoken to the dean of the Hopkins medical school to secure Henry junior's admission, and the son had subsequently chosen to enroll there over Columbia, New York, and Harvard. His father had expressed great pleasure at this decision: "I still think Hopkins has a more stimulating effect upon students than other institutions and I am especially pleased that he will enjoy your stimulating influence. He is especially fortunate to be able to come under such good influence so early in his career." In his own case, Cotton noted, "I did not have that opportunity until long past my medical schooling, but I continue to be extremely grateful for my associations with you. It has meant a great deal to me and I feel I owe you a debt of gratitude for all you have done for me personally and professionally."[8]

Meyer professed himself delighted at the news, and basked in the accompanying flattery: "I appreciate the remarks of allegiance and appreciation of our longtime relations which have always been those of a warm relation of personal and professional nature." He waxed nostalgic about their long association: "I wonder whether you remember giving Mrs. Meyer and me a good lift on the skates. It is hard to believe that it is 23 years since we talked about Trenton in my office on Ward's Island. What you have made of that place!"[9]

Flattery was thus a two-way street. And Henry junior and Meyer's namesake, Adolph Cotton, helped to cement the bonds between the two men. Over the years, Henry senior had made a particular point of keeping Meyer apprized of his younger son's achievements and interests, to Meyer's evident delight. The professor now took an avuncular interest in Henry junior as well, he and Mrs. Meyer entertaining the young man at their home, and Meyer informing his father that, "it is a real pleasure to have him in our school." But it was young Adolph whom Meyer watched over most closely, and when Henry senior told him of the young man's career plans on completing his Princeton degree, Meyer professed himself well satisfied: "Adolph's desire to go in for architecture brings many thoroughly worthwhile interests into your life. Mrs. Cotton must be pleased too . . . Now that Henry is here, I hope you and Mrs. Cotton will come occasionally, and perhaps Adolph will find some interests as well."[10]

A few weeks after this exchange of intimate correspondence, an extended visit to Trenton by another of Adolf Meyer's assistants, the young Swiss psychiatrist Solomon Katzenelbogen, provided an outsider's perspective on the daily routine at the hospital in the aftermath of the administrative changes and Cotton's move to his new post as director of research. Meyer had hired Katzenelbogen "to be the head of our Internal Medicine Laboratory and internist of the Phipps Psychiatric Clinic" in June of 1928,[11] and it seems that the visit to Trenton some eighteen months later was undertaken at the young associate's own initiative, for over the ensuing decade, one of his major interests would turn out to be the assessment of a whole array of new physical treatments for psychosis that now began to enter psychiatry. Katzenelbogen provided a copy of his written report to Meyer, and this gave the professor his first independent assessment of conditions at Cotton's hospital since Greenacre had completed her work there in 1925.[12] It made for sobering reading.

To assess the situation at the state hospital, Katzenelbogen indicated that he had attended staff meetings, accompanied Cotton and the staff on ward rounds, examined the laboratories for diagnosis and treatment, and observed the routine handling of the patients. He also visited "Charles Hospital (Private Hospital in Trenton which is provided almost entirely with Dr. Cotton's private patients)." He began by noting at both hospitals the "strikingly high percentage of cases in which infection was found in one or another system, as indicated by Dr. Cotton's statistics . . . He claims that infection of the teeth occurs in practically 100 percent of his patients; infected tonsils in about 80 percent; involvement of the gastro-intestinal tract with consecutive toxemia in about 88 percent of cases," all figures that would have been familiar to those who had followed Cotton's publications. Perhaps, as Cotton suggested to him when he raised the matter, these extraordinary numbers reflected the fact that "hardly any one has been so persistent and thorough in searching for infections of different organs, as Dr. Cotton has proven to be." Surely, Katzenelbogen continued, given that the surgery that followed such diagnoses was "drastic and risky," patients would be subjected to such "dangerous operations only as a last resort" and "after a very cautious consideration of each individual case."

On the contrary, however, when he made his own observations, Katzenelbogen was struck by "the very unsatisfactory examination of the mental status" of patients, something that cast serious doubt on "the statistics referring to the recovery rates in certain psychotic types." Nor were the means for evaluating the improvement of patients' psychiatric states any more careful or satisfactory, and, "I was told by the members of the staff who worked for years under Dr. Cotton that there has been absolutely no change in the formulation of the cases since his resignation." In their eyes, "the accurate discrimination between different types of psychosis matters very little, for the reason that *any psychosis would be of septic origin* and the type of psychosis would be determined by the individual predisposition." More remarkably yet from his point of view, Katzenelbogen reported that, though a variety of X-ray and laboratory work was completed as a matter of routine on virtually all admissions by a staff Cotton boasted did "real medical work, not like in other psychiatric institutions," the testing was slipshod and badly performed, by medical staff not "sufficiently trained in physiopathology." Worse still, he observed that when even careless work did not suffice to demonstrate pathology, Cotton and his staff simply manipulated the accepted boundaries of what constituted an abnormal reading: "if it seems logical that that infection should induce certain blood alterations, and the latter cannot be elicited in the light of the generally accepted normal standards, then it is again logical to admit that there is something wrong with the normals."

Defocalization was thus the universal therapy, and Katzenelbogen next visited the wards to view the results. In the surgical division, "patients who had their teeth and tonsils removed, or had other surgical interventions kept quiet. The operation," he commented, "plus the anesthesia and the consecutive sickness quiets them." Everywhere, he saw maimed patients:

> I felt sad, seeing hundreds of people without teeth. Only a very few have sets of false teeth. The hospital takes care as to the pulling out of teeth, but does not provide false teeth ... The extraction of the teeth does great harm to those who cannot afford to pay for a set of false teeth, and these patients are numerous. While in the hospital they suffer from indigestion ... not being able to masticate their food. At home, recovered, these poor people have the same troubles, not being in a position to choose food which they would be able to eat without teeth. In addition, they are ashamed of being without teeth, since in their communities it is known to be a token of a previous sojourn in the State Hospital. They abstain from mixing with other people, refuse to go out and look for a job ... Thus, many of those recovered develop a reactive depression.

Elsewhere in the hospital, he observed the use of "malarial therapy," which had been introduced into psychiatry some years earlier as a treatment for tertiary syphilis "in manic depressive psychosis," and "the indiscriminate use of typhoid vaccine for intravenous injection in order to make the patient more manageable" – a practice he labeled "unfortunate." "The patients," he observed, "have fever, chills, and they quiet down. Those who have insight and had once the injection [*sic*] are threatened with being given a second one if they do not behave. The menace works well." In perhaps a quarter of patients, sinuses were punctured, washed, and drained, and, in female cases, cervixes were treated with electrical coagulation "quite frequently." Most patients, of both sexes, could also look forward to repeated "colonic irrigations (sodium bicarbane 50 gr. in 8 gallons of water) during 15 minutes or more every other day." As for colectomy, "I know that in general pathology it is being resorted to only in cases of carcinoma." At Trenton, where its employment had been routine, Cotton continued to boast of its efficacy, and to insist, as well, on the need to employ laparotomies, "to release intestinal adhesions." Constipation provided evidence that "the intestines are infected by stasis," but these less extensive operations were also "being done in cases in which there are no marked functional distur- bances of the g.i. tract or none at all." The failure to recover was itself seen as sufficient grounds for widening the sphere of surgical interference, and there appeared to be a blithe "certainty of finding abnormalities in the removed colons and adhesions on laparotomy."

Cotton insisted on the remarkable therapeutic benefits of these interven- tions, in at least some cases. Katzenelbogen, by contrast, was clearly skeptical, suggesting that to the extent that the abdominal surgery had any positive effect, these apparent improvements could instead be attributed to the powerful placebo effect that inevitably accompanied such a drastic procedure: "The treatment induces pain, fever, chills. The patient feels quite badly during the treatment and when he comes back to the *status quo ante*, he feels compara- tively improved. Also the relatives are hopeful." Any positive change is then attributed to the elimination of "the almighty 'focal infection.'" Worse still, besides the steep mortality rates associated with operative interference, there was a further iatrogenic complication of a singularly ironic sort, the creation of the very problem one purported to be relieving: "In resorting to such an oper- ation one should bear in mind that any surgical abdominal intervention may be followed by adhesions."

There had been, so it seemed, some changes in therapeutic practices since Cotton had been forced to step down as medical director. "Not infrequently [the staff] are prevented from pulling out all the teeth by the patient or by the relatives. This happens now much more frequently than it used to be with Dr. Cotton . . . for he invariably succeeded in getting permission in those cases where nobody else on the staff could."[13] And in the few weeks since Cotton's status had changed, colectomies "have so far not been done," Dr. Stone con- tenting himself with the less drastic laparotomies.

Whether this more conservative approach would persist was initially unclear. Cotton complained directly to Katzenelbogen that he "had a hard time to persuade the dentist to adopt his views on the indications of extractions . . . but I felt from my interviews with [Dr. Fischer] and from following his work that he also is quite badly infected with the idea of focal infection and is extremely easy in deciding upon extraction." For years, too, Stone had been Cotton's most devoted acolyte on the Trenton medical staff, though now he was himself in charge, he "does not seem to be enthusiastic about" the most radical abdominal surgeries. Katzenelbogen concluded his assessment of what he had seen by remarking that, "for my part, I would say without malice, that in their sacred efforts to do something for the patients since 'psychiatrists do nothing for them' they resort to laparotomies because there are no other available points of attack of 'septic foci' after the teeth and tonsils are removed and the cervix coagulated. The colon can be removed, at a high cost of human life, it is true, but still it can be done, why not try it since the conviction is absolute that the survived patients will get well?"

But in some quarters it turned out that the conviction about the value of colectomies was not so absolute after all. Though the staff Katzenelbogen spoke with did not trouble to "conceal their contempt for psychiatry, *in so far as it does not subordinate the psychic status to the physical condition*," he suspected that a number of them had previously suppressed doubts about some aspects of Cotton's approach, realizing that they "must do away with their 'phantasies and talking heresies' if they want to hold their position and make advancement." More importantly still, Katzenelbogen's observations had persuaded him that both the hospital's board of managers and the state bureaucrats had at last developed some qualms about the program of major abdominal surgery. Perhaps, like the patients' relatives who now had the temerity to reject suggestions that all their nearest and dearest's teeth should be extracted, the removal of Cotton from his position of unquestioned power emboldened them to adopt a more cautious course.

To Cotton's fury, his protégé and former chief assistant Robert Stone, now installed as director in his place, bent with the changing wind and abandoned the most elaborate and extensive abdominal surgery. Cotton tried browbeating him, and lobbying the managers themselves, but to no effect. In Cotton's private practice at the Charles Hospital, his interventions remained as aggressive as before, but, though teeth extractions, tonsillectomies, colonic irrigations, fever treatments, and the like continued to be part of the routine at the state hospital, and Stone even chose to perform a certain number of Lane's operations to relieve intestinal adhesions, Cotton's attempts to garner permission to resume his more radical surgery were consistently rebuffed. Neither his new title as "director of research" nor his characteristic attempts to bully and bluster past the opposition of Stone and his board of managers appeared to be of any avail.[14]

Cotton's threat to launch a campaign to reinstate a fully fledged war on sepsis was no idle one. With the ear of sympathetic state legislators, he sought to bring political pressure to bear in order to whip hospital managers and medical staff back into line. A resolution in the state senate lauded the vast sums of money his cures had saved the state, and urged a prompt resumption of his full

31 Dr. Robert Stone was Cotton's chief assistant physician in the 1920s and under-took most of the gynecological surgery performed at Trenton State Hospital. When Cotton was shunted sideways from the superintendency and given the post of head of research, Stone replaced him as head of the hospital, and immediately reined in the more controversial abdominal surgery, much to Cotton's dismay.

therapeutic program. Behind the scenes, too, he was composing a new assess-ment of the impact of his years in the front lines of the fight against pus infec-tion. The hospital authorities might deny him access to the operating theater, but as director of research, he still had access to the institution's records. Focus-ing entirely on the impact of surgery on the colon, Cotton sought once more to lay out "the facts," and to force the opposition to let him resume his life's work.

On November 15, 1932, he presented Joseph Raycroft, president of the board of managers, with an eight-page "Report on the Operative Procedures on the Colon in Mental Disorders."[15] By turns a polemic, a review of what Cotton claimed were the results of abdominal surgery at Trenton, and a summary of his more recent work with his private patients, the report ploughed much familiar ground. Yet it also revealed a major revision in his theory and practice, hinging upon a discovery that he claimed could sharply mitigate the one objec-tion to colectomies to which he gave any credence, the high mortality associ-ated with the operation. Claiming to be armed with a new understanding of why so many of his early patients had perished, he insisted he was now in a position to exploit the operation's therapeutic potential, without the risk of an untoward number of deaths.

Cotton's early publications on colectomies had in passing acknowledged a mortality rate associated with the surgery that approached 30 percent, a figure that prompted remarkably little public comment or criticism at the time. His new report, intended only for internal consumption, prominently acknowledged the issue of elevated patient mortality. "After determining in 1918 to hunt for chronic infection in our patients, I became convinced that many of these cases had serious gastro-intestinal stasis and possibly intestinal toxemia." Having attracted the New York surgeon John Draper to undertake the necessary surgery, "from 1918 to 1925 . . . some 300 cases suffering from so-called functional disorders, mainly dementia praecox cases, were operated upon and their colons either wholly or partially removed. Out of this number, 75 cases recovered both mentally and physically," though some of them only after two rounds of surgery. "These patients were all suffering from chronic mental disorders and in all probability would never have recovered their mental condition or left the hospital if the surgical methods had not been employed."[16]

But there was a dark side to this tale of success: "In this pioneer work the mortality rate was about 33⅓ percent, which means that one third of our cases died, usually of peritonitis." Worse still, "there seemed to be no definite explanation for this mortality. The technique used was the same in all cases. Yet frequently when such an operation was performed and no contamination was evident and we considered the operation perfect, the patient developed peritonitis and died." With some asperity, Cotton acknowledged that "we were criticized for this high mortality rate, although, as stated heretofore, the patients would never have been well mentally and we felt that under the conditions the risk was justified."[17]

Convinced of the need to eradicate contamination via the colon, yet aware that such a high mortality rate might not be regarded so complacently by others, Cotton had felt trapped in a painful dilemma. However, the way forward soon seemed clear. "In 1923," when he had first traveled to Britain to be hailed for his pioneering assault on focal sepsis, he was "fortunate enough to spend several months in London with Sir Arbuthnot Lane who was one of the first men to call attention to the importance of the colon and intestinal stasis and toxemia." At the great man's side, Cotton had learned of a new and less invasive form of surgery, the release of "congenital bands of adhesions" in the digestive tract, and had discovered that "gastro-intestinal X-ray studies of these patients showed very definitely where these bands were located and the resulting constrictions caused by them. In the fall of that year we adopted his method of releasing adhesions around the appendix, terminal ileum, ascending colon, hepatic flexure, splenic flexure and descending colon," with happy results, "because the mortality was reduced from 33⅓ percent to about 19 percent, and the recovery rate was 37 percent."[18]

Over the next seven years, Cotton recorded that he had undertaken 493 such operations at the state hospital, and in the process, he asserted, "148 patients permanently recovered." And yet the 19 percent mortality rate "we still considered too high" – and a puzzle besides, "because the colon was not opened and there were no visible sources of contamination or infection." Compounding the mystery, from his point of view, was the fact that some patients only improved temporarily, and others not at all. "We have since learned that although the condition of the colon at the time of operation apparently was good, very frequently it was so badly diseased that the adhesions re-formed and the intestinal toxemia went on as before. This fact was discovered in 1929 when we operated the second time on a number of patients" – releasing the new adhesions in some, and removing colons entirely in others.[19]

Alongside all this work at the state hospital, Cotton reminded the board that he had also been treating private patients in the city, at the Charles Hospital, where the use of abdominal surgery had continued unabated even after the managers had pushed him aside as medical director. Fortunately so, apparently, for he announced triumphantly that his work there had finally allowed him to uncover the reasons for the uncomfortably high mortality rates associated with both colectomies and Lane's operation. Moreover, having grasped the mortality's etiology, he had been able to solve the problem once and for all.

In all, he had conducted 148 operations to eliminate intestinal adhesions in his private facility between 1928 and 1932, and only 7 of these had died, "or a mortality rate of 4.8 percent." He had also resected, or removed, 18 colons, "with only 4 deaths, or 22 percent mortality," and "two of these deaths occurred in 1930 before we had changed our methods of technique." Those 2 deaths, to be sure, were, like the deaths that had occurred in the early 1920s, the result of post-surgical peritonitis, but the two most recent were not, both dying instead of chronic myocarditis, "so that the deaths from resections due to peritonitis were only 11 percent, contrasted with the rate of 33⅓ per cent at the State Hospital for cases from the earlier period of 1918 to 1923." As Cotton's ability to transform a 22 percent death rate to "only" 11 percent suggests, and as the following sentence of his report makes clear, so far as he was concerned, post-operative death from causes other than peritonitis could be dismissed as coincidental, unrelated to his surgical interventions. And in his eyes, this breakthrough had momentous implications: "Now that we have eliminated the mortality rate from operations on the colon, either for release of adhesions or resection, which was the principal objection raised against them, we see no reason why this procedure should not be adopted as a routine measure in the treatment of mental patients where it is indicated."[20]

What, for Cotton, explained this remarkable turnaround? The crucial clue, he informed the board of managers, had surfaced on July 2, 1929, when he had operated on two of his private patients on the same day. B.S., a 30-year-old who had been paranoid for two years, showed "very marked evidences of a chronic infection. Tonsils had been previously removed. Teeth were badly infected. She took my advice and had them all extracted." Operated upon "for a very serious stasis due to adhesions . . . she made an uneventful surgical convalescence and was discharged from the hospital three weeks following the operation." The second patient, E.L., was 55 years of age, and had been insane for three years. "In this case only the molars and bicuspids in the upper and lower jaw were extracted, leaving about 8 upper and 8 lower front teeth *which did not appear to be infected*. This patient developed peritonitis and died within a week."[21]

For Cotton, this coincidence was a eureka moment:

Here we have a condition which was almost experimental in character although it was not planned as such. Two patients having the same operation on the same day, similar pathological conditions and similar technique, with practically the same sterilization. The one with all teeth extracted made an uneventful convalescence and the other developed peritonitis and died. The only difference noted in these two cases was the fact that all teeth have been removed in one and in the other only the suspected infected teeth had been extracted. But those remaining were later found to be badly infected although not apparent in the X-rays.

Not only was the failure to render the second patient edentulous the obvious source of the differential outcome in this instance, but retrospectively, as he reflected on the situation, Cotton realized that here lay the source of "our high mortality from 1918 to 1923."[22]

Once the full significance of what Cotton saw as this unimpeachable discovery had sunk in, he did not hesitate to pursue its logic: "I soon made it a rule to not operate for either resection or release of adhesions in these patients until all teeth were extracted, irrespective of the age of the patient."[23] Failure to follow this rule in a handful of cases, which resulted in either patient death or the need to re-operate, only confirmed the linkage in his own mind, and demonstrated "without any question of a doubt that we were making serious mistakes by leaving teeth which were supposed to be normal, but in reality were infected even though the X-rays did not indicate it." For example, in "113 operations performed for releasing adhesions in the colon, only three patients have died . . . and in these three cases, infected teeth were present."[24]

The implications of these findings, Cotton was convinced, were enormous, and extended even beyond the psychiatric realm. Except where an emergency existed, "such as an acute appendicitis . . . I am convinced that no patient should have a serious abdominal operation, or any operation, without all infected teeth being extracted."[25] Within psychiatry, though, the way forward was clearer still: full dental extraction followed by abdominal surgery. And just how routine such surgery would need to be was made clear in the closing lines of his report, where he noted "that 80 percent of the so-called functional group [of mental patients] suffer from pathological conditions in the colon which must be surgically corrected before they will recover their mental condition."[26]

A few years earlier, the Trenton board of managers might have swallowed these arguments without a second thought, as they had done for years while Cotton headed the institution over which they nominally presided. But his loss of the medical directorship, and the bully pulpit it represented, seems to have encouraged them to react with greater skepticism. Indeed, hearing that Cotton planned to campaign for an expanded program of abdominal surgery, and perhaps to get his old job back, the board had taken the precaution of commissioning their own study of his prior results.

Beginning in June 1932, Emil Frankel, who served as the director of research of the New Jersey Department of Institutions and Agencies, began to comb through the hospital records, and to compile a systematic account of the fate of the several hundred patients who had been subjected to abdominal surgery while at Trenton, comparing their fate to that of a sample of patients whom he listed as "non-operative cases." To be sure, Frankel's definition of "major surgery" was somewhat idiosyncratic, for his "non-operative" control group consisted of patients who had routinely seen teeth and tonsils disappear (often along with other lesser organs like cervixes, gall bladders, stomachs, and spleens). Mrs. Lewis, for example, who was twice admitted to Trenton for "depression and anxiety" had the following surgeries: a gastroenterostomy to treat a stomach ulcer, an operation to repair the iatrogenic hernia the first operation left her with, a thyroidectomy, a double oophorectomy [removal of both ovaries] and salpingectomy [removal of the fallopian tubes], and enucleation of her cervix.[27] Using his standard definition Frankel would have assigned her to his "non-operative cases," except that her failure to improve also led to her being given a right-side partial colectomy, and then, when she still resisted being cured, a total colectomy.

Still, the "non-operative" cases were patients whose bowels, at least, had been immune from surgical assault, and it was colon operations that Cotton insisted were most frequently required if cures were to be obtained, with infected colons to be found in 80 percent of those suffering from serious mental disorders. What sorts of patients, Frankel wondered, had been subjected to surgery on their colons? And how did the outcomes among these contrasting groups of patients compare with the results Cotton had previously claimed, and now truculently reiterated, that he had achieved?[28]

To arrive at his answers, Frankel chose to look at the entire population of patients who had undergone colectomies and "pericolic membranotomy" (or Lane's operation), a total of some 645 cases. For comparison, he sampled 407 other patients from the files, taking "all functional cases admitted (and *not later operated upon*)" – again in Frankel's idiosyncratic definition of that category – "during one month of each year covered by this study. For instance, the admissions for the month of January, 1918, February, 1919, and so through each of the years to 1930. It is to be understood that all functional cases not receiving major surgical treatment, *during these months*, were used in this comparative group. No attempt at selection was made."[29]

Frankel's findings were potentially explosive, though, like Phyllis Greenacre's report, his typescript never circulated beyond a tightly controlled group of insiders. Greenacre's report had, in fact, been provided to Frankel, and he recorded that his own careful examination of the data led him to conclusions that "are substantially in agreement with those reached in Dr. Greenacre's special study made in 1925."[30] By contrast, his statistics systematically conflicted with those provided by Cotton, and decisively undercut Cotton's claims.

Cotton, for example, had justified colectomies as a "last resort" operation, reserved for chronic patients, "mainly dementia praecox cases" with an exceedingly poor prognosis. Frankel's re-examination of the data revealed that only 105 of the 309 colectomy cases had been given that diagnosis. As many again had been assigned to the category of manic depression, widely regarded as a condition from which many made temporary or permanent recoveries. Still others who had lost their colons had been labeled psychoneurotic or psychopathic, and a half-dozen had even been diagnosed as "without psychosis," that is, sane, but had been operated upon anyway. Cotton had claimed 75 recoveries in this group of 309 cases; Frankel (or rather the assistant psychiatrist at Trenton State Hospital) found that recoveries amounted to only 24 patients, with an additional 22 listed as "improved."

Similar patterns prevailed with the group of 336 patients who had been subjected to the less extensive pericolic membranotomies. Here, 139 patients had
come from those diagnosed as manic depressive, compared with 113 recorded
as suffering from dementia praecox. Yet only 42, or 12.5 percent, of these cases
had been reported as cured, and a further 45 (13.4 percent) as improved – far
fewer than Cotton's claim of *"148 patients permanently recovered."*[31] By contrast,
among those spared both forms of bowel surgery, more than half were living
back in the community, and 105 of these, or more than 25 percent of those in
the control group, were considered to be cured. Again contrary to the impression Cotton had cultivated, the patients in the surgical group were as a whole
much younger than those spared these particular operations: 42 percent of
those spared the surgery were over the age of 40, compared with 22.1 percent
among those whose colons were excised. Without comment, Frankel also
recorded that 77.9 percent of the colectomies had been performed on women
patients; and an even higher percentage of the pericolic membranotomies,
some 83.6 percent, were visited upon female bodies. By contrast the female to
male ratio in the control group was 53.3 to 46.7. Quite what might explain this
startling discrepancy was left wholly unexplored in his report, though presumably toxic colons were not disproportionately present in the female of the race.

But more disturbing than the extremely low cure rates he had uncovered
among those subjected to these forms of surgery, and more sobering than the
finding that it was "the non-operative cases [that] show the most favorable
results,"[32] were still another set of statistics Frankel had compiled: the death
rates associated with these operations. In the text of his report, Frankel
recorded that, "of the 309 patients who had colectomies performed, 138 or 44.7
percent died; 101 or 32.7 percent are still confined in mental hospitals; leaving
only 70 or 22.6 percent who are living outside of a mental hospital" – a number
of them in other types of institution.[33] Among those receiving the less-
extensive operation, it was true that "only" 13.7 percent had died, but 186, or 55.4
percent remained in a mental hospital, and a further 13 were in prisons or institutions for the feeble minded.[34] Thus, "the reduction in the mortality of those
patients who had pericolic membranotomies resulted merely in a larger
number of patients remaining in a mental hospital."[35] And to drive home the
connection between the elimination of colons and the elimination of patients,
Frankel proceeded to present the statistics he had compiled in bar graph form
as well as in the body of his text.

Finally, Frankel examined whether this frightful mortality – all the more
striking for occurring among a group of patients 77.9 percent of whom were
aged 39 or younger – was to some degree an unfortunate coincidence. He found
it easy to show that it was not. Leaving aside the potentially devastating, even

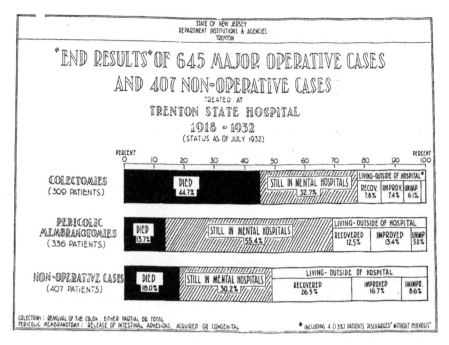

32 *"End Results" of 645 Major Operative Cases and 407 Non-Operative Cases.*

fatal, long-term health effects of the whole series of other surgical procedures to which these patients had been subjected,[36] effects whose impact on mortality rates was difficult to quantify, most of the deaths recorded in the hospital records, particularly among those whose colons were removed, came about "as a direct consequence of the surgical operation. The death certificates give the causes of death as peritonitis, post-operative pneumonia, hemorrhage, etc."[37]

Immediately and unambiguously, therefore, the most salient effect of the surgery was to kill a third or so of those who went under the knife. Had matters improved over time? Indeed,

> Dr. Cotton has maintained that as the operative work on the colon at the Trenton State Hospital progressed there has been secured an improvement in the excessively high death rate of patients. The present study shows that there has been some decrease in the death rate considering all patients on whom colectomies had been performed in the period under consideration, but that there has been *no appreciable decrease* in the relative number of surgical deaths. The hospital records show that the surgical deaths in colectomies for the period 1918–1921 were 28.2 percent, for the period 1922–1925 they were 27.8 percent and for the period 1926–1932 they were 26.3 percent."[38]

If Cotton had reacted to the pressures of the Bright Committee's inquiries with a mental breakdown, and to Greenacre's findings with undisguised fury, he appears to have responded to Frankel's refutation of his claims by simply ignoring it. Drawing support from sympathetic state politicians, who remained convinced by his claims to save the state substantial sums of money with his surgical treatments, he continued to bring pressure on the hospital board to allow him to resume colectomies. In the closing months of 1932, he wrote yet another summary of his theories of insanity and their practical application. Designed to appeal to a broad lay audience, it was submitted to H. L. Mencken for possible publication in the latter's widely circulated monthly, *The American Mercury*.[39]

"The Physical Causes of Mental Disorders" was all familiar stuff, designed to "educate" the literate public about the sources of the scourge of insanity, and to encourage them to demand access to the new curative regime. Cotton rehearsed his standard objections to hereditarian theories of insanity. "We are now in a position to say, with reasonable confidence if not with absolute finality, that mental disease *per se* cannot be transmitted from one generation to another. The doctrine of hereditary insanity at last has been judged in the light of sound biological knowledge and has been found wanting." As for the notion that "mental disorders are in fact disorders of the mind . . . mental factors undoubtedly have their place. But they are of secondary importance to the toxic factors."[40] And so to a survey of some cases of successful treatment by defocalization, an insistence on the dangers of rotten teeth and tonsils, and a frank acknowledgment of the need to attend to infected colons in some 80 percent of mentally ill patients – coupled with a warning that "partial resection of the colon" was "a procedure successful only in the hands of a well-trained abdominal surgeon."[41] Cotton recognized that his audience might have had some concerns about permitting such drastic surgery, but he hastened to reassure them that "the generally accepted idea that people are unable to live without a colon is disputed . . . by many of our patients who had their colons removed as far back as 1918 [and] are still living and are normal both mentally and physically . . . Improvement in the technique has lowered the operative fatalities so that at the present time such an operation is no more dangerous than a normal appendectomy." Moreover, subsequent research had apparently shown that a more limited operation to release adhesions in the bowel often sufficed to produce a recovery, and in these cases, "the mortality is negligible, especially when all infection of teeth and tonsils has been removed."[42] At the other extreme, in more advanced cases, "if the infection is very extensive, involving more of the bowel than it is considered wise to remove, the disease must be attacked by either vaccine or serum."[43] Mencken apparently found the essay very much to his taste. He requested a few minor cuts and the addition of a short section on the feeble minded, and then he accepted it for publication.[44]

It was with Meyer, significantly, that Cotton chose to vent some of his frustrations about his loss of authority at the hospital, clearly anticipating a sympathetic response. A whole series of events since the tense meeting with Greenacre in early 1926 about her report made this a not unreasonable assumption. Meyer had, of course, suppressed that damaging document, and refused to allow any public or private discussion of its contents. He had repeatedly resisted all efforts to get him to comment on the value or limitations of Cotton's work on focal sepsis, and though some of that resistance had occurred in private, Cotton was well aware of the public occasions where Meyer had refused to enter the fray. Meyer had maintained the warmest of personal relations with Cotton, and despite regularly being kept abreast of Cotton's continued commitment to a program of thorough cleansing and aggressive surgery, he had uttered not a word urging restraint or a change of course to his protégé.[45] Then, too, in the late spring of 1933 came another indication of the professor's continued support. Cotton was contacted by H. H. McClellan, "formerly the superintendent of the Dayton State Hospital. He, for a while, attempted to carry on similar work in Dayton as our work in Trenton and made some progress." McClellan was now seeking to become "Mental Hygiene Director for the State of Ohio and has asked me to have you write to Governor George White at Columbus, O., recommending him for the position." Remarkably, though Cotton acknowledged that "this is rather an imposition on your good nature as you do not know the man,"[46] Meyer complied.[47]

In his April 29 letter, Cotton had discussed at length a patient whom Meyer had formerly treated "at the Phipps Clinic for nearly a year." Charlotte Surtees had subsequently been treated at the Bloomingdale asylum, and had been in correspondence with one of Meyer's staff concerning her subsequent treatment by Cotton. "Although she had been growing violent and it had not been possible for her to see her parents for a year or more, three weeks after the extraction of her teeth," Cotton proudly reported, "she apparently became absolutely normal. She met her father, kissed him, called him 'Daddy' and spent an hour in a very profitable conversation." Subsequently, though, "her X-ray studies showed a bad colon condition and we operated for release of adhesions. She did very well, sent out Christmas cards to all her friends, and seemed to be on the road to recovery. However, she slipped back to some extent but did not develop the many delusions of persecution which she had against her parents. She became more or less indifferent and physically lost weight and was somewhat anemic." Cotton was convinced that untreated sepsis must still lurk somewhere in her body. "Another series of X-rays showed that she had some post-operative adhesions and [she] was operated on again last Monday. We found several interesting things, one was that the tubes and ovaries on the left side were the seat of chronic infection and had become attached to the mesentery of the descending colon. On the right side they were attached to a knuckle of the small intestine. There were some adhesions around the terminal ileum and the ascending colon was very badly damaged as well as obstructed." For some reason, "we did not take the right side of the colon out although I think it should have been done. We felt that with the removal of the other conditions the function of the colon could be established without a partial resection. She has done very well since the operation and I shall be glad to give you further accounts."[48]

Meyer professed to find all this of interest, yet another indication of his continuing fascination with Cotton's work on focal sepsis. He wrote back to Cotton that the young woman's father had separately informed him about other patients under Cotton's care, "three particularly interesting cases of recovery in apparently chronic Dementia Praecox," and Meyer wondered if Cotton could send him the details of these cases. "I consider it of great value for the members of staff to get as much possible first-hand data concerning the cases that should figure in their thought and reasoning concerning a condition too readily handled fatalistically."[49]

Cotton scrambled to oblige. "Of course, I have some two hundred cases which have recovered but I thought you knew about them." One such, Miss A. A., was a case "I first reported at the meeting of the New York Psychiatric Society in April 1918." He now added some more details: "She remained well until 1926 at which time she had a slight recurrence which I attributed to her colon condition as only the left side had been removed at the first operation." Accordingly, he had decided to re-operate. Unfortunately for Miss A. A., though, "we were not insisting then on the removal of all infected teeth before operation. She had several infected teeth and died of peritonitis following the second operation." There was a considerable consolation, however. "She had practically ten years of normal life . . . following her six years' confinement in a hospital."[50]

At that time, Cotton conceded, "the mortality rate . . . was high, about 30 percent," but in recent years, he had dramatically reduced it.

In fact, I have done 22 consecutive cases without a death. Last year, for instance, I did 30 operations for the release of adhesions in mostly chronic dementia praecox cases, and out of that number we had twenty recoveries, both surgically and mentally . . . In some few cases a resection has to be done later, but the recovery rate has increased while the mortality rate has decreased. Out of the thirty cases, three died. Two as a result of heart conditions and one of peritonitis, the latter case being one where the family refused to have all the teeth extracted."[51]

Yet despite what any impartial observer must surely acknowledge was a spectacularly improved record, "unfortunately," he complained to Meyer,

> things have not gone as well here at the hospital as I anticipated when I retired in 1930. I found that by retiring I had literally walked into a trap because as soon as I gave up the directorship, Dr. Raycroft, who has been very luke-warm toward the work and greatly influenced by Greenacre's report, immediately began to discredit the work as far as possible. As a result of this, since 1930 there have been practically no operations for release of adhesions or colectomies. This, in spite of the record we made for over thirteen years when we had at least seventy-five recoveries.[52]

It was a denouement that Cotton simply refused to accept. After all, "there is no question but that I saved the State over three million dollars due to the elimination of chronic foci of infection in thirteen years." While he had run Trenton, the hospital population had increased at only a third of the rate in New York State. Since 1930, however, the hospital census at Trenton had increased almost four times as fast as in his time. All this meant that "I have had to get back into the fight again."[53] He simply could not allow his therapeutic breakthroughs to be compromised by the pusillanimity of his successor and the spinelessness of the hospital board, so "instead of spending my time on research work I have had to be more active in protecting my work, otherwise it would be entirely discredited, and this," he noted bitterly, "by Raycroft."[54]

As part of his campaign, Cotton had rallied his considerable support among the state's politicians. "I am enclosing," he informed Meyer, "a copy of a resolution passed recently by the Legislature [encouraging the renewed reliance on colectomies] which is now being considered by the State Board." Passed by a 12–0 vote in the Senate, and endorsed by the State House of Representatives, this document had lamented the "population increases . . . experienced at the Trenton State Hospital since the retirement of Dr. Henry A. Cotton" and urged that "his ability and initiative be utilized to a greater extent in an effort to improve conditions [there]."[55] And the resolution received a prompt endorsement from the *Trenton Evening Times'* editors, who declared it "decidedly in the public interest." It could only be a matter of regret, they informed their readers, that "since [Cotton's] retirement as active head of the hospital in 1930, the great work which he publicly launched in 1918 and promoted with results that attracted international attention has been largely pushed aside . . . [Yet] his theories as to the role of chronic infections in the deterioration of brain structure have been accepted by many leading psychiatrists both here and abroad," and they held out the very real promise of tremendous cost savings to the state's taxpayers. It was time, the editors insisted, to get "professional jealousy and departmental politics" out of the way, and to bring back Dr. Cotton "for successful waging of the war on insanity."[56]

Cotton's *American Mercury* article, defiantly rehearsing the value of a wide-ranging attack on focal sepsis, finally appeared in print in June 1933. Mencken described Henry Cotton in his section on that month's authors as "one of the leading psychiatrists of the United States,"[57] and Cotton had obviously hoped that the propaganda value of this piece would prove to be of inestimable value to him as he sought to extend his surgical assault on pus infection.[58] And so perhaps it might have, except for one inconvenient fact: by the time "The Physical Causes of Mental Disorders" appeared in print, the erstwhile "leading psychiatrist of the United States" was dead.

The announcement of Cotton's death came in a brief front-page story in the *Trenton Evening Times* on May 8, the very day he had written to Meyer to outline his proposed campaign to compel the hospital authorities to reinstitute colon surgery. "World Famous Alienist Drops Dead," read the headline. "There were," the story reported, "few men in the public life of the State who could point to a record so replete with notable achievements." His vigorous efforts on behalf of the mentally ill had brought "generous appropriations from the legislature with which to carry on his splendid work" and had made Trenton State Hospital "equal to the foremost hospitals of its kind in the country." At his hands, the recovery rate among the state's mentally ill had risen as high as 87 percent, and "high officials of the State Department of Institutions and Agencies repeatedly have declared that the Cotton methods were saving the State millions of dollars."[59] The *Times*'s obituary the following day was more fulsome still: "Thousands of people who have suffered mental affliction," it informed its readers, "owe [Dr. Cotton] an enduring debt of gratitude for . . . displacing confusion and despair with hope and confidence. [All must lament the loss of] this great pioneer whose humanitarian influence was, and will continue to be, of such monumental proportions."[60]

Apprized of the news,[61] Adolf Meyer hastened to offer his condolences to Cotton's widow. Within three days of Henry's death, she received a note from the Baltimore professor lamenting "the abrupt and deplorably premature" death of her husband. Meyer consoled her by praising what had been "a remarkable and noble life and then [an] end like that of the soldier in action." (Actually, Cotton had died of a heart attack at his Trenton club, shortly after lunch – though perhaps Meyer might be forgiven the military metaphor, given what he knew of his protégé's plans.) Cotton's was, he assured her, "a life and work that will live on and will lead to more fruitions."[62]

It would be easy to assume that these were simply the sort of diplomatic words of consolation anyone might offer in private to a grief-stricken friend of many years' standing, no more to be taken seriously as a measure of a person than most utterances at such a moment. Rather more difficult to explain away in this fashion, though, were Meyer's considered remarks published in the *American Journal of Psychiatry* some eight months later, in a lengthy obituary for his protégé. "Among 1933's losses from the ranks of psychiatrists," he informed his professional colleagues, "there is an outstanding and premature one, that of Henry A. Cotton." Meyer recalled Cotton's days as his student at the Worcester State Hospital, spoke of the close relationship they had developed in those years, with Cotton turning to him for advice, and remembered how, "on each occasion [in his fledgling career] he would only become more determined to make a mark in psychiatry."[63]

And make his mark he certainly had. Meyer recalled his further training in Munich under Kraepelin and Alzheimer, and his contributions to the study of the neuropathology of the "insane brain." Most centrally, though, he focused on Cotton's subsequent elevation to the superintendency of the Trenton State Hospital, his abolition of mechanical restraint, his experimental treatment of general paresis, and his move from those efforts to his work as "the protagonist of focal infection theory." Though initially relying on the New York surgeon, J. W. Draper, "after the death of Dr. Draper, Dr. Cotton practically took over the entire responsibility and actual work."[64]

Meyer now turned to his considered assessment of that work. Cotton, he concluded, had been "a man of action and of results," and "he made an extraordinary record of achievement. His views and practices were a vigorous challenge which stood non-compromisingly for an almost unitary explanation by focal infections, supported by the testimony of number patients and a number of colleagues." To be sure, Meyer conceded (as how could he not), Cotton's views had been controversial. They had inspired "an equally non-compromising attitude of non-surgically inclined colleagues in the rising wave of variously inclusive psychogenic interpretations." Implicitly, however, to represent the opposition to Cotton in this fashion was to suggest subliminally that the objections to his work were founded in ideological difference, rather than more substantive concerns about his therapeutics. And Meyer then proceeded to lament the fact that, "the hope that Dr. Cotton himself might obtain the support of one or another of the foundations promoting research was only partially fulfilled and the analysis of the tremendous amount of work was but slowly progressing at the time of his death and will now have to be carried on without the leading and active spirit of the sincere and convinced protagonist." Still, notwithstanding the need for more research, it was quite clear that, "the history of the developments at the Trenton State Hospital is a most remarkable achievement of the pioneer spirit, and the history of Dr. Cotton one of a remarkable example of energy, purpose, and wholeheartedness."[65] With not a sideways glance at what Meyer knew to be, in reality, a history of more than a decade of forced treatments, mass maiming, and deaths in the service of a therapeutically bankrupt ideal, the dean of American psychiatrists concluded with words of unalloyed praise: "As a physician, and as a friend and colleague, [Henry Cotton] will always be remembered as one of the most stimulating figures of our generation."[66]

Indeed. So he undoubtedly will.

Epilogue:
Psychiatry and Its Discontents

How easy it would be to dismiss the tale of Henry Cotton and his enthusiasm for focal sepsis as a momentary aberration in the march of psychiatric progress, the product of a lone obsessive, himself of uncertain mental status. Perhaps, as the medical historian Edward Shorter would have it, one can safely marginalize Cotton as a "maniacal Trenton psychiatrist" who embarked on a program of medical malpractice on a grand scale in an obscure "psychiatric Sleepy-Hollow," an insignificant figure who ought to be seen as a crazed creature blundering down a biological blind alley.[1] After all, Cotton did suffer some form of psychotic breakdown in the summer of 1926, when the political pressures on him grew acute, and his ideas do in hindsight have a peculiarly monomaniacal cast to them. All we have here, then, is a strange story of a psychopathological psychiatrist, one with its own particular horrors and charms, but one of no larger import or intellectual interest.

Not unreasonably, given this assessment of the case, one might prefer to pass over the whole episode in silence. So historians and the profession itself have mostly elected to do. Except that such an account is surely too simple, and too readily assumes that such unpleasant episodes can be safely forgotten.

Freud, we may recall, famously saw the selectivity of our individual recall as anything but accidental. Painful or unpleasant memories, unable to find conscious expression, were dealt with by repression, strangled when they sought to become overt. But murdered memories, on his account, were not so easily disposed of. Still lurking ominously beneath one's attempts to sustain the simulacrum of normality, they displaced themselves in striking and symbolically resonant directions, surfacing as strange and disabling symptoms whose meanings were recoverable only through the mysterious alchemy of psychoanalysis, albeit through a process perhaps interminable. Even on the analytic couch, rendering the unconscious conscious was, he insisted, a deeply and necessarily fraught process, for the psyche resisted any simple substitution of one for the other, employing all sorts of defenses against a reality it found too painful to contemplate.

History, which we may consider our collective memory, is inevitably a narrative that is also constructed on a foundation of forgetfulness.[2] To remember too well, to carry with us the full burden of the past, would surely prove cognitively and emotionally overwhelming, to say nothing of being profoundly disturbing and disorienting existentially. Remembrance of things past thus always occurs against a background of shadows and darkness, a casting of much of our shared experience into oblivion, and a recasting of what we do remember into mythological portraits that transfigure and transform the reality they purport to recreate. Like the selective forgetfulness of the individual, cultures and social institutions cling to retrospective illusions, substitute them for a fuller record of the past, and fiercely resist reconstructions that would disturb and displace the myths we all necessarily live by. To put it another way, our collective "forgetfulness" is, like our individual memories, anything but random.

As this gothic tale has reminded us, however, repression in the collective context is the product of conscious quite as much as unconscious processes. If, as Marx once famously remarked, men (our more egalitarian age would prefer to say persons) make their own history, but not under circumstances of their own choosing, we need to add an important caveat: the making of history takes place on many levels. It embraces not just actions themselves, but their authors' attempts to manage and manipulate the interpretations and meanings ascribed to actions, both contemporaneously and by posterity. And since history is also made by its historians, one has to consider, too, the preferences, prejudices, and predilections of those of us who write it, the ways in which our own biases and blindnesses, selective attention and inattention, shape still further the history we collectively make.

Henry Cotton's experiments on his Trenton patients were not an isolated and transient phenomenon. The notion of focal sepsis upon which he seized to explain psychosis and to promote his campaign for surgical bacteriology, was embraced by some of the best medical minds of his era, and its significance and practical application extended far beyond the marginal realm of psychiatry. In general medicine over several decades, millions of tonsils were sacrificed on this particular altar, and major figures in physic and surgery accepted the basic idea that focal sepsis could cause chronic disease as plausible and promising.

And what many found plausible was not just this general idea, but its specific applications to psychiatry. On at least two occasions, as we have seen, the best and the brightest – or rather, the most prestigious and most prominent, at least in British medicine – flocked to sing Henry Cotton's praises and embrace his theories and therapeutics as a signal contribution to twentieth-century medicine. They did so at length and in very public settings, and with scarcely a whisper of dissent, even when the object of their hosannas acknowledged that his most drastic interventions killed almost a third of those he treated. Visitors from three continents descended on Trenton. All pronounced themselves profoundly impressed by what they had seen. In Britain, T. C. Graves, who had independently happened upon and embraced the focal sepsis hypothesis, actively and aggressively treated *all* the mental patients hospitalized in the Birmingham area along Cotton's lines. He presided over all the mental hospitals in England's second city till well after the end of the Second World War, and continued assaulting sepsis during the four years he occupied the post of president of the Royal Medico-Psychological Association in the 1940s (the longest period anyone has ever held this position).

And Cotton was by no means a prophet without honor in the United States. A substantial number of his fellow asylum superintendents visited Trenton in the twenties and lamented that the parsimony of their local state legislators kept them, too, from embarking on so ambitious, so laudable, so desirable an antiseptic program. Respectable figures like Hubert Work, the president of the American Medical Association, and Stewart Paton, author of perhaps the most influential American textbook of psychiatry in the early twentieth century, blessed Cotton's endeavors, as did medical men whose expertise was of more dubious provenance but whose public influence was large: the nation's most famous medical agony aunt, Senator Royal Copeland, and the entrepreneur who had built the country's most lucrative funny farm for the fashionably nervous and the prostrated neurasthenic, John Harvey Kellogg of the Battle Creek Sanitarium. Cotton's assistant physicians at Trenton included at least two Hopkins-trained psychiatrists who went on to very prominent careers in North American psychiatry – Clarence Farrar, editor of the *American Journal of Psychiatry* from 1931 to 1965,[3] and Franklin Ebaugh, director of the Division of Psychiatric Education at the National Committee for Mental Hygiene and chair of the Department of Psychiatry at the University of Colorado. Neither of them is known to have objected to what went on, either then or later. Indeed, during his time at the Trenton hospital, Ebaugh gave every sign of being a willing and enthusiastic participant in the search for sepsis.[4] Right down to Cotton's premature demise, for a period of more than a decade and a half, the moneyed classes flocked to the doubtful charms of New Jersey's capital city, bringing loved ones whose teeth, tonsils, and colons were willingly sacrificed in a frantic search for sanity – a practical (and profitable) endorsement of Cotton's theoretical claims.

As we have seen, Cotton had his critics, even at the time, and while he attracted support, and some of that support came from prominent and powerful people, his ideas never came close to becoming the ruling orthodoxy in American psychiatry. But how muted the criticism remained. It was confined for the most part to backstage grumbling and the exchange of critical correspondence. And how limited were the grounds of criticism. The empirical critiques of George Kirby and his associates were the exception rather than the rule, and even Kirby and Kopeloff felt compelled to acknowledge that eliminating sepsis in mental patients was a desirable goal. Others found Cotton's relentlessly monocausal account of psychosis implausible, and of course the psychodynamically inclined greeted his claims with hostility and unbelief. But scarcely anyone doubted his right to experiment on his patients, or raised in any serious or sustained manner any questions about the propriety of maiming and mangling the bodies of the mad – not even when Cotton confessed, on occasion, that his surgical interventions proceeded notwithstanding verbal and physical resistance from their victims. Published mortality rates exceeding 30 percent drew neither significant reproof nor efforts at restraint.

As members of a healing profession that likes to trace its lineage back at least as far as classical Greece and the fabled Hippocrates, physicians pronounce themselves the guardians of our physical welfare – and, in the case of that subordinate branch once called by the derisive term of "mad-doctors" and now preferring to own to the title "psychiatrist," our mental welfare as well. Like all of those who make the most well-founded and broadly socially accepted claim to the title of professional, medical men (and these days medical women) operate in an arena where the ordinary disciplines of the marketplace seem to fail, or to perform poorly. As lay people, we lack access to their specialized knowledge and expertise, even though the content of their cognitive world may be quite literally of life and death importance to us. In a poor position to second guess their expert judgments or even, in many instances, to grasp the foundations on which their diagnoses and prescriptions are based, and ill-equipped to assess the quality of the care we are about to receive, we are perforce at their mercy. Elaborate social rituals persuade us to grant these strangers our trust, and reassure us that they are motivated, not by the self-interest of the marketplace – the hidden hand that allegedly guides so much of civil society – but by a higher ethical standard, a genuine concern for our well-being and survival and a willingness to subordinate their interests to ours. And so it sometimes proves.

And sometimes not.[5]

For seventeen years, from 1916 until Cotton's collapse and death in 1933, the thousands of patients who swarmed Trenton's wards and the hundreds of affluent patients who sought his ministrations at his private facility, the Charles Hospital, were abandoned to their fate. That remained the case even after America's leading psychiatrist, Adolf Meyer, learned definitively in 1925 that Cotton's whole enterprise was built on a foundation of sand. Not only was Meyer more concerned with protecting his protégé than with protecting the patients, but his role went beyond a complicit silence to embrace a desire to see the surgical experiment carried out to its logical extreme (fearing, as he put it, that the opportunity to explore the potential value of eliminating sepsis would otherwise never recur). His suppression of Phyllis Greenacre's report, and his silencing of Greenacre herself, kept the most thorough and systematic review of Cotton's activities from public view, and, together with Meyer's deliberate avoidance of the highly publicized discussion of focal sepsis by the British medical profession in 1927, permitted Cotton to proceed unchecked for a further half-dozen years. On Cotton's death, Greenacre's and Katzenelbogen's reports safely buried in his voluminous files, Meyer did more than cover up the parade of death and debility that Cotton had left behind him. Knowing that what had resulted at Trenton was a piling up of the edentulous, the eviscerated, and the extinguished, Meyer chose the most prominent of professional platforms, the *American Journal of Psychiatry*, to praise the whole enterprise as "a most remarkable achievement of the pioneer spirit," to laud Cotton as "one of the most stimulating figures of our generation," to call for his work "to be carried on" through "prolonged observation and comparison"; and to lament that further exploration of this therapeutic approach "now will have to be carried on without the leading and active spirit of the sincere and convinced protagonist."[6]

No, dismissing Cotton's surgical assaults as an aberration is not the lesson we should draw from these events. On the contrary, this long-suppressed story demonstrates the extraordinary vulnerability of the mentally ill to victimization and the hollowness of professionals' claims to police themselves. Morally, socially, and physically removed from the ranks of humankind, locked in institutions impervious to the gaze of outsiders, deprived of their status as moral actors, and presumed by virtue of their mental state to lack the capacity to make informed choices for themselves, patients were helpless to resist the interventions of those who controlled their very existence. Many must have succumbed to the pressures to admit that what was being done to them was right and appropriate, to believe that their treatment was dictated by the impersonal god of science. In any event, those who resisted swiftly learned that their resistance was futile. Cotton boasted in print that he had operated on resisting bodies, and drew neither criticism nor reproof from peers. He acknowledged astonishingly high rates of mortality accompanying his most extensive interventions, and found himself praised by the very professionals before whom he had acknowledged these deaths as a new Lister. He proclaimed cure rates in excess of 80 percent – claims one might have thought would have beggared belief – and was able to shrug off criticism that others were unable to replicate his findings by dismissing their interventions as insufficiently radical and thoroughgoing.[7]

We live, as Cotton's contemporaries already did, in an age of experts, professionals who loudly proclaim their disinterestedness, their benevolence, the grounding of their actions in the neutral territory that is science. Theirs is a universe of progress, moral quite as much as cognitive and technical, with the professions presenting themselves as the priests of that progressive universe. Yet in a wide variety of contexts, events of the twentieth century stretched such claims to the breaking point and beyond. Nowhere was that more apparent than when the apostles of rationality confronted the irrational, presuming to divide the mad from the sane and to minister to minds diseased.

Cotton is by no means the only therapeutic enthusiast who makes plain the pitfalls of progress and expertise. Nor were the patients who thronged the wards of Trenton State Hospital somehow uniquely vulnerable to experimental treatments. The desperation felt by the families of those whose minds were unhinged, to say nothing of the fiscal pressures that the burden of chronic madness visited upon the body politic, were everywhere familiar features of the twentieth-century psychiatric landscape. Thus it was that Cotton's desperate remedies had their analogues in other places and other times.

Psychiatrists, who claimed to serve as guardians of collective sanity, sought throughout the century either to encapsulate the crazy or to transform them to normalcy. Confronting a recalcitrant patient population resistant to their remedies, many were willing to embrace somatic therapies with little more than their inventors' enthusiasm to support them – treatments that often proved to have profoundly bad effects on the lives of those subjected to the psychiatrists' science once the initial enthusiasm surrounding their introduction began to wane.

Central, after all, to the medical identity of psychiatry for most of its history has been its metaphysical embracing of the body. From the humoral accounts of the origins of mania and melancholia that underpinned medical claims to comprehend and treat mental disorder in the eighteenth century, to the declaration by the paymaster of American academic psychiatry, the National Institute of Mental Health, that the 1990s marked "the decade of the brain," alienists have repeatedly tried to account for mental disorder in somatic terms.

Recurrently, the profession has clung to claims about the bodily basis of insanity as the securest anchor of its objectivity and scientific status, the uniquely potent guarantor of its privileged role in the diagnosis and disposition of the lunatic. The attribution of madness to disorders of the body has, unsurprisingly, led to a recurrent fascination with somatic treatments for the presumed underlying pathology.

At least one of these therapeutic interventions, albeit a particularly dramatic one, was devised by a former assistant physician to Cotton, and followed from the logic of his experiments. In the early 1920s, R. S. Carroll induced "aseptic meningitis" in a number of his patients to "combat the dementia praecox problem," using injections of horse serum into the spinal canal. He argued that the resultant fevers and inflammation of the brain would stimulate the body's immune system and help resolve the infective processes that were at the root of the psychotic break. As the body's defenses attacked the meningitis, "the scavenger action of these cells would rid the central nervous system of toxins which were deleterious to its proper functioning."[8] Others were persuaded to try the same tactic, but high mortality among those subjected to the treatment, and the strange inability of the treatment to show any therapeutic results, led to its rapid abandonment.[9]

During the First World War, armies on both sides routinely employed electric shocks to punish and "treat" shell-shocked soldiers, forcing the mute to speak, the deaf to hear, the lame to walk.[10] Never routinely used outside the military context, the treatment was still occasionally revived in civilian mental hospitals. A paper in the *Lancet* in 1939, for example, matter of factly records the use of electrodes that were attached to patients' foreheads and necks and then used to deliver electric shocks of up to 20,000 volts for one second each, the treatment to be repeated ten to twenty times daily in an effort to force functional psychotics to return to "sanity." The author dispassionately reported that at each administration, "the patient's eyelids and facial muscles twitch, the head jerks, and evidence of fear and pain is exhibited"[11] – a description more sanitized than some of the reports from wartime administrations of shock.[12] But outside a military context, there was little enthusiasm for so transparently brutal a therapy, which overtly sought to inflict pain and fear on resisting subjects.

The same Julius Wagner von Jauregg who had faced criminal prosecution for his enthusiastic wartime deployment of electricity on Austrian shell-shocked troops seized upon the diminished constraints on the battlefield to redeploy another weapon in the fight against madness, the fever therapy to which I alluded in chapter 5. Before the war, he had tried such dangerous tactics as injecting his patients with erysipelas in order to raise their temperatures,[13] but in 1917 a more attractive febrile agent came to his attention when he came across a soldier suffering from tertian malaria. Though he had earlier touted fever therapy as a remedy for "melancholy, manic states, and acute mania," he now focused his attentions on tertiary syphilis and the psychiatric and neuro-logical catastrophes that accompanied it. Ten years later, he received the Nobel Prize in Medicine for his innovation.[14]

Wagner von Jauregg's fever treatment for neurosyphilis spread rapidly in North America and elsewhere. For a uniformly fatal disease usually associated with a steep physical decline and a particularly nasty end,[15] even a therapy that promised marginal improvements had obvious attractions.[16] Soon, hospitals were using paretics with malaria as a source of infected blood,[17] and the pre-cious liquid was passed among them in thermos flasks sent through the mail.[18] Others began experimenting with alternative means of inducing fever, and sought to explore whether febrile reactions might not cure other varieties of mental disturbance. Injections of colloidal calcium[19] or rat bite fever organ-isms[20] were tried on occasion, but such exotica were generally discarded in favor of "diathermy machines," sweat cabinets that artificially broke down the body's homeostatic mechanisms.[21] But though fever therapy continued to be endorsed by many clinicians as a last-ditch treatment for tertiary syphilis, there was a broad consensus that other forms of psychosis did not respond to this approach.

If heat and fever failed to work in cases of schizophrenia or the affective psy-choses, perhaps chilling and cold might offer therapeutic possibilities. Two Harvard psychiatrists decided to experiment. In a handful of patients at the McLean Hospital, the private resort for disturbed Boston Brahmins, body tem-peratures were deliberately lowered to 85 degrees Fahrenheit and below – tem-peratures barely consistent with and, as it turned out, sometimes inconsistent with life. The death of one of the patients, and the failure of any of the subjects to show anything more than a minor and temporary therapeutic response to cold rapidly terminated the experiment.[22] Not to be outdone, others experi-mented with cyanide injections, first in psychotics, and when results with them proved dismal, in cases of psychoneurosis.[23]

With the partial exception of fever therapy, these various experiments were isolated and rarely replicated, but it would be a mistake to think that there were no interventions that continued as long as, and drew as many and more adher-ents as, Cotton's defocalization. One of the most widely employed techniques made use of the recent discovery of insulin. Administered in large doses, insulin induced shock and coma, but having begun by using this approach to treat drug addicts, a Polish psychiatrist, Manfred Sakel, began to experiment with the deliberate use of insulin coma therapy in Vienna in 1933. Like Cotton, he proclaimed the results of his approach were miraculous, and the technique rapidly spread, with Sakel himself coming to the United States to demonstrate the therapy.[24]

Injected with insulin, patients were placed in a series of medically induced comas that were often accompanied by convulsions (some of them deliberately induced, after patients had become stuporous, by adding metrazol into the therapeutic mix). Sakel himself thought that, "the mode of action of the epileptic seizure is on the one hand like that of a battering ram which breaks through the barriers in resistant cases, so that the 'regular troops' of hypoglycemia can march through" and felt that "the epileptic seizure also affects the psychosis . . . by means of the retrograde amnesia it produces." Only such radical and risky measures could hope "to break through the fixated and petrified psychotic processes and to devitalize them."[25] At constant risk of dying or slipping into an irreversible coma as the "treatment" proceeded, patients required close monitoring at all times, prior to being revived through the administration of glucose.[26]

Almost contemporaneously, in Hungary, convinced (falsely) that schizophrenia and epilepsy could not co-exist, Ladislaus Meduna began to experiment with ways to induce convulsions artificially, trying and rejecting camphor in oil because after the injections, "anxiety amounts to panic and is associated with assaultive and suicidal behavior."[27] After some trials with injections of strychnine, Meduna settled on pentathylenetetrazol, soon known in the United States as metrazol, as his drug of choice.

After inducing a convulsion in his first patient on January 23, 1934, Meduna reportedly "was so distressed that he had to be supported to his room by nurses."[28] Perhaps his reaction should not occasion surprise. Metrazol, while somewhat more predictable in its effects, had scarcely less savage consequences than camphor for those injected with it. Meyer's assistant, Katzenelbogen, reported that, "outstanding among other very marked reactions are the patients' facial and verbal expressions testifying to their feelings of being excessively frightened, tortured, and overwhelmed by fear of impending death."[29] And this existential terror was not the only, or even the most severe of the side-effects. As another psychiatrist observed, "the most serious drawback to this treatment is the occurrence of such complications as joint dislocations, fractures, heart damage, permanent brain trauma, and even an occasional death. Because of the extreme fear and apprehension shown by most patients towards the treatment and because of the violent convulsions and serious complications which result at times, an extensive search for some satisfactory substitute is in progress"[30] – a search that would conclude with the invention of electroshock or electro-convulsive therapy a few years later. Thereafter, the use of metrazol diminished quite rapidly. In the intervening years, however, it had been widely used in both Europe and North America.

Meduna soon backed away from his claim that there was an antagonism between epilepsy and schizophrenia. Instead, he contended that both metrazol and insulin shared a common mode of action. Attacking entrenched psychosis, he argued, required the application of "brute force . . . we act with both [insulin and metrazol] as with dynamite, endeavoring to blow asunder the pathological sequences and restore the diseased organism to normal functioning . . . we are undertaking a violent onslaught with either method we choose, because at present nothing less than such a shock to the organism is powerful enough to break the chain of noxious processes that leads to schizophrenia."[31]

Such assessments of these two therapies were broadly shared, even among those actively endorsing their use. Charles Burlingame, head of the expensive private asylum that disguised itself as the Institute for Living, in Hartford, Connecticut, acknowledged that "certainly it is true that the human system takes a terrific battering during the process of insulin shock. If it were not for the amnesia concerning these episodes it would be difficult to get anyone to submit willingly to the treatment . . . one cannot help wondering . . . what damage is possibly being done to parts of that body. Sufficient information is not yet available to answer that question"[32] – but he proceeded to use the treatments anyway. Stanley Cobb, professor of psychiatry at Harvard, dissented forcibly from such insouciance. Citing a variety of animal experiments to show that brain damage followed the administration of insulin and metrazol, he commented that

> Such evidence makes me believe that the therapeutic effect of insulin and metrazol may be due to the destruction of great numbers of nerve cells in the cerebral cortex. This destruction is irreparable . . . the physician recommending these radical measures should do so with his eyes open to the fact that he may be removing the symptoms by practically destroying the most highly organized part of the brain. The use of these measures in the treatment of psychoses and neuroses from which recovery may occur seems to me entirely unjustifiable.[33]

Sakel himself did not dispute that his technique produced brain damage. Indeed, he concluded that such damage was central to insulin's therapeutic effect. The comas, he speculated, reflected the decreased supply of oxygen to the brain, an anoxia that he thought selectively killed brain cells, attacking the most recently established (and thus pathological) pathways that had been established in the brain, allowing the pre-psychotic personality to re-emerge.[34] This, he suggested, accounted for the 70 percent remissions his treatment produced in patients whose schizophrenia was less than six months in duration.[35] And regardless of the purely speculative character of these claims, it was Sakel's, not Cobb's, view of the utility of insulin comas that carried the day for another decade and more.[36] Politicians were solemnly assured, following the trail Cotton had blazed, that an investment in this miracle cure would pay off in dollars and cents. In California, for example, Aaron Rosenoff, who was busy lobbying the state legislature for funds for an acute-care psychiatric hospital for the University of California, claimed that insulin comas for schizophrenics at the new facility would save the state upwards of $2 million a year.[37]

Once its Italian inventors, Cerletti and Bini, had shown that electric shocks to the brain could be reliably and easily reproduced, with very low mortality rates and without the most extreme side effects associated with Meduna's pharmacological approach, electricity quickly displaced metrazol as the preferred mode of inducing convulsions. As metrazol fell into disuse, very much to the dismay of its inventor, Meduna turned to other techniques to affect his patients' brains. Harold Himwich and his colleagues, who accepted the notion that insulin coma therapy and metrazol "worked" by producing anoxia in the brain, had experimented in the late 1930s with using nitrogen as a "safer and more controllable" means of producing the same effect, and boasted that, "unlike previous attempts of other workers, the anoxia was intense. At the height of the bout the patient was respiring almost pure nitrogen," producing "respiratory stimulation, tachychardia, cyanosis, spasms, and convulsive jerkings."[38] A decade later, Meduna followed their lead, using carbon dioxide instead. "In developing my method," though, he confessed, "I made initial mistakes: to my first few patients I gave 100 per cent carbon dioxide to inhale. The results were formidable: massive motor discharges, decerebrate fits on the objective level, and horrifying dream experiences on the subjective level. None of these patients ever permitted a second experiment. One of them, in fact, still in a half daze, jumped off the treatment table and began to run out of the laboratory at such speed that only at the door were we able to catch him and hold him by force until he had calmed down enough to be permitted to leave the building."[39] Undeterred by either these reactions or by the absence of clinical response, Meduna continued to enthusiastically advocate further experimentation along similar lines, cautioning only that the patient not be given pure carbon dioxide to breathe. On this occasion, however, he found few followers.

Rather, it was electroconvulsive therapy, or ECT, and an operation that overtly aimed to damage the frontal lobes of the brain, dubbed lobotomy or leucotomy depending upon which side of the Atlantic one inhabited, that became the most widely used somatic treatments for psychosis. By their thousands, and tens of thousands, patients received these treatments. Lobotomy would win for its inventor, the Portuguese Egas Moniz, a Nobel Prize in medicine, some thirteen years after its introduction, and during the 1940s attracted much favorable publicity, as well as more than a modicum of criticism. Eventually, it was viewed as the very symbol of psychiatry run amok and largely abandoned.[40] ECT, by contrast, as empirical and mysterious in its operations as any of these therapies we have surveyed, has survived into the twenty-first century, albeit controversially, still touted by many psychiatrists as a valuable remedy in the treatment of mood disorders.

Along the way, some of ECT's proponents have experimented with some exotic variants of the original shock treatment, including something called "regressive electroshock" or "blitz therapy." First attempted in 1946, this involved giving patients as many as seven electric shocks a day, with thirty to sixty minutes between each one, until "the patient was in a state of complete confusion and utter apathy, mute, incontinent, and unable to take food without assistance."[41] The outcomes were uniformly disastrous: at Mapperly Hospital in Nottingham, England, for instance, of eighteen chronic schizophrenics treated in this fashion, none demonstrated any sustained improvement, and two died.[42] Yet in the early 1960s, and again in the '70s, still further experiments were made along these lines, in the former instance by someone who would serve as president of both the World and the American Psychiatric Association and was repeatedly honored by his fellow professionals, the Montreal psychiatrist D. Ewen Cameron.[43]

As historians have begun to undertake serious work on these somatic therapies that were so notable a feature of early twentieth-century psychiatry, they have sought to place what may now seem crude and barbaric interventions into their contemporary context. We must, so they rightly argue, avoid anachronistic judgments and seek to understand why many therapeutic regimens we now dismiss as useless or actively harmful were once endorsed as efficacious and employed by some of the most highly regarded medical practitioners of their era. There are obvious echoes here of Charles Rosenberg's seminal attempt to understand how, for millennia, a traditional therapeutics of bleedings, purges, vomits, counter-irritation, and the like – the whole painful, nauseating, and to our eyes useless armamentarium of humoral medicine – *worked*: how it made sense to both doctor and patient, illuminated their mutual understandings of the nature of disease and its appropriate treatment, and reassured both parties that something useful could and was being done to ward off disease, debility, death.[44] Employing a similar approach to examine, for example, the uses, rationalizations, and impact of sterilization as a form of psychic cure, or of malaria as a remedy for the ravages of tertiary syphilis, or of passing electric currents through the brains, first of schizophrenics, and then of those suffering from profound depression, has illuminated the discovery, flourishing, and in some instances decline, of these desperate remedies, and provided us with a far more sophisticated grasp of their natural history than could possibly be generated by those who simply resort to moral condemnation.[45] A far harder case, and certainly one that has to contend with still more deeply rooted assumptions that it was an aberrant treatment, wholly without merit, mutilating, and verging on the criminal, has been psychosurgery. Even here, though, Jack Pressman has made a spirited attempt to revise our easy moral certainties, going so far as to proclaim that lobotomy "worked" in 1949, if not in our time.[46]

Pressman's is a subtle and nuanced argument, one that has had a powerful appeal for academics who delight in well-wrought accounts that appear to contradict received wisdom and turn common sense on its head. In important ways, he complicates the story we thought we knew, and he manages to suggest moral ambiguity where others have simply seen science run amok. And yet, I think that ultimately, he goes too far, as contextualizing arguments are prone to do, and his detailed reconstruction topples over into apologetics. Lobotomy, in my judgment, even by the standards of the 1940s ought ultimately to be seen as indefensible, as a number of informed and perspicacious critics argued at the time.[47]

But a proper examination of that issue is a debate for another place and another time. Here I want to note that placing the rise and fall of a particular therapeutic intervention in its cultural, political, and scientific context may in some circumstances, so far from serving to rationalize and explain away what occurred, instead succeed in demonstrating the full enormity of what its proponents and their fellow-travellers wrought. In the case of focal sepsis, it is those who seek to minimize the significance of what occurred at Trenton who avoid a detailed encounter with the historical record, for thereby it becomes much easier, as the example of Edward Shorter shows, to dismiss the whole episode as an aberration, a momentary lapse with no connections to the main actors and strands of psychiatric history. But, as I have already indicated, Cotton was among the best-trained psychiatrists of his era, his career blessed and protected by the man who was arguably the leading American psychiatrist of the first four decades of the twentieth century. His initial hypothesis relied upon a set of ideas that attracted many leading medical thinkers on both sides of the Atlantic, and his efforts to provide bodily cures for mental ills must be understood, as we have seen, as part of a far broader pattern of seeking somatic cures for psychosis that dominated institutional psychiatry for decades, beginning in the 1910s. Nor were Cotton's activities hidden or undertaken in secret, and if the full scope of the horrors he unleashed were known only to a handful of people, what was revealed in the published literature, both his own and the papers produced by his critics, ought amply to have sufficed to call a halt to procedures that maimed and killed, and were practiced on vulnerable, often resisting bodies.

What of the fate of some of the principal actors in this real-life gothic tale? Adolf Meyer, the revered leader of his profession, continued as professor of psychiatry at Johns Hopkins till 1941, stepping down only with great reluctance at the age of 74, long past the normal age of retirement. Over the years, in the words of Smith Ely Jelliffe, editor of the *Journal of Nervous and Mental Disease*, he had "put partly castrated pupils in professional chairs" all across the United States,[48] which perhaps explains why, when he was finally forced to retire, Hopkins looked elsewhere for his successor. But John C. Whitehorn, imported from his position as director of laboratories at the McLean Hospital in Boston, had no formal training in psychiatry, and did little to justify his appointment in the two decades he occupied the chair at Hopkins. Meyer, having accepted his retirement with ill-grace, insisted on maintaining an office at the Phipps, and until his death in 1950, his looming presence had much the same effect on his successor as it had previously had on many of his former students.[49] Whitehorn was an unsophisticated Nebraska farm-boy who was still addicted to barnyard humor; a man who loathed, and was incapable of, small talk; a dullard who was profoundly uninterested in culture and proud of his lack of it – and he proceeded to fritter away his time on meaningless make-work.

Before his retirement, Meyer had played a crucial role in the survival and deployment of perhaps his profession's most notorious flirtation with somatic remedies for psychosis. In the late 1930s, Walter Freeman and James Watts sprung upon their astonished colleagues the news that they had experimented with Moniz's technique of damaging the frontal lobes of the brain to treat the mad. Freeman's announcement of what they had done at the November 1936 meeting of the Southern Medical Society in Baltimore was greeted in many quarters with fury and denunciation. Freeman's presentation, the reporter from the *Baltimore Sun* recorded, had been received with "sharp criticism and

cries of alarm," and for much of the discussion period, "one man after another
. . . joined in the chorus of the hostile cross-examiners." Benjamin Wortis from
New York University pointedly demanded to know "where Dr. Freeman
obtained his evidence that obsessions are located three to four centimeters deep
in the frontal lobes," and in an obvious attempt to draw a parallel between
lobotomy and Cotton's surgical interventions, added "I can only hope this
report will not start an epidemic of progressive evisceration experiments."[50]
Meyer at once stepped into the fray, using his prestige in an attempt to calm the
crowd. "I am not antagonistic to this work," he informed his assembled colleagues, "but find it very interesting." Though it was important not to promise
miracles to the laity, experiments with the new procedure should continue, for
certainly "the available facts are sufficient to justify the procedure in the hands
of responsible persons" – as he testified Freeman and Watts most certainly
were.[51] A handful of others then followed his lead, prompting the *New York
Times* to run a story proclaiming the advent of a new operation pioneered by
"Washington scientists" that "eased . . . abnormal worry, apprehension, anxiety,
sleeplessness, and nervous tension."[52]

Years later, Freeman credited Meyer's support as playing a vital role in
encouraging him to continue: "Adolf Meyer, bless him, wrote out a judicious
statement indicating that this method had possibilities, that it was based on
some of the information we were gaining about the frontal lobes, and he
adjured us to 'follow each case'" – a classic Meyerian injunction! – "with a view
to determining the eventual results. Had it not been for his sympathetic and
helpful discussion, the advance of lobotomy would probably have been much
slower than it was."[53] In the months and years that followed, Meyer continued
to provide private support and encouragement to Freeman, and the two men
met on a number of occasions to examine the brains of lobotomized patients
who had died during or immediately after the operation.[54]

In retirement, Meyer was elected as a foreign corresponding member of the
Royal Medico-Psychological Association of Great Britain, an honor one of the
psychiatrists nominating him, R.G. Gordon, felt was only appropriate for "one
whom in this country we all regard as the foremost psychiatrist of the century."[55]
But once severed from the power that stemmed from his position at Hopkins,
Meyer quickly sank into merited oblivion, at least in North America. In part, the
temporary rise of psychoanalysis to dominate American psychiatry helped to
ensure his eclipse, for Meyer's hostility to Freud did not sit well with the high
priests of the new orthodoxy, and his eclecticism, which had once added much
to his appeal, was scorned by a generation of true believers.[56] More significant,
in the long run, was the obscurity, the logical inconsistencies, and the confusions

that riddled his writings, the crude empiricism and emphasis on collecting fact on fact, resulting in the accumulation of immense amounts of data devoid of any organizing framework or theoretical point.[57] Absent his intimidating presence to direct attention away from its content, and Meyerian psychiatry turned out to be as intellectually empty as its author was ethically blind.

Phyllis Greenacre, in her New York exile, slowly and painfully rebuilt her career. Financially pressed and emotionally distraught, she survived the first miserable months and years after her flight from Baltimore by taking a position as a consulting psychiatrist to the juvenile court in suburban White Plains, a post Meyer had helped her to obtain. Cut off from the world of academic medicine, and having entered a personal analysis in an effort to cope with her own looming depression, she found herself trapped in an endless round of mundane activities of a purely routine sort:

> Nearly one half the time is given up to acting as examiner and adviser to the Juvenile Court – and the recommendations of the psychiatrist are followed by the court in something over 90% of the cases in which recommendations are asked for. The chief drawback is that the accessory investigation is usually scant and not always reliable; so that it gives one at times a horrible feeling of absolutism in dealing with human destinies. The rest of the time, I spend as adviser to the department of child welfare for this county – being consulted on a strange gamut of problems arising in all sorts of situations.[58]

It was, perhaps, all she could cope with at the time,[59] something "I could carry . . . adequately even through a period of intense personal preoccupation," but three years on, as her depression lifted and her energy returned, she lamented to Meyer that the post "furnishes relatively little opportunity for developement [*sic*] and I do not feel that I can stick by it indefinitely without danger of atrophy." And she directly appealed to him: "Since you know my capacities and limitations better than anyone else, I would appreciate very much your advice and help if you know of any opening which I might satisfactorily fill."[60]

Meyer initially did little more than to write to suggest some prominent figures on the New York psychiatric scene whom she might contact – Russell, Wells, Stevenson, and Hinkle. Ultimately, though, he did intervene more forcefully, helping her to obtain a post at the Cornell Medical Center in New York, as director of outpatient treatment. It was a gesture for which, she indicated at the time, "I am ever so grateful,"[61] though years later, both Phyllis and her son Peter saw Meyer's patronage as prompted by guilt.[62]

Throughout these years, and beyond, Greenacre said nothing of the nightmare situation she had encountered at Cotton's hospital. Meyer had insisted that the whole matter was to remain confidential, and to ignore him would have been to court professional suicide. "I was so glad," she wrote to me, more than a half century later, "to get away from both the Trenton horrors and the complexity in the relation to Meyer, that I played ostrich and buried my head in the sand in New York."[63] She was, besides, initially too depressed and upset to take any substantial initiative on this or any other matter.

When the vogue for other forms of physical treatment in psychiatry gathered steam in the late 1930s, however, it brought back uncomfortable, long-repressed memories for Greenacre. In November 1937, after a decade of silence on the issue, she wrote to Meyer to express her misgivings and to suggest that in the present climate it might be time to air her findings on focal sepsis. "I have recently been considering again the Trenton focal infection work," she informed him. "It has been brought to my mind, especially by the present therapeutic enthusiasm about the use of insulin, metrazol, and camphor in the treatment not only of schizophrenia, but of almost anything else in the field of psychiatry." Her qualms arose from the fact that,

> the present epidemic seems to be following quite closely in the lines that the Cotton one went; – with similar premature claims of cures; confusion between therapeutic hopes and results; – the utilization of manic-depressive remissions in the interest of 'proving' and demonstrating 'results' in schizophrenia, etc., etc. I have naturally watched it with considerable interest, and recently have thought of writing up the Cotton material in such a way as to picture what happens in a 'wave' of this kind, and to emphasize the need for a critical evaluation of therapeutic results, and the danger of early publicizing of one's enthusiasm.

With considerable understatement, she added that, "while one does sympathize with the urge to 'do something,' it seems that the landslide which is sometimes set in motion has some dangers too."[64] During the preceding decade, however, much of the Trenton material she had gathered had vanished. "I have case reports and some manuscript; but not the summary report that I made then." Could she, she asked Meyer, consult his copy?[65]

Meyer responded that he was "not at all surprised that with the very searching experience you have this work of 1925 looms up in the present situation." Perhaps mindful that almost five years had now passed since Cotton's death, he indicated that "I am very glad to put anything at your disposal," and indicated that he was sending along his own copy of her report. But he signaled his own pragmatic embrace of the new physical treatments: "I must confess . . . that in general I have the impression that these non-bloody onslaughts upon the person have given some very interesting results." To be sure, "I do not believe that we have as yet reached anything that strikes at the core of the difficulties." Nonetheless, in a situation "where one is almost powerless with regard to the inability to get out of the daydreaming or scattering conditions," there was something to be said for the new techniques, though "it is unfortunate that it is so hard for some patients to get en rapport along less aggressive lines."[66]

In the end, Greenacre's proposal came to naught, and her findings in the Cotton matter remained safely buried in the archives at Hopkins and Trenton. Increasingly drawn to psychoanalysis, which by the 1940s would become the dominant strand in American psychiatry, she left more traditional approaches to the field behind. She became an expert on the psychoanalytic study of childhood and adolescence,[67] and wrote psychohistorical studies of Jonathan Swift, Lewis Carroll, and Charles Darwin.[68]

Rather remarkably, in New York psychoanalytic circles that were otherwise dominated by European refugees, she became steadily more prominent, eventually coming to be widely regarded as one of the most powerful figures in the inner circle of analysts, a position signaled by her election as president of the New York Psychoanalytic Institute for 1948–50, and president of the New York Psychoanalytic Society for 1956–7. When Arnold Rogow surveyed a number of psychiatrists in 1970, Greenacre was ranked the fourth most influential living psychoanalyst (behind only Anna Freud, Heinz Hartmann, and Erik Erikson), and was the only one of those named who was not a European or a European refugee.[69]

There was an ironic feature of these years, an incident that on a smaller scale recalled her prior involvement in the Cotton case, and one which once again left her with guilty knowledge. In the early 1940s, the prominent New York analyst Gregory Zilboorg was accused of misconduct with his patients, seducing and sleeping with some and pocketing the fortunes of others in the guise of serving simultaneously as analyst and financial advisor. As rumors of these ethical improprieties began to swirl, threatening a devastating scandal for the analytic community, Greenacre was appointed to a panel to investigate the charges. She had no doubt of their truth, not least because a fellow analyst with whom she was close had confessed to an affair with Zilboorg, with whom she had undertaken a training analysis. But as Meyer had done with Cotton, the refugee analysts closed ranks to protect one of their own, and at the secret meeting where the findings of the investigation were discussed, Greenacre's friend got up and defended Zilboorg ardently – a development the cognoscenti dismissed as an understandable transference phenomenon.[70] The Rasputin of the Dakotas, as Zilboorg was perhaps not so fondly called, survived essentially unscathed.[71]

In the decades that followed, Greenacre was constantly on the move from one New York City apartment to another, restless and never content or able to settle down. She did, however, create some semblance of stability in her domestic arrangements by buying a house in the country, in Garrison, New York, and this became the place where she spent the summers. Greenacre furnished this country house to look like her childhood home near Chicago, from which she had fled in 1916 to start her career in Baltimore.[72] And when she finally retired from practice in 1984, it was to move to Garrison, where she died on October 24, 1989, at the age of 95.[73]

Adolph Cotton, Henry's younger son, soon abandoned his plans to become an architect. He chose instead to join a Princeton archeological expedition to Antioch, Syria, for which he left in 1933.[74] The following year, he returned to Princeton to take a course in the fine arts, and then left for London to obtain further training in archeology at the British Museum. And then, in February 1936, en route back to America on a North German Lloyd liner, the SS *Bremen*, he disappeared overboard. In the newspapers, it was reported as an accident: Henry Cotton junior "said that he could only think that his brother might have been blown off the ship during a storm or have slipped on wet decks and fallen overboard" and that "it is unthinkable that his loss might have resulted from any action of his."[75] But in reality, the death was a suicide.[76]

Attempting to cope with the loss of both his father and his younger brother, Henry Cotton junior completed his own medical training in psychiatry at Johns Hopkins. At one point, he had contemplated switching to surgery as his specialism, something Meyer thought suited him better,[77] but in the end, he chose to follow in his father's footsteps. It was not an easy passage. Recommending him for his first job at the Essex County Juvenile Clinic in Newark, New Jersey, Meyer commented that the younger Cotton "has had to undergo a rather exacting transformation with us, inasmuch as his father's crusader's spirit in the fight with mental disease had to be adjusted to our local perspective and sense of proportions."[78]

Privately, Meyer knew that the transformation was far from complete. One of his subordinates had reported just days before that "[Cotton] hasn't found himself yet, but is still struggling with the crumbling of his adoration for his father (complicated here by his brother's death and a love affair with a SG nurse)."[79] It can scarcely have helped matters, then, that in 1938, young Henry returned to the hospital in whose grounds he had grown up. Here he served first as assistant director and then director of the Trenton State Hospital Mental Hygiene Clinic.[80]

The outbreak of war brought a temporary change of scene when he joined the Army medical corps. But with the end of hostilities, he returned to New Jersey once more, securing an appointment in the Department of Institutions and Agencies, where he was supposed to act as liaison between the state hospital superintendents and the commissioner. It was a difficult role, for the more senior state hospital staff resented having to communicate through an intermediary for the first time, and they made their discomfiture plain. Whether this accounts for the younger Cotton's growing alienation is unclear, though he complained of disturbed sleep and grew depressed. One day in June 1948, he was found dead in his office, having taken an overdose of "sleeping powder."[81] Prophylactic teeth extractions notwithstanding, both of Henry Cotton's sons thus ended up committing suicide.

Ferdearle Fischer, the dentist who had been appointed by Cotton to head the dental department at Trenton State Hospital, remained in post until 1960, busily pulling teeth.[82] It was he whom Mrs. Cotton entrusted with the task of going to the New York docks to retrieve her son Adolph's personal effects from the SS *Bremen*, thus enabling her to avoid the crowds of journalists. Fischer's forty-two years of service were marked by the sacrifice of literally hundreds of thousands of other people's teeth, as part of his continuing war on sepsis. When I interviewed him in retirement at Leisure World in Orange County – a bizarre encampment where the affluent elderly live behind barbed wire in what for all the world resembles a giant and luxurious concentration camp, except that the barbed wire is to keep outsiders out, not insiders in – he waxed nostalgic about his years in the hospital, and was still convinced that the world would eventually recognize Henry Cotton for the great man he undoubtedly was.[83]

Thomas Chivers Graves outlived Cotton by many decades. He continued to preside over all the mental hospitals in the Birmingham area until the late 1940s, finally retiring to write his memoirs in 1950, shortly after the advent of the National Health Service brought about a reorganization of the old county and borough asylums. Graves remained unflinching in his faith in focal sepsis, and his election as president of the Royal Medico-Psychological Association in 1940 gave him a platform he did not hesitate to use to promote his views.[84] The vagaries of the war against Hitler and Hirohito, which drew off most skilled psychiatric manpower to cope with the renewed problem of mental breakdowns among the troops, left a skeletal profession behind to manage the home front, and in this environment, there was little thought given to the problems of professional societies. The upshot was that Graves served as president for four successive terms, making him the longest serving head of the profession in the history of British psychiatry. Oddly, though, by the time he succeeded to the post, he had largely lost whatever influence he had once possessed over his professional brethren. His continued belief in fighting focal sepsis was increasingly seen as a harmless eccentricity, and though he organized symposia of ear, nose, and throat specialists to proclaim the importance of the fight, he found himself without much in the way of support. In his own eyes, the discovery of antibiotics opened up the possibilities of a remarkable new assault on psychosis, one that would no longer have to rely on surgery. But penicillin was precious and in short supply – far too precious to waste on the mentally ill. Imperious to the last, and not to be deprived of the glorious therapeutic breakthrough that surely awaited the first psychiatrist to inject his patients with the new miracle remedy, Graves elected to produce his own, growing mold in jam jars in the Hollymoor Hospital basement and injecting the slurry that he harvested into a series of his patients. His detailed description in the *Medical Press and Circular*[85] of how others might follow in his footsteps unaccountably failed to generate enthusiasm in the profession at large, and the patients who were offered the fruits of his ingenuity inexplicably remained as mad as ever. After fourteen years of retirement, during which he vainly sought a publisher for his memoirs, Graves died on June 6, 1964, aged 81, his last months spent in a nursing home.

Joseph Raycroft, who had served as president of the board of managers at Trenton in Cotton's last years at the hospital, continued to serve on the board for almost two more decades, helping to cement the hospital's continued commitment to rooting out focal infection, albeit without resorting any longer to abdominal surgery. He remained on the faculty at Princeton for much of this period, being responsible for student health and physical education. By February of 1949, however, his memory was reported to be failing "badly,"[86] and the meeting of July 21 of that year to endorse the appointment of Harold Magee as superintendent of Trenton State Hospital was the last he was able to attend.[87] Eventually, as his dementia worsened, Raycroft was certified as being in need of psychiatric care and treatment. In an ironic twist of fate, the former president of the hospital's board of managers, the man who had done so much to facilitate Cotton's experiments, ended his days on the back wards of Trenton State Hospital, where he died on October 1, 1955.[88]

Burdette Lewis, the quintessential Progressive-era bureaucrat who had served as the head of New Jersey's Department of Institutions and Agencies in the critical years from 1918 through 1925, had provided vital support for Cotton's radical assault on focal sepsis. His professed admiration for modern advertising and public relations, coupled with Cotton's own incorrigible desire for self-promotion, had at times provoked grumblings from psychiatrists who apparently saw "ethical" lapses of this sort as a far more serious breach of professional decorum than forced treatment of resisting patients, or the repeated resort to experimental treatments that maimed and killed. But the publicity he had obtained had done much to draw attention to Cotton's work, and to draw in the legions of private paying patients, many from across the country, who sought out, or whose families sought out, a surgical remedy for their psychiatric troubles.

Lewis's high-handed manner, and his visible contempt for the politicians with whom he was forced to interact, had helped to bring about his ouster from state government in 1925. The boy wonder, who had risen rapidly from deputy commissioner of corrections in New York City to head New Jersey's penal and welfare apparatus on the strength of his embrace of modern business practices and their application to public administration, now secured a lucrative post in the private sector, as an executive with the Penney-Gwinn Corporation. His flirtation with the world of business did not last long, however. In 1932, he went to Washington to join the State Department, and from 1941 to 1945, he was seconded to Iran, to serve as chief economist to its puppet government. The end of the Second World War brought the opportunity to practice his old skills. The military authorities occupying Japan installed him as their chief prison administrator, a post he occupied until 1951.

Shortly after his return from Japan, though, a life of achievements in the public eye all abruptly came crashing down, as mental troubles led to his admission to the very state hospital that he had once regarded as the leading institution in his empire. Ferdearle Fischer, the dentist who had known him in his salad days, recalled the sadness of seeing the man who had headed all New Jersey's state hospitals, prisons, and reformatories when he had joined Cotton's staff in 1918 now reduced to a mental wreck, just one more chronic patient shuffling around the back wards, and queuing up for his daily meals. And it was at Trenton that Burdette Lewis lived out the last years of his life. His tenure on the back wards extended even into the years after Fischer at last retired, and he gradually sank into obscurity: so much so that the passing of the man once listed in *Who's Who in America* merited the briefest of stories in the *New York Times*, and a three-line death notice a day later, alongside those of a host of others whose lifelong anonymity brought them a similar fate.[89]

Martha Hurwitz, the intermittently depressed Jewish patient whom we last saw being released back to the care of her parents, "cured" for the second time by a course of surgical bacteriology, had a third mental breakdown in 1932. Returned to the hospital on April 4, she remained there for five years, being discharged once more on March 31, 1937. Again, though, the remission was short-lived, and less than a year later, she appears in the hospital records.[90] Her admission on March 14, 1938, was to prove her last and for decades she languished on Trenton's back wards, haunting its halls, and being subjected to most of the panoply of new experimental treatments that characterized American psychiatry in these years.

On September 13, 1938, she is recorded as having been on a course of insulin coma therapy. The transcript in her notes records her as commenting that, "she can't stand this place. This is a boarding house and the people here resent the fact that she is so healthy so they give her needles to make her sick" – an interesting commentary on her interpretation of the coma "therapy" – "She is sure she will be killed in time." By January 20, 1940, her case notes reveal that she had been given fifty insulin treatments, and her condition was deteriorating. She displayed a flattened emotional tone, stamped her feet during the interview, and remained largely mute. An order was made transferring her to a continuous treatment ward.

In 1943, her doctors tried inoculating her with malaria, but she remained mute and inaccessible, seemingly indifferent and out of touch with her environment. Case notes henceforth become more intermittent. In mid-1949, she was given a series of electric shocks, which had no discernible impact on her by now chronic condition. On September 18, 1951, she was reported to be "greatly deteriorated," uncooperative, and confused, but presumably not troublesome enough to join the ranks of those the new superintendent, Harold Magee, was selecting for lobotomies. Two and a half years later, on March 5, 1954, her pathologies were still more in evidence: her case notes record her as disoriented as to time and place. On being questioned, she claimed to have been born at Trenton State Hospital, and to have lived there since the age of three. Separately, her attendants reported that she was uncooperative and quarrelsome on the ward.

These years saw the introduction of the new drugs for the treatment of psychosis, and early on, the withdrawn and deteriorated Martha was selected for experimental treatment with Reserpine. Her treatment began on September 28, 1955, when she was given the then-standard dose of 4 mg of the drug by mouth.[91] But the Trenton psychiatrists had a different treatment plan in mind for her and for a number of other patients treated alongside her. At frequent intervals, the dosage she was given was doubled, until on October 31, 1955, she was reported to have been given 164 mg in a single day. By November 24, 1955, her dosage was increased yet again – not quite doubled, this time, but at 236 mg a day, she was now receiving about seventy times the standard "therapeutic" dose. Finally, after forty-two doses, the treatment was terminated, and the still psychotic Martha was temporarily left alone. Not for long. On September 9, 1956, she began a similar trial of Thorazine, and then on June 15, 1957, was given another rapidly escalating course of Reserpine.

None of this was to any avail. Throughout the 1960s, she was reported to be withdrawn and passive, her affect was "grossly inappropriate and her insight and judgment seem to be severely defective." (No similar judgment was rendered about those treating her.) She had become cleaner and more cooperative, however, though she "does not talk." Finally, in the early 1980s, it appeared that she might be the dubious beneficiary of a new wave of enthusiasm that had been sweeping American psychiatry. Notwithstanding the fact that she was now a burnt-out case, a demented old woman who had somehow survived repeated surgeries, the extraction of all her teeth and tonsils, fever therapy, insulin comas, electric shocks, and massive overdoses of drugs, during a confinement that had stretched over five decades, her case notes recorded that she was scheduled to be "deinstitutionalized," released back into a "community" she had last seen in 1938, a fate she was scheduled to share in common with thousands of other long-stay patients as states abrogated any responsibility for the fate of the chronically crazy. But it never happened. In the last year of her life, Martha fell and broke her hip. Riddled with bed sores that proved resistant to treatment, she contracted pneumonia. She gradually deteriorated, and on May 7, 1982, fifty-four years after her first admission to the hospital, she was pronounced dead, her age variously calculated as being 80 or 86.[92]

And what of Trenton itself? For decades after Cotton's departure and death, it continued to be administered by those he had trained, and who had served as his subordinates, and Drs. Raycroft and Mecray provided yet a further layer of continuity as members of the board of managers until after the Second World War. (Paul Mecray, indeed, was eventually succeeded by his son, Paul Mecray junior, who remained on the Board until 1978.) Robert Stone, who succeeded Henry Cotton in 1930, made the political decision to abandon the abdominal surgery he had previously participated in with enthusiasm. (Stone had done most of the tonsillectomies and gynecological surgery in the 1920s, and he remained active on these fronts.) But though he ceased performing colectomies, Stone professed himself still convinced of the importance of seeking out and eliminating focal sepsis, and the hospital's operating theater and its dentist's chair, to say nothing of its apparatus for performing colonic irrigations, reflected that conviction, remaining almost as busy as ever.[93] Stone's annual report for 1934, for instance, noted that the hospital had given 16,247 colonic irrigations that year, and was making extensive use of castor oil therapy, electrotherapy, and a whole array of hydrotherapies, and 1938 saw the extraction of 7,258 teeth, and 160 tonsillectomies.[94] Stone's special enthusiasm, though, was for fever therapy,[95] and he sought to interest both the Rockefeller Foundation and (inevitably) Adolf Meyer in his experiments, claiming remarkable successes for the treatment.[96] On this occasion, however, neither party would be drawn into the fray.

On Stone's retirement because of heart problems in 1944, he was succeeded by yet another of Cotton's assistants, J. B. Spradley. Spradley served for only four years, but during his tenure, "therapeutic activism reached its greatest degree of intensity."[97] When ill health forced Spradley, too, into retirement, he joined Raycroft and Mecray on the board of managers. In his place, in 1948, the superintendency was bestowed on Harold Magee, the youngest and last of the generation who had worked under Cotton. Every year, the hospital's annual report under Magee continued to express the administration's continued belief in the vital significance of searching out sepsis, and teeth and tonsils were extracted just as before.[98] But Magee was especially enamored of the new psychiatric panacea, lobotomies, and with the assistance of Dr. Michael Scott and then Dr. William W. Wilson, Philadelphia neurosurgeons, the hospital embarked on an extensive series of brain operations,[99] and continued to embrace the surgery into the second half of the 1950s.

As with other state hospitals, rather quickly Trenton's preferred means of severing patients' frontal lobes became the transorbital lobotomy Walter Freeman had pioneered just a few years before, not the so-called "precision" operation he and Watts had originally used. Those first operations, which required the services of a neurosurgeon and a whole team of assistants, and took two to four hours and more to perform, had proved far too costly and time consuming to serve as the mass-market solution to the problems of mental disease that Freeman sought.[100] By contrast, Freeman's revised approach, which he boasted was so simple to use that even a state hospital psychiatrist could be taught the technique in a matter of hours,[101] employed electroshock to render the patient unconscious, after which an ice-pick could be inserted into the brain via both eye sockets, and frontal lobes severed before the patient once more became conscious of his or her surroundings.[102] It was, as even Freeman conceded, an operation attended with certain unfortunate sound-effects: as the leucotome, the modified and calibrated ice-pick that Freeman had devised to allow the operator to observe how far the instrument had penetrated into the skull, was driven through the bone, the cracking sound tended to disturb the naive observer: "The fracture of a thick orbital plate is not infrequently accompanied by a rather horrifying snap and sometimes by a gush of blood and extreme swelling of the eyelids that is definitely disturbing to both psychiatrists and surgeons until they have become accustomed to it."[103] But fortunately, the patient was unconscious, and he assured his professional colleagues that the ease and speed of the operation,[104] and results that rivaled or exceeded those associated with the more elaborate standard operation, would convince them to tolerate what was no more than a momentary aesthetic annoyance and to embrace a procedure amply justified by the benefits, managerial and therapeutic, that damaged frontal lobes brought in their wake.

In 1958, following the introduction of the phenothiazines, lobotomies finally ceased at Trenton. Magee, though, praised the operation as "a good procedure, giving unexpectedly good results when applied as a therapy to unresponding aggressive and assaultive patients," and he insisted that, "it is entirely likely that in some instances, after careful review by the Psychosurgery Review Board, that this procedure will again be activated."[105] With few exceptions, it was not.

Only in 1960, though, with the joint retirements of Harold Magee and Ferdearle Fischer, can one say with assurance that Cotton's posthumous

33 *The Cotton Award for Kindness: an official picture commemorating the presentation of the award to a member of the staff of Trenton State Hospital in the early 1950s.*

influence and the sustained assault on focal sepsis finally drew to a close at Trenton. Through all these years – through the addition to the hospital's therapeutic armamentarium of such wonders of twentieth-century psychiatric science as insulin shock, camphor and metrazol-induced convulsions, electroshock machines, histamine shock, inoculation with malaria and typhoid vaccine, lobotomy in both its standard and transorbital forms, and massive doses of the new neuroleptic drugs – Cotton remained the hospital's guiding genius and patron saint. Madness was still seen as rooted in bodily pathology, and aggressive efforts continued to be made to drive out the demons of insanity. Meanwhile, every year, thanks to the grieving widow who had provided the necessary endowment, the contribution to the welfare of the hospital's patients of the great man who had once presided over the establishment was symbolically recognized – with the bestowal on an outstanding member of the staff of "the Cotton Award for Kindness."[106]

Notes

Prologue

1 *Trenton Evening Times*, August 5, 1925.
2 "Warden's Report to the Board of Managers of the New Jersey State Hospital at Trenton for July 1925," Trenton State Hospital (hereafter TSH) Archives.
3 Cotton's erratic behavior before and during the proceedings was recounted in some detail in both the *Trenton Evening Times* and the *Newark Evening News* for August 5, 1925. For Leedom's testimony, see *Trenton Evening Times*, August 6, 1925.
4 *Trenton Evening Times*, August 5, 1925.
5 Ibid.
6 *Trenton Evening Times*, August 7, 1925; *New York Times*, August 7 and 8, 1925.
7 *Trenton Evening Times*, August 13, 1925.
8 *Trenton Evening Times*, August 12, 1925.
9 *Trenton Evening Times*, August 26, 1925.
10 *Trenton Evening Times*, August 13, 1925.
11 *Trenton Evening Times*, August 19, 1925.
12 Raycroft to Meyer, September 12, 1925, Meyer Papers, Chesney Archives Johns Hopkins University (hereafter CAJH) 3215/1.
13 Ibid.

Chapter 1

1 Lord Shaftesbury, *Diaries*, September 5, 1851, University of Southampton Library, Special Collections, SHA/PD.
2 William Pargeter, *Observations on Maniacal Disorders* (Reading: for the author, 1792), p. 123.

3 Andrew Wynter, *The Borderlands of Insanity*, 2nd ed. (London: Renshaw, 1877), p. 112.
4 See Francis B. Lee (ed)., *Genealogical and Personal Memoir of Mercer County, New Jersey* (New York: Lewis, 1907), vol. 1, pp. 200–01.
5 Minutes of the Board of Managers, November 27, 1901, TSH Archives.
6 *Trenton Evening Times*, July 24, 1907.
7 *Trenton Evening Times*, July 20 and 24, 1907.
8 *Trenton Evening Times*, July 24, 26, 27, and 29, 1907.
9 The progress of the typhoid epidemic and the exposé of conditions in the asylum may be followed in the *Trenton Evening Times*. See, for example, the issues for July 9, 16, 17, 19, 20, 23, 24, 26, 27, 29, and 31, and then August 1, 2, 3, 5, 6, 8, and 12, 1907. No grand jury indictment of Ward was actually forthcoming.
10 *Trenton Evening Times*, August 15, September 2, 1907.
11 *Trenton Evening Times*, October 5, 19, and November 1, 1907.
12 Minutes of the Board of Managers, October 18, 1907, TSH Archives.
13 Cotton to Meyer, October 19, 1907, Meyer Papers, CAJH I/767/3.
14 See Adolf Meyer, "Requirements for the Establishment of Scientific Work at the Worcester State Lunatic Hospital," undated [*c*.1895], Meyer Papers, CAJH Series X.

15 See Gerald Grob, *The State and the Mentally Ill: A History of the Worcester State Hospital in Massachusetts, 1830–1920* (Chapel Hill: University of North Carolina Press, 1966), pp. 287, 297–8. Two of the twenty-nine junior physicians who trained under Meyer in his years at Worcester were women.

16 Charles G. Hill, "How Can We Best Advance the Study of Psychiatry?," *American Journal of Insanity* 64 (1907), p. 6.

17 Henry Maudsley, *The Pathology of Mind* (London: Macmillan, 1879), p. 88. For Maudsley and his influence, see Andrew Scull, Charlotte MacKenzie, and Nicholas Hervey, *Masters of Bedlam: The Transformation of the Mad-Doctoring Trade* (Princeton, N.J.: Princeton University Press, 1996).

18 See, for example, the discussions in Bonnie Blustein, "'A Hollow Square of Psychological Science': American Neurologists and Psychiatrists in Conflict," in *Madhouses, Mad-Doctors, and Madmen: The Social History of Psychiatry in the Victorian Era*, ed. Andrew Scull, pp. 241–70 (Philadelphia: University of Pennsylvania Press, 1981); Scull, MacKenzie, and Hervey, *Masters of Bedlam*, chapter 9.

19 George A. Tucker, *Lunacy in Many Lands* ([Birmingham?], 1885), pp. 24–5.

20 Edward C. Spitzka, "Reform in the Scientific Study of Psychiatry," *Journal of Nervous and Mental Diseases* 5 (1878), pp. 206–10. Nearly three decades later, the situation did not appear to have changed. Charles Hill's presidential address urged his colleagues to "get away from the growing of pumpkins, the rearing of pigs, and the planting of potatoes, close our old text-books, always ten years behind the times, and study the latest clinical diagnosis, physiological and pathological chemistry, bacteriology, toxicology, and metabolism." *American Journal of Insanity* 64 (1907), p. 8.

21 Meyer shared – indeed actively promoted – such an outlook. In 1895 he even founded a (largely ineffectual) new professional organization, the Association of Assistant Physicians of Hospitals for the Insane, explicitly as a forum for the discussion of scientific rather than management issues.

22 Edward Cowles, "The Relation of Mental Diseases to General Medicine," *Boston Medical and Surgical Journal* 137 (1897), pp. 277–82.

23 On Meyer's move to New York, and his role as director of what he soon renamed the Psychiatric Institute, see Gerald Grob, *Mental Illness and American Society, 1875–1940* (Princeton, N.J.: Princeton University Press, 1983), pp. 128–31.

24 See Meyer Papers, CAJH I/767/1–32 for their correspondence.

25 Cotton to Meyer, October 25, 1905, Meyer Papers, CAJH I/767/2.

26 Cotton to Meyer, May 9, 1903, Meyer Papers, CAJH I/767/1.

27 Cotton to Meyer, February 3 and March 13, 1905, Meyer Papers, CAJH I/767/1.

28 The standard discussion of this scholarly migration is Thomas Henry Bonner, *American Doctors and German Universities* (Lincoln, Nebr.: University of Nebraska Press, 1963). At least 15,000 American medical students studied in German universities between 1870 and 1914.

29 Cotton to Meyer, September 19, 1905, Meyer Papers, CAJH I/767/2.

30 Wilhelm Griesinger, *Der Pathologie und Therapie der psychischen Krankheiten* 2nd ed. (Stuttgart: Krabbe, 1861).

31 On Cotton's departure for Europe, see his letter to one of his rivals for prominence in American psychiatry, Clarence Farrar. Cotton to Farrar, Novmber 6, 1905, Farrar Archive, Toronto, Canada. Farrar had preceded Cotton to Germany between October 1902 and May 1904, sponsored by a mentor they shared in common, Stewart Paton of Johns Hopkins University. He would

later serve as editor of the *American Journal of Psychiatry* for more than three decades, and was director of the Toronto Psychiatric Hospital from its opening in 1925 until 1947. For a biographical sketch of Farrar, see Edward Shorter, "C. B. Farrar: A Life," in *TPH: History and Memories of the Toronto Psychiatric Hospital, 1925–1966*, ed. Edward Shorter (Toronto: Wall and Emerson, 1966), pp. 59–96.

32 Kraepelin had published a minor textbook, *Compendium der Psychiatrie* (Leizig: Abel), in 1883, but his major influence began with its third edition, which appeared in 1893 and provided an extended discussion of premature dementia, or dementia praecox (relabelled schizophrenia in 1908 by the Swiss psychiatrist Eugen Bleuler). Neo-Kraepelinian ideas lie at the core of the various versions of the American Psychiatric Association's *Diagnostic and Statistical Manual*, at least since its third edition in 1980.

33 *Trenton Evening Times*, November 1, 1907.

34 Cotton to Meyer, October 3, 1907, Meyer Papers, CAJH I/767/2. See also Cotton to Meyer, October 19, 1907, Meyer Papers, CAJH I/767/3.

35 He promptly shared the news with Meyer: Cotton to Meyer, October 14, 1907, Meyer Papers, CAJH I/767/2.

36 Cotton to Meyer, November 21, 1907, Meyer Papers, CAJH I/767/2.

37 Silas Weir Mitchell, "Address Before the Medico-Pychological Association," *Journal of Nervous and Mental Diseases* 21 (1894), p. 19.

38 See Nancy Tomes, "The Great Restraint Controversy: A Comparative Perspective on Anglo-American Psychiatry in the Nineteenth Century," in *The Anatomy of Madness*, ed. W. F. Bynum, R. Porter, and M. Shepherd (London: Routledge, 1988) vol. 3, pp. 190–225.

39 Dr. Harold Magee, interview with James Leiby, March 10, 1961, quoted in

James Leiby, *Charity and Correction in New Jersey: A History of State Welfare Institutions* (New Brunswick, N.J.: Rutgers University Press), 1967, p. 121.

40 These volumes are still preserved in the hospital's archives.

41 Farrar stayed only three years, finding that he hated life as an underling at a state hospital. In 1916, with Stewart Paton's help, he successfully sought a post elsewhere, leaving just as Cotton began to implement a new, surgically based approach to the therapeutics of mental disorder. See Shorter, "C. B. Farrar," pp. 72–4. Shorter attributes Farrar's unhappiness with his position at Trenton to his concern about Cotton's "massive looming malpractice," but he provides no evidence to support this claim. Cotton's interventions at this time were limited to the removal of some patients' teeth and it is unlikely that these procedures were enough to unnerve Farrar. Abdominal and other surgeries did not commence for another two years and it is more likely that Farrar tired of his subordinate position and of the monotony of asylum life. Certainly, Shorter notwithstanding, there is no evidence that Farrar was especially concerned on his departure about Cotton's activities (the two men kept up, for example, a friendly correspondence in the years after he left) and it is hard to see why he would have been.

42 The occasion of a congratulatory note from pupil to master. See Cotton to Meyer, June 24, 1908, Meyer Papers, CAJH I/767/3.

43 See Cotton to Meyer, October 6, 1909, Meyer Papers, CAJH I/767/4. In response, Meyer sent Cotton a christening cup and his congratulations.

Chapter 2

1 On the expansion of surgery and the growing recourse of the wealthier classes to the hospital for treatment, as

its technical advantages for antiseptic and aseptic surgery were ever more broadly grasped, see Joel Howell, *Technology in the Hospital: The Transformation of Patient Care in the Early Twentieth Century* (Baltimore: Johns Hopkins University Press, 1995); Rosemary Stevens, *In Sickness and in Wealth: American Hospitals in the Twentieth Century* (New York: Basic Books, 1989), pp. 33–4; William Frederick Braasch, *Early Days in the Mayo Clinic* (Springfield, Ill.: Charles Thomas, 1969).

2 Edwin F. Hirsch, *Frank Billings: The Architect of Medical Education* (Chicago: University of Chicago Press, 1966), pp. 12, 19.

3 See Robert Kohler, *From Medical Chemistry to Biochemistry: The Making of a Biomedical Discipline* (Cambridge: Cambridge University Press, 1982); Andrew Cunningham and Perry Williams (eds.), *The Laboratory Revolution in Medicine* (Cambridge: Cambridge University Press, 1992); Braasch, *Mayo*.

4 Henry Maudsley, *Body and Mind: An Inquiry into their Mutual Influence, Specially in Reference to Mental Disorders* (London: Macmillan, 1870), p. 61.

5 Richard Greene, "The Care and Cure of the Insane," *Universal Review*, July 1889, p. 503.

6 G. Alder Blumer, "Presidential Address," *American Journal of Insanity* 60 (1903), pp. 1–18.

7 George Henry Savage and Edwin Goodall, *Insanity and its Allied Neuroses* 4th ed. (London: Cassell, 1907), p. 44.

8 S. A. K. Strahan, "The Propagation of Insanity and Allied Neuroses," *Journal of Mental Science* 36 (1890), p. 334.

9 Ibid., p. 331.

10 G. Alden Blumer, "Marriage in its Relation to Morbid Heredity" (1900), quoted in Ian Dowbiggin, *Keeping America Sane: Psychiatry and Eugenics in the United States and Canada, 1880–1940* (Ithaca, N.Y.: Cornell Uni-

versity Press, 1997), p. 84. See also Charles Rosenberg, "The Bitter Fruit: Heredity, Disease, and Social Thought in Nineteenth Century America," *Perspectives in American History* 8 (1974), pp. 189–235.

11 Henry Maudsley, *The Pathology of Mind*, p. 115. As the founder of the Salvation Army summed up the consensus, "it is a crime against the race to allow those who are so inveterately depraved the freedom to wander abroad, infect their fellows, prey upon Society and to multiply their kind." General W. Booth, *Darkest England and the Way Out* (London: Salvation Army, 1890), pp. 204–5.

12 See Joel Braslow, "In the Name of Therapeutics: The Practice of Sterilization in a California State Hospital," *Journal of the History of Medicine and Allied Sciences* 51 (1996), pp. 29–51; idem., *Mental Ills and Bodily Cures* (Berkeley: University of California Press, 1997); Philip Reilly, *The Surgical Solution: A History of Involuntary Sterilization in the United States* (Baltimore, Md.: Johns Hopkins University Press, 1991). Involuntary sterilizations continued in California into the 1960s. In Europe, the Swedes and the Swiss, among others, ventured down this path, though the British resisted, and the advocacy of forced sterilization came from self-professed progressives, liberals, and socialists, as well as Fascists and the Right. See Mark Mazower, *Dark Continent: Europe's Twentieth Century* (New York: Knopf, 1999), pp. 77–8; M. E. Kopp, "Eugenic Sterilization Laws in Europe," *American Journal of Obstetrics and Gynecology* 34 (1937), pp. 499–504; Mathew Thomson, *The Problem of Mental Deficiency: Eugenics, Democracy, and Social Policy in Britain, c.1870–1859* (Oxford: Clarendon Press, 1998).

13 It was left to their German counterparts, a few decades later, to discard these alientists' scruples, to translate the

logic of their arguments into a program for action, and to opt for euthanasia and systematic medicalized mass-murder – actions a number of modern historians have rightly refused to see as "an incomprehensible excess" or the product of "individual aberrations." The "extermination" the American and British psychiatrists had previously spoken of as no more than a theoretical possibility was here transformed into legitimate medical practice and appalling reality. See Robert Proctor, *Racial Hygiene: Medicine Under the Nazis* (Cambridge, Mass.: Harvard University Press, 1988); Paul Weindling, *Health, Race, and German Politics between National Unification and Nazism, 1870–1945* (Cambridge: Cambridge University Press, 1988); idem., "Psychiatry and the Holocaust," *Psychological Medicine* 22 (1992), pp. 1–3; Michael Burleigh, *Death and Deliverance: 'Euthanasia' in Germany c.1900–1945* (Cambridge: Cambridge University Press, 1994); idem., *Ethics and Extermination: Reflections on Nazi Genocide* (Cambridge: Cambridge University Press, 1997), esp. chapter 4, "Psychiatry, German Society, and the Nazi 'Euthanasia' Program"; Hugh Gregory Gallagher, *By Trust Betrayed: Physicians and the License to Kill in the Third Reich* (New York: Holt, 1990); Götz Aly, Peter Chroust, and Christian Pross, *Cleansing the Fatherland: Nazi Medicine and Racial Hygiene* (Baltimore: Johns Hopkins University Press, 1994); Volker Roelcke, Gerrit Hohendorf, and Maike Rotzoll, "Psychiatric Research and 'Euthanasia': The Case of the Psychiatric Department at the University of Heidelberg, 1941–1945," *History of Psychiatry* 5 (1994), pp. 517–32. The key to the differential outcome in the three countries, one suspects, is not some ethical difference between the profession in Germany, Britain and America. One notes that many of Germany's leading psychiatrists and major academic departments at German universities joined enthusiastically in the mass killing, and certainly there was no difference in the language and theoretical conclusions of these men and their Anglo-American counterparts. Rather, I suggest, what differentiated the actions of the two groups of professionals was the rise of the Nazi state, which at once removed the practical obstacles that democratic societies thankfully erected against such horrors, and provided state-sponsored incentives to embark upon a policy of *Desinfektion* (disinfection) that cost upwards of a hundred thousand lives. Henry Cotton, as we shall see, practiced his own version of "disinfection," and used the term in a more straightforward, less Orwellian, sense.

14 The micro-organism that caused syphilis had been identified in 1905 by two German researchers, Fritz Schaudinn and Eric Hoffmann, and Wassermann's test for the presence of the syphilitic spirochete was developed the following year. See Ludwig Fleck, *The Genesis and Development of a Scientific Fact* (Chicago: University of Chicago Press, 1979).

15 A British physician later commented that this approach required only "a knowledge of anatomy, a steady hand, and a stout heart," in response to which one of his critics, the wonderfully named Farquhar Buzzard, retorted that "the stout heart is required by the patient as much as by the physician!" Sir James Purves-Stewart, "The Treatment of General Paralysis," *British Medical Journal*, March 22, 1924, p. 509.

16 Frank Billings, *Focal Infection: The Lane Medical Lectures* (New York: Appleton, 1916); see also Hirsch, *Billings*, pp. 60, 85; James Bowman, *Good Medicine: The First 150 Years of Rush-Presbyterian-St. Luke's Medical Center* (Chicago: Chicago Review Press, 1987).

17 For Billings' role in fundraising and building medical education and institutions in Chicago, see Hirsch, *Billings*, pp. 109–13, 117–21.

18 Billings, *Focal Infection*, p. 144.

19 Ibid., p. 130. Röntgen rays, named after the man who discovered them, are better known today as X-rays.

20 Ibid., p. 131.

21 Ibid., pp. 128–9.

22 Ibid., p. 129.

23 Ibid., pp. 132–3.

24 For discussion of these developments, see Braasch, *Mayo*, pp. 33, 47–50, 68–9, 74–5.

25 Cotton noted the exception in one of his numerous letters to his mentor, Adolf Meyer: "I realize that the question of focal infection has not been accepted by everyone and that the Hopkins men, under the influence of Janeway, have not accepted the views of Hastings, Billings, and others. The only exception, however, is Dr. Barker." Cotton to Meyer, April 8, 1918, CAJH I/767/14.

26 Howell, *Technology in the Hospital*, esp. pp. 60–65.

27 The notion of a "surgical bacteriology" was a commonplace of the era, equally central to American surgery. John Chalmers Da Costa's *A Manual of Modern Surgery* (Philadelphia: Saunders, 1894) would eventually go through 10 editions and opens with a discussion of bacteriology; and William Williams Keen's and James William White's *An American Textbook of Surgery*, one of its main rivals, titled its opening section "Surgical Bacteriology." Cotton later adopted the term in his own publications.

28 See W. Arbuthnot Lane, *The Operative Treatment of Chronic Constipation* (London: Nisbet, 1909); idem., "The Consequences and Treatment of Alimentary Toxaemia from a Surgical Point of View," *Proceedings of the Royal Society of Medicine* 6, no. 5 (1913), pp. 49–117, and discussion, pp. 121–380;

idem., "The Sewage System of the Human Body," *American Medicine*, May 1923, pp. 267–72; Arbuthnot Lane Papers, Wellcome Trust Contemporary Medical Archives, London, GC/127/A2. By the 1930s, having made a fortune from his society practice, Lane had freed himself from the constraints of "medical ethics" by removing his name from the General Medical Register and had launched his New Health Society, urging an assault on constipation, dietary reform, and a redesign of the water closet to create a more "natural" position for the necessary twice or thrice daily defecation. See Arbuthnot Lane Papers, Wellcome Trust Contemporary Medical Archives, London, Box 1, GC/127/B15, 18, and Sir W. Arbuthnot Lane, *An Apple a Day* (London: Methuen, 1935).

29 Moynihan's 1905 textbook, *Abdominal Operations* (Philadephia: W. B. Saudders), had, in Gerald Grob's words, "helped to define his specialty," and, in the process, "gave him an international reputation because, in the words of a colleague, 'it literally threw open the abdomen to all surgeons.'" Gerald Grob, "The Rise of Peptic Ulcer, 1900–1905," *Perspectives in Biology and Medicine* 46 (2003), p. 553, internal quotation from B. G. A. Moynihan, *Selected Writings of Lord Moynihan: A Centenary Volume* (London: Pitman, 1967).

30 Arbuthnot Lane Papers, Wellcome Trust Contemporary Medical Archives, London, Box 1, GC/127/A2/1.

31 See John Harvey Kellogg, *Autointoxication or Intestinal Toxemia* (Battle Creek, Mich., 1919), passim, esp. pp. 131, 311; idem., *The Itinerary of a Breakfast* (Battle Creek, Mich., 1919), pp. 25, 36, 82. For commentary, see especially James C. Whorton, *Crusaders for Fitness: The History of American Health Reformers* (Princeton, N.J.: Princeton University Press, 1982); and Stephen Nissenbaum, *Sex, Diet and Debility in Jacksonian*

America: Sylvester Graham and Health Reform (Westport, Conn.: Greenwood, 1980.

32 Whorton, *Crusaders for Fitness*, p. 204. Kellogg's patients included President Taft, John D. Rockefeller Jr., Alfred DuPont, J. C. Penney, Montgomery Ward, and a host of the rich and famous.

33 Frank Billings, "Chronic Focal Infections and their Etiologic Relations to Arthritis and Nephritis," *Archives of Internal Medicine* 9 (1912), pp. 484–98.

34 Henry A. Cotton, *The Defective Delinquent and Insane* (Princeton, N.J.: Princeton University Press, 1921).

35 Henry A. Cotton, "The Relation of Chronic Sepsis to the So-Called Functional Mental Disorders," *Journal of Mental Science* 69 (1923), pp. 434–65.

36 Henry Maudsley, *The Physiology and Pathology of Mind* (London: Macmillan, 1867).

37 William Hunter, "Oral Sepsis and Antiseptic Medicine," *Faculty of Medicine of McGill University*, Montreal, 1910, quoted in Cotton, "The Relation of Chronic Sepsis to the So-Called Functional Mental Disorders."

38 Henry S. Upson, "Nervous Disorders Due to the Teeth," *Cleveland Medical Journal* 6 (1907), p. 458; idem., "Dementia Praecox Caused by Dental Infection," *Monthly Cyclopedia and Medical Bulletin* 2 (1909), pp. 648–51; idem., "Serious Mental Disturbances Caused by Painless Dental Lesions," *American Quarterly of Roentgenology* 2 (1910), pp. 223–43; idem., "Dental Disease as it Affects the Mind," *Monthly Cyclopedia and Medical Bulletin* 5 (1912), pp. 129–41.

39 Lewis Campbell Bruce, *Studies in Clinical Psychiatry* (London: Macmillan, 1906), p. 227; see also pp. 6, 8–10.

40 Ibid., pp. 5, 37–8.

41 Cotton, *The Defective Delinquent and Insane*, p. 41.

42. Trenton State Hospital *Annual Report*, 1916, p. 15.

43 Cotton, "The Relation of Chronic Sepsis to the So-Called Functional Psychoses," p. 437. The treatment of paresis continued to receive substantial attention, and Cotton reported that they were now using "an Albee electric drill" to make holes in patients' skulls under local anesthetic, thus allowing the intracranial administration of Salvarsan in a manner "that saves considerable time." Trenton State Hospital *Annual Report*, 1917, p. 13.

44 Personal interview with Dr. Ferdearle Fischer, Leisure World, Laguna Hills, Orange County, California, February 20, 1984.

45 Cotton to Meyer, April 8, 1918, Meyer Papers, CAJH I/767/14.

46 Cotton to Meyer, July 1, 4, 1918, Meyer Papers, CAJH I/767/15.

47 Meyer to Cotton, July 14, 1918, Meyer Papers, CAJH I/767/15.

48 Burdette Lewis to Seymour Cromwell, September 5, 1918; Lewis to Dwight Morrow, March 28 and November 29, 1919, July 30 and August 4, 1920, in Dwight Morrow Papers, Amherst College Library, Amherst, Massachusetts; Burdette Lewis, manuscript autobiography, revealingly titled "The Truth Shall Set You Free," esp. pp. 3–10, in Burdette Lewis Papers, State Archives, Trenton, New Jersey.

49 Cotton to Meyer, October 13, 1918, Meyer Papers, CAJH I/767/15.

50 Ibid.

51 See Trenton State Hospital *Annual Reports*, 1919, 1920, and 1921.

Chapter 3

1 "Report of the Medical Director," Trenton State Hospital *Annual Report*, 1919, p. 10.

2 Henry A. Cotton and J. W. Draper, "What is Being Done for the Insane by Means of Surgery: Analysis of One Hundred and Twenty Five Laparotomies: Importance of Preventive Psychiatry," *Transactions of the Section on*

Gastroenterology and Proctology of the American Medical Association 71 (1920), pp. 143–57.

3 Martin Stone has estimated that 80,000 cases of "shell-shock" were treated in the British Army hospitals. "Shell Shock and the Psychologists," in *The Anatomy of Madness*, ed. W. F. Bynum, R. Porter, and M. Shepherd, vol. 2 (London: Tavistock, 1985), p. 249. Paul Lerner has estimated that the German total was approximately 200,000 ("From Traumatic Neurosis to Male Hysteria: The Decline and Fall of Hermann Oppenheim," in *Traumatic Pasts: History, Psychiatry, and Trauma in the Modern Age, 1870–1930*, ed. M. S. Micale and P. Lerner [Cambridge: Cambridge University Press, 2001], p. 141); and Marc Roudebush has suggested that "the numbers in France were as high as those in Germany, or higher." "A Battle of Nerves: Hysteria and Its Treatment in France During World War I," in ibid., p. 254. To these, of course, one must add the psychiatric casualties among the Austrians, the Italians, the Americans, and others.

4 The British War Office officially banned the use of the term in 1917. See Ruth Leys, "Traumatic Cures: Shell Shock, Janet, and the Question of Memory," *Critical Inquiry* 20 (1994), p. 29, footnote.

5 Ibid., p. 1.

6 Trenton State Hospital *Annual Report*, 1920, p. 18.

7 Trenton State Hospital *Annual Report*, 1919, p. 8.

8 Ibid.

9 Cotton, "The Relation of Chronic Sepsis to the So-Called Functional Psychoses," p. 438.

10 Trenton State Hospital *Annual Report*, 1921, p. 16.

11 Ibid., p. 16. Cotton repeatedly trumpeted these notional savings, though his estimate of their size varied considerably from publication to publica-

tion. See, for example, Cotton, *The Defective Delinquent and Insane*, p. 80; idem., "The Etiology and Treatment of the So-Called Functional Psychoses," *American Journal of Psychiatry* 79 (1922), p. 188; Trenton State Hospital *Annual Report*, 1920, p. 14.

12 Trenton State Hospital *Annual Report*, 1921, pp. 7–8.

13 Meyer to Cotton, April 4, 1918 and Cotton to Meyer, April 8, 1918, Meyer Papers, CAJH I/767/14.

14 Cotton, *The Defective Delinquent and Insane*, p. 77.

15 Henry A. Cotton, "The Relation of Oral Infection to Mental Diseases," *Journal of Dental Research* 1 (1919), p. 289.

16 Cotton and Draper, "What is Being Done for the Insane," p. 7.

17 Trenton State Hospital *Annual Report*, 1919, p. 17.

18 Cotton, *The Defective Delinquent and Insane*, pp. 120, 122.

19 Cotton, "The Etiology and Treatment of the So-Called Functional Psychoses," p. 163.

20 Cotton and Draper, "What is Being Done for the Insane," pp. 2–3.

21 Ibid., p. 10.

22 Cotton, *The Defective Delinquent and Insane*, p. 74; see also idem., "The Relation of Oral Infection to Mental Diseases," p. 287.

23 Cotton, *The Defective Delinquent and Insane*, p. 72.

24 Cotton, "The Relation of Oral Infection to Mental Diseases," p. 287.

25 Cotton and Draper, "What is Being Done for the Insane," p. 7.

26 Trenton State Hospital *Annual Report*, 1920, p. 20.

27 Ibid., p. 4.

28 Cotton, "The Relation of Oral Infection to Mental Diseases," pp. 286–7.

29 Cotton, "The Etiology and Treatment of the So-Called Functional Psychoses," p. 163.

30 Cotton, "The Relation of Oral Infection to Mental Diseases," p. 301.

31 Ibid., p. 308.
32 Cotton, *The Defective Delinquent and Insane*, p. 57; see also idem., "The Relation of Oral Infection to Mental Disease," p. 279; idem., "Oral Diagnosis: An Essential Part of Medical Diagnosis," *Journal of Oralogy* 1 (1922), p. 10; Trenton State Hospital *Annual Report*, 1921, p. 21.
33 Cotton, "The Etiology and Treatment of the So-Called Functional Psychoses," p. 164.
34 Cotton, *The Defective Delinquent and Insane*, p. 53.
35 Ibid., p. 95.
36 Ibid., p. 46.
37 Cotton, "The Relation of Oral Infection to Mental Diseases," p. 292.
38 Trenton State Hospital *Annual Report*, 1919, p. 12.
39 Ibid., p. 42.
40 Cotton, "The Relation of Oral Infection to Mental Diseases," p. 292.
41 Howell, *Technology*, passim.
42 Trenton State Hospital, *Annual Report*, 1921, p. 30.
43 Ibid.
44 Cotton, *The Defective Delinquent and Insane*, p. 54. He preferred to average out the number of extractions over the entire hospital population, thereby reducing the mean number taken out to approximately 5 per capita.
45 Cotton, *The Defective Delinquent and Insane*, p. 42.
46 Trenton State Hospital *Annual Report*, 1920, p. 18.
47 Cotton, *The Defective Delinquent and Insane*, p. 42.
48 Cotton, "The Relation of Oral Infection to Mental Diseases," p. 270.
49 Cotton, *The Defective Delinquent and Insane*, p. 42.
50 Ibid., p. 300. For similar sentiments, see also Trenton State Hospital *Annual Report*, 1919, pp. 20–21.
51 Cotton, *The Defective Delinquent and Insane*, p. 269.
52 Ibid., p. 300.
53 Ibid., p. 74.
54 Trenton State Hospital *Annual Report*, 1920, p. 18.
55 Trenton State Hospital *Annual Report*, 1919, p. 13.
56 Trenton State Hospital *Annual Report*, 1920, p. 8; 1921, p. 30.
57 Cotton, "The Etiology and Treatment of the So-Called Functional Psychoses," p. 166.
58 Ibid., pp. 166–7.
59 Cotton, "The Relation of Oral Infection to Mental Diseases," pp. 284–5.
60 Trenton State Hospital *Annual Report*, 1919, p. 13; Cotton, "The Relation of Oral Infection to Mental Diseases," p. 294.
61 Trenton State Hospital *Annual Report*, 1919, p. 15.
62 Cotton and Draper, "What is Being Done for the Insane," p. 6.
63 Cotton to Farrar, November 4, 1919, Farrar Archive, Toronto, quoted in Shorter, "C. B. Farrar," p. 92. In an independent review of all Cotton's major abdominal surgery over a fourteen-year period, Emil Frankel of the New Jersey Department of Institutions and Agencies found that "the cases selected by Dr. Cotton for colectomies were *not* 'mainly dementia praecox cases,' since the records show that only about one-third of the total number were dementia praecox cases," another third being manic-depressive cases, and the remainder suffering from a wide range of generally milder disorders. Emil Frankel, "Study of 'End Results' of 645 Major Operative Cases and 407 Non-operative Cases Treated at Trenton State Hospital 1918–1932," unpublished report, 1932, State of New Jersey, Department of Institutions and Agencies, in TSH Archives, p. 17.
64 Frankel, "Study of 'End Results,'" p. 17.
65 Henry A. Cotton, J. W. Draper, and J. Lynch, "Intestinal Pathology in the Functional Psychoses: Preliminary Report of Surgical Findings, Proce-

dures, and Results," *Medical Record* 97 (1920), p. 5.

66 Trenton State Hospital *Annual Report*, 1919, pp. 19–20.

67 J. F. Ewing, a consulting pathologist from Cornell University Medical School had now been brought in to examine "sections of the intestinal tract removed by operations." Trenton State Hospital *Annual Report*, 1920, p. 15.

68 Cotton, Draper, and Lynch, "Intestinal Pathology in the Functional Psychoses," p. 8.

69 Cotton, *The Defective Delinquent and Insane*, p. 101.

70 Cotton and Draper, "What is Being Done for the Insane," p. 14.

71 Ibid., p. 12.

72 Cotton, "The Etiology and Treatment of the So-Called Functional Psychoses," p. 180.

73 Ibid., pp. 23, 24. In his 1920 paper with J. W. Draper, "What is Being Done for the Insane," Cotton had spoken of having performed 125 laparotomies on functionally psychotic patients and he reported that in all cases, the bowel showed evidence of infection.

74 Cotton, Draper, and Lynch, "Intestinal Pathology in the Functional Psychoses," pp. 719–25.

75 Cotton, "The Etiology and Treatment of the So-Called Functional Psychoses," p. 186.

76 Cotton and Draper, "What is Being Done for the Insane," p. 12.

77 Cotton, Draper, and Lynch, "Intestinal Pathology in the Functional Psychoses," p. 724.

78 Cotton, *The Defective Delinquent and Insane*, p. 101. As we shall see, Cotton's surgical mortality rates were actually considerably higher than the extraordinary 25 to 30 percent he acknowledged in his publications. Consistently and with good reason, however, he sought to play down the problem. In his 1921 *Annual Report*, for example, he at one

point claimed that there had been "only one death [as a direct result of] operation." But elsewhere in the same report, he acknowledges that, in addition to one patient who died on the operating table, two others succumbed the following day, and a fourth four weeks post-operatively of broncho-pneumonia.

79 Between July 1, 1920, and June 30, 1921, for example, among 70 colon operations, "we can report only thirteen cases recovered." Trenton State Hospital *Annual Report*, 1921, p. 25.

80 Trenton State Hospital *Annual Report*, 1921, p. 23.

81 Ibid., p. 22.

82 Cotton, "The Etiology and Treatment of the So-Called Functional Psychoses," p. 186.

83 Ibid., p. 182.

84 Cotton, Draper, and Lynch, "Intestinal Pathology in the Functional Psychoses," p. 724; see also Cotton, "The Etiology and Treatment of the So-Called Functional Psychoses," p. 186; Trenton State Hospital *Annual Report*, 1921, p. 25.

85 Cotton, "The Etiology and Treatment of the So-Called Functional Psychoses," p. 185.

86 Trenton State Hospital *Annual Report*, 1921, p. 21.

87 Trenton State Hospital *Annual Report*, 1921, p. 26.

88 Cotton, *The Defective Delinquent and Insane*, p. 66.

89 Trenton State Hospital *Annual Report*, 1921, p. 30.

90 Cotton, "The Etiology and Treatment of the So-Called Functional Psychoses," pp. 182–3. Elsewhere, he reported that an infected cervix was found in "at least sixty percent of the female patients." Trenton State Hospital *Annual Report*, 1921, p. 23. Retrospective re-examination of Cotton's clinical records demonstrates that 78 percent of his colectomies were per-

formed on female patients. Subsequently, in the late 1920s, he was to opt for a last drastic procedure pioneered by the British surgeon Arbuthnot Lane. "Lane's operation" was designed to eliminate so-called "intestinal adhesions," and in this later phase the proportion of intestinal surgery being performed on women rose to some 84 percent. See Frankel, "Study of 'End Results.'"

91 On this episode, see Andrew Scull and Diane Favreau, "'A Chance to Cut is a Chance to Cure': Sexual Surgery for Psychosis in Three Nineteenth Century Societies," in *Research in Law, Deviance, and Social Control*, ed. Andrew Scull and Steven Spitzer, vol. 8 (Greenwich, Conn.: JAI Press, 1986), pp. 3–39.

92 Trenton State Hospital *Annual Report*, 1921, p. 21.

93 Cotton, *The Defective Delinquent and Insane*, p. 70.

94 Ibid., p. 185; see also Henry A. Cotton, "The Relation of Focal Infections to Crime and Delinquency," *Proceedings of the 49th Annual Session of the American Association for the Study of the Feeble-Minded*, Raleigh, North Carolina, 1925, p. 73; Trenton State Hospital *Annual Report*, 1920, p. 20.

95 Trenton State Hospital *Annual Report*, 1920, p. 24.

96 Mikhail Rotov, "The History of Trenton State Hospital, 1848–1976: An Interpretative Essay," unpublished paper, no date, p. 43. Rotov records this polysurgery as "typical"; in fact, few patients were operated upon quite this often.

97 Rotov, "A History of Trenton State Hospital." I am most grateful to Dr. Rotov, formerly chief psychiatrist for the State of New Jersey, for sharing this paper with me, and for facilitating my access to many other relevant materials at the Trenton State Hospital.

98 Cotton, "The Relation of Oral Infec-

tion to Mental Diseases," p. 273.

99 Quoted from an unspecified Trenton State Hospital *Annual Report* in Rotov, "The History of Trenton Psychiatric Hospital."

100 Trenton State Hospital *Annual Report*, 1920, p. 25; 1921, p. 20.

101 Cotton to Meyer, September 19, 1921, CAJH I/767/18. As usual, I have changed the patient's name here so as to protect her identity, but have kept her correct initials.

102 Ibid., pp. 21–2.

103 Ibid., p. 22.

104 Cotton, "The Relation of Chronic Sepsis to the So-Called Functional Mental Disorders," p. 460.

105 Cotton, *The Defective Delinquent and Insane*, pp. 120, 122.

106 Trenton State Hospital *Annual Report*, 1921, p. 25.

107 Cotton, *The Defective Delinquent and Insane*, p. 173.

108 Ibid., p. 174

109 Ibid., p. 11.

110 Trenton State Hospital *Annual Report*, 1921, pp. 36–47.

111 Ibid., pp. 46-47.

112 Ibid., p. 25.

113 Cotton, "The Relation of Focal Infections to Crime and Delinquency," p. 18.

114 Ibid., p. 13.

115 Ibid. In fact, Clarence Darrow, grasping at any straw to save his widely reviled young clients from the electric chair, had embraced, if not Cotton's theory of the physical roots of their moral depravity, any possible sign of physical abnormality that could be used to reduce their culpability in the eyes of the judge and jury, ordering, for example, studies of their "basal metabolism" to find evidence that their monstrous acts were the product of physical defect rather than moral depravity. Alvin V. Seller, *The Loeb-Leopold Case* (Brunswick, Ga.: Classic Publishing Co., 1926); Maureen McKenrnan, *The Amazing Crime and*

Trial of Leopold and Loeb (Chicago: Plymouth Court Press, 1924).

116 Cotton, "The Relation of Focal Infections to Crime and Delinquency," p. 76–7.

117 Ibid., p. 68.

118 Personal interview with Dr. Ferdearle Fischer, who served as the head of the dental department at Trenton State Hospital from 1918 to 1960, extracting teeth possibly numbering in the hundreds of thousands during his long career, Leisure World, Laguna Hills, Orange County, California, February 20, 1984. (At the time of my interview with him, Dr. Fischer still believed completely in Cotton's theories and thought that his former chief would eventually be recognized as the genius he was.) Cotton's operations on his children (and his pressure on his wife to have her teeth attended to as well) provoked a rare estrangement between the married couple. As Mrs. Cotton subsequently confessed to Adolf Meyer in 1927, abdominal surgery, in particular, was for a time "a topic on which my husband and I were unable to speak." Delha Cotton to Meyer, January 25, 1926, Meyer Papers, CAJH I/767/23. Clarence Farrar, who spent time on Cotton's staff at Trenton, informed his wife that Mrs. Cotton succumbed to the pressure and had all her teeth extracted as well. See Shorter, "C. B. Farrar," p. 92, citing an interview with Joan Farrar, July 10, 1992.

119 Cotton, "The Relation of Focal Infections to Crime and Delinquency," p. 17.

120 Maudsley, *The Pathology of Mind* (1895 edn.), p. 563. On Maudsley, see Scull, MacKenzie, and Hervey, *Masters of Bedlam*, chapter 8.

121 Greene, "The Care and Cure of the Insane," p. 503.

122 Strahan, "The Propagation of Insanity and Allied Neuroses," p. 337.

123 Ibid., p. 331.

124 See Grob, *Mental Illness*, pp. 15–71.

125 Norman Dain, *Clifford Beers: Advocate for the Insane* (Pittsburgh: University of Pittsburgh Press, 1980), p. 146.

Chapter 4

1 Trenton State Hospital *Annual Report*, 1920, p. 29.

2 Henry A. Cotton, "The Relation of Focal Infection to Mental Diseases," *New York Medical Journal* 111 (1920), p. 672.

3 Trenton State Hospital *Annual Report*, 1920, pp. 8, 33–4; 1921, p. 30.

4 Trenton State Hospital *Annual Report*, 1920, p. 29; 1921, p. 34.

5 Trenton State Hospital *Annual Report*, 1921, p. 34.

6 Trenton State Hospital *Annual Report*, 1920, p. 28.

7 In the twelve-month period between July 1, 1920 and June 30, 1921, Cotton recorded visits from the superintendent, staff, and board members of New Jersey's other state hospital for the insane, in Morristown; "frequent" visits from trustees and staff of the Norristown State Hospital in Pennsylvania; hospital superintendents from Georgia, South Carolina, Virginia, and New York; the director of the psychopathic clinic in Chicago; several neurologists; the superintendent of charities for the state of Illinois; and a variety of others, capped by a visit from Adolf Meyer of Johns Hopkins, who pronounced himself "especially interested in the methods in use and in the pathology of focal infection, which we have demonstrated, especially in the intestinal tract." Trenton State Hospital *Annual Report*, 1921, p. 35.

8 Trenton State Hospital *Annual Report*, 1920, p. 29.

9 Ibid., p. 17.

10 Cotton, *The Defective Delinquent and Insane*, p. 185.

11 Ibid., pp. 80-81.

12 Ibid.

13 Ibid., p. 185.

14 Ibid., p. 19.

15 Ibid., p. 21.

16 Cotton to George S. Kirby, January 8, 1919, copy in Meyer Papers, CAJH I/2110/9.

17 Ibid.

18 Kirby to Meyer, January 13, 1919, Meyer Papers, CAJH I/2110/9.

19 Meyer to Kirby, January 15, 1919, Meyer Papers, CAJH I/2110/9.

20 Cotton to Meyer, January 18, 1919; Meyer to Cotton, January 21, 1919, Meyer Papers, CAJH I/767/16. See Henry A. Cotton "The Role of Focal Infections in the Psychoses," *Journal of Nervous and Mental Disease* 49 (1919), pp. 177–207.

21 See the *Daily Princetonian*, April 7, 1921.

22 Terms of the bequest were published opposite the title page of Cotton's and other volumes of the printed lectures.

23 Cotton, *The Defective Delinquent and Insane*, pp. 1–3.

24 Ibid.

25 Ibid., p. 1.

26 Adolf Meyer, "Foreword" to Cotton, *The Defective Delinquent and Insane*, p. v.

27 Ibid.

28 Ibid., p. vi.

29 "Psychopathic" was here used not in its modern sense, but as meaning an acute treatment facility for recent cases of insanity. Beginning with the opening of the Michigan Psychopathic Hospital at Ann Arbor in 1905, a number of specialized institutions of this sort had been created: in Boston, in Baltimore, in Chicago, and in Iowa. Cotton's innovation was to create these intensive treatment facilities as part of a traditional mental hospital.

30 Cotton to Meyer, September 19, 1921, Meyer Papers, CAJH I/767/18.

31 Speech at the opening of the new psychopathic wards at Trenton State Hospital, quoted in Burdette G. Lewis, "Winning the Fight Against Mental Disease," *Review of Reviews* 65 (April 1922), p. 11.

32 "Association and Hospital Notes and News," *American Journal of Insanity* 79 (1922), pp. 114–15.

33 Hubert Work, "The Sociologic Aspect of Insanity and Allied Defecs," *American Journal of Insanity* 69 (1912), pp. 1–15.

34 "Association and Hospital Notes and News," *American Journal of Insanity* 79 (1922), pp. 120–22.

35 Ibid., p. 122. Stewart Paton's invitation to this august occasion is carefully preserved in the faculty records now housed in the archives of the Mudd Library at Princeton University.

36 Lewis, "The Winning Fight Against Mental Disease," pp. 411–18.

37 Ibid.

38 Ibid.

39 It was Shaw who edited Wilson's papers and speeches: Albert Shaw (ed.), *President Wilson's State Papers and Speeches* (New York: Review of Reviews Company, 1918); idem., *The Messages and Papers of Woodrow Wilson*, 2 vols. (New York: Review of Reviews Company, 1924).

41 Shaw's books included *Municipal Government in Great Britain* (New York: The Century Company, 1895), *Municipal Government in Continental Europe* (London: Macmillan, 1901), and *The Business Career in Its Public Relations* (San Francisco: Elder, 1904).

41 Albert Shaw, "Physical Treatment for Mental Disorders: A Summary of Expert Comments Upon Dr. Cotton's Work at Trenton," *Review of Reviews* 66 (December 1922), pp. 625–36.

42 Ibid., pp. 625–6.

43 Ibid., p. 627.

44 Ibid., pp. 627–8.

45 Ibid., p. 628, quoting Dr. Robert T. Morris.

46 Ibid., p. 629, quoting Dr. Royal S. Copeland.

47 Ibid., p. 629, quoting Dr. H. S. MacAyeal, director of the Department of Public Welfare in Ohio.

48 Ibid., pp. 628–9, quoting Dr. John R. Oliver, chief of the Medical Service of the Supreme Bench of Baltimore.

49 Ibid., p. 630.

50 Ibid., pp. 631–2, quoting Dr. Charles W. Page, former superintendent of Danvers Asylum in Massachusetts.

51 Ibid., p. 632, quoting Dr. William C. Garvin, superintendent of King's Park State Hospital in New York.

52 Ibid., pp. 632–3, quoting Dr. C. C. Kirk, superintendent of Little Rock State Asylum in Arkansas.

53. Ibid., pp. 630–31, quoting Dr. Paul E. Bowers of the Palo Alto Veteran's Hospital.

54 Ibid., pp. 631–2, quoting Dr. D. E. Drake, head of the Idylease Inn.

55 Ibid., pp. 635–6, quoting Drs. Mayo and Stewart Paton, and Professor Edwin G. Conklin.

56 Ibid., p. 636, quoting Dr. Frank Billings.

57 Ibid., p. 634, quoting Dr. Richard Hutchings, superintendent of the New York State Hospital at Utica.

58 Ibid., pp. 634–5.

59 Ibid., p. 635.

60 Ibid.

Chapter 5

1 See the discussion in Andrew Scull, *The Most Solitary of Afflictions: Madness and Society in Britain, 1700–1900* (New Haven and London: Yale University Press, 1993), pp. 355–63. For an American example of this phenomenon, see the case of the heir to the McCormick Harvest Machine Company (later International Harvester) fortune, Stanley McCormick, examined in chapters 9 and 10.

2 Joseph Schumpeter, *Ten Great Economists from Marx to Keynes* (New York: Oxford University Press, 1951), p. 223.

3 Cotton, *The Defective Delinquent and Insane*, p. 157. Margaret Fisher is identified here as "Case 24." I am most grateful to Sylvia Nasar, who first drew my attention to Margaret Fisher's encounter with Henry Cotton, who identified case 24 as Margaret, and who has, with immense generosity, shared with me items from Fisher's family correspondence bearing on the case. I am greatly in her debt for this and other assistance.

4 Ibid.

5 Bloomingdale clinical records, as summarized in Cotton, *The Defective Delinquent and Insane*, p. 158.

6 Ibid.

7 Robert Loring Allen, *Irving Fisher, A Biography* (Oxford: Blackwell, 1993), p. 139.

8 Cotton, *The Defective Delinquent and Insane*, pp. 158–9.

9 Ibid., p. 159.

10 Irving Fisher to Margaret Hazard Fisher, August 16, 1919, Fisher Papers, Yale University.

11 I. Fisher to M. H. Fisher, August 18, 1919, Fisher Papers, Yale University.

12 Ibid. Draper was the Columbia surgeon who at this stage was undertaking the abdominal surgery at Trenton.

13 I. Fisher to M. H. Fisher, August 20, 1919, Fisher Papers, Yale University. Colax is still advertised on the web as a "herbal colon cleanser," a product that allows one to "maintain regularity and cleanse the body of harmful toxins. Detoxification is the process of neut-ralizing and eliminating toxins that have accumulated in the body . . . The special fibre blend gently sweeps un-healthy toxins from your system." See www.opnetint.com/colax.htm.

14 Cotton, *The Defective Delinquent and Insane*, p. 159.

15 I. Fisher to M. H. Fisher, October 7, 1919, Fisher Papers, Yale University.

16 Cotton, *The Defective Delinquent and Insane*, p. 159.

17 Allen, *Fisher*, p. 159.

18 See the portraits drawn in Allen, *Fisher*, and in the memoir written by Fisher's son, Irving Norton Fisher, *My Father,*

Irving Fisher (New York: Comet Press, 1956).

19 Edward Brush, editor of the *American Journal of Psychiatry*, complained that he and his colleagues "find ourselves told by the friends of patients, people who have heard of these activities and this theory, not through medical publications, seldom through their family physicians, but through lay journals and the daily press, that something is being done at Trenton by Dr. Cotton and his associates which the rest of us are not doing, and they are demanding that we shall adopt these theories and follow the methods pursued at Trenton." "Discussion – Functional Psychoses," *American Journal of Psychiatry* 79 (1922), p. 199. In the course of the same discussion, Bernard Glueck, director of the Bureau of Children's Guidance at the New York School of Social Work, spoke of "the thousands of lay-people who have become interested in this subject ... some of whom occupy important positions of public trust." Ibid., p. 204.

20 Rudolph Kampmeier, "Wagner von Jauregg and the Treatment of General Paresis by Fever," *Sexually Transmitted Diseases* 7 (1980), p. 143.

21 For recent scholarship examining the differential responses to shell-shock in a variety of national and cultural contexts, see Micale and Lerner (eds.), *Traumatic Pasts*.

22 See Sigmund Freud, "A Memorandum on Electrical Treatment," in *The Complete Psychological Works of Sigmund Freud*, vol. 17, ed. A. and J. Strachey (London: Hogarth Press, 1955), pp. 211–15.

23 Julius Wagner von Jauregg, "The Treatment of General Paresis by Inoculation of Malaria," *Journal of Nervous and Mental Disease* 55 (1922), pp. 369–75. In 1927, Wagner von Jauregg was awarded the Nobel Prize in medicine for his accomplishment.

24 "The Treatment of Paresis by Malaria," *American Journal of Psychiatry* 79 (1922), pp. 721–3.

25 See Braslow, *Mental Ills and Bodily Cures*, chapter 4.

26 I am here paraphrasing and quoting Braslow's conclusions about the impact of malaria therapy.

27 Lewis, "Winning the Fight Against Mental Disease," p. 416.

28 Meyer to Cotton, March 26, 1921, Meyer Papers CAJH I/767/17.

29 William A. White to L. M. Jones, September 26, 1919, William Alanson White Papers, National Archives, Washington, D.C.

30 White to J. G. Whiteside, November 22, 1922, White Papers, National Archives, Washington, D.C. White's use of the female pronoun surely did not reflect a premature political correctness. His was an era when generically the male stood for the human. However, the patients on the receiving end of Cotton's attentions, particularly the most serious operations, were, as we shall see, disproportionately female, and given White's intellectual proclivities, one is tempted to term this linguistic solecism a Freudian slip.

31 J. K. Hall to Albert Anderson, July 27, 1922, J. K. Hall Papers, Southern Historical Collection, University of North Carolina, Chapel Hill, quoted in Gerald Grob, *The Inner World of American Psychiatry, 1890–1940: Selected Correspondence* (New Brunswick, N.J.: Rutgers University Press, 1985), pp. 110–11.

32 Ibid.

33 Nicholas Kopeloff and Clarence O. Cheney, "Studies in Focal Infection: Its Presence and Elimination in the Funcional Psychoses," *American Journal of Psychiatry* 79 (1922), pp. 141, 143. The double-blind controlled experiment that is now the "gold standard" for evaluating therapeutic innovations in medicine was not broadly accepted until

after the Second World War. See Harry Marks, *The Progress of Experiment: Science and Therapeutic Reform, 1900–1990* (New York: Cambridge University Press, 1997).

34 Kopeloff and Cheney, "Studies in Focal Infection," pp. 145, 154–5, emphasis in the original.

35 Cotton, "The Etiology and Treatment of the So-Called Functional Psychoses," 1922, pp. 170–71, 190–91.

36 Ibid., pp. 157–8.

37 Ibid., p. 158.

38 Ibid., p. 162.

39 "Discussion – Functional Psychoses," *American Journal of Psychiatry* 79 (1922), pp. 198–9.

40 Ibid., p. 202.

41 Ibid., p. 195.

42 Ibid., pp. 200–02.

43 Ibid., p. 195.

44 Ibid., pp. 199, 200.

45 Ibid., p. 202.

46 Ibid., p. 203.

47 Ibid.

48 Ibid., p. 207.

49 The idea of a committee to investigate was suggested by Dr. Glueck, and supported to varying degrees by Brush and Francis Devlin from Quebec. See ibid., pp. 204, 206. Cotton's endorsement of the idea appears on p. 204.

50 Ibid., p. 207.

51 Ibid., pp. 205–7.

52 Ibid., pp. 197, 198, 200.

53 Ibid, p. 206.

54 Ibid., pp. 208–9.

55 Ibid., p. 209.

56 Ibid., p. 210.

57 Cotton to Meyer, June 20, 1922, Meyer Papers, CAJH I/767/18. Characteristically, Meyer's response was to urge that the differences with Kirby be worked out between the two of them, and to insist that, in the latter's work, "I do not believe that there is any tendency to hang back or distort." Meyer to Cotton, June 22, 1922, Meyer Papers, CAJH I/767/18.

Chapter 6

1 "Notes and Comment: the Seventy-Eighth Annual Meeting of the American Psychiatric Association," *American Journal of Psychiatry* 79 (1922), pp. 108–9.

2 Ibid., p. 110.

3 Ibid.

4 Ibid., p. 111.

5 Cotton to Meyer, June 20, 1922, Meyer Papers, CAJH I/767/18.

6 Meyer to Cotton, June 22, 1922, Meyer Papers, CAJH I/767/19.

7 Frankel, "Study of 'End Results.'"

8 Cotton, "Oral Diagnosis," pp. 4, 10.

9 "The dentist today must be extremely cautious in treating healthy individuals, for it must be remembered that in many of our patients who had the wrong kind of dental work, it was done at the time when they were perfectly healthy and from five to ten years prior to the onset of the mental symptoms. For this reason we are compelled to condemn the practice in general of trying to save devitalized teeth." Ibid., p. 4.

10 Cotton to Henry J. Fernald, December 8, 1922, TSH Archives.

11 For some critical comments made in passing, see, for example, Albert M. Barrett, "Presidential Address: The Broadened Interests of Psychiatry," *American Journal of* Psychiatry 79 (1922), p. 10; the unsigned editorial, "State Hospital Physicians and the Recognition and Diagnosis of Physical Disorders in their Patients," *American Journal of Psychiatry* 79 (1922), pp. 346–8; C. McFie Campbell, "The Psychoneuroses," *American Journal of Psychiatry* 79 (1922), p. 369; H. W. Mitchell, "Presidential Address," *American Journal of Psychiatry* 80 (1923), pp. 4–5.

12 Lewis was appalled at this recalcitrance, and urged Marcus Curry, the newly appointed superintendent, to bend his every effort to bring his staff "into line." The innate conservatism of those "who have been there for years and who will

very naturally question the desirability of all the new medical work" could not be allowed to impede the march of progress. Burdette G. Lewis, "Log," December 21, 1922, Lewis Papers, New Jersey State Archives.

13 E. D. B[rush], "Review of *The Defective Delinquent and Insane*," *American Journal of Psychiatry* 79 (1922), pp. 124–5.

14 The Association had severed its connection with the *Journal of Nervous and Mental Disease* when its editor, Smith Ely Jelliffe, embraced psychoanalysis, an approach to nervous diseases that mainstream, somatically orientated neurology regarded as a form of charlatanism.

15 [Edward] Strecker, "Abstracts from Current Literature," *Archives of Neurology and Psychiatry* 9 (1923), pp. 223–7.

16 Smith Ely Jelliffe and William Alanson White, *Diseases of the Nervous System: A Textbook of Neurology and Psychiatry* 4th ed. (Philadelphia and New York: Lea and Febiger, 1923), p. 752.

17 See the letters exchanged between the two men and preserved in the Meyer Papers, CAJH I/2110/2–3.

18 Ibid. These files contain a number of draft letters from Meyer written in pencil that he evidently did not send, but the two men did eventually meet to discuss the issue, and Kirby acceded to his wishes.

19 See Kirby to Meyer, October 25, 1917; Kirby to Meyer, November 26, 1918; Meyer to Kirby, December 2, 1918; Meyer to Kirby, January 30, 1920, Meyer Papers, CAJH I/2110/9 and I/2110/12. Meyer was well aware of the problems of the New York mental hospital system, but not sanguine about the alternatives. Again, the ethnic prejudices of the time surfaced, as they had with Kirby's proposed marriage: "The Worcester plant might be ideal but for the uncertainties of the human material in New England. A numerically declin-

ing race overwhelmed by New Ireland? At any rate nothing very inspiring." As for private practice, "the expenses are great and one must have a feeling of great stability and confidence on that score, with regard to being able to face certain fluctuations of income with equanimity and sagacity ... For the peace of my own mind I should choose Worcester ... The missionary spirit and the bigger style of possibilities would hold me at the Institute." Meyer to Kirby, December 2, 1918.

20 Cotton to Meyer, May 16, 1923, Meyer Papers, CAJH I/767/19.

21 Nicholas Kopeloff and G. Kirby, "Focal Infection and Mental Disease," *American Journal of Psychiatry* 80 (1923), p. 149.

22 Ibid., p. 169.

23 Ibid., p. 190.

24 Ibid., p. 171.

25 Ibid., p. 186.

26 Ibid., pp. 186, 187, 190.

27 Ibid., p. 190.

28 Here they made reference to Kopeloff's detailed previous examination of this issue: Nicholas Kopeloff, "Studies in the Rehfuss Fractional Method of Gastric Analysis Applied to the Psychosis," *New York State Hospital Quarterly* 7 (1922), pp. 326–416.

29 Kopeloff and Kirby, "Focal Infection," pp. 187, 188.

30 Ibid., p. 191.

31 Ibid., p. 193.

32 Ibid., p. 166.

33 Ibid., p. 170.

34 Ibid., p. 193.

35 Ibid., p. 170.

36 Henry A. Cotton, "Discussion," *Archives of Neurology and Psychiatry* 9 (1923), pp. 392–3, quoted in ibid., p. 170.

37 Ibid., p. 171.

38 Ibid., p. 163.

39 Ibid., p. 166.

40 Ibid., pp. 169, 191, emphasis in the original. One should note, however, that Kirby, too, was enamored of the idea of

discovering somatic treatments for mental disorder. His institute was among the first establishments in the United States to experiment with von Jauregg's malarial treatment for general paresis, and after rejecting focal infection theory, Kirby proceeded to experiment with using prolonged narcosis with barbiturates, hormone preparations, oxygen injections, and strychnine, all in vain. See Walter Bromberg, *Psychiatry Between the Wars: A Recollection* (Westport, Conn.: Greenwood, 1982), pp. 70–71.

41 Kopeloff and Kirby, "Focal Infection," pp. 194–7.

42 Ibid., p. 192.

Chapter 7

1 Cotton to Meyer, June 22, 1922, Meyer Papers, CAJH I/767/18.

2 "Association and Hospital Notes and News," *American Journal of Psychiatry* 80 (1923), p. 137.

3 Adolf Meyer Cotton to Meyer, May 29, 1923. Meyer Papers, CAJH I/766/1. The older man took a continuing interest in Cotton's son, sending him books periodically, providing long-distance advice about his schoolwork, and listening to his young correspondent's complaints about being lonely when his parents were away. See ibid., and A. M. Cotton to Meyer, February 11, 1923.

4 "Notes and News," *Journal of Mental Science* 69 (1923), p. 557.

5 See, for example, J. M. Wolfson, "The Pre-Disposing Factors in War Psychoneurosis," *The Lancet* 2 (Feburary 1918), pp. 177–80; Frederick W. Mott, *War Neurosis and Shell Shock* (London: Hodder and Stoughton, 1919). Sir Frederick Mott, pathologist in charge of all the laboratory work for the London-area asylums, would become a convinced proponent of focal sepsis in the years immediately after the war.

6 Graves had two sons in later years and both of them became doctors, one a urological surgeon, the other a distinguished general practitioner who was awarded an OBE for his services to continuing medical education. In interviews with Frederick Chivers Graves (July 31, 1986) and Valerie Graves (July 28, 1986), the widow of his general practitioner son John, both independently told me that the elder Graves was convinced that the only real medicine was surgery, and that even in John's later years, when he had achieved considerable renown, his father continued to badger him about practicing "real" medicine and to label him a failure for persisting in his chosen branch of practice.

7 Having joined the Royal Army Medical Corps in 1914, Graves almost immediately encountered his first cases of mental breakdown, and by 1915 he had become a member of the Medico-Psychological Association.

8 As a medical student at University College London, Graves had won gold medals in Anatomy, Physiology, Pharmacology, Hygiene, and Public Health, and the Liston Gold Medal in Surgery, and he had become a Fellow of the Royal College of Surgeons in 1914, at the age of 31.

9 The appointment of an outsider to such a post must obviously have come as a bitter blow to aspiring assistant physicians. Three such doctors had once ruefully compared their situation with that of "dutiful relatives, most patiently await[ing] the falling in of their estate." They felt that the contrast of "the fat salaries of the Superintendents with the lean ones of the assistants" had perhaps been bearable "when the Assistant Medical Officers were few and superintendencies ripened in four or five years, but [their elders' counsel to be patient] loses all its sweet reasonableness when we have to wait ten, twelve, or more years for the golden fruit, and even run the risk" – they prophetically added –

"of its being plucked by some outsider from over the wall just as we thought it about to drop." Dr. Dodds, Dr. Strahan, and Dr. Greenlees, "Assistant Medical Officers in Asylums: Their Status in the Specialty," *Journal of Mental Science* 36 (1890), pp. 43–50.

10 "Obituary: Thomas Chivers Graves," *British Medical Journal* 1 (1964), p. 1711.

11 His obituarists discreetly termed him "stimulating, but at times overwhelming." (*British Medical Journal* 1 [1964], p. 1711.) His daughter-in-law more bluntly informed me that he was "a bit of a bully," and Dr. D. W. Millard (personal communication), who became consultant psychiatrist at Rubery a few years after Graves's retirement found that "T. C. seemed to have been capable of inducing real terror among the staff" – a reaction Millard attributes to the "fact that he was an absolute tyrant."

12 A. H. Ogden, "T. C. Graves and Focal Sepsis Theory," unpublished paper presented to the Midlands Division of the Royal College of Psychiatrists, 1983, p. 3.

13 "Obituary," *British Medical Journal* 1 (1964), p. 1711; interview with Dr. Valerie Graves, August 28, 1986; A. Ogden, "T. C. Graves," p. 4.

14 On the sources and extent of this hostility, see Michael Clark, "The Rejection of Psychological Approaches to Mental Disorder," in *Madhouses, Mad-Doctors, and Madmen*, ed. A. Scull, pp. 71–101; and Malcolm Pines, "The Development of the Psychodynamic Movement," in *150 Years of British Psychiatry, 1841–1991*, ed. G. E. Berrios and Hugh Freeman (London: Gaskell, 1991), pp. 206–31.

15 "Obituary," *The Lancet* 1 (1964), p. 1400.

16 T. C. Graves, "Colloidal Calcium in Malnutrition, Chronic Sepsis, and Emotional Disturbance," *The Lancet* 2 (1922), p. 957.

17 Chalmers Watson, "The Role of Auto-Intoxication or Auto-Infection in Mental Disorders," *Journal of Mental Science* 69 (1923), pp. 52–77.

18 T. C. Graves, "The Relation of Chronic Sepsis to So-Called Functional Mental Disorder," *Journal of Mental Science* 69 (1923), p. 471.

19 Watson, "The Role of Auto-Intoxication," pp. 63, 75.

20 "Obituary," *British Medical Journal* 1 (1964), p. 1711.

21 William Hunter, "Oral Sepsis as a Cause of Disease," *British Medical Journal* 2 (1900), pp. 215–16.

22 On Friday, the day after the temperature had soared to 96 degrees Fahrenheit in Camden Square near central London, a *Times* leader advised that Englishmen should keep a stiff upper lip even as they sweltered. The heatwave would finally begin to abate on the Saturday. *The Times*, July 13, 1923, p. 11, col. D.

23 See B. Prichard, "London's Top Ten Thunderstorms in the Twentieth Century," *Journal of Metereology* 24, no. 243, (November 1999), pp. 354–8, which ranks the storm of July 9/10 as London's top thunderstorm of the century. I am very grateful indeed to Trevor Harley for this reference.

24 "Notes and News," *Journal of Mental Science* 69 (1923), p. 560.

25 Cotton, "The Relationship of Chronic Sepsis to the So-Called Functional Mental Disorders," p. 435.

26 Ibid., pp. 346–7.

27 Ibid., pp. 434–5. Cotton was quoting here from a source he cites as William Hunter, "Oral Sepsis and Antiseptic Medicine," *Faculty of Medicine of McGill University, Montreal*, 1910. I have not been able to trace this paper.

28 Cotton, "The Relationship of Chronic Sepsis to the So-Called Functional Mental Disorders," p. 438. Later in his paper, Cotton contrasted the recovery rate at Trenton between 1908 and 1918 (38 percent), with the rate between 1918 and 1922, which corresponded to the implementation of a radical programme of eliminating sepsis (87 per-

cent, or "a total of 1,412 successfully treated cases"). Ibid., pp. 458–9.

29 Ibid., p. 439. Elsewhere he had claimed that "modern biological research tends to show that the inheritance of mental disorders ... is next to impossible." Cotton, "The Etiology and Treatment of the So-Called Functional Psychoses," p. 158.

30 Ibid., p. 440.

31 Ibid.

32 "Functional," as distinct from "organic," psychoses were those severe mental disorders (such as dementia praecox, or schizophrenia, and manic-depressive psychosis) with no known structural or organic cause. Cotton referred to them as "so-called functional psychoses" because, of course, he believed he had uncovered their physical etology.

33 Ibid., p. 443.

34 Ibid., pp. 443, 444.

35 Ibid., pp. 444–5.

36 Ibid., p. 445.

37 Ibid., p. 444.

38 Ibid., pp. 454, 457.

39 "Notes and News," *Journal of Mental Science* 69 (1923), pp. 555–7.

40 See John Crammer, "The Maudsley Hospital," in *150 Years of British Psychiatry*, vol. 2, *The Aftermath*, G. E. Berrios and Hugh Freeman (London: Athlone, 1996), pp. 237–42; Trevor Turner, "James Crichton-Browne and the Anti-Psychoanalysts," in ibid., pp. 145–7.

41 "Notes and News," *Journal of Mental Science* 69 (1923), pp. 557–9.

42 Ibid., p. 553.

43 Ibid., p. 555.

44 Goodall's own presidential address, "Considerations, Bacteriological, Toxicological, and Hæmatological, and Others Thereto Akin, Bearing Upon the Psychoses" (*Journal of Mental Science* 69 [1923], pp. 417–34), was an impenetrable, rambling affair that verged upon, if it did not wholly degenerate into, incoherence. To the extent that it had a discernible point, it appeared to focus upon the somatic roots of psychoses. Though at various points he urged that the possible toxic origins of psychosis should be explored, he elsewhere appeared to voice considerable skepticism, as in the following striking passage: "Some people seem to be on terms of familiarity with the toxins of the psychoses, as others are with money-lenders, and others again with their lackeys. Especially as regards the toxins hailing from the bowel ... These gentlemen might with advantage be afforded a moratorium, if not a crematorium." Ibid., p. 418.

45 "Notes and News," *Journal of Mental Science* 69 (1923), pp. 553–8.

46 Ibid., pp. 558–9.

47 Ibid., p. 560.

48 Ibid., pp. 569–70. Cotton made one more intervention on the following day, Thursday July 12. Commenting on a paper by Sir Frederick Mott and I. M. D. Robertson on the histology of the pituitary gland among deceased mental patients, he suggested that the pathology they claimed to have located was itself the product of other, septic processes. Most importantly, while many of his American colleagues were disposed to regard the manic depressives and dementia praecox cases Mott examined as "functional, with practically normal physical conditions," he was delighted to see that it "was an opinion which did not seem to be at all prevalent in London. His association with members during the last few days made him feel that English psychiatrists were on a much firmer foundation with regard to the physical defects in these psychoses ... they were dealing with an etiological unit – with an individual who had a mind, it is true, but who also had a body, which admittedly, had been very much neglected in the past. It was essential to study the individual below the eyebrows, as well as above that limit, remembering that the part above was

only a small part of the anatomy." Ibid., p. 575.

49 Henry A. Cotton, "Chronic Sepsis and Mental Disease," *Journal of Mental Science* 69 (1923), pp. 502–4.

50 Ibid.

51 Ibid., pp. 502–3.

52 Ibid., p. 502.

53 White to Jelliffe, December 20, 1923, Jelliffe Papers, Library of Congress, Washington, D.C.

54 White to Hobbs, March 7, 1924, William Alanson White Papers, National Archives, Washington, D.C.

55 Cotton, "The Relationship of Chronic Sepsis to the So-Called Functional Disorders," p. 440

56 See Scull and Favreau, "'A Chance to Cut is a Chance to Cure,'" pp. 3–39.

57 A. T. Hobbs, "A Survey of American and Canadian Psychiatric Opinion as to Focal Infections (or Chronic Sepsis) as Causative Factors in the Functional Psychoses," *Journal of Mental Science* 70 (1924), p. 550.

58 Ibid., pp. 550–51.

59 Ibid., p. 552.

60 Ibid., p. 549.

61 Ibid.

62 Ibid., p. 550.

63 Ibid., p. 553.

64 Cotton, "Relation of Focal Infections to Crime and Delinquency," p. 11.

65 Frankel, "Study of 'End Results,'" p. 18, quoting Henry A. Cotton, "Report on the Operative Procedures on the Colon in Mental Disorders," presented to the Board of Managers of Trenton State Hospital, November 15, 1932, TSH Archives.

66 Ibid., pp. 2, 15. Cotton's own internal estimate of the results in 1932, less optimistic than his earlier published claims, was that "this operation [membranotomy] was attended with more success than the operation for resection, or total removal of the colon, because the mortality was reduced from 33½ percent to about 19 percent, and the recovery rate was 37 percent." "Report on the Operative Procedures on the Colon," quoted p. 18. Frankel's own re-examination of the data on outcomes disputed this last claim: "In comparison with Dr. Cotton's recovery rate of 37 percent the hospital records reveal that of the total number who had pericolic membranotomies only 42 (12.5 percent) patients may be regarded as recovered." p. 19.

67 Ibid., pp. 2, 4.

68 Ibid., p. 3.

69 Cotton, "Relation of Focal Infections to Crime and Delinquency," p. 72.

70 Ibid.

71 Ibid., p. 65.

72 Ibid.

73 Ibid., pp. 63–4.

74 Ibid., p. 65.

75 Ibid., pp. 66–7.

76 Ibid., p. 69.

77 Ibid., p. 70.

78 Ibid., pp. 76–8.

79 Ibid., p. 78.

80 Ibid., pp. 73, 74.

81 Ibid., p. 73.

82 Ibid., p. 78.

83 Ibid., p. 79.

Chapter 8

1 Until her death, Phyllis kept a copy of the undertaker's bill for the burial of "baby Greenacre," gender not specified. And she told her son in later years that she recalled her father bending over her when she was bed-ridden with scarlet fever and saying, "she's going to die too." I am grateful to her son, Peter Richter, for sharing this information with me.

2 See the brief biography of Phyllis Greenacre posted by the New York Psychoanlytic Institute and Society on its web site, http://www.psychoanalysis. org/bio_gree.htm.

3 My discussion of Phyllis Greenacre's upbringing and the circumstances surrounding her departure for Baltimore

are based upon my own interview with her, and on my subsequent discussions with her son, Peter Richter, who has been enormously kind and helpful to me in a multitude of ways as my research has proceeded.

4 Greenacre to Meyer, November 16, 1915, Meyer–Greenacre Correspondence, Meyer Papers, CAJH Series XV. See also *Chicago Transcript*, November 18, 1915, filed in Adolf Meyer's papers, presumably as part of the dossier on Phyllis Greenacre, Meyer–Greenacre Correspondence, Meyer Papers, CAJH Series XV. A bachelor's degree prior to proceeding to an MD, while routine in the United States now, was quite unusual in the early twentieth century. When Rush had affiliated with the University of Chicago in 1898, the university's president, Andrew Harper, had insisted that the medical school require at least two years of college pre-med courses prior to admission to a forty-five-month-long MD programme. Greenacre's scientific credentials, therefore, considerably exceeded the norm for the period, and made her a distinctly more appealing candidate for a position at Hopkins, which prided itself on being at the forefront of the drive to link science and medicine ever more tightly together.

5 See Greenacre to Adolph Meyer, November 10, 1915, Meyer Papers, CAJH Series XV.

6 John M. Dodson to Adolph Meyer, November 15, 1915, Meyer Papers, General Correspondence, CAJH Series XV.

7 Meyer to Greenacre, January 8, 1916, Meyer–Greenacre Correspondence, Meyer Papers, CAJH Series XV.

8 Greenacre to Meyer, January 12, 1916, Meyer–Greenacre Correspondence, Meyer Papers, CAJH Series XV.

9 John Noland Mackenzie, "The Physiological and Pathological Relations Between the Nose and the Sexual Apparatus of Man," *Johns Hopkins Hospital Bulletin* 9 (1898), p. 100.

10 Dorothy Reed, quoted in A. McGehee Harvey, *Adventures in Medical Research: A Century of Discovery at Johns Hopkins* (Baltimore: Johns Hopkins University Press, 1976), pp. 229–30.

11 On the pattern of restricting all but a handful of junior appointments to "Hopkins men," see Thomas B. Turner, *Heritage of Excellence: The Johns Hopkins Medical Institutions, 1914–1947* (Baltimore: Johns Hopkins University Press, 1974), pp. 234–37.

12 Norman Dain, *Beers*, pp. 151, 359.

13 Smith Ely Jelliffe to Harry Stack Sullivan, June 1, 1937, Jelliffe Papers, Library of Congress.

14 Curt P. Richter, autobiographical reminiscences, reprinted in Harvey, *Adventures in Medical Research*, pp. 341–2.

15 Greenacre to Meyer, June 24, 1919, Meyer Papers, CAJH Series XV.

16 On the general prohibition of marriages among the junior staff, see Turner, *Heritage of Excellence*, pp. 237–8. As late as 1935, the medical board reiterated its policy that, "an unmarried intern may not change his status during the period of his internship. Should he or she do so, this will automatically mean a resignation from the Staff. Under no circumstances will the Hospital allow both husband and wife to serve on the Resident Staff at the same time, even though they be assigned to different services." Officially, the policy remained intact until the Second World War.

17 Meyer to Greenacre, undated [late June, 1919], Meyer Papers, CAJH Series XV.

18 Greenacre to Meyer, August 14, 1919, Meyer Papers, CAJH Series XV.

19 Meyer to Greenacre, July 1, 1919, Meyer Papers, CAJH Series XV.

20 Meyer to Greenacre, undated [late June, 1919], Meyer Papers, CAJH Series XV.

21 Ibid.

22 Ibid.

23 Ibid.

24 Greenacre to Meyer, July 18, 1919, Meyer

Papers, CAJH Series XV.

25 Meyer to Greenacre, July 24, 1919, Meyer Papers, CAJH Series XV.

26 Greenacre to Meyer, August 14, 1919, Meyer Papers, CAJH Series XV. Meyer's undated response to this letter renews his plea that she not rush into a premature marriage, but is otherwise full of reassurances about his high regard for her talents, and his "desire to see you both lastingly and safely happy."

27 Greenacre to Meyer, September 8, 1919, Meyer Papers, CAJH Series XVH.

28 Meyer to Greenacre, no date, Meyer Papers, CAJH Series XV.

29 See Bertram M. Bernheim, *The Story of the Johns Hopkins* (New York: McGraw-Hill, 1948), chapter 13; Turner, *Heritage of Excellence*, pp. 441–4 (who judges that "Meyer seems to have done very little research in the accepted sense after coming to Hopkins" and seems unable to discern "any direct contribution to knowledge in the field" – a damning assessment of a Hopkins professor). The silence about Meyer in McGehee Harvey's *Adventures in Medical Research* (he receives only the most glancing of mentions when Harvey discusses Ritcher's researches) likewise speaks volumes about the low regard in which psychiatry was held among the medical leaders at Hopkins. For outside criticism over a period of several decades about the confusion and obscurities endemic to Meyer's writings, see, for example, Arthur Lovejoy to Meyer, February 25, 1916; Edward B. Tichener to Meyer, September 19, 20, 25 and October 26, 1909; Walter B. Cannon to Meyer, May 13, 1931, all in Meyer Papers, CAJH Series I. (As Gerald Grob notes, "The efforts that Meyer made to clarify his views invariably created only greater confusion." *Mental Illness*, p. 118.)

30 See Alfred Lief (ed.), *The Commonsense Psychiatry of Adolf Meyer: Fifty-Two Selected Papers* (New York: McGraw Hill, 1948).

31 Turner, *Heritage of Excellence*, p. 268 (attributing the story to Richter).

32 See, for example, Meyer to Watson, May 29, 1916; Watson to Meyer, June 1, 1916, Meyer to Watson, June 3, 1916, Meyer Papers, CAJH I/3974.

33 Quoted in David Cohen, *J. B. Watson: The Founder of Behaviorism* (London: Routledge and Kegan Paul, 1979), p. 151.

34 Quoted in Kerry W. Buckley, *Mechanical Man: John Broadus Watson and the Beginnings of Behaviorism* (New York: Guilford, 1989), p. 124.

35 A small portion of Watson's correspondence with Rosalie Rayner was submitted in evidence in his wife's divorce petition, and has thus survived. The quotations which follow are from Mary Watson's exhibit in Watson v. Watson, #B680/1920 B-21779, Circuit Court of Baltimore City, Baltimore, Maryland, December 24, 1920. Watson's prominence and the prurient appeal that sexual scandal always has for a broad audience ensured extensive press coverage of his "sinful" behavior, not just in the local press, but nationally. See the *Baltimore Sun*, November 27, 28, 29 and December 26, 1920; *Baltimore Evening Sun*, November 20 and December 24, 1920; *New York Times*, November 27 and December 25, 1920; *Washington Post*, November 27, 1920.

36 Meyer to Goodnow, September 29, 1920, Hamburger Archives. See also Meyer to Watson, August 17, 1920, Meyer Papers, CAJH I/3974/19.

37 Curt P. Richter, *A Behavioristic Study of the Activity of the Rat* (Baltimore: Williams and Wilkins, 1922).

38 Greenacre to Meyer, January 5, 1922, Meyer Papers, CAJH Series XV.

39 Ibid.

40 Meyer to Greenacre, no date [July 1919], Meyer Papers, CAJH Series XV.

41 Greenacre to Meyer, January 5, 1922, Meyer Papers, CAJH Series XV.

42 Ibid.

43 Greenacre to Meyer, August 23, 1923,

Meyer Papers, CAJH Series XV.

44 Greenacre to Meyer, September 5, 1923, Meyer Papers, CAJH Series XV.

45 Ibid.

46 When I interviewed Phyllis Greenacre in her penthouse apartment on Manhattan's East Side, more than sixty years had passed since this episode had taken place. Her vivid memories of Meyer's behavior and the obvious emotion with which she invested the tale made manifest just how much she had resented being treated in this fashion.

47 Phyllis Greenacre, *Emotional Growth*, (New York International University Press, 1971), p. xxii.

48 Adolf Meyer, "The Scope and Teaching of Psychobiology," in *The Commonsense Psychiatry of Dr. Adolf Meyer*, (ed.) Alfred Lief (New York: McGraw-Hill, 1948), p. 436.

49 Greenacre, *Emotional Growth*, p. xxii.

50 I am grateful to Dr. Peter Richter for information on these matters.

51 Meyer to Greenacre, July 3, 1924, Meyer Papers, CAJH Series XV.

52 Greenacre to Meyer, July 18, 1924, Meyer Papers, CAJH Series XV, emphases in the original.

53 Meyer to Greenacre, July 29, 1924, marked "not sent," Meyer Papers, CAJH Series XVH.

54 Ibid.

55 Ibid.

56 See Meyer to Cotton, September 11, 1924, Meyer Papers, CAJH I/767/20.

Chapter 9

1 For the internal debate over setting up an external review of Cotton's work on focal sepsis, see Raycroft to Cotton, March 1, 1924; Raycroft to Paul M. Mecray, March 11, 20 and April 2, 1924; Mecray to Raycroft, March 14, 24, 1924, TSH Archives.

2 Mecray to Raycroft, March 24, 1924, TSH Archives. Mecray was a Camden physician and he and Raycroft together formed the medical subcommittee of

the hospital board.

3 Raycroft to Mecray, March 11, 1924, TSH Archives.

4 Raycroft to Mecray, April 2, 1924, TSH Archives.

5 See Raycroft to Cotton, March 1, 1924, TSH Archives.

6 Raycroft to Mecray, March 20, 1924, TSH Archives.

7 For the conversations between Lewis, Cotton, and Raycroft, and the negotiations with Meyer, see memoranda dated February 28 and June 10, 1924, and Raycroft to Meyer, June 30, 1924; Meyer to Raycroft, July 10, 1924, TSH Archives.

8 Raycroft to Meyer, June 30, 1924, Meyer Papers, CAJH I/767/20.

9 Meyer to Raycroft, July 10, 1924, Meyer Papers, CAJH I/767/20.

10 On Meyer's instructions to Greenacre about the conduct of the inquiry, see Meyer to Raycroft, September 15, 1925, TSH Archives.

11 Meyer's notes on his two-day visit to Trenton, dated September 8, 1924, are in his papers, CAJH I/767/21.

12 Meyer to Cotton, September 11, 25, 1924, CAJH I/767/20.

13 See Cotton to Meyer, September 12, 1924. Meyer Papers, CAJH I/767/20.

14 I rely here upon my extended discussion with Phyllis Greenacre herself about her journey to Trenton and her reception once she arrived. Greenacre's recollection of these and other aspects of her time at Trenton was detailed and precise, and in those cases where I could check her recollections against other contemporary sources, such as the notes she made at the time on her work, her memory proved to be exceptionally accurate. In an earlier interview with Ruth Leys of Johns Hopkins University, Greenacre's recollections of Cotton and Trenton, while less detailed, were of a very similar sort. I am very grateful to Dr. Leys for sharing her notes on this conversation with me.

15 Personal interview with Phyllis

Greenacre, December 22, 1983; letter to the author from Phyllis Greenacre, March 20, 1984.

16 Again, this account of Greenacre's work at Trenton rests largely upon her own recollections, supplemented by my access to the report she wrote in late 1925.

17 Adolf Meyer to Hermann Meyer, December 5, 1924, Meyer Papers, CAJH IV/3/229.

18 Cotton to Meyer, December 4, 1924, Meyer Papers, CAJH I/767/21.

19 This report, along with those that follow, is taken from patient records annexed to Phyllis Greenacre's report on Cotton's activities at Trenton State Hospital, TSH Archives.

20 In reconstructing this particular case, I have drawn on Greenacre's very detailed memory of the visit, some sixty years after the fact. The exact correspondence between her later account of the extraordinary incident and her contemporary notes were a measure of her impressive memory for detail. My assessment of her emotional response rests, of course, on my face-to-face discussion with her.

21 *Trenton Evening Times*, July 8, 1925.

22 Ibid.

23 *Trenton Evening Times*, July 22, 1925; *New York Times*, July 23, 1925.

24 *Trenton Evening Times*, July 23, 1925; *New York Times*, July 24, 1925.

25 *Trenton Evening Times*, July 29, 1925.

26 Ibid.

27 Ibid.

28 Cotton to Lewis, July 26, 1925, TSH Archives.

29 *Trenton Evening Times*, August 4, 5, 1925; *New York Times*, August 5, 1925.

Chapter 10

1 Relations between Stanley's wife and his mother, in particular, had been frigid from the outset, but once he had gone mad, the two sides were scarcely on speaking terms. Meyer had early on thrown in his lot with Stanley's mother

Nettie and her children, and had urged the patient's wife, the formidable Katherine Dexter McCormick, to agree to an annulment and a suitably generous financial settlement – advice Katherine scornfully dismissed. For years, she and her husband's mother and sisters fought bitterly over the living corpse, and in 1927 Katherine would finally resort to the courts in an effort to assert her own claims to control Stanley's treatment, spending upwards of half a million dollars in legal fees, only to find the whole issue remain stalemated. For Meyer and the other psychiatrists lucky enough to be brought on board as consultants by one side or the other (and these included the eminent Kraepelin, lured from Germany to examine Stanley in 1908 by fees of $2,000 a week), it was like winning the lottery. The whole sorry episode is documented in the Cyrus Hall McCormick Jr. Papers, housed at the Wisconsin Historical Society Archives in Madison, Wisconsin. See especially Boxes 86–97, and the papers relating to the lawsuit in Box 98. There is some elliptical discussion of Stanley's breakdown and treatment in Gilbert A. Harrison, *A Timeless Affair: The Life of Anita McCormick Blaine* (Chicago: University of Chicago Press, 1979), esp. pp. 159–62, 196–200. And for a gothic, fictionalized portrait of Stanley and Katherine's fate, see T. Coragessan Boyle's *Riven Rock* (New York: Viking, 1998).

2 Greenacre to Meyer, July 25, 1925, Meyer Papers, CAJH I/767/21.

3 Meyer to Greenacre, August 15, 1925, Meyer Papers, CAJH I/767/21.

4 Raycroft to Meyer, September 12, 1925, Meyer Papers, CAJH I/3215/1.

5 On Meyer's abhorrence of exposés and scandals, see Dain, *Beers*, p. 290.

6 Meyer to Raycroft, September 15, 1925, TSH Archives.

7 Raycroft to Meyer, September 16, 1925, TSH Archives.

8 Ruth Leys, who interviewed Greenacre a year and a half before I did, noted that, "my impression was that Greenacre still felt emotional about some of things that happened to her at the Phipps." "Impressions of My Evening with Phyllis Greenacre," unpublished manuscript, June 16, 1982. (I am most grateful to Dr. Leys for sharing this document with me.) The more extensive interview I conducted with Dr. Greenacre in December 1983 focused closely on the events at Trenton, which was clearly one of those things about which she still felt strong emotions. My discussion of Greenacre's reaction to the crisis surrounding the Bright Committee's inquiries is derived from my conversation with her on that occasion.

9 This was an impression confirmed in some of Meyer's later correspondence, and also, indirectly, in the obituary of Cotton he wrote for the *American Journal of Psychiatry* in 1934.

10 On this point, Greenacre had been equally emphatic when she discussed Meyer with Ruth Leys. See Ruth Leys, "Impressions of My Evening with Phyllis Greenacre," p. 5: "The thing that she stressed again and again was that Meyer had a saviour [*sic*] complex, which meant that he would lean over backwards to save second-rate people, people who needed saving at the expense of first rate people ... Esther Richards was much disliked, very cold, often cruel in front of patients, much disliked by the staff ... She had scoliosis, a kind of hunch-back. Ruth Fairbanks was another person who had been as it were rescued by Meyer." To this list, we may obviously add Henry Cotton.

11 Meyer to Raycroft, September 15, 1925, TSH Archives.

12 Meyer to Cotton, September 15, 1925, Meyer Papers, CAJH I/767/21.

13 James Leiby, *Charity and Correction*, p. 223.

14 A copy of the typescript report, "Summary of Investigation made by Board of Managers of Trenton State Hospital with Regard to Testimony Concerning the Work of this Hospital to the Joint Legislative Investigating Committee," can be found in the Meyer Papers, CAJH I/767/21.

15 *Newark Evening News*, September 23, 1925.

16 For a detailed account of the day's developments, including the text of the hospital board's statement, see *Trenton Evening Times*, September 23, 1925.

17 Raycroft to Meyer, September 25, 1925, Meyer Papers, CAJH I/3215/1.

18 "Statement by the Board of Managers," *Trenton Evening Times*, September 23, 1925.

19 See Cotton to Burdette Lewis, July 24, 1925, TSH Archives.

20 *Trenton Evening Times*, September 23, 1925.

21 Ibid.

22 *New York Times*, September 24, 1925.

23 Royal S. Copeland, "Your Health: Inviting the Peril of Pus Infection," *Trenton Evening Times*, October 21, 1925.

24 *Trenton Evening Times*, September 23, 1925; *New York Times*, September 24, 1925.

25 *Newark Evening News*, September 24, 1925.

26 *Trenton Evening Times*, September 24, 1925.

27 *New York Times*, September 24, 1925.

28 *Trenton Evening Times*, September 30, 1925.

29 Raycroft to Meyer, September 25, 1925, Meyer Papers, CAJH I/325/1.

30 Cotton to Meyer, September 30, 1925, Meyer Papers, CAJH I/767/22.

31 Meyer to Cotton, October 3, 1925, Meyer Papers, CAJH I/767/22.

32 Cotton to Meyer, October 10, 1925, Meyer Papers, CAJH I/767/22.

33 Meyer to Cotton, October 14, 1925, Meyer Papers, CAJH I/767/22.

34 Cotton to Meyer, October 23, 1925,

Meyer Papers, CAJH I/767/23.

35 Cotton to Meyer, December 17, 1925, Meyer Papers, CAJH I/767/23.

36 Meyer to Cotton, October ?, 1925, Meyer Papers, CAJH I/767/23.

37 Cotton to Meyer, December 30, 1925, Meyer Papers, CAJH I/767/23.

38 Cotton to Meyer, January 6, 1926, Meyer Papers, CAJH I/767/23.

Chapter 11

1 Meyer to Raycroft, January 18, 1926, TSH Archives.

2 Ibid.

3 Here again, my account rests principally on my December 22, 1983, interview with Phyllis Greenacre, supplemented on this occasion by the penciled notes Meyer kept of the meeting on a set of index cards, Meyer Papers, CAJH I/767/23.

4 I am grateful to Dr. Peter Richter once more, for sharing this revealing anecdote about his mother. Interview, February 4, 1996.

5 Meyer to Raycroft, January 18, 1926, Meyer Papers, CAJH I/767/23.

6 Meyer's notes, from which I quote here, survive in his papers at Johns Hopkins, Meyer Papers, CAJH I/767/27.

7 Ibid.

8 Meyer to Raycroft, January 18, 1926, Meyer Papers, CAJH I/767/23.

9 Ibid.

10 Meyer's notes, Meyer Papers, CAJH I/767/25.

11 Meyer to Raycroft, January 18, 1926, Meyer Papers, CAJH I/767/23.

12 Meyer's notes, Meyer Papers, CAJH I/767/25.

13 Ibid.

14 Ibid.

15 Meyer to Raycroft, January 18, 1926, Meyer Papers, CAJH I/767/23.

16 [Henry A. Cotton,] "Conference with Dr. Adolf Meyer and Dr. Phyllis Greenacre, Phipps Clinic, January 14th, 15th & 16th, 1926," unpublished manuscript, TSH Archives, pp. 13, 14.

17 Meyer to Raycroft, January 18, 1926, marked "confidential," TSH Archives.

18 Ibid.

19 Knight to Meyer, January 26, 1926, Meyer Papers, CAJH I/2152/1.

20 Ibid.

21 Meyer to Knight, January 27, 1926, Meyer Papers, CAJH I/767/25. Disingenuously, Meyer added: "I absolutely take for granted your impartial attitude as well as I take my own for granted, and as the sole directing factor in this whole matter."

22 Baillie to Meyer, February 11, 1926, Meyer Papers, CAJH I/767/25.

23 Meyer to Baillie, February 18, 1926, Meyer Papers, CAJH I/767/25.

24 "Trenton State Hospital Survey – 1924–1926," made by Dr. Phyllis Greenacre with the cooperation of Dr. Adolf Meyer, The Johns Hopkins Hospital, Baltimore, Maryland, unpublished typescript [1926], p. 1. As well as her own copy of her findings, copies of Greenacre's report were originally given to Meyer, Cotton, and the Trenton State Hospital board. Three of these copies subsequently appear to have vanished. I was given a photocopy of the remaining copy of the report, together with copies of Greenacre's typed follow-up notes on the patients she studied.

25 Ibid., pp. 1–2.

26 Ibid., p. 16.

27 Ibid., pp. 8–11.

28 Ibid., p. 19, emphasis in the original.

29 Ibid., pp. 20–24, emphasis in the original.

30 Ibid., pp. 27–8.

31 Ibid., p. 25, emphasis in the original.

32 Ibid., p. 37.

33 Ibid.

34 Ibid., p. 38.

35 Ibid., p. 34, emphasis in the original. Thorough to a fault, Greenacre had also taken the time to study a select group of patients whom Cotton identified as his best results. She then undertook to visit and examine all 21 of them. Of these, 16 were cases of manic-depressive

psychosis, and all but 2 had recovered, the others being greatly improved. At first blush, these results might seem impressive, but, as Greenacre pointed out, this "was a group in which recovery is the expected and chronicity the unexpected result, even without 'detoxication treatment.'" Of the epileptic patients, 4 seemed improved, but all had had previous periods of remission without surgery, making the results in these cases difficult to interpret. Finally, there was a single patient whom Cotton had diagnosed as suffering from dementia praecox, and who was now recovered. Her case notes, however, provided "no record of distortions or dissociations such as delusions or hallucinations" and Greenacre was clearly sceptical of just how serious her disturbance had ever been. Even here, therefore, taking the most favourable examples imaginable, careful follow-up work could document no connection between surgery and recovery. Ibid., pp. 40–46.

Chapter 12

1 Meyer to Mrs. Henry A. Cotton, January 18, 1926, Meyer Papers, CAJH I/767/24, emphases in the original.

2 Mrs. Henry A. Cotton to Meyer, January 25, 1926, Meyer Papers, CAJH I/767/24.

3 Meyer to Mrs. Henry A. Cotton, n.d., manuscript in Meyer Papers, CAJH I/767/24, emphasis in the original.

4 Ibid.

5 Nearly six decades later, Phyllis Greenacre commented that, "Mrs. Cotton is still an enigma to me. She came to me after the results were in. She was a little woman, very friendly and a nice hostess. Mrs. Cotton pleaded with me to change my findings. It was a very naive attempt, although Mrs. Cotton was not a stupid woman. It seemed that she had no idea that what she was asking me to do was an improper thing. For years afterwards, I would get

friendly messages from her. She was a very shallow person. She wanted Henry to be a famous doctor. I could not understand why she tried to stay in contact with me." Interview with Phyllis Greenacre, New York City, December 22, 1983.

6 A copy remains in the Trenton Archives: See p. 326, note 16.

7 Raycroft to Meyer, January 25, 1926, Meyer Papers, CAJH I/3215/1.

8 Ibid.

9 Ibid.

10 Cotton, "Conference with Dr. Adolf Meyer and Dr. Phyllis Greenacre," p. 6.

11 Ibid., p. 2.

12 Ibid.

13 Ibid., pp. 3–6.

14 Ibid., p. 8.

15 Ibid., pp. 9–10, 12.

16 Ibid., pp. 13–14.

17 Meyer to Raycroft, January 27, 1926, Meyer Papers, CAJH I/3215/1.

18 Meyer to Raycroft, January 27, 1926, Meyer Papers, CAJH I/3215/1, emphases in the original.

19 Raycroft to Meyer, January 28, 1926, Meyer Papers, CAJH I/3215/1.

20 Meyer to Raycroft, February 1, 1926, Meyer Papers, CAJH I/3215/1.

21 Raycroft to Meyer, November 8, 1926, Meyer Papers, CAJH I/3215/1.

22 Cotton to Raycroft, March 6, 1926, TSH Archives.

23 John Harvey Kellogg to Cotton, March 26, 1926, TSH Archives. With his own obsessions with dietary reform and frequent defecation, Kellogg was particularly interested in Cotton's emphasis on intestinal toxaemia: "What dietetic measures do you find most effective? What success do you have in changing the [intestinal] flora and what results have you seen? In what proportion of patients do you seem necessary [sic] to resort to radical surgery?"

24 D. M. Baillie to Cotton, March 22, 1926, TSH Archives.

25 Meyer to Raycroft, June 7, 1926, Meyer Papers, CAJH I/3215/1.

26 Raycroft to Meyer, June 9, 1926, Meyer Papers, CAJH I/3215/1.

27 Meyer to Cotton, October 23, 1926, Meyer Papers, CAJH I/3215/1.

28 Raycroft to Meyer, October 28, 1926, Meyer Papers, CAJH I/3215/2.

29 See Cotton to Meyer, November 19, 1926; Meyer to Cotton, November 22, 1926, Meyer Papers, CAJH, I/767/27–8.

30 Manuscript notes in Meyer's handwriting, dated Nov[ember] 18, [19]26, and headed "Interview with Dr. Cotton," Meyer Papers, CAJH I/767/27.

31 Typescript of meetings of November 17 and 18, Meyer Papers, CAJH I/767/28.

32 Raycroft to Meyer, May 17, 1927, Meyer Papers, CAJH I/3215/2.

33 Meyer to Raycroft, May 19, 1927, Meyer Papers, CAJH I/3215/2.

34 Cotton to Meyer, May 28, 1927, Meyer Papers, CAJH I/3215/2.

35 Ibid.

36 Ibid.

37 Manuscript notes dated May 30, [19]27, Meyer Papers, CAJH I/767/28.

38 Undated manuscript notes headed "Visit of Dr. Cotton," Meyer Papers, CAJH I/767/28.

39 Ibid.

40 Ibid.

41 Raycroft to Meyer, June 3, 1927, Meyer Papers, CAJH I/3215/2.

42 Interview with Phyllis Greenacre, New York City, December 22, 1983. The substance of Greenacre's memory of her reactions on this occasion was confirmed in a contemporaneous letter from Meyer to Raycroft dated June 4, 1927, Meyer Papers, CAJH I/3215/2.

43 Meyer to Raycroft, June 4, 1927, Meyer Papers, CAJH I/3215/2.

44 Ibid.

45 Meyer to Cotton, June 8, 1927, Meyer Papers, CAJH I/767/28.

46 Ibid.

47 Cotton to Meyer, June 10, 1927, Meyer Papers, CAJH I/767/28.

48 Ibid.

49 Draft letters from June 11, addressed but not sent to Henry Cotton, Meyer Papers, CAJH I/767/28.

50 Cotton to Meyer, June 10, 1927, Meyer Papers, CAJH I/767/28.

51 Unsent draft of a letter to Cotton, June 11, 1927, Meyer Papers, CAJH I/767/28.

52 Meyer to Cotton, June 11, 1927, Meyer Papers, CAJH I/767/28.

Chapter 13

1 Quotations from Cotton's own typewritten notes of his trip, preserved in the Trenton State Hospital Archives under the winsome title of "European Rambles of a Psychiatrst," p. 1. Pinel, one of the great French physicians of the Revolutionary age, had served as physician to the vast Salpêtrière in the 1790s. One of the founding myths of modern psychiatry proclaims that in the midst of the Terror, with thousands going to their deaths at the guillotine, Pinel took one of the most bloodthirsty of the revolutionary leaders with him to the hospital, and there terrified *him* by striking off the shackles and chains that had hitherto bound the raving mad. The painting of the grand event that Cotton viewed on this occasion had been made by Robert-Fleury. All this made for a pretty story and a striking shrine. The only trouble is that (Cotton's garbling of place names and dates aside) the events in question never happened. Robert-Fleury's painting dates from 1878, more than three quarters of a century after the events it purports to record, and it puts on display a purely imaginary scene, actions that simply never happened but which, in the 1920s and now, are routinely invoked by those who seek to establish the humanitarian impulses allegedly at the root of the modern psychiatric enterprise. J. M. Charcot, the most eminent French neurologist of the late nineteenth century had legitimized the treatment of hysteria with hypnosis, turning his

grand rounds into a hysterical circus where his mostly female patients acted out a stylized and eroticized *mise en scène* that drew crowds of onlookers including the young Sigmund Freud. "Acted out" is the all-too-appropriate phrase, for it turns out that these scenes were every bit as spurious as Pinel's renowned gesture, though Charcot himself can most probably be numbered among the duped. Perhaps it is appropriate that the profession of mad-doctoring should rely on such wish-fulfilling fantasies for some of its cultural authority.

2 "European Rambles," p. 1.

3 Ibid.

4 Henry Devine, "Presidential Address on Psychiatry and Medicine," *British Medical Journal* 2 (December 6, 1924), p. 1033.

5 "European Rambles," p. 2.

6 Ibid.

7 Ibid., pp. 2, 3.

8 Ibid., p. 3.

9 Ibid.

10 Ibid., p. 4.

11 Ibid., pp. 4–5.

12 Ibid., pp. 5–6.

13 William Hunter, "Chronic Sepsis as a Cause of Mental Disorder," *Journal of Mental Science* 73 (1927), pp. 549–50.

14 Ibid., p. 550.

15 Ibid., p. 552.

16 Ibid., p. 556.

17 Ibid., p. 561.

18 Ibid., p. 551.

19 Ibid., pp. 561–2.

20 Ibid., p. 562.

21 "Discussion: Chronic Sepsis as a Cause of Mental Disorder," *British Medical Journal* 2 (November 5, 1927), p. 817.

22 "European Rambles," p. 8.

23 Ibid., pp. 6–8. See also the account of the discussion printed in the *Journal of Mental Science* 73 (1927), pp. 716–28.

24 Sir Berkeley Moynihan, "Relation of Aberrant Mental States to Organic Dis-

ease," *British Medical Journal* 2 (November 5, 1927), pp. 815, 817. The *Daily Telegraph*'s report of the occasion (July 21, 1927) recorded that these remarks were greeted with "loud cheers" by the assembled throng of medical men.

25 D. K. Henderson, in "Discussion on Chronic Sepsis as a Cause of Mental Disorder," *Journal of Mental Science* 73 (1927), pp. 721–2.

26 Ibid., p. 722.

27 "Decayed Teeth and Mental Disorder: Doctors' Sepsis Theory," *Daily Telegraph*, July 21, 1927.

28 Ibid.

29 William Hunter, in "Discussion of Chronic Sepsis as a cause of Mental Disorder," p. 726.

30 Ibid., p. 727.

31 See "Decayed Teeth and Mental Disorder," *Daily Telegraph*, July 21, 1927; "Mind and Body," *Daily Telegraph*, July 22, 1927; "Sepsis and Mental Disorder: Work of a New Lister," *Times* (London), July 21, 1927.

32 See, for example, "Bad Teeth as Cause of Insanity: Dr. William Hunter Holds Septic Poison Rises and Affects the Brain," *New York Sun*, August 10, 1927. To his further delight, the *Sun* emphasized that "Dr. Hunter paid a tribute to, and told a remarkable story of, the pioneer work in this field of Dr. Cotton, director of the New Jersey Hospital."

33 "European Rambles," p. 11.

34 Ibid., pp. 11–12.

35 Ibid., p. 14.

36 Ibid., pp. 16–18. In 1936, Gjessing would become a Rockefeller Foundation Fellow, and from 1939 was in receipt of a substantial series of grants from the foundation. He remained a devoted adherent to the doctrine of focal sepsis, noting in a letter to Daniel P. O'Brien, the foundation's European officer, that, "the first stage in our activities is concerned with the picking up and locating chronic infection," adding that he was

following in the footsteps of Cotton and Graves. "All patients sent here are extremely carefully somatically examined and treated. Cleaning out foci and cure of chronic infections are aimed at with all possible means at hand." And later in the same letter he defended Cotton's colectomies, even with their high mortality, as justified by the desperation of the cases. Such sentiments did not seem to trouble O'Brien in the least. Following a visit to Dikemar Hospital the following spring, he wrote back to headquarters in extremely positive terms, noting that Gjessing was "a superior person with a great capacity for work and an unusual persistence in his efforts to clear up the largest problem in psychiatry today, namely the etiology of schizophrenia." See Gjessing to O'Brien, March 6, 1938; O'Brien to Alan Gregg, March 3, 1939, Record Group 1.1, Series 767, Box 1, Folder 3, Rockefeller Archives, Tarrytown, New York.

37 "European Rambles," pp. 18–19.

Chapter 14

1 A copy of the resolution is preserved in Adolf Meyer's papers, CAJH III/114/1.

2 Sanger Brown, "Presidential Address," *Psychiatric Quarterly* 1 (1927), p. 9.

3 Meyer's files contain his invitation to attend the British Medical Association's Annual Dinner at the Edinburgh meeting, held on Thursday, July 21, but he elected to remain in London rather than attend.

4 Kopeloff to Meyer, Meyer Papers, CAJH I/2179/1.

5 Meyer to Kopeloff, January 12, 1928, Meyer Papers, CAJH I/2179/1, emphasis in the original.

6 Adolf Meyer to Hermann Meyer, October 27, 1927, Meyer Papers, CAJH IV/3/239.

7 A. Meyer to H. Meyer, April 10, 1927, Meyer Papers, CAJH IV/3/237.

8 Adolf Meyer, manuscript notes on Curt

Richter dated May 1928, Meyer–Greenacre correspondence, Meyer Papers, CAJH Series XV.

9 Greenacre to Meyer, September 10, 1928, Meyer Papers, CAJH Series XV.

10 Ibid.

11 A. Meyer to H. Meyer, October 27, 1927, Meyer Papers, CAJH IV/3/239.

12 Ibid.

13 A. Meyer to H. Meyer, November 17, 1927, Meyer Papers, CAJH IV/3/240.

14 A. Meyer to H. Meyer, December 12, 1927, Meyer Papers, CAJH IV/3/240. Some months later, he confessed somewhat guiltily, in a private note to himself, that "Dr. Greenacre should have been . . . instructor and director of the lab . . . Justly or unjustly, I considered her as a potential rather than fully active member of the staff, on account of the family responsibilities." Meyer–Greenacre correspondence, note, no date [1928], Meyer Papers, CAJH Series XV. For all her experience, and the invaluable work she had done for him, he had neglected to advance her over the years, so that both her title and her income had lagged far behind her responsibilities.

15 See Greenacre to Mrs. Meyer, January 3, 1928, thanking her "for your very practical help just at the time I left. It relieved me very much in more ways than you can know . . . my first reaction has been to *sleep*, hard, long, and imperiously . . . The children . . . have, on the whole, taken the move with a minimum of distress." Meyer Papers, CAJH Series XV.

16 It was, she noted, "a far cry from the intensive work of the Phipps." Greenacre to Meyer, January 17, 1928, Meyer Papers, CAJH Series XV. Her sense of alienation only deepened over time.

17 Telephone interview with Dr. Peter Richter, August 15, 1996. Much to Meyer's discomfiture, a number of his students drifted into psychoanalysis

after leaving Baltimore, a development that heightened his own estrangement from Freud and his doctrines.

18 He tried hard to tempt her to accept this offer, appending a handwritten note to his letter offering her the position: "The work nat[ural]ly could not begin before Oct. I may say that Miss B. will leave end of Sept. Whether Dr. R. had best go too is a question. I wish he wd go to Russia where he wd like to see the Pavlov lab – and stay there to prepare for another place in this country. I shd find it hard to find anyone in his place just yet; but—I am terribly anxious to make possible having a harmonious active group during the rest of my working years at Hopkins and shall bend all my energy in that direction." But in the body of the letter, he had all but acknowledged the impossibility of the situation: "I naturally feel all the more distressed over your departure. Yet if it must be – you clearly had to look for the peace of your mind." Meyer to Greenacre, June 15, 1928, Meyer Papers, CAJH Series XV.

19 On being invited to the Phipps staff reunion, Greenacre responded that, "I want if possible to attend, for the Phipps will always have my loyalty and interest ... [But] I do not know whether I shall find it possible to face again, in the setting of a family reunion, the whole physical situation which swamps me with such painful conflicts and memories ... the thought of this past year and a half gives me a comprehensive shudder." Greenacre to Meyer, Feburary 29, 1928. Six weeks later, she had made up her mind: "there is much that draws me and I should like to come. But I have about decided not to attempt it, because it still stirs me up too much, – and in addition I do not know that I should really be able to live up to the conventional surface demanded ... I do not want to take the risk of exposing my personal feelings in

a general gathering of that kind." Greenacre to Meyer, April 17, 1928, Meyer Papers, CAJH Series XV. For the invitation to return to direct research on schizophrenia, see Meyer to Greenacre, June 15, 1928, Meyer Papers, CAJH Series XV.

20 For a brief summary of Richter's scientific influence and standing, and of the defining characteristics of his work, see Jay Schulkin, Paul Rozin, and Eliot Stellar, "Curt Richter, Feburary 20, 1894 – December 21, 1988," in *Biographical Memoirs*, vol. 65 (Washington, D.C.: National Academies Press, 1994). The authors claim that "Richter stands as America's foremost psychobiologist in the twentieth century."

21 In typically opaque Meyerian prose, he commented that, "Dr. R has evidently changed his attitude towards my courses and instead of a cold blanket, the students with whom he deals seem to fall in line with a more favorable spirit – both the 1st and the 2nd year classes. I do not think it is mere policy. I really feel it is the first time that he has approached the teaching with a fairer spirit, and I myself seem to feel the relief, in the rather heavy load I have taken on." Meyer to Greenacre, Feburary 20, 1928, Meyer Papers, CAJH Series XV.

22 A point Phyllis Greenacre made to me several times in the course of my interview with her in December, 1983.

23 In a letter to Meyer written on February 29, 1928, Greenacre commented that "the Phipps ... stands more in the place of familial roof to me than any other place can." Meyer Papers, CAJH Series XV.

24 See Greenacre to Meyer, January 17, 1928; February 29, 1928; March 6, 1928; April 17, 1928; May 15, 1928; September 10 and 19, 1928; October 2, and 25 1928; May 15 and 27, 1929; June 3 (telegram) and 20, 1929; June 18 and 21, 1930, Meyer Papers. CAJH Series XV. See also copies

of letters from Richter to Greenacre, August 23, 1928, and Greenacre to Richter, September 13, 1928 in Greenacre's handwriting, sent to Meyer later in September. Meyer Papers, CAJH Series XV. As this correspondence makes clear, there were also a number of meetings between Greenacre and Meyer to discuss her situation, and on at least one occasion, Meyer, Greenacre, and Richter had a joint meeting in an effort to resolve issues of child support and custody.

25 Meyer to Greenacre, n.d., [January 1927]; February 20, 1928; [May?], 1929; June 21, 1929; August 28, 1929, Meyer Papers, CAJH Series XV.

26 He did insist to Richter that he must arrange for "the departure of Miss B.," his mistress, whom he referred to as "a foolish young girl ... while I did not want to pounce on the girl I felt she had to retire in due time, notwithstanding my appreciation of what she had achieved in the laboratory. He [Richter] has asked her to find another position and she will not be here next year." Meyer to Greenacre, February 20, 1928, Meyer Papers, CAJH Series XV. But a year and more later, he remained completely passive when Richter first informed him that he had decided to leave Hopkins and then announced he had changed his mind and would be staying.

27 Greenacre informed Meyer that, "I find that going back there [to Baltimore] even for a short time, precipitates depression that takes several weeks to deal with. I know that ultimately I will come to a better immunization, but it seems to be a bewilderingly slow process ... In addition, I would hesitate before taking the children back now into an atmosphere in which there would be the possibility of stirring up further conflict for them. They accept Curt's not living with us now, – as we are on new ground, but they think that

if we went back to Baltimore, it would mean a re-establishment of joint family life." Greenacre to Meyer, September 10, 1928, Meyer Papers, CAJH Series XV.

28 Meyer to Raycroft, December 1, 1927, Meyer Papers, CAJH I/3215/3.

29 Raycroft to Meyer, December 8, 1927, Meyer Papers, CAJH I/3215/3. Raycroft's report of the proceedings included a stock promise that "I am going to take up again with Dr. Cotton and Dr. Stone the question of working out the hospital's answer to Dr. Greenacre's study along the lines we agreed upon so long ago. I am quite unwilling to allow the matter to remain where it is." But remain there it did, with neither party raising the matter in their further correspondence.

30 Leiby, *Charity and Correction*, p. 223.

31 Trenton State Hospital, case notes, patient record 26359. (As always, I have retained the patient's first and last initials, but changed the name to a pseudonym to protect her privacy.)

32 Trenton State Hospital, case notes, patient record 27156. (On each admission, a patient received a new record number.)

33 Henry A. Cotton, "Oral Infection," reprint of an address to the 55th Annual Meeting of the New Jersey Public Health and Sanity Association, Asbury Park, December 3, 1929, p. 6.

34 Ibid., p. 9.

35 Ibid., p. 10.

36 Ibid., pp. 7, 3.

37 Ibid., p. 8.

38 Ibid., pp. 8–9.

39 Ibid., p. 7.

40 Ibid., pp. 3–5.

41 Ibid., p. 3.

42 Ibid., p. 4; See also Henry A. Cotton, "Gastro-intestinal Stasis in the Psychoses," *Proceedings of the Fifth International Congress of Physiotherapy*, 14–18 September, 1930, pp. 1–2.

43 Ibid., p. 10.

44 Cotton, "Gastro-intestinal Stasis," p. 6.

45 Ibid., p. 1.

46 Ibid., p. 8.

47 Ibid., p. 2.

48 Ibid., p. 4.

49 Ibid. "Morse Sine Wave" refers to efforts to stimulate sluggish colons using electricity.

50 Ibid., p. 6. The King–Scheerer Table and double stop-cock were the apparatus used in colonic irrigation.

51 Ibid., p. 2.

52 Ibid., p. 5.

53 Ibid.

Chapter 15

1 Henry Cotton, quoted in Leiby, *Charity and Correction*, p. 223.

2 Minutes of the Board of Managers, New Jersey State Hospital at Trenton, July 1, 1930 to June 30, 1934, TSH Archives.

3 Comments made a year later by the head of all the state's mental health system, Commissioner John Ellis, suggest that he also continued to support Cotton's program, and to endorse the need to root out focal sepsis. In an address at the celebration of the twenty-fifth anniversary of the Vineland Training School, he complained about the difficulties of conducting research in state institutions, and suggested that, in Cotton's case, "people who should have been patient and understanding, and who should have withheld hasty judgments have not done so." See Edgar A. Doll (ed.), *Twenty-Five Years: A Memorial Volume in Commemoration of the Twenty-Fifth Anniversary of the Vineland Laboratory, 1906–1931* (Vineland Training School: Department of Research Series, No. 2, 1932), pp. 20–22, quoted in Leiby, *Charity and Correction*, p. 286.

4 Cotton to Meyer, October 18, 1930, Meyer Papers, CAJH I/767/30.

5 Ibid.

6 Ibid.

7 Meyer to Cotton, October 24, 1930, Meyer Papers, CAJH I/767/30.

8 Cotton to Meyer, March 20, 1930, Meyer Papers, CAJH I/767/30.

9 Meyer to Cotton, no date, handwritten response appended to Cotton's letter of March 20, 1930, Meyer Papers, CAJH I/767/30.

10 Meyer to Cotton, October 24, 1930. See also Meyer to Cotton, January 15, 1931, addressed, most unusually for the extremely formal and normally distant Meyer, "My dear friend." Meyer Papers, CAJH I/767/30.

11 Meyer to Henry M. Fitzhugh (secretary of the Board of Medical Examiners of Maryland), June 18, 1928, Meyer Papers, CAJH III/285/30.

12 Solomon Katzenelbogen, "Trenton State Hospital," unpublished typescript, n.d. [late 1930], Meyer Papers, CAJH I/2024/20. The following quotations are all taken from this report. I am most grateful to Gerald Grob for drawing my attention to this document, and for kindly sharing his photocopy of it with me.

13 Actually, Cotton had boasted more than once in print that he did not trouble himself overmuch about such niceties as consent. One of the many advantages of a surgical approach, he suggested, was that if a patient became resistive and objected to an operation, one could simply administer anesthesia and proceed with "deseptization" anyway.

14 In early 1932, for example, Raycroft warned Paul Mecray, the other medical man on the Trenton State Hospital board of governors, that "we may look forward to a discussion that will be somewhat unpleasant . . . It looks to me as though we were [*sic*] in for a rumpus unless Henry's emotional state is distinctly modified in the meantime." Raycroft's anxiety had been prompted by a chance encounter: "In my optimism I had come to feel that the question of resuming the major operation policy at the hospital had been dropped by Dr. Cotton. I saw him the other day,

however, and he raised the question as to why no major operations were being done and was inclined to complain in view of the fact that there were in the hospital some thirty patients from whose friends permission had been gained to perform an operation. He was quite critical of Stone, said he had been unable to get any satisfaction from him." Raycroft to Mecray, February 10, 1932, TSH Archives.

15 Raycroft's copy, annotated in his own handwriting, still survives in the TSH Archives.

16 Ibid., p. 1.

17 Ibid., pp. 1–2. Cotton was scarcely unique in suggesting that desperate remedies could be legitimately employed in such circumstances. Employing a remarkably similar logic, the eminent late nineteenth-century gynecologist William Goodell had rationalized the removal of apparently healthy ovaries in female mental patients in an effort to use sexual surgery to cure their madness. Whatever the outcome of the operation, he suggested, whether it were mental recovery, sterilization, or death, the intervention could be accounted a success: "For, in the first place, an insane woman is no more a member of the body politic than a criminal; second, her death is always a relief to her dearest friends; third, even in the case of her recovery from her mental disease, she is liable to transmit the taint of insanity to her children, and to her children's children for many generations." William Goodell, "Clinical Notes on the Extirpation of the Ovaries for Insanity," *Transactions of the Medical Society of the State of Pennsylvania* 13 (1881), p. 639.

18 Henry A. Cotton, "Report on the Operative Procedures on the Colon," unpublished paper, November 15 1932, TSH Archives, p. 2.

19 Ibid., pp. 2–3. In all likelihood, the adhesions Cotton discovered on this second occasion were iatrogenic, the product of the surgery he had previously inflicted on these patients.

20 Ibid., p. 3.

21 Ibid., pp. 3–4.

22 Ibid., p. 4.

23 Ibid.

24 Ibid., p. 5.

25 Ibid., p. 7.

26 Ibid., p. 8.

27 Case quoted in Rotov, "History of Trenton State Hospital."

28 See Emil Frankel to Raycroft, June 10, 1932; Raycroft to Frankel, December 5, 1932; Frankel to Raycroft, January 7, 1933, TSH Archives.

29 Frankel, "Study of 'End Results,'" pp. 2–3.

30 Ibid., p. 22.

31 Ibid., p. 20, emphasis in the original, a quote from Cotton's own 1932 report.

32 Ibid., p. 23.

33 Ibid., p. 9.

34 Ibid., p. 10,

35 Ibid., p. 19.

36 Though the death rates among the control group were far lower, 18 percent of the total, this was still an extraordinarily high figure, considering that 58 percent of these patients were under the age of 40. Frankel did not examine this statistic further, but remembering that virtually all of the patients he misleadingly referred to as "non-operative cases" had had their teeth extracted, their tonsils removed, and in many cases spleens, stomachs, cervixes, and other organs "attended to," one has to wonder whether some of the apparent excess mortality in this group of patients was not also due to the treatment regime at Trenton.

37 Frankel, "Study of 'End Results,'" p. 14.

38 Ibid., p. 15.

39 Cotton to Mencken, December 13, 1933, Mencken Papers, New York Public Library. I am most grateful to Stephen Cox for alerting me to this correspondence.

40 Henry A. Cotton, "The Physical Causes of Mental Disorders," *The American Mercury* 29, no. 114 (June 1933), p. 221.

41 Ibid., pp. 222–3.

42 Ibid., p. 223.

43 Ibid., p. 224.

44 See Cotton to Mencken, December 19, 28, 1932; January 4, 26, 1933, Mencken Papers, New York Public Library.

45 In January 1931, for example, Cotton had written a letter to Meyer, congratulating him on receiving "the First Award under the Thos. Salmon Fund." He seized the occasion to complain of the "ignorance" that was displayed in recent criticism of the focal sepsis hypothesis, and boasted that "we have 250 cases recovered following the removal of either the colon or the release of adhesions or high colon irrigations in the milder cases." Meyer had responded that he found the latest criticism of Cotton's work "not very illuminating . . . I hope, with the gain of a certain leisure you will be able to organize your experiences with the necessary documentation. I doubt whether anyone has anywhere like the material you have . . . I wish," Meyer continued, "that there were a way to get a well-trained man into your laboratory to collect and organize the material and correlate it with the clinical data. I should be greatly interested." Again, this letter contained no hint of criticism. See Cotton to Meyer, January 13, 1931; Meyer to Cotton, January 15, 1931, Meyer Papers, CAJH I/767/30.

46 Cotton to Meyer, April 29, 1933, Meyer Papers, CAJH I/767/31.

47 Meyer to Cotton, May 6, 1933, Meyer Papers, CAJH I/767/32.

48 Cotton to Meyer, April 29, 1933, Meyer Papers, CAJH I/767/31.

49 Meyer to Cotton, May 6, 1933, Meyer Papers, CAJH I/767/32.

50 Cotton to Meyer, May 8, 1933, Meyer Papers, CAJH I/767/32.

51 Ibid.

52 Ibid.

53 Cotton to Meyer, April 29, 1933; May 8, 1933, Meyer Papers, CAJH I/767/31–2.

54 Cotton to Meyer, May 8, 1933.

55 *Trenton Evening Times*, April 11, 1933, p. 3.

56 *Trenton Evening Times*, April 12, 1933, p. 6. Raycroft, who from 1927 had headed the Trenton State Hospital board of governors, and who had now lost some of his earlier confidence in Cotton's methods, "asked John Ellis [Commissioner of Institutions and Agencies] what had happened to bring forth this panegyric and he sent [Raycroft] a copy of the resolution referred to in the newspaper accounts." Worried by "this latest evidence of Dr. Cotton's publicity methods," Raycroft wrote to his fellow board member, Paul Mecray, suggesting that "we should be thinking it over with the idea of deciding at the next meeting whether or not we are going to continue to tolerate this kind of thing, or whether we shall make some definite reply for the purpose of correcting the impressions which have been sown in the minds of our undiscriminating legislators." Raycroft to Mecray, April 14, 1933, TSH Archives.

57 *The American Mercury* 29, no. 114 (June 1933), p. 256.

58 He had sought to purchase 2,000 reprints of his piece, which he planned to use in his political fight, only to be informed by Mencken that the *American Mercury* did not provide reprints. "Under its copyright it holds its monopoly on [articles] for six months. At the end of that time all rights are transferred to the author. He is then free to reprint the article as he pleases, but The American Mercury can't furnish him with the reprints." See Cotton to Mencken, January 30, 1933; Mencken to Cotton, Feburary 3, 1933, Mencken Papers, New York Public Library.

59 "World Famous Alienist Drops Dead,"

Trenton Evening Times, May 8, 1933, pp. 1, 14.

60 *Trenton Evening Times,* May 9, 1933, p. 6.

61 Cotton's secretary, Mrs. M. A. Hulfish, had received the news of his demise by mid-afternoon, and hastened to inform Adolf Meyer in a note she enclosed with Cotton's last letter to him: "Since writing the enclosed letter to you from Dr. Cotton, I have heard of his sudden death at the Trenton Club this afternoon at 2.15. I know this will be as great a shock to you as it is to me, and I felt you would want to know it." Hulfish to Meyer, Meyer Papers, CAJH I/767/32.

62 Meyer to Mrs. Henry A. Cotton, May 10, 1933, Meyer Papers, CAJH I/767/32.

63 Adolf Meyer, "In Memoriam: Henry A. Cotton," *American Journal of Psychiatry* 13 [old series, 90] (1934), p. 921.

64 Ibid., p. 922.

65 Ibid., pp. 922–3.

66 Ibid., p. 923.

Epilogue

1 Edward Shorter, *A History of Psychiatry: From the Era of the Asylum to the Age of Prozac* (New York: Wiley, 1997), p. 112; idem., *TPH: History and Memories of the Toronto Psychiatric Hospital, 1925–1966,* pp. 72–5.

2 I draw here on some remarks by the French social theorist, Robert Castel, "Moral Treatment, Moral Therapy and Social Control in the Nineteenth Century," in *Social Control and the State: Historical and Comparative Essays,* ed. Stanley Cohen and Andrew Scull, (Oxford: Martin Robertson, 1983), pp. 248–9.

3 Farrar left Trenton in 1916 for a position in Canada, just months after Cotton had first begun to explore the idea of focal sepsis and extract teeth from a handful of patients. It was one of Farrar's former patients, a Mrs. Florence P., who was subsequently, in 1918, the first of Cotton's patients to undergo a colectomy. Admitted on February 26, 1916, after a brief depression and an attempt at suicide, she had come under Farrar's care, and he had paid particular attention to her "intestinal condition" and history of constipation. Edward Shorter, from whose book on the Toronto Psychiatric Hospital I take these details, suggests quite plausibly that this focus on the bowels, otherwise uncharacteristic of Farrar's clinical work, reflects Henry Cotton's growing interest in focal sepsis. But Shorter's further suggestion that Farrar "fled in horror" from Cotton's planned abdominal surgery, "in the face of such massive looming medical practice," is nothing more than speculation, and far-fetched speculation at that. Cotton's abdominal surgery did not commence until two years after Farrar had left Trenton, and the Trenton annual reports for 1916 and 1917 show no evidence that such surgery was contemplated – indeed, their tone and substance are quite tentative by comparison with the truculent language in the 1918 report. Quite how Farrar could have possibly known what Cotton planned to do two years after he departed for Canada, Shorter leaves wholly unexplained. As it happens, Florence P. died as a direct consequence of the removal of her colon, and Cotton reported as much to Farrar: "Our surgical work at the present time is developing quite nicely . . . Our first patient was one in which you were interested, that of Florence P. . . . She never got any better, in fact got very much worse and it was the first case on which we . . . operated, resection of the colon. Unfortunately, her physical condition was so bad and her heart so weak that she did not survive, although she lived a week. It served to confirm my opinion, however, that her trouble was largely in the intestinal tract . . . I think our statistics show conclusively that the manic-depressive

and dementia-praecox groups are toxemias due to chronic infections." Cotton to Farrar, November 4, 1919, Farrar private archive, 20 Oriole Road, Toronto, Canada. I know of no objections to these claims or activities on Farrar's part, either then or subsequently. For Shorter's discussion of these issues, see *TPH*, pp. 72–5, 92–3.

4 In his years at Trenton, Ebaugh enthusiastically adopted Cotton's approach. Charged with the task of examining the juvenile delinquents at the Jamesburg Reformatory, he reported in 1921 that "focal infections have played a very definite role" in their anti-social behavior, claiming that he had found that 75 percent of them had infected teeth and tonsils. Trenton State Hospital *Annual Report*, 1921, p. 45. Ebaugh's enthusiasm was almost certainly feigned, a careerist move designed to curry favor with Cotton, for almost as soon as he moved on from Trenton, he abandoned his apparent faith in surgical excision as the pathway to the cure of madness. Cotton complained to Meyer that immediately after Ebaugh departed for Philadelphia, he became an apostate, and "has fallen back upon the psychogenic explanations." Cotton to Meyer, n.d., Meyer Papers, CAJH I/767/28. Yet despite being present during some of the busiest periods for colectomies, tooth extractions, and the like, Ebaugh never uttered public criticism of the hospital's therapeutics.

5 Lest anyone be tempted to think that these problems belong only in some mythical medical dark ages, or are to be found only among such marginal figures as psychiatrists, I suggest a perusal of Henry K. Beecher's seminal paper on "Ethics and Clinical Research," *New England Journal of Medicine* 74 (1966), pp. 1354–60. The specialties represented in Beecher's survey include surgery, cardiovascular physiology, oncology, virology, and infectious diseases – anything but marginal fields. The investigators he surveyed displayed no qualms about experimenting upon their patients, even "when the hazard may be per-manent injury or death." Yet, so far from being marginal or disreputable figures, they were members of the elite of the American medical profession. And though, like Cotton, they publicly acknowledged what they were up to (injecting cancer cells into healthy patients, for example, to observe what happened to them, or feeding live hepatitis viruses to children), they drew neither negative reactions nor reproof from their colleagues and professional peers. To the contrary, they were praised, and their careers advanced, for engaging in these kinds of behavior. David Rothman rightly remarks that it will not do "to dismiss them as less moral or trustworthy than their colleagues. They were too well-supported, too integral to the research establishment, too much honored to be characterized as aberrant or deviant." See the discussion in his *Strangers at the Bedside: A History of How Law and Bioethics Transformed Medical Decision Making* (New York: Basic Books, 1991), esp. chapter 4, "The Doctor as Whistle Blower," which provides a valuable overview of the events surrounding the publication of Beecher's paper. I wish I could share Rothman's faith that the bioethical enterprise, spawned in part by Beecher's courage, has substantially changed things for the better. I fear, however, that much of it represents an employment relief act for second-rate philosophers and theological types, and a piling up of bureaucratic rules and make-work committees designed to salve institutional consciences and minimize legal liability, rather than a major reorientation of professional conduct.

6 "In Memoriam: Henry A. Cotton,"

American Journal of Psychiatry 13 (1934), pp. 922, 923.

7 Of Cotton's sincerity and self-belief there can be no doubt. He was, after all, willing to sacrifice his wife and his children's teeth (and in the case of his youngest son, part of the bowel), to his beliefs – and on more than one occasion, to insist that teeth of his own must be pulled to allow him to recover or maintain his own sanity.

8 R. S. Carroll, "Aseptic Meningitis in Combating the Dementia Praecox Problem," *New York Medical Journal,* October 3, 1923, pp. 407–11; E. S. Barr and R. G. Barry, "The Effect of Producing Aseptic Meningitis upon Dementia Praecox," *New York State Journal of Medicine* 26 (1926), p. 89.

9 Barr and Barry, "The Effect of Producing Aseptic Meningitis upon Dementia Praecox," pp. 89–92. Barr and Barry injected 20cc of horse serum into the spinal canals of their patients, producing a temperature of 103 degrees Fahrenheit that persisted for three or four days. Severe headaches and backaches were common, and many patients showed evidence of edema of the brain, which was treated with adrenaline.

10 Such tactics were widely employed by British, French, Italian, German, and Austrian physicians, and more occasionally by Americans. See Micale and Lerner (eds.), *Traumatic Pasts.* Julius Wagner von Jauregg, professor of psychiatry at the University of Vienna, even stood trial after the war for using this approach, only to be acquitted, in part because of defense testimony from none other than Sigmund Freud. See Kurt Eissler, *Freud as an Expert Witness: The Discussion of War Neuroses Between Freud and Wagner-Jauregg* (Madison, Conne.: International Universities Press, 1986).

11 N. J. Berkwitz, "Faradic Shock Treatment of the 'Functional' Psychoses," *Lancet* 2 (1939), pp. 351–5.

12 See, for example, A. D. Adrian and L. R. Yealland, "Treatment of Some Common War Neuroses," *Lancet* 1 (1917), pp. 867–72; L. R. Yealland, *Hysterical Disorders of Warfare* (London: Macmillan, 1918); Clovis Vincent, *Le Traitement des phénomènes hystériques par la rééducation intensive* (Tours: Arrault, 1916).

13 Erysipelas, or St. Anthony's Fire, is a bacterial infection usually caused by *Streptococcus pyogenes.* It consists of a rapidly developing skin disorder accompanied by pain, fever, chills, and shivering, and can cause lymphatic damage. In a pre-antibiotic era, there was no effective treatment for the disease.

14 See Wagner von Jauregg's comments in W. Simpson and W. Bierman (eds.), *Fever Therapy: Abstracts and Discussions of Papers Presented at the First International Conference on Fever Therapy* (New York: Hoeber, 1937), p. 2; and Julius Wagner von Jauregg, "The History of Malarial Treatment," *American Journal of Psychiatry* 102 (1946), pp. 577–8.

15 Frederick Mott, who served as pathologist to London's mental hospitals, drew from repeated first-hand experience when he informed readers of his six-volume *System of Syphilis* in 1910 that "there is nothing more pitiable or degrading than the sight of a number of these wrecks of humanity sitting in a row, their heads on their breasts, grinding the teeth, saliva running out the angles of the mouth, oblivious to their surroundings, with expressionless faces and cold, livid, immobile hands." Quoted in Hugh Pennington, "Can You Close Your Eyes Without Falling Over?" *London Review of Books,* September 11, 2003, p. 31.

16 A review of 35 studies in 1926 gave an average "complete" remission rate of 27.5 percent. J. R. Driver, J. A. Gammel, and L. J. Karnosh, "Malarial Treatment

of Central Nervous System Syphilis," *Journal of the American Medical Association* 87 (1926), pp. 1821–7. Notwithstanding the substantial clinical consensus on the value of the malarial treatment, the intermittent and uncertain course of the underlying disease, the absence of any clear criteria of what constituted improvement, and the wholly uncontrolled character of the evaluations of therapeutic outcomes make it very difficult at this remove to assess whether the therapy actually "worked." Contemporaries, however, were generally convinced of its efficacy, and its existence dramatically altered the way doctors and patients afflicted with the disorder interacted with one another. The best discussion of these issues is Braslow, *Mental Ills and Bodily Cures*.

17 There were major ethical problems with this approach, not least the certainty, given the absence of a wholly reliable means of diagnosing general paresis, that misdiagnosed patients could be given syphilis as well as malaria. William Alanson White, the superintendent of St. Elizabeth's Hospital in Washington, D.C., was unusual in acknowledging the problem, and in refusing sometimes importunate requests from underlings who sought to embrace a clinical practice widely used elsewhere. See W. Watson Eldridge to W. A. White, June 21, 1930; White to Eldridge, June 24, 1930; Eldridge to White, June 27, 1930; White to Eldridge, June 28, 1930, William Alanson White Papers, Record Group 418, National Archives, Washington, D.C. These letters are reproduced in Gerald N. Grob, *The Inner World of American Psychiatry: Selected Correspondence* (New Brunswick, New Jersey: Rutgers University Press, 1985), pp. 124–5.

18 On July 7, 1941, for instance, White's successor as superintendent of St. Elizabeth's Hospital, Winfred Overholser, noted that he had shipped quartan malarial blood, taken "from one of our paretics," in thermos flasks, and the same file records exchanges of malarial blood between state hospitals in Illinois, Tennessee, New Mexico, Pennsylvania, Indiana, Maryland, and Connecticut, as well as the Boston Psychopathic Hospital, Westbrook Sanitarium in Richmond, Virginia, and the mental hospital in Puerto Rico. Overholser to Ernesto Quintero, July 7, 1941; Seth Howes to W. Overholser, October 6, 1943, St. Elizabeth's Hospital, Treatment Files, Entry 18, National Archives, Washington, D.C. (White's concerns about the ethical problems of injecting patients with paretic blood were evidently not shared by his successor.)

19 Here, Cotton's key ally in the fight against focal sepsis, T. C. Graves, took the lead. See his "A Short Note on the Use of Calcium in Excited States," *Journal of Mental Science* 65 (1919), p. 109. One explanation offered at the time for the therapeutic effect of malarial therapy was that it somehow stimulated the immune system, a line of reasoning that may have commended fever therapy to Graves.

20 Illinois Department of Public Welfare, *Annual Reports* 11 (1927–8), pp. 12, 23; 1928–9, p. 23.

21 For the first report of the employment of such a device, see C. A. Neymann and S. L. Osborne, "Artificial Fever Produced by High-Frequency Currents, Preliminary Reports," *Illinois Medical Journal* 56 (1929), pp. 199–203. Such devices were not without their hazards. The superintendent of the Arizona State Hospital complained to Winfred Overholser, superintendent of St. Elizabeth's Hospital in Washington, D.C., that at his establishment, "as sometimes happens, the first patient treated [in this fashion] died. Since that time the few graduate nurses we

have have refused to operate the cabinet and I am in no position to force them to do so ... [for the moment] we will be obliged to use malarial therapy." Seth Howes to Overholser, October 6, 1943, St. Elizabeth's Hospital Treatment Files, Entry 18, National Archives, Washington, D.C.

22 J. H. Talbott and K. L. Tillotson, "The Effects of Cold in Mental Disorders: A Study of Ten Patients Suffering from Schizophrenia and Treated with Hypothermia," *Diseases of the Nervous System* 2 (1941), pp. 116–26; J. H. Talbott, "The Physiologic and Therapeutic Effects of Hypothermia," *New England Journal of Medicine* 224 (1941), pp. 281–8.

23 These experiments are recorded in passing (their uniformly negative results having presumably precluded separate publication) in L. J. Meduna, "The Carbon Dioxide Treatment: A Review," *Journal of Clinical and Experimental Pschopathology and Quarterly Review of Psychiatry and Neurology* 15 (1954), pp. 235–6. On Meduna's account, these included "about 40 schizophrenic patients [at the Illinois Neuropsychiatric Institute], each of whom received a fairly long series of cyanide injections ... None of these patients, however, recovered from their illness." Cyanide injections were also being tried elsewhere, for example by Solomon Loevenhart of the University of Wisconsin in the late 1920s.

24 Later, as a Jewish refugee from the Nazis, Sakel took up an appointment at the Harlem Valley State Hospital in New York.

25 Benjamin Wortis, translation of a lecture by Sakel delivered in Paris at the University Clinic, July 11, 1937, and distributed when Sakel lectured again at the Harlem Valley State Hospital in New York on November 18, 1937. St. Elizabeth's Hospital Treatment File, Entry 18, National Archives, Washington, D.C.

26 Charles Burlingame provided a vivid description of what occurred, in a text designed to portray the heroic psychiatrist daringly jousting with death in an effort to reclaim his patient: "There are few scenes that can match the dramatic intensity of the insulin treatment room in a modern psychiatric center. Here, each day, the patient is brought to the very fringe of life and allowed to hover there for several hours; sometimes he even starts to slide across the border, and only heroic measures, applied without delay, bring him back. Only the immeasurable reward of a mind restored could possibly justify the extremity of the method. From the moment the insulin is injected into the muscle of the patient, he is under the most careful scrutiny. A special nurse is assigned to him. Pulse and temperature are taken every few minutes, and the physician is constantly nearby, ready to go into action at any sign of danger. The nurse looks up from her patient: 'Doctor, I can detect no respiration.' The doctor moves to the side of the patient and speaks sharply in attempt to arouse him. There is no response, nor is there any visible sign of breathing; a few moments ago the breathing was sterterous, but now the patient is silent and limp. Meanwhile, artificial respiration is being given. It is a matter of seconds before the sterilized needle is given and the adrenalin is injected. Breathing follows almost instantly. Then follows the administration of sugar. The effect is quick. In five minutes the patient is sitting up in bed, smiling and, fortunately, remembering nothing of what has taken place. So it goes, this skilful sparring with death, where a few moments of neglect, inattention, or inadverdence may cost a life." "Insanity and Insulin: Shock Treatment for Schizophrenia," *The Forum* (1937), pp. 98–102. (Copy in Meyer Papers, CAJH I/557/2.)

Controlled studies eventually demonstrated that insulin coma therapy was useless, though claims to this effect were initially greeted by leading psychiatrists with fury. See Harold Bourne, "The Insulin Myth," *Lancet* 2 (1953), pp. 964–8; and the discussion in Michael Shepherd, "Neurolepsis and the Psychopharmacological Revolution: Myth and Reality," *History of Psychiatry* 5 (1994), pp. 90–2.

27 L. J. Meduna and E. Friedman, "Convulsive-Irritative Therapy of Psychoses: Survey of More Than 3,000 Cases," *Journal of the American Medical Association* 112 (1939), p. 509. See also L. Meduna and B. Rohny, "Insulin and Cardiazol Treatment of Schizophrenia," *Lancet* 1 (1939), pp. 1139–42. Kalinowski and his associates reported that camphor had other drawbacks as well. It was frequently associated with nausea and vomiting, and its effects were so unpredictable that clinicians were unable to anticipate the timing of the subsequent convulsions, which might occur from fifteen minutes to three hours later, or not at all. See Lothar Kalinowski, Hans Hippius, and Helmfried Klein, *Biological Treatments in Psychiatry* (New York: Grune and Stratton, 1982), pp. 217–18.

28 S. Brandon, "The History of Shock Treatment," in *Electronconvulsive Therapy: An Appraisal*, ed. R. L. Palmer (Oxford: Oxford University Press, 1981), p. 8.

29 Solomon Katzenelbogen, "A Critical Appraisal of the 'Shock Therapies' in the Major Psychoses and Psychoneuroses, III – Convulsive Therapy," *Psychiatry* 3 (1940), pp. 412, 419. See also Kalinowski, Hippius, and Klein, *Biological Treatments in Psychiatry*, pp. 218–19. As they report, "the patient has an amnesia for the convulsion, but unfortunately, he remembers the feeling of deadly fear that he experienced between injection and convulsion. If

no convulsion takes place, anxiety, restlessness, and general discomfort may continue for hours."

30 Berkwitz, "Faradic Shock Treatment," p. 351.

31 L. J. Meduna, "General Discussion of Cardiazol [Metrazol] Therapy," *American Journal of Psychiatry* (Supplement) 94 (1938), p. 50.

32 Burlingame to Adolf Meyer, 1938, Meyer Papers, CAJH I/55/2.

33 S. Cobb, "Review of Neuropsychiatry," *Archives of Internal Medicine* 62 (1938), p. 897.

34 Sakel actually advanced a whole series of "theories" about why his therapy worked over the years, most of them incompatible with each other, none of them grounded in anything more than his fertile imagination. On one occasion, he alleged that neurons were like engines and produced psychotic thought patterns when over-supplied with fuel. Insulin comas, on this account, worked by starving the brain of fuel; on another, that madness was produced by the overactivity of the sympathetic system, and that insulin acted by increasing the "tone" of the parasympathetic system. See M. Sakel, "The Nature and Origin of the Hypoglycaemic Treatment of Psychoses," *American Journal of Psychiatry* (Supplement) 94 (1938), pp. 24–40; idem., "The Classic Sakel Shock Treatment: A Reappraisal," in *The Great Physiodynamic Therapies in Psychiatry: A Reappraisal*, ed. Arthur M. Sackler (New York: Hoeber-Harper, 1956), pp. 13–75.

35 M. Sakel, "The Influence of Pharmacological Shocks on the Psychoses," *Journal of Mental Science* 84 (1938), pp. 626–36. Others claimed cure rates as high as 80 to 90 percent, emulating Cotton's claimed cure rates using defocalization.

36 In 1941, for instance, a national survey reported that 72 percent of 305 public and private mental institutions used

insulin shock therapy. See U.S. Public Health Service, *Shock Therapy Survey* (Washington, D.C.: Government Printing Office, 1941). However, the expense of administering the treatment, and the large demands it made on staff time, meant that most hospitals used the therapy on only a small scale, and largely as a symbolic gesture.

37 State of California, Department of Institutions, *Report for the Governor's Council on Activities During May 1939* (Sacramento: California State Printing Office, 1939), cited in Braslow, *Mental Ills and Bodily Cures*, p. 201, n. 15. The acute care facility, the Langley Porter Neuropsychiatric Institute, was funded and built, though, of course, neither the cures nor the promised savings materialized.

38 H. E. Himwich, F. A. D. Alexander, and B. Lipetz, "Effect of Acute Anoxemia Produced by Breathing Nitrogen on the Course of Schizophrenia," *Proceedings of the Society for Experimental Biology and Medicine* 39 (1938), pp. 367–9.

39 L. J. Meduna, "The Carbon Dioxide Treatment: A Review," p. 236.

40 The standard surveys of the lobotomy episode are Eliot Valenstein, *Great and Desperate Cures: The Rise and Decline of Psychosurgery and Other Radical Treatments for Mental Disorders* (New York: Basic Books, 1986); and Jack Pressman, *Last Resort: Psychosurgery and the Limits of Medicine* (Cambridge: Cambridge University Press, 1998).

41 P. L. Weil, "'Regressive' Electroplexy in Schizophrenics," *Journal of Mental Science* 96 (1950), pp. 514–20. See also W. L. Milligan, "Psychoneuroses Treated with Electrical Convulsions: The Intensive Method," *Lancet* 1 (1946), pp. 516–20; E. A. Tyler, "Polydiurnal Electric Shock Treatment in Mental Disorders," *North Carolina Medical Journal* 8 (1947), pp. 577–82.

42 Weil, "'Regressive' Electroplexy in Schizophrenics," pp. 517, 520.

43 D. E. Cameron, J. G. Lorentz, and M. D. Hancock, "The Depatterning Treatment of Schizophrenics," *Comparative Psychiatry* 3 (1962), pp. 65–7; L. G. Murillo and J. E. Exner, "The Effects of Regressive ECT with Process Schizophrenia," *American Journal of Psychiatry* 130 (1973), pp. 269–73. Cameron's experiments were secretly funded by the CIA, and years later, when this emerged, a major diplomatic incident ensued.

44 Charles Rosenberg, "The Therapeutic Revolution: Medicine, Meaning, and Social Change in Nineteenth Century America," in *The Therapeutic Revolution: Essays in the Social History of American Medicine* eds Charles Rosenberg and Morris Vogel (Philadelphia: University of Pennsylvania Press, 1979), pp. 3–25.

45 Braslow's *Mental Ills and Bodily Cures*, provides an admirable discussion of these phenomena.

46 Pressman, *Last Resort*.

47 See, for example, the comments of the British psychiatrist Clifford Allen: "There is no doubt that with sufficient destruction of the cerebral tissue one can 'cure' any psychosis by replacing it with dementia ... It is obvious that such a patient is more manageable and easier to nurse than one who is violent, shouting, and restlessly psychotic ... Deterioration of the personality always occurs to a greater or lesser degree, and is shown in what may be called 'emotional dementia.' The patient has a diminished judgment, behaves unsuitably, lacks interest, is childish and unselfconscious. His conduct may be careless, filthy, and disgusting, owing to his lack of appreciation of what he should do. He is not the man he was, and has lost much that he had before ... How far it is ethically permissible to mentally maim a patient in order

that he may be nursed more easily is still unsettled." As for treating ambulatory patients, and those in the early stages of their mental illness (something Freeman did and repeatedly urged others to do), "such precipitancy is little less than criminal." "An Examination of Physical Methods of Treatment in Mental Disease," *The Medical Press and Circular*, June 5, 1946, p. 377.

48 Smith Ely Jelliffe to Harry Stack Sullivan, June 1, 1937, Jelliffe Papers, Library of Congress, Washington, D.C.

49 Franklin Ebaugh, one of Meyer's former students, recognized from the outset the problem Meyer's continued presence would represent. In conversation with Alan Gregg, the shrewd director of the Rockefeller Foundation's medical sciences program, he lamented "Adolf Meyer is staying on with a room at the Phipps – this will be hard for Whitehorn" – but Ebaugh's efforts to lure Meyer away to Colorado were unavailing. Alan Gregg, "Diary," September 10, 1941, Rockefeller Foundation Archives, Tarrytown, New York.

50 "Brain Surgery Feat Arouses Sharp Debate," *Baltimore Sun*, November 21, 1936, pp. 1, 9. Years later, when he wrote an account of his life and adventures for his children, each of whom was given a copy, Walter Freeman still vividly recalled that "the reaction of most of the discussors was . . . unfavorable." Walter Freeman, "Autobiography," unpublished typescript, *c.*1970, chapter 14, p. 5. I am most grateful to Freeman's son, Franklin, for arranging to provide me with a copy of this fascinating document.

51 See the discussion of Walter Freeman and James Watts, "Prefrontal Lobotomy in the Treatment of Mental Disorders," *Southern Medical Journal* 30 (1937), pp. 23–31. The published version of the events at the session omits much of the controversy that erupted, including the attempt Dexter Bullard made to shout down Freeman's presentation. A better guide to the hostility Freeman and Watts faced in many quarters is provided in the newspaper account of the session in the *Baltimore Sun*, November 21, 1936, cited above. Freeman's subsequent presentation on "surgery for the soul sick" at the American Medical Association's annual meeting in Atlantic City in June 1937 provoked further hostilities, the *New York Times* noting on this occasion (in an otherwise favorable article) that "some leading neurologists are highly skeptical of it." William L. Laurence, "Surgery on the Soul-Sick: Relief of Obsessions Is Reported," *New York Times*, June 7, 1937, pp. 1, 10.

52 "Find Surgery Aids Mental Cases," *New York Times*, November 26, 1936, p. 10. Freeman had planted a longer and even more favorable story in the Washington *Evening Star* where it appeared on the front page under the byline of Thomas R. Henry, the President of the National Association of Science Writers. Containing pictures of the local heroes, Freeman and Watts, it described the operation as "one of the greatest surgical innovations of this generation . . . [which] seems to establish, among other things, that there is an actual, tangible, physical basis in the brain for various mechanisms of both normal and abnormal personality which can be attacked with the surgeon's knife as easily as can an inflamed appendix or diseased tonsils." "Brain Operation by D.C. doctors Aids Mental Ills," *Evening Star*, November 20, 1936. Watts sent a copy of this piece to his mentor, John Fulton, at Yale, where it is preserved in the Fulton Papers. Freeman's characteristically boastful account of how he stage managed its production a month in advance of the meeting, and collaborated in the writing of the text, is to be found in chapter 4 ("The Fourth Estate") of his

unpublished manuscript, "Adventures in Lobotomy," pp. 7–10. Copies of all but two chapters of this manuscript are held in the Archives of the George Washington University Medical School, Washington, D.C.

53 W. Freeman, "Autobiography," unpublished manuscript, January 1972, chapter 14, p. 5. Like Cotton, incidentally, Freeman had himself had a psychotic episode. His breakdown, however, occurred *before* he adopted his chosen therapeutic panacea. Freeman became manic and delusionary, convinced he was dying of cancer. He subsequently boasted that he avoided a relapse by taking Nembutal nightly for 30 years, substituting an addiction to barbiturates for his previous mental instability.

54 See Freeman to Meyer, November 17, 1937; Meyer to Freeman, November 18, 1937; Freeman to Meyer, March 1, 1938; Meyer to Freeman, March March 2, 1938; Meyer to Freeman, May 25, 1938; Freeman to Meyer, May 25, 1938; Freeman to Meyer, February 3, 1941; Meyer to Freeman, February 4, 1941. Meyer Papers, CAJH I/1256/1.

55 R. G. Gordon to Meyer, April 22, 1949; Charles Hill to Meyer, March 28, 1949. Meyer Papers, CAJH II/137/12.

56 It did ensure, however, a continued reputation across the Atlantic, where the heads of the English profession embraced a similar eclecticism. The influence of the sharp-tongued Aubrey Lewis, once Meyer's student, certainly helped to keep potential critics in line. On Meyer and British psychiatry, see Michael Gelder, "Adolf Meyer and his Influence on British Psychiatry," in *150 Years of British Psychiatry 1841–1991*, ed. Berrios and Freeman, pp. 419–435.

57 See Gerald Grob's only slightly kinder assessment of Meyer, which cites an array of contemporaries making these and similar points. *Mental Illness and American Society*, pp. 116–18. In Grob's words, "That [Meyer] had so few com-petitors within psychiatry [in the first four decades of the twentieth century] reflected the weakness rather than the vitality of the specialty within the United States." A summary of what Meyer meant by "psychobiology" amply illustrates the problem: it was, in the words of his student and Cotton's one-time assistant, Franklin Ebaugh, "a science of personality formation and personality-function, objective and yet reflecting all of man's subjectivity, keeping close to a common ground of generally accessible facts and concepts . . . mental disorders are considered to result from the gradual accumulation of unhealthy reaction tendencies . . . [which requires] the study of all previous experiences of the patient, the total biography of the individual, and the forces he may be reacting to, whether physical, organic, psychogenic, or constitutional." "The Crisis in Psychiatric Education," Chairman's address read before the section on Nervous and Mental Diseases, American Medical Association, New Orleans, May 12, 1932. Copy in the Commonwealth Fund Mental Hygiene Program, Box 17, Folder MH 271, Rockefeller Foundation Archives, Tarrytown, New York. While this Sisyphean task promised to keep practitioners busy on the impossible task of piling up fact on fact, with no criteria of relevance and no means of distinguishing patterns of causation, it was a labor without point, as well as without end.

58 Greenacre to Meyer, January 17, 1928, Meyer Papers, CAJH Series XV.

59 Not that she didn't from time to time voice her displeasure, even early on in her tenure: "Work goes along *very* actively. I miss most frightfully the intensive psychiatric work and I do not know how well I shall be able to reconcile myself to this particular branch of work – necessary and useful

as I recognize it to be." Greenacre to Meyer, April 17, 1928, Meyer Papers, CAJH Series XV.

60 Greenacre to Meyer, December 13, 1930, Meyer Papers, CAJH Series XV.

61 Greenacre to Meyer, September 18, 1931, Meyer Papers, CAJH Series XV.

62 Interviews with Peter Richter, February 4, August 15, 1996; Interview with Phyllis Greenacre, December 22, 1983. Some time after her Cornell appointment, Greenacre informed Ruth Leys, an attempt was made to fire her, and Meyer once more intervened, this time to safeguard her position. Greenacre recalled that when she left Baltimore, Meyer "told her at that time that he had not treated her correctly. She felt that this was true, and that he would therefore do anything for her." Ruth Leys, "Impressions of My Evening with Phyllis Greenacre," unpublished paper, pp. 6–7, quoted by kind permission of the author.

63 Greenacre to the author, March 8, 1985.

64 Greenacre to Meyer, November 21, 1937, Meyer Papers, CAJH Series XVH.

65 Ibid.

66 Meyer to Greenacre, November 22, 1937, Meyer Papers, CAJH Series XV.

67 See, for example, Phyllis Greenacre, *Trauma, Growth, and Personality* (New York: Norton, 1952).

68 Phyllis Greenacre, *Swift and Carroll* (New York: International Universities Press, 1955); idem., *The Quest for the Father: A Study of the Darwin-Butler Controversy as a Contribution to the Understanding of the Creative Individual* (New York: International Universities Press, 1963).

69 Arnold Rogow, *The Psychiatrists* (New York: Putnam, 1970), p. 109.

70 I rely here on accounts provided by Peter Richter and Ruth Leys, which were based upon their conversations with Phyllis Greenacre. Ruth Leys, "Impressions of My Evening with Phyllis Greenacre, 16 June 1982,"

unpublished paper, cited by kind permission of the author; interview with Dr. Peter Richter, February 4, 1996.

71 For a confused and partial account (in more than one sense) of the Zilboorg affair, see John Frosch, "The New York Psychoanalytic Civil War," *American Psychoanalytic Association Journal* 39 (1991), pp. 1051–3. Characteristically, the aftermath of the failure to discipline Zilboorg was one of a whole series of schisms in the New York analytic community.

72 I am grateful to Peter Richter for this information.

73 The dilemmas Greenacre faced as a would-be whistleblower have many analogues today, where to go public with information that threatens to tarnish the carefully cultivated ideological image of how medicine and science are actually practiced is to court personal and professional disaster. David Rothman, for example, provides an instructive account of "The Doctor as Whistle Blower" in his *Strangers at the Bedside*, pp. 70–84. Though the example he focuses on, Henry Beecher, was a senior figure at Harvard Medical School, and chair of its department of anesthesiology, his attempts to draw attention to major ethical violations by other physicians were met with ostracism and attempted humiliation, as well as thinly veiled efforts to censor his findings. The David Baltimore affair, involving charges of misconduct that were directed against a Nobel Prize-winning figure who was then the head of Rockefeller University, is perhaps a more interesting example of the phenomenon. The alleged scientific lapses here were brought to light by a junior female collaborator on the research. Baltimore eventually survived the scandal and became president of the California Institute of Technology, while the whistle blower, Margot O'Toole, saw her career ruined.

A wide-ranging discussion of the case by a major historian of science purported to vindicate Baltimore of the charges. See Daniel Kevles, *The Baltimore Case: A Trial of Politics, Science, and Character* (New York: Norton, 1998). For a highly skeptical critique of Kevles's brief for Baltimore's defense, see the review by C. K. Gansalus in the *New England Journal of Medicine*, January 21, 1999; and for a very different assessment of the whole affair, see Judy Sarasohn, *Science on Trial: The Whistle Blower, The Accused, and the Nobel Laureate* (New York: St. Martin's Press, 1993). For a muckraker's examination of the general phenomenon, see Robert Bell, *Impure Science: Fraud, Compromise, and Political Influence in Scientific Research* (New York: Wiley, 1992). As these instances document, for Phyllis Greenacre silence was almost certainly her only route to professional salvation.

74 Cotton to Meyer, April 29, 1933, Meyer Papers, CAJH I/767/31.

75 "Adolph Cotton is Reported Lost at Sea," *New York Times*, Feburary 9, 1936, p. 1. There were follow-up stories over the next two days, the last one finessing the issue of suicide but quoting a "mysterious remark" by Adolph: one of his fellow passengers had commented, "I suppose you are going to New York as we are all going?" to which he replied, "I don't know about that." *New York Times*, February 10, 1936, p. 19; February 11, 1936, p. 6.

76 This was confirmed by Ferdearle Fischer when I interviewed him in Orange County.

77 Meyer to Raycroft, November 11, 1935, Meyer Papers, CAJH I/3215/4.

78 Meyer to James S. Plant, Feburary 16, 1937. Meyer Papers, CAJH I/768/1.

79 W.M. to Meyer, n.d., Meyer Papers, CAJH I/768/1.

80 Leiby, *Charity and Correction*, p. 235.

81 Ibid., p. 334; "Dr. Henry A. Cotton Dies," *New York Times*, June 22, 1948. The *Times*, in keeping with contemporary taboos about suicide, reported that his death had been "ascribed to an inadvertent overdose of a sleeping powder."

82 His retirement, as of April 15, 1960, was announced in the Trenton State Hospital *Annual Report*, 1960, p. 6.

83 Interview with Dr. Ferdearle Fischer, Leisure World, Laguna Hills, California, February 20, 1984.

84 See T. C. Graves, "Diphasic Vascular Variation in the Treatment of Mental Inefficiency Arising from a Common Somatic Cause," *Journal of Mental Science* 86 (1940), pp. 751–66; and "Symposium on Ear, Nose and Throat Disease in Mental Disorder," *Journal of Mental Science* 87 (1941), pp. 477–528.

85 T. C. Graves, "Penicillin in the Psychoses," *The Medical Press and Circular*, March 13, 1946, pp. 172–8.

86 See John M. Durrie to Professor T. J. Zender-Browne, February 28, 1949, copy in Princeton University Faculty Records, Mudd Library, Princeton University, A-142.

87 The Raycroft Papers in the Mudd Library, Princeton University, A-142, contain copies of the minutes of the New Jersey State Hospital Board of Managers' Minutes for July 21, November 17, 1949 and February 16 and April 20, 1950.

88 Princeton University Faculty Records, Mudd Library, A-142. Raycroft had been appointed to the faculty on June 13, 1911, and had retired on June 15, 1936. The biographical sketch housed at the Mudd Library indicates that he served as a member of the United States Olympic Committee in 1932 and 1936, accompanying the American team on the latter occasion to the infamous Olympic Games in Hitler's Berlin. See also "Obituary," *New York Times*, October 20, 1955.

89 *New York Times*, April 16, 1966, p. 28; April 17, 1966, p. 87.

90 On each occasion, she was assigned a different patient number, so tracing her moral career, to use Erving Goffman's term, requires one to consult Trenton State Hospital, Case Records, Case numbers 26,359; 27,156; 29,775, and 34,871.

91 Joel Braslow (personal communication) has confirmed for me that among his patient sample at Stockton State Hospital in California in this period, the daily dosage of Reserpine (which was soon abandoned as a possible treatment for psychosis in favor of Thorazine, and then later generations of the phenothiazines), ranged from 2.5 to 5 mg.

92 Trenton State Hospital Case Records, Case number 34,871.

93 The 1935 *Annual Report*, for instance, records 528 tonsillectomies and 62 circumcisions (p. 3).

94 Trenton State Hospital *Annual Report*, 1934, p. 5; 1938, p. 5. Insulin coma therapy, camphor, and metrazol were all introduced in 1937–8, though the two latter therapies were rapidly discontinued. Trenton State Hospital *Annual Report*, 1938, pp. 1, 5.

95 In 1935, for instance, more than 1,500 patients were given some form of fever therapy, most getting 10 injections of typhoid vaccine, others 5 or more diathermy treatments, or inoculation with malaria. Trenton State Hospital *Annual Report*, 1935, p. 3. In 1938, "almost all functional cases" received fever therapy. *Annual Report*, 1938, p. 5.

96 Raycroft had sent some of the details of Stone's use of fever therapy to Meyer, who responded that the material "shows a rather aggressive policy ... apparently with remarkably little hazard to the patient. The figures are more moderate in their claims than those of Dr. Cotton, and perhaps somewhat better than the average State Hospital results, which may be due as much to the general atmosphere produced as to the specific procedures employed." Meyer to Raycroft, November 11, 1935, Meyer Papers, CAJH I/3215/4. Raycroft's parallel correspondence with the Rockefeller Institute met with a rather chillier response. See Raycroft to Herbert S. Gasser, November 8, 1935; Gasser to Raycroft, November 9, 13, 1935; Raycroft to Gasser, November 15, 1935, TSH Archives.

97 Rotov, "A History of Trenton State Hospital," p. 57.

98 See, for example, *Trenton Sunday Times Advertiser*, September 26, 1948; Trenton State Hospital *Annual Reports*, 1950, p. 3; 1951, p. 17; 1952, p. 2; 1955, p. 2; 1956, p. 8.

99 The Raycroft Papers in the Mudd Library at Princeton University contain a copy of the minutes of the Trenton State Hospital Board meeting for July 21, 1949, at which, "the Medical Director informed the Board that the performance of lobotomys [*sic*] upon selected patients at the Institution had been authorized by the State Board, and requested that he be authorized to employ Dr. Michael Scott of Temple University for the performance of the same, he to be paid at the rate of $50 a day, the total not to exceed $2,500. Raycroft Papers, A-142, p. 5. The first transorbital lobotomy was performed in November 1949, "on one of our patients who was a problem from a management standpoint. The immediate results were so gratifying that plans were formulated in January 1950 to continue this type of operation on a larger scale." By the end of June, 36 standard or "precision" lobotomies had been performed, together with a further 57 transorbital operations. Trenton State Hospital *Annual Report*, 1950, pp. 12, 21. As this report indicates, the primary goal of the lobotomy program at Trenton was the behavioral

control of the most difficult patients, and success was defined as the reduction of violence and increased manageability of those subjected to the surgery. The *Annual Report* for 1952, for example, reported that "during the past fiscal year, 147 Transorbital Leucotomies were followed through with gratifying results" (p. 3.). In 1956, the total was 49. *Annual Report*, 1956, p. 9. But by the following year, it had fallen to 11: 6 women and 5 men. *Annual Report*, 1957, p. 16.

100 He lamented, towards the close of his career, that even with the introduction of the transorbital lobotomy, "the 20,000 lobotomies done in this country to date are a small proportion of the 600,000 patients in mental hospitals" – most of whom, presumably, might once have benefited from his favorite operation. Walter Freeman, "Adventures in Lobotomy," unpublished manuscript, copy in George Washington University Medical Library, Psychosurgery Collection, chapter 6, p. 26.

101 Freeman delighted to perform demonstrations to show off his new technique. In July 1950, for example, he was invited to deliver the McGhie Lecture for the following year at the University of Western Ontario, and was delighted when his hosts asked for "an actual demonstration of a transorbital lobotomy." He hastened to offer far more than that: "I hope you have a sufficient number of patients to make things interesting for your staff. Ten operations is a fairly good number and I have done as many as twenty-one in an afternoon with time out for lunch. This requires a fair amount of teamwork. I shall bring instruments so that the two sets can be sterilized alternating, and will require a hammer ... I trust one or more of the capable staff will be interested in doing a few operations under my direction. Since transorbital lobotomy is a closed operation and has no exposed operative wound, you may reassure the operating room nurse that gowns, masks, and gloves are not necessary for the operator or for the audience. Some of the operations might be done under local anesthesia if the patients are cooperative ... but I have recently found an additional reason for using electroshock; namely, that it increases the speed of coagulation of the blood." In a previous letter, he had specified the sorts of patients he had in mind: "I would prefer a most violent schizophrenic and the most agitated involutional, but if you do have a completely helpless obsessional or anxiety state of long duration, that patient might be good for demonstration of transorbital lobotomy under local anesthesia. Otherwise, I expect to employ electroshock to produce the few moments of coma necessary for the operation." George H. Stevenson to Walter Freeman, July 28, 1950; Freeman to Stevenson, December 12, 1950; January 3, 1951. Psychosurgery Collection, George Washington University Medical School. Some months after Freeman had performed the surgeries, Stevenson informed him that they had done little good: "I am afraid there is very little to report about the patients on whom you operated when you were here. Our four schizophrenic patients are much the same. The coloured girl, X, has relapsed to her former mute condition. Y is rather acutely disturbed much of the time. Z continues on our convalescent ward and I think she has shown definite somatic improvement." Regrettably, he added, "our Head Office does not give us any encouragement to do transorbital lobotomies so long as Dr. McKenzie can do a reasonable number of standard lobotomies for us." A later report was, if anything, still more negative. Stevenson to

Freeman, April 4, 1951; January 29, 1952. Psychosurgery Collection, George Washington University.

102 On occasion, not even this much instruction was required: "I learned with some astonishment," the not easily astonished Freeman recorded, after a visit to the State Hospital at Evanston, Wyoming, in the summer of 1951, that "Dr. J. S. Walen had used transorbital lobotomy in nearly 200 cases, just from reading the published reports and working out what should be done." Another disciple, Dr. Paul Schrader at the State Hospital Number 4 in Farmington, Missouri, had performed more than 200 lobotomies, and "all but solved the problems of the disturbed ward at that particular hospital." Clearly, some first-hand instruction by the master was desirable before such extensive replication was attempted, but it could be quite slight: another former student of Freeman's, Dr. Harry Elder, brought in a patient for Freeman to demonstrate on, and then did 101 all by himself at the Sacramento State Hospital in California, including some re-operations on patients Freeman had previously treated without success. W. Freeman, "Adventures in Lobotomy," chapter 6, pp. 18–19.

103 Walter Freeman, "Adventures in Lobotomy," chapter 6, p. 59.

104 Just how quickly the operation could be performed is outlined in a report Freeman sent to lobotomy's inventor, Egas Moniz, in 1952. Freeman had collected patients from West Virginia's three state mental hospitals. "I began operating by the transorbital route on July 18, and when the study was closed on August 7 the total number of operations was 228. Only twelve days were devoted to operating . . . I mention this matter to reveal how mass surgery can

be carried out against a background of shortages of everything except patients . . . I followed the technic developed over the past year and more, first making the patient unconscious with electric convulsive shocks, usually three at intervals of two minutes . . . On one occasion when the team was working to perfection I routinely administered two shocks and then proceeded immediately with operation. Upon this day I operated upon 22 patients in a total of 135 minutes, about six minutes per operation . . . When the patient had stopped convulsing I had the nurse hold a towel firmly over the nose and mouth of the patient. I then elevated the eyelid and inserted the point of the instrument into the superior conjunctive sac, being careful not to touch the skin with the point. I felt for the vault of the orbit, about 3cm. from the midline and then aimed the shaft of the instrument parallel with the bony ridge of the nose. I drove the point of the instrument through the orbital plate to a depth of 5cm. . . . When the instrument was thus in place on one side I inserted the other instrument in the same fashion on the other side. This maneuver not only makes for greater symmetry in the lesions, but also prevents the frontal lobes from moving laterally with the moving of the instruments. It also hastens the operation." Sweeping motions with the two instruments then sliced through sections of the patient's brain. Freeman to Moniz, September 9, 1952, Psychosurgery Collection, George Washington University.

105 Trenton State Hospital *Annual Report,* 1958, p. 8.

106 The prize was first given in 1951, funded by Delha Cotton's donation of $5,000. See Trenton State Hospital *Annual Report,* 1951, p. 37.

Index

abdominal surgery 9, 49–50, 52, 53, 55, 58, 71, 84, 90, 102, 120, 127, 170, 201–2, 212, 249, 250; abandonment of at Trenton 256, 257, 259, 269, 296; and women 309*n*90, 314*n*30

Adams, W. S. 227

Aiken, Thomas B. 62

Alienists 29; *see also* psychiatry

Allen, Clifford 342*n*47

Alzheimer, Alois 23, 24, 66, 271

Alzheimer's disease 24

American Academy of Applied Dental Science 61

American Association for the Study of the Feeble-Minded 127

American Journal of Psychiatry 88, 92, 101, 103, 125, 271, 275, 277, 284

American Medical Association 32, 62, 68, 69, 275

American Medico-Psychological Association 20, 29, 69, 94, 98, 99

American Mercury, The 266, 270

American Neurological Association 101, 234

American Psychiatric Association xi, 20, 52, 62, 68, 102, 108, 122, 125, 284

American Psychopathological Association 235

antisepsis 28

Archives of Neurology and Psychiatry 64, 65, 101, 106

Arkansas State Hospital 92

arthritis 31, 36

aseptic Meningitis 279, 338*n*9

Association of American Physicians 32

asylum superintendencies 317*n*9

Atchley, Samuel 1–3, 6, 19

Baber, Armitage 93

Backes, Theodore 9

bacteriology 28, 31, 34, 45, 51, 57, 90, 96, 104–5, 227, 230, 232

Bailey, Pearce 87

Baillie, D. M. 198, 212

Baltimore 138–9, 286

Baltimore Sun 286

barbiturates 317*n*41, 344*n*53

Barker, Llewellys 33, 36, 124, 230

Barrett, Albert 68, 94, 125

Battle Creek Sanitarium 35, 36, 82, 83, 84, 85, 212, 275

Beers, Clifford 60

Bernard, Helen 176

Bethlem Hospital 121

Billings, Frank: and Cotton 78; and focal sepsis 32–3, 36, 230

Billings, John Shaw 139

Bini, Lucio 283

biochemistry 45

biological reductionism xi, 63

biology: and mental illness xii, 25–6, 29, 30, 63, 66, 73, 75, 79, 91, 112, 120, 226–7, 279, 299

blood, malarial 280, 339*m*17–18; tests 84

Bloom, Leah 5, 6, 8, 177, 178

Bloomingdale Asylum 83, 125, 154, 188, 267

Blumer, G. Alder 29

Bond, Hubert 222

Boston Psychopathic Hospital 125

Boutroux, Emile 65

brain anoxia 283

Braslow, Joel 86, 88

Bright, William 1, 3, 6, 8, 174, 175, 176

Bright Committee 1, 3, 4, 5, 8, 9, 10, 174, 175, 181, 184–6, 187, 188, 203, 208, 250, 266

Bright's disease 7, 8

Brill, A. A. 92

British Medical Association 222, 225, 229, 233, 236

British Medical Journal 236

British Neurological Association 234

British psychiatry 109

Brooklyn State Hospital 92

Brown, Sanger 235

Bruce, Lewis 37

Brush, Edward 91–2, 95, 101, 125, 314*m*19

Burlingame, Charles 282, 340*n*26

Butler Asylum 29

Byberry State Hospital 242

Cameron, D. Ewen 284, 342*n*43

Campbell, Macfie 125

camphor 281, 299, 341*n*27

Canadian Medical Association 212

carbon dioxide 283

Carroll, R. S. 279

castration 55, 185

Cerletti, Ugo 283

cervix: enucleation of 84, 95, 100, 105, 185, 245, 247, 248, 255, 257, 262; and infection 54, 55, 83, 117; *see also* gynecological surgery

Charcot, J. M. 225, 328*m*

Charles Private Hospital 9, 85, 176, 241, 250, 251, 254, 260, 277

Cheney, Clarence 90, 95, 96, 98, 101, 103, 104, 106, 232

Chicago 133–4, 137

children: and focal sepsis 57, 58, 247–8; and surgery 58

chilling the body 280

cholera 28

Christian Science 62–3

CIA and regressive ECT 342*n*43

Clare, Harvey 93

Clark, William 7

Cleveland State Hospital 37

Cobb, Stanley 282, 283

Colax 84, 313*m*13

colectomies 51, 54, 55, 56, 59, 95, 100, 102, 105–6, 125, 128, 129, 163, 169, 186, 201, 205–6, 215, 230, 248, 249, 252, 256, 257, 260–61, 262, 263, 265, 266, 268, 296

colloidal calcium 280, 339*m*9

colon: developmental reconstruction of 52, 53, 163

colon bacillus 84

colonic irrigation 218, 227, 245, 246, 247, 249, 255–6, 257, 296

Columbia University 50, 253

community care 15, 296

Conklin, Edwin G. 79

consent: absence of 55, 56, 64, 185, 276, 277, 333*m*13

constipation: as cause of mental illness 84, 90, 105; as indication for surgery 52, 57, 83, 248, 256

Copeland, Royal 76, 186–7, 275

Copp, Owen 94

Corman, Dr. 220–21

Corman, Miss 217, 220–21

Cornell University 39, 41, 288

Costill, Henry 69, 185

Cotton, Adolph Meyer 27, 109; abdominal surgery on 58, 206; and Adolf Meyer 253, 317n3; career plans 253, 291; removal of teeth 57, 205, 248; suicide 291, 292, 346n75

Cotton, Henry xi; anniversary of appointment at Trenton 235, 241; appointment to Trenton 19, 24; and Bright Committee 1–4, 10, 175, 176, 178, 179, 188–9, 235; and Charles Private Hospital 9, 85, 176, 241, 250, 251, 254, 260; criticisms of 75, 79–80, 88–9, 90–92, 95–6, 97, 98–9, 101, 102, 103, 104, 105–7, 123–5, 176–9, 197, 232–3, 235–6, 262–6, 269–70, 276; death of 270, 271, 336n61; early training 19, 24, 285–6; and Edinburgh meeting 222, 225, 229–33; and focal sepsis 36, 37–8, 45–9, 50, 56, 63, 66–70, 88, 96, 112, 114–19, 126–7, 178–9, 245–9, 250, 252, 269–70, 274, 305n25; and Freudian theories 58, 62, 63, 118; and Germany 23–4, 117, 122; and T. C. Graves 109, 112, 226–9; and Phyllis Greenacre 153–4, 157–8, 161, 163, 164, 175, 188–91, 192–6, 206–7, 208–24, 236, 249, 267; and heredity 63, 118; and laboratory 30, 73, 91, 95, 252; and Burdette Lewis 39, 41, 61, 178, 293; in London 113–14, 225, 234, 273; loss of superintendency 250–52, 256–9; and H. L. Mencken 266, 267, 335n58; mental breakdown of 1–4, 6, 7, 10, 179, 184, 185, 188, 189, 190, 235, 266; and Adolf Meyer 20, 22, 23, 27, 38, 39, 43, 56, 64–5, 66, 67–8, 80, 88, 96, 100, 163, 175, 184, 188–91, 192–6, 203–9, 212, 213–23, 241, 249, 251–2, 267–8, 271–2, 277, 335n45; and Norway 225, 234; in Paris 225; and patients' families 8, 81,

256; personality 108; and Princeton University 65–7; and private patients 9, 81–6, 236, 241, 250–51, 258, 275, 276–7, 294; and publicity 61, 62, 63, 64, 65, 66, 67, 70–71, 80, 97, 100, 126, 293–4, 335n56; and reform of Trenton State Hospital 24–6, 27; support for 75, 76–9, 80, 93–4, 95, 119–121, 123, 212, 225, 230–31, 232, 233, 235, 236, 241, 274–5, 278; and surgery 9, 50–51, 52, 53, 54, 55, 56–7, 58, 72, 73, 118, 125–6, 176, 249, 250, 252, 256, 258, 259, 260–62, 266–7, 277–8, 333n4; and Worcester State Hospital 20, 22, 102, 271

Cotton, Henry Jr.: birth 24; and brother's suicide 291; and Johns Hopkins University 253, 291; and Adolf Meyer 253, 291–2; psychiatric career 291–2; removal of teeth, 58, 205, 248; suicide 292, 346n81

Cotton, Mrs. Henry (Alice Delha Keyes): 22, 192, 196, 203–6, 207, 221, 252, 270, 271; and Cotton Award for Kindess 198–9; and Phyllis Greenacre 205, 327n5; sacrifice of teeth 205, 248; 311n118; and suicide of Adolph Meyer Cotton 292; and surgery 205–6, 311n118

Cotton Award for Kindness 298, 299, 349n106

Court of Chancery 9

Cowles, Edward 21

Crick, Francis 65

cure rates at Trenton 52, 53, 67, 71, 91, 92, 93, 99, 106, 118, 122, 123, 175, 207, 259, 278, 318n28; doubts about, 200, 201; Frankel's reassessment of 263–5

cyanide injections 280, 340n23

Dain, Norman 60

Danvers State Hospital 19, 24, 77

Darrow, Clarence 310n115

Dayton State Hospital 93, 267
De Lisi, L. 87
degeneration 18, 21, 29, 30, 42, 59, 63, 81, 109, 121, 303*n*11
delusions 30, 50, 86, 174
dementia 30, 53, 102
dementia praecox *see* schizophrenia
depression xi, 30, 55, 86, 169, 247, 262; and Greenacre family 136, 141
Diagnostic and Statistical Manual of Mental Disorders xi
diathermy 248, 249, 280
dietary reform 82, 85
Dikemark Asylum 234
diphtheria 28, 72
Dix, Dorothea 16, 68, 70, 164
Dodson, Dean 135, 136
double-blind experiments 314*n*33
Draper, John W. 41, 50, 51, 52, 53, 78, 84, 106, 259, 271
Dudley, Emelius 186

Ebaugh, Franklin 275, 337*n*4, 343*n*49
Edinburgh Royal Infirmary 112
Edinburgh University 233
Edmunds, James 8
Ehrlich, Paul 56, 72
electric shocks 87, 279
Electro-Convulsive Therapy (ECT) 284, 285, 295, 297, 299
Ellis, William John 197, 216, 221, 333*n*3
Epilepsy: and schizophrenia 282, 283; and sepsis 228
Erikson, Erik 290
Erysipelas 280, 338*m*3
ethics, medical 337*n*5
eugenics 30, 59, 69, 70, 82
experts and their clients 276, 278
experimentation on patients 278, 283, 287, 295, 337*n*5; at Trenton 14, 95, 97, 174, 176, 202, 235, 241, 274, 276, 277, 278, 286, 294, 295–7

Fairbank, Ruth 141, 145, 325*m*0
Fall, Albert 69
Farrar, Clarence 26, 27, 51, 275, 301*n*31, 302*n*41, 311*m*18, 336*n*3
Fernald, Henry J. 100, 101
fever therapy 86–8, 297, 339*n*21, 347*n*96
Fields, Grace 9
First International Congress on Racial Betterment 83
First World War 42, 82, 87, 109, 279
Fischer, Ferdearle x, 38, 100, 256, 292, 294, 298, 311*m*18
Fisher, Irving 81, 82, 83, 84, 85
Fisher, Margaret 81, 82, 83, 84, 85
Fletcher, Horace 34
Florence B. 51
focal sepsis: British views of 108, 111–13, 117–18, 122–3, 225–9, 230–33, 236–7, 274–5, 293, 319*n*48; Canadian interest in 198; and children 127–9; and crime and delinquency 57, 65, 66; and dental profession 48–9; and John Harvey Kellogg 83; and medicine 31, 32, 33, 34, 36, 274; and mental illness 37, 38, 43–4, 45, 50–51, 54, 55–6, 59, 66–7, 69, 70–71, 78, 80, 83, 90–91, 98, 106–7, 114–19, 228–9, 274–5, 276, 289; and Norway 234; savings from eliminating 73, 186, 307*m*1
Foscarini, E. 87
Frankel, Emil 262–6, 308*n*63, 320*n*66, 334*n*36
Freeman, Walter 286, 287, 297, 343*n*50–52, 344*n*53, 348*m*100–01, 349*m*02, 349*m*04
Freud, Anna 290
Freud, Sigmund xi, 62, 76, 86, 87, 89, 273, 287, 338*m*0
Freudian theories *see* psychoanalysis
frontal lobes 286, 287, 297
functional mental illness 78, 118, 319*n*32

Garvin, William C. 77

gender: and Johns Hopkins 140, 141; and surgery at Trenton 54, 126

General Paralysis of the Insane 24, 30, 44, 56, 86, 91, 339*n*17; *see also* syphilis

Geraghty, John 178

germ theory of disease 17, 19, 66, 86

German medicine 23

Gill, Dr. 251

Gjessing, Rolf 218, 234, 329*n*36

Glueck, Bernard 95

Goodall, Edwin 121, 222, 319*n*44, 334*m*7

Gordon, R. S. 287

Gosline, Howard 94, 106

Graby, Henry 177

Graham, Sylvester 34, 36

Graves, Frederick x, 317*n*6

Graves, John 317*n*6

Graves, Thomas Chivers x, 109–12, 117, 123, 226–9, 231, 232, 237, 275, 292–3, 317*n*6, 318*m*1, 339*m*9

Graves, Valerie x, 318*m*1

Great Depression 251

Greenacre, Isaiah 133–4, 135

Greenacre, Phyllis x; at Cornell 288, 345*n*62; and Delha Cotton 207–8, 327*n*5; and Henry Cotton 153–4, 157–8, 161, 163–74, 192–6, 203–10, 212–23, 236, 288; depression 143, 145, 155, 156, 169, 238, 239, 288, 289, 290; divorce 238–41; early life 133–5, 320*n*2–3; Johns Hopkins career 151, 152–3, 156, 157, 239, 321*n*4, 325*n*8; last years 291; marriage 321*m*6, 322*n*26; and Adolf Meyer 135–6, 142–3, 144–5, 153, 154–5, 156–7, 167–8, 181–3, 192–6, 236–41, 288, 323*n*46, 325*m*0, 330*m*14, 331*m*8–19, 337*n*4, 344*n*62; and psychoanalysis 239, 290, 291; and Curt Richter 143–5, 146, 148, 149, 151, 152, 155, 156, 238–41, 332*n*27; and therapeutic enthusiasm 289; and Trenton study 161, 163,

164–74, 181–3, 184, 190–93, 196, 197, 198–202, 203–23, 263, 289–90, 323*n*14, 326*n*24, 326*n*35; at White Plains 239, 288, 344*n*59; and Gregory Zilboorg 290–91

Gregg, Alan 343*n*49

Greystone Park State Asylum 196

Griesinger, Wilhelm 23

Grob, Gerald 344*n*57

gynecological surgery: in Canada 124; at Trenton 54, 55, 201, 262

Hall, J. K. 89, 90

hallucinations 82, 86, 172, 244

Harding, Warren 69

Harlem Valley State Hospital 340*n*24–25

Hartmann, Heinz 290

Harvard University 253, 282

Hastings, T. W. 41

Hayes, William 16, 18

Healy, David xi

Henderson, D. K. 232, 233, 234

heredity: and mental illness 59, 63, 118, 266, 319*n*29

Hereford County Asylum 109

Hill, Charles 20, 21, 301*n*20

Hill, Frank 10

Himwich, Harold 283

Hinkle, Beatrice 239, 288

Hippocrates 276

history and memory 274

Hobbs, A. T. 123,

Hoch, August 63, 64, 65

Hollymoor Hospital 109, 227, 293

Homewood Sanitarium 124

Hoover, Herbert 69

Hot Springs, Arkansas 190

Howell, Joel 33

Hubble, Edwin 65

Hulfish, Mrs. M. A. 336*n*61

Hunter, William 37, 112, 117, 212, 222, 225–6, 229, 230, 231, 232, 233, 237

Hurd, Henry 19, 140
Hurwitz, Martha 241–5, 294–6
Hutchings, Richard 79, 80
hydrotherapy 82, 85, 227, 297

Idylease Inn 78
Indiana Board of State Charities 77
Institute of Living 282
Institute of Psychiatry ix
insulin shock 280–81, 282, 283, 295, 299, 341*n*34–36; and cost savings 283; description of 340*n*26
intestinal pathology: and psychiatry 52
intestinal stasis 32, 34, 85, 128, 248, 255, 259

Jacobson, Edith 239
Jamesburg State Home for Boys 57, 127
Jelliffe, Smith Ely 65, 102, 123, 143, 286, 316*m*5
Johns Hopkins University 10, 19, 26, 33, 39, 70, 124, 133, 135, 136, 139, 140–41, 150–51, 207, 239–41, 252–3
Journal of Dental Research 61
Journal of Mental Science 122, 124
Journal of Nervous and Mental Disease 65, 286, 316*m*5
juvenile delinquency: and focal sepsis 57

Kankakee State Hospital 20
Katzenelbogen, Solomon 253–7, 281
Kaufmann, Fritz 87
Kellogg, John Harvey 34, 35, 36, 82, 83, 84, 85, 212, 275, 327*n*23
Kempf, Edward J. 162
Kilbourne, Arthur 94
King's Park State Hospital 77
Kirby, George 64, 90, 102–3, 104, 105–6, 232, 276, 317*n*41
Kirk, C. C. 77, 92
Knight, Augustus 196–7
Koch, Robert 25, 87

Kopeloff, Nicholas 90, 95, 96, 98, 101, 102, 103, 104, 105–6, 232, 236–7, 276
Kraepelin, Emil x, 23, 44, 66, 103, 118, 163, 271, 302*n*32, 324*m*1

laboratory: and psychiatry 30–31, 50, 51
Lancet 112, 279
Lane, Sir Arbuthnot 34, 126, 245, 259, 305*n*28
Lane's operation 126, 201, 245, 259–60, 262, 264, 320*n*66
laparotomy 50, 51, 62, 83, 169, 256, 309*n*73
lay opinion 75, 76, 93, 99, 100
Leedom, Detective 4
Leisure World 292
Leopold and Loeb case 58
Lewis, Aubrey 344*n*56
Lewis, Burdette 39, 41, 57, 64, 70–71, 74, 75, 76, 78, 81, 88, 99, 100, 127, 159, 174–5, 178, 293–4, 315*m*3
Leys, Ruth 325*n*8
Lister, Lord 25, 28, 34, 112, 229, 230, 231, 278
Literary Digest 64
Llewellyn, Mrs. 55
lobotomy 284, 285, 295, 297, 343*n*50, 343*n*52; contemporary criticism of 342*n*47, 343*n*51; at Trenton 347*n*99
lockjaw *see* Tetanus
Ludwig, Anna 171–2
Lynch, Jerome 41, 50, 51, 105

mad-doctors 14, 276
madhouses 13–14, 81
Magee, Harold 243, 293, 295, 297, 298
malaria 28, 87, 228, 255, 280, 299, 317*n*41, 338*m*6, 339*m*7–19
Manhattan State Hospital 104
mania 86, 280
manic-depressive psychosis 44, 50, 53, 78, 106, 119, 123, 125, 255, 263, 264, 265

Mann, Thomas 65
Mapperly Hospital 284
Marx, Karl 274
masturbation 129
Maudsley, Henry 37, 59, 120
Maudsley Hospital 120
Mayo, Charles 33, 78, 230
Mayo, Will 33
Mayo Clinic 33, 36, 50, 78
McClellan, H. H. 267
McCormick, Katherine Dexter 161, 162, 324*n*
McCormick, Stanley 161, 162, 180, 324*n*
McGregor, Mrs. 217
McLean Asylum 21, 161, 280, 286
mechanical restraint 25, 71, 74–5
Mecray, Paul 160, 251, 296, 333*n*4, 335*n*56
Medical Press and Circular 293
Medical Society of London 113, 114
Medicine: humoral 284; status of 28, 64, 66, 97–8
Medico-Psychological Association of Great Britain and Ireland 108, 112, 113, 222, 225, 233; *see also* Royal Medico-Psychological Association
Meduna, Ladislaus 281
Mencken, H. L. 266, 267, 335*n*58
mental hygiene 42, 59, 66
mental illness: and heredity 29, 30, 43, 81
mental patients: in Nazi Germany 303*n*3; vulnerability of 277–8
Metchnikoff, Elie 34
metrazol 281–2, 299, 341*n*29
Meyer, Adolf 10, 14, 21, 165; and Adolph Meyer Cotton 317*n*3; and Delha Cotton 191, 196, 203–8; and Henry Cotton 20, 22, 23, 27, 38, 39, 43, 56, 64–5, 67–8, 80, 88, 98, 99, 100, 102, 157–8, 163, 168, 181–3, 184, 189–90, 192–6, 198, 203, 206–9, 212–13, 236–7, 241, 251–2, 253, 267–8, 269–70, 277, 335*n*45, 336*n*61; and Henry Cotton Jr.

253; early training 20; and Edinburgh meeting 222, 223, 234, 236, 277; and Phyllis Greenacre 135–6, 142–3, 144, 145, 154–5, 156–7, 158, 167–8, 181–3, 184, 190, 192–6, 206–7, 212–14, 216, 217–18, 219–23, 238, 239–41, 254, 277, 330*n*4, 331*n*8–19, 332*n*27; and D. K. Henderson 232, 236–7; and Johns Hopkins University 27, 146–8, 239–40, 252–3, 286, 322*n*29; and Solomon Katzenelbogen 253–4, 277; and George Kirby 90, 102–3; and Nicholas Kopeloff 236–7; and lobotomy 286, 287; and Stanley McCormick 160, 161, 162, 180, 324*n*; and mental hygiene 59–60; obituary of Cotton 271–2, 277; professional standing 287, 344*n*56–57; and psychoanalysis 330*n*17; and retirement 286, 287; and Curt Richter 143–4, 146, 147, 148–9, 151, 155–6, 238–41, 331*n*21; and scandal 183, 184, 188, 277; tooth abscess of 217, 218; and Trenton study 157, 158, 160, 161, 162, 163, 192–6, 197–8, 199, 203–12, 213, 214, 215–24, 238–9, 277, 332*n*29; trip to Britain 220, 222; and John B. Watson 146–7, 150–51, 239, 240; at Worcester State Hospital 20, 21–2
Meyer, Hermann 168, 238
Meyerian psychiatry 288
Michigan Psychopathic Hospital 68, 312*n*29
Milledgeville State Hospital 62, 93
Mills, C. K. 125
Mitchell, Charles 5, 8
Mitchell, Henry 17
Mitchell, Silas Weir 24
Moniz, Egas 284, 286, 349*n*04
Moore, J. W. 31
Morgan, Thomas Hunt 65
Morris, Robert T. 75
Morse sign wave 249

mortality rates at Trenton 51, 52, 53, 64, 72, 95, 119, 126, 127, 163, 168–9, 177, 215, 249, 276, 278, 309*n*78, 334*n*36; claimed improvement of 258–61, 262, 268–9; criticism of 102, 200–01, 202, 256, 257, 259, 262–6; Frankel's data 263–5; manipulation of 185–6
Mott, Sir Frederick 120, 317*n*5, 319*n*48, 338*m*5
Mount Hope Retreat 20
Moynihan, Sir Berkeley 34, 222, 230, 231, 232, 233, 237, 305*n*29
multiple sclerosis: and focal sepsis 56

National Committee for Mental Hygiene 41, 60, 125, 194–5, 275
National Institute of Mental Health 278
nephritis 31
nervous breakdown 78
neurasthenia 78, 275
Neurological Association 61
New Health Society 34
New Jersey State Board of Charities and Corrections 64
New Jersey State Medical Society 61, 69, 251
New York Hospital 33
New York Medical Journal 61
New York Psychiatric Institute 22, 63, 90, 102, 103, 105, 316*n*20
New York Psychoanalytic Institute 290
New York Psychoanalytic Society 290
New York State Medical Society 61
New York State Pathological Institute *see* New York Psychiatric Institute
New York Times 1, 176, 186, 287, 294
New York University 253, 287
New York World 181
Newark Evening News 187
Nissl, Franz 23, 24
nitrogen 283
Nobel Prize in medicine 284

Noguchi, Hideyo 31
Norris, Stella 169
Norristown State Hospital 62

Oliver, John 76
Oppenheimer, Robert 65
Osler, William 33
Overholser, Winfred 339*m*8, 339*n*21
Oxford University Press 67

P., Mrs Florence 336*n*3
Palo Alto Veterans' Hospital 78
paraldehyde 165
paranoia 92, 119, 123
Parent, Edward 8
Parent, Mrs. 177
paresis *see* General Paralysis of the Insane
Pargeter, William 14
Pasteur, Louis 25, 28
Pasteur Institute 34
Paton, Stewart 19, 36, 39, 60, 65, 66, 68, 69–70, 79, 275
Pauling, Linus 65
penicillin 293
Pennsylvania Hospital 33, 101; Nervous and Mental Disease Department of 94
pericolic membranotomies *see* Lane's operation
peritonitis 52, 169, 215, 259, 260, 265
Phillips, Georgiana 4–5, 9
Phillips, Porter 121
Phipps Clinic 135, 142, 147, 150, 151, 154, 156, 165, 239, 254, 267, 286, 343*n*49
Pickworth, F. A. 227
Pinel, Philippe 78, 328*m*
Powell, Clifford 185
Pressman, Jack 285
Princeton University 7, 65, 66, 70, 127, 187, 206, 242, 253, 293, 346*n*88
Princeton University Press 67
professional ethics 64, 97, 98, 99, 276–7

Progressive era 74, 82
prohibition 82, 122
prophylaxis 46–7, 49, 57, 58, 60, 127–8, 247–8
Prozac xi
Psychiatric Bulletin 64
psychiatric nosology 23–4
psychiatry: and the body 278; relations with medicine 21, 42, 226–7, 229; status of 28, 113, 141, 147
psychoanalysis 55, 58–9, 62, 63, 89, 118, 147, 273, 290–91
psychobiology 27, 146, 147, 239–40, 331*n*20, 344*n*57
psychodynamic psychiatry 109
psychoneuroses 123, 280
psychopharmaceutical industry xii
psychosurgery 285
public health 75, 76

Quackenbush case 175
quinine 87

Rahway Prison 57, 58, 127
rat-bite fever 280
Raycroft, Joseph: and the Bright Committee 181–3, 184, 185–6, 187, 188; and Henry Cotton 211–12, 221, 241, 242, 258, 269, 333*n*14, 335*n*56; and Henry Cotton's breakdown 7, 10; later years and death 293; and Adolf Meyer 196; 208–9, 210–11, 212, 213, 215–16, 218, 219, 220, 241, 251, 332*n*29; and Princeton 242, 346*n*88; and Trenton study 157, 159, 160, 166, 218, 222, 332*n*29
Rayner, Rosalie 149, 150, 322*n*35
Reed, Dorothy 140, 153
regressive ECT 284
Rehfuss method 50, 104
Reserpine 295–6, 347*n*91
Review of Reviews 70, 74, 80, 88, 100

rheumatic fever 31
Rhode Island State Hospital 94, 106
Richards, Esther 141, 157, 183, 325*m*10
Richter, Curt 143–4, 146, 147, 148–9, 151, 155–6, 238–41, 331*n*20–21, 332*n*26–7
Richter, Peter x, 288
Riven Rock 161, 180
Robertson, George 112, 233
Robertson, White 225
Rochester State Hospital 94
Rogers, Annie 9
Rogow, Arnold 290
Rolleston, Sir Humphry 122
Röntgen Rays *see* X-rays
Rosenberg, Charles 284
Rosenoff, Aaron 283
Rosenow, Edward 33, 36
Ross, Bessie 177–8
Rothman, David 337*n*5
Royal College of Physicians 122
Royal College of Surgeons 231
Royal Medico-Psychological Association 229, 275, 287, 292–3; *see also* Medico-Psychological Association of Great Britain and Ireland
Royal Society of Medicine 233
Rubery Hill Mental Hospital x, 109, 226
Rue, Mrs. 163, 166, 167, 199, 207
Rush, Benjamin 78
Russell, William 288

Sabin, Florence 140
Sakel, Manfred 281, 282, 283, 340*n*24–5
Salpêtrière 225, 328*m*
Salvarsan 31, 56, 72, 73, 306*n*43
San Quentin Prison 80
sanitariums 81
Santa Barbara earthquake 180
scarlet fever 87
schizophrenia xi, 44, 50, 78, 83, 90, 92, 106, 123, 125, 162, 180, 239, 242, 243, 263, 264, 268, 283, 285

Schumann, Elsie 56
Schumpeter, Joseph 82
science and mental illness 72, 75, 76, 77, 86, 227
Scott, Michael 297, 347*n*99
septic heredity 228
septic psychosis 230, 232, 233, 242, 243, 254
serums *see* vaccines
Seventh Day Adventists 36
Shaftesbury, Lord 13
Shaw, Albert 70, 74, 75, 78, 80, 88
shell-shock 41–2, 87, 109, 279
Sheppard and Enoch Pratt Hospital 19
Shorter, Edward 273, 285, 302*n*41, 336*n*3
Silzer, Governor 174
sinuses, infected 66, 100, 117, 227, 228, 230, 245, 247, 255
Sleber, Iola 8
Smith, Gertrude 9
somatic therapies 278, 286
Southern Medical Society 286
Spitzka, Edward 21
spleens 100, 201, 262
Spradley, J. B. 243
Squibb Company 50
St. Bartholomew's Hospital 41
St. Elizabeth's Hospital 89, 339*n*17–18, 339*n*21
Stanford University 32
sterilization 30, 69, 303*n*12
Stevens, Alice 171–2
Stewart, George 82
stigma: and mental illness 81–2, 86
Stokes, Governor 19
stomach: dispensability of 54; infection and 66, 71, 84, 100, 117, 230, 262
Stone, Robert 5, 9, 58, 84, 170, 216, 218, 220, 222, 228, 251, 256, 258, 296–7, 347*n*96
Strecker, Edward 101, 102, 106–7
streptococcus 84, 87, 169

Striefler, William 41
Strong, Edith 176, 177, 178, 181
surgical bacteriology 43, 49, 54, 66–7, 78, 86, 236, 274, 305*n*27
Swint, Roger 93
syphilis 30, 31, 56, 72, 73, 86, 88, 153, 158, 228, 255, 280, 285, 304*n*14, 338*n*15

Tabes dorsalis 24
Teapot Dome scandal 69
teeth: extraction of 37, 38, 46–9, 67–8, 79, 90, 100, 105, 212, 229, 232, 243, 244, 246, 247, 248, 252, 256, 257, 261–2, 275, 292, 297; extracted without anesthetic 228; infected 66, 84, 86, 88, 90, 117, 228, 229, 230, 268, 315*n*10
tetanus 28, 31
therapeutics 10, 20, 59
Thompson, Julia 169
Thorazine xii, 296
thyroid 54
thyroidectomy 55, 262
tonsillectomies 32, 33, 38, 49, 58, 69, 73, 90, 105, 169, 185, 212, 227–8, 229, 243, 246, 247, 248, 257, 261, 275, 297
tonsils: infected 32, 46, 62, 66, 79, 86, 90, 117, 228, 229, 230
Toronto Hospital for the Insane 93
toxic overload 228, 229, 246
transmissible familial infection 228
transorbital lobotomy 297–8, 299, 347*n*99, 348*n*100–01, 349*n*102; description of 349*n*104
Trenton Evening Times 269, 270
Trenton State Hospital xi, 1, 7, 16, 68, 164–74, 187–8; board of managers 10, 19, 36, 38, 39, 139, 167, 185, 249, 251, 293, 296, 297; clinical records 167–8; current state of 15; edentulous patients 165, 170, 255, 277; and focal sepsis 42, 45, 56, 68, 105–6, 230–31, 245–6, 257–9, 276–7, 293, 298–9;

forensic unit 15–16, 165–6, 171; and
Solomon Katzenelbogen 253–7, 277;
and outside consultants 39–40, 65;
patient abuse at 1–2, 4, 5, 8, 9, 10, 17,
18, 19, 24–5, 177, 187; private patients at
43, 83, 250; reform of, 24–6, 27;
statistics 166–7, 193–4, 199–202, 208,
209–12, 214–15; study of 157–8, 159,
163, 164–74, 203–24, 326*n*24; surgery
at 9, 14, 38, 53–5, 62, 73, 100, 101, 245,
249, 293; therapeutic changes after
Cotton 256, 257, 258, 259, 296–9,
347*n*95–96, 347*n*99; visits by
psychiatrists 311*n*7
Trenton State Prison 57, 127
trust 276
tuberculin 87
typhoid fever 16, 17, 18, 19, 50, 120; cause
of 28; vaccine as febrile agent 228,
243, 246, 255, 299

University of California 283
University of Chicago 32, 33, 135, 139, 141,
321*n*4
University of Colorado 275
University of Pennsylvania Medical
School 69
Upson, Henry 37
Urey, Harold 65
Utica State Hospital 79

vaccines: in psychiatry 50, 57, 72, 84, 85,
248, 267
Van Cleve, Mrs. Samuel 19
Vanuxem lectures 65, 66–8, 88
Vincent, Clovis 87
Volterra, Vito, 65
Von Jauregg, Julius Wagner 86, 279–80,
333*n*10

Ward, John Wesley 16, 17, 18, 19
Wasserman, August von 31
Watson, Chalmers 112, 119, 212, 222, 230
Watson, John B. 143, 146, 148–9; affair
with Rosalie Rayner 149–51, 238,
322*n*35
Watson, Mary 150
Watts, James 286, 297, 343*n*50–52
Welch, William 136
whistle-blowers x, 345*n*73
White, Connover 4
White, Ellen 34, 35
White, Emmeline 4
White, William Alanson: and Cotton 89,
102, 123, 124; and malaria therapy
339*n*7–18
Whitehead, A. N. 65
Whitehorn, John C. 286, 343*n*49
Wilcox, Franklin 125
Williams, Eric Watson 232
Williams, Frankwood 125
Wilson, William 297
Wilson, Woodrow 73
Wittels, Fritz 239
Woodcroft Asylum 69
Wootton, William Turnor 190
Worcester State Hospital 19, 37, 102,
103
Work, Hubert 68, 69, 275
World Psychiatric Association 284

X-rays 32, 38, 42, 45, 46, 47, 57, 58, 73,
90, 128, 227, 232, 245, 248, 254, 261,
262

Yale University 82
Yealland, Lewis 87

Zilboorg, Gregory 290–91